Buddhist Monks and the Politics of Lanka's Civil War

Oxford Centre for Buddhist Studies Monographs

Series Editor: Richard Gombrich, Oxford Centre for Buddhist Studies

The Oxford Centre for Buddhist Studies promotes teaching and research into all Buddhist traditions, as found in texts and in societies, and is equally open to the study of Buddhism by methods associated with the humanities (philology, philosophy, history) and the social sciences (anthropology, sociology, politics). It insists only on using sources in their original languages and on aiming at the highest scholarly standards.

The series was previously published by Routledge.
Books published:

Ronkin, Noa. *Early Buddhist Metaphysics: the making of a philosophical tradition* (2005)

Phuntsho, Karma. *Mipham's Dialectics and the Debates on Emptiness: to be, not to be, or neither* (2005)

Gombrich, Richard F. *How Buddhism Began: the conditioned genesis of the early teachings*. 2nd ed. (2005)

Shaw, Sarah. *Buddhist Meditation: an anthology of texts from the Pali Canon* (2006)

Tuladhar-Douglas, Will. *Remaking Buddhism from Medieval Nepal: the fifteenth-century reformation of Newar Buddhism* (2007)

Roberts, Peter Alan. *The Biographies of Rechungpa: the evolution of a Tibetan hagiography* (2007)

Hwang, Soon-il. *Metaphor and Literalism in Buddhism: the doctrinal history of nirvana* (2006)

Wynne, Alexander. *The Origin of Buddhist Meditation* (2007)

Kuan, Tse-fu. *Mindfulness in Early Buddhism: new approaches through psychology and textual analysis, of Pali, Chinese and Sanskrit sources* (2007)

Published in the series from Equinox Publishing Ltd:

Gombrich, Richard. *What the Buddha Thought* (2009)

Seongcheol, Venerable. *Sermon of One Hundred Days: Part One* (2010)
Soonil, Hwang (translator), Covill, Linda (editor)

Jungnok Park. *How Buddhism Acquired a Soul on the Way to China* (2012)

Buddhist Monks and the Politics of Lanka's Civil War

Ethnoreligious Nationalism of the Sinhala *Saṅgha* and Peacemaking in Sri Lanka, 1995–2010

Suren Rāghavan

equinox

SHEFFIELD UK BRISTOL CT

Published by Equinox Publishing Ltd.

UK: Office 415, The Workstation, 15 Paternoster Row, Sheffield S1 2BX
USA: ISD, 70 Enterprise Drive, Bristol, CT 06010
www.equinoxpub.com

First published, 2016. First printing in paperback, 2018

ISBN 978-1-78179-078-6 (hardback)
ISBN 978-1-78179-574-3 (paperback)

British Library Cataloguing-in-Publication Data

A catalogue record for this book is available from the British Library.

Library of Congress Cataloging-in-Publication Data

Raghavan, Suren, author.
Buddhist monks and the politics of Lanka's Civil War : ethnoreligious nationalism of the Sinhala sangha and peacemaking in Sri Lanka, 1995–2010 /
Suren Raghavan.
pages cm. — (Oxford centre for Buddhist studies monographs)
Includes bibliographical references and index.
ISBN 978-1-78179-078-6 (hb)
1. Buddhism and politics—Sri Lanka—History. 2. Buddhist monks—Political activity—Sri Lanka—History. 3. Sri Lanka—History--Civil War, 1983-2009. 4. Peace-building—Sri Lanka—History. I. Title.
BQ4570.S7R34 2014
954.9303'2—dc23

2014011969

Edited and Typeset by Queenston Publishing, Hamilton, Ontario, Canada

Index by Jane Read, www.readindexing.co.uk

Printed by Lightning Source Inc. (La Vergne, TN), and
Lightning Source UK Ltd. (Milton Keynes)

Dedicated to
අජිත් අයියා
in deep gratitude for his
contributions in my life

and to

all the unarmed children, women and men who
died as Tamils, Sinhalas and Muslims because we
failed to avoid an ethnic war

Contents

Preface xi

Acknowledgements xv

Notes on Translation of Pāli and Sinhala Words xvii

1 A Paradise Poisoned? 1
Burden of the Past—Blunder of the Present
- Introduction 1
- The conflict in Lanka: The burden of the past 11
- The Tamils: A different history 13
- Federalism in Lanka 25
- Federalism rejected 34

2 The Social and Political Role of the Saṅgha in Lanka 43
- Introduction 43
- Buddha, the Saṅgha and politics 47
- The first Saṅgha: A social background 49
- *Mahāvaṃsa* and its impact 63
- The Sinhala Saṅgha 70
- The Saṅgha under colonial rule 75
- The Saṅgha and post-Protestant Buddhism 79

The Sinhala Saṅgha and the Tamils of Lanka 85
Conclusion 87

3 An Army in Yellow Robes: Saṅgha Political Resistance 1815–2010 91
Introduction 91
Saṅgha and Śāsana in Lanka 97
Restoration of Śāsana 1750–1815 102
Redeeming the Sinhala Land 1815–1948 104
Defining the Sinhala Nation 1948–1983 115
Conclusion 127

4 Three Saṅgha Activists and Their Politics 133
Introduction 133
Sinhala Saṅgha Activists 134
Venerable Walpola Rāhula (1907–1997) 137
Venerable Gaṅgoḍawila Sōma (1948–2003) 152
Venerable Athuraliyē Rathana (1966–) 167
Conclusion 179

5 Federalism and Sinhala Buddhist Nationalism 183
Introduction 183
Defining federalism 183
Federalism without indigenous owners 187
Conclusions 194

6 Epilogue 203

Appendices 205
References 207
Index 267

List of Figures

1. Venerable Elle Gunawansa pictured preparing the newly appointed Army Commander Lieutenant-General Jagath Jayasuriya the blessings of the Triple Gem. 92
2. Venerable Buddharakkhita handcuffed and led away from the courts. 119
3. Venerable Walpola Rāhula. 138
4. Venerable Gaṅgoḍawila Sōma in Sakman meditation. 153
5. Venerable Athuraliyē Rathana. 168

Preface

In December 2007, on my way home from the United Kingdom after my scholarship on Peace Studies, the passenger next seat in the plane was a Cambodian. Soon our exchanges reveled that we have some common ground in experiencing ethnic wars and suffered personally as much as collectively as societies. Inevitably, our conversation turned to the reality of conflicts and war in human history and how even in the twenty-first century the human conditions are often unable to avoid preventable wars. Being Cambodian and Sri Lanka, we both had another strong common link—Buddhism—the overarching philosophy, historical narrative, popular culture, socio-political structure and the ethical fabric of both our societies. There, we both were further astonished to learn the abysmal level of personal and collective violence our societies had propagated, produced and justified. How did Buddhism especially the Theravāda Buddhism, generally perceived as a philosophy of Ahiṃsā—the non-violent engagement—became the basis for protracted violence or least could not prevent such. Further, how did the majority of its monks—the Mahā Saṅgha became active agents or passive supporters of such crimes? The usual chorus of a nine-hour flight disturbed our exchanges. Nevertheless, the question that surfaced became a turning point in my research interest for the following four years.

Back at home in Colombo, like many million Lankans I had to share a society that had entered a new level of civil war what later became the dramatic final stages of one of Asia's brutal ethnic conflicts that lasted for 30 years. The key to this dramatic transformation of the war was the unprecedented level of support and justification it galvanized amongst the majority Buddhists. The dominant role of key Saṅgha activists became the pathfinder for what came to be a "just war." I felt my fate had commanded me to an inescapable reality question. How do I live in a Buddhist society and respect its venerable Saṅgha, when the majority of them have willingly become chanters of a war cry? How to understand their role in society? Is it a counter-reaction to an external threat? If so what are the historical patterns? What factors makes a section of the (southern) Sinhala Saṅgha embedded in ethnoreligious nationalism to a level that calls for a war against the "other"? As often, happened unanswered questions do not leave you easily unless you start working on them.

During the period of 2008–2012, my research became even more complex as the dramatic theatre of war and the highly questionable way it was brought to an end with the cost of thousands of human lives be there soldiers, rebels or the ever-suffering civilian caught between.

This book is by no means a comprehensive answer to the philosophy, politics or the practice of violence in Buddhist societies. Rather it is one case study based on Lankan civil war and the role of the Sinhala Saṅgha. My aim was not to provide solutions. That is the job of a politician. Yet I wanted to present a framework of understanding for the historical and contemporary role of the Saṅgha in Sinhala (and other Theravāda) society. By which, collectively we can find a path of dialogue with Saṅgha and their lay followers. This is even more important as of 2014, when this book is coming to print—the Saṅgha in Lanka have become even more militant and radical in the interpretation of their role in society.

While this is not a textbook, I believe will provide a deeper understanding to policymakers towards peacebuilding in Lanka and other deeply ethnoreligious societies. As we have firmly argued, the ignorance and willful rejection of the role of Saṅgha in Lanka by many western peace promoters not only destabilized the once possible negotiated settlement but also deepened the violent crisis. Book also offers analyses how Buddhism—as against the popular belief—is never a global one-text philosophy but becomes an indigenous ideology cross-fertilized by the local ethnic cultural structures. Thus, this has insights for students of Buddhism as well cross discipline practitioners of political anthropology.

One challenge the new readers will face is the not so familiar and often difficult to pronounce Pāli, Sinhala and Tamil names of people and places. I have kept them to the minimum. However, some are unavoidable. Hope this will not be a major hindrance but your interest on the subject will only deepen. The maps, pictures are provided to make the reading a relaxed one. Those who are familiar with the Lankan conflict and its recent history can skip some sections as they are provided only to construct the needed context.

The war ended in May 2009. But hardly anyone—be they Tamils, Sinhalas or the concerned outsider, genuinely believe that peace has returned to this beautiful island because mere absence of war is never the actual peace. Lanka continues to struggle with multiple challenges. A strong and victorious military that is spreading its roots to every aspect of civil society. An elite defined development agenda, growing anger on corruption and eroding democratic freedom and the multiple minority identities that are now facing even greater anxiety, are all posing formidable challenges to which Lanka needs to find sustainable answers collectively and fairly soon if she desires to arrest and reverse democratic decomposition of the last few decades. Our hope is that at least a section of the venerable Mahā Saṅgha will come forward to provide leadership to such new directions.

August 2015
Colombo

Acknowledgements

Researching on a topic that is concurrent and ever changing with multiple dynamics is never easy. Beside no research ever is a solo effort. Like in a symphony, while the conductor takes the responsibility of the composition it is a collective effort of every small and big instrumentalist alike. I have had the generous benefit of numerous individuals during these trying research years. To mention all of them is a long list and some in their compassionate attitude wish to remain unnamed.

The research was possible because of the generous grant that primarily came from two sources. The James Madison Trust of UK and the Overseas Research Scholars Award of the British government. My research supervisor Professor Michael Burgess provided strategic directions as the director of the Centre for Federal Studies under which the research funds were managed. Dr. Stephan Rossbach of University of Kent became a friend, helper and a scholar of rare category by spending long hours re-reading my drafts and debating them for days. His extraordinary commitment to scholarship and his intellectual sharpness is a rare combination in modern academia. He was more than a supervisor to me and was a role model of the scholastic life.

The accidental friendship I found with Richard Gombrich—world class Buddhist scholar and Professor emeritus at University of Oxford was a turning point in my life. His compassion towards my research, and to me, was a constant solace I found in the UK. He facilitated part of my research at the Oxford Centre for Buddhist Studies by which I was able to accesses the unmatched resources at the Bodleian library. Professor Gombrich remains a friend whose life and intellectuality constantly challenges me. After my PhD defense, he painstakingly corrected my colonial English—which is in fact my fourth language.

My stay in the UK and this research would have not been possible if not for the absolute generosity of Wendy and Steve Morrell. They housed me, made me a member of their family for three full years. I need a long time to pass such kindness to others. Professor Matthew Pepper and Rosemary offered such rare friendship that made deep impressions. Eliot Hamberstone—the first Britain who came forward to help me back in 2005 remained my constant companion at often so frustrating and humiliating conditions. His genuine selfless friendship was a gift.

Janet Joyce of Equinox publishers believed that this is a solid contribution to the scholarship of Buddhist studies and was supportive and encouraging to the idea of this book. My editor, Dr Russell Adams took painstaking long hours to recorrect my bibliographic references and other aspects of the book.

In Colombo at the last stage of this book my friends Sājāni Amaratunga and Dilshān Muhājarīne helped with many things to improve the final draft.

Venerable Khammai Dhammasami the chief of Oxford Vihāra—a true Saṅgha—was often my counselor. My stay at the beautiful Vihāra was always pleasant. A medical doctor opened her so beautiful home during my time at Oxford. Her kind friendship was beautiful and rare in the so busy western world.

Many more friends and supporters helped me in numerous ways. They all did so in the expectation that we all will find sustainable solutions in Lanka and bring peace to the most deserving often-marginalized people of that land.

Finally like any researcher, the biggest support came in the form of the price paid by my immediate family. Sherine, Sumedh and Vishwa helped me in my lonely journey as a peacemaker even when they did not understand and bore numerous costs. My academic life would have not come this far without them.

Notes on the Translation of Pāli and Sinhala Words

This book contains numerous Sinhala, Tamil, Pāli, and Sanskrit words. Except for popularly Anglicized terms such as karma, Buddha, Colombo, and Tamil, we have adopted the convention used by scholars in the field of Buddhist studies. This book uses the convention adopted by the Oxford Dictionary of Buddhism 2004 edition for transliterating Buddhist/Theravādin terms and concepts.

There are differences in the way a Pāli word appears in its original form and how it is used in Sinhala. For example, the word Bhikkhu in Pāli is Bhikshu in Sinhala. We have used the original Sinhala form, as the context demands it and most references are in Sinhala texts. In regards to the names of Saṅgha, we have used the transliterations done by scholars such as Kitsiri Malalgoda (1976) and Ann Blackburn (2010). Names of popular/political figures are abbreviated as they are used in popular discourse in Sri Lanka, such as SWRD for S. W. R. D. Bandaranaike, JR for J. R. Jayawardene and NM for N. M. Perera. Throughout this book, the term Saṅgha is used both in singular and plural and we use Sinhala and Sinhalas to refer to the ethnic Sinhalas as against the traditional Anglicization of the same as Sinhalese.

Tamil words and pronunciation are used as they are in the Sri Lankan Tamil tradition, which may be different to that of Tamil Nadu. Where there was no original English translation, we have ourselves translated some Sinhala and Tamil texts.

— 1 —

A Paradise Poisoned?
Burden of the Past—Blunder of the Present

Introduction

Sometimes called the "Pearl of the Indian Ocean," Sri Lanka has during the last 40 years often drawn attention to herself for reasons other than her tropical beauty.[1] Violence has been a constant feature in the history of the country since 1958, when Buddhist monk Thudawē Sōmārāma assassinated Prime Minister Bandaranaike. The 1971 Sinhala youth rebellion, led by the Maoist Janathā Vimukti Peramuna (JVP), and the state's violent response killed at least 50,000 people. The ethnic pogrom of 1983 killed at least 4,000 Tamil civilians and displaced over 150,000 Tamils in the south of Lanka. The second JVP uprising, in 1988–1989, is estimated to have led to the death of over 60,000 (largely Sinhala) youth including some 5000 bhikkhus or Buddhist monks. From the 1980s to 2009, the war between the separatist rebels, the Liberation Tigers of Tamil Eelam (தமிழீழ விடுதலை புலிகள்) (LTTE), and the state military claimed over 150,000 lives [2](Goodhand, Hulme and Lewer 2000; Radhakrishnan 2010; Senarathne 1997; Spencer 1990b; Kapferer 1988).

On 22 March 2012, the United Nations Human Rights Council in Geneva adopted a resolution (A/HRC/19/L.2/Rev1) regarding Lanka. In its resolution, "the Council called on the Government to implement the recommendations made in its previous report and to present as expeditiously as possible a comprehensive action plan detailing the steps it has taken and will take towards that end, and also to address alleged violations of

1. The island is referred to by various names throughout its turbulent history—Tabrobane, Seylan and Ceylon are just a few names given to it by western travelers. Ceylon was renamed as Sri Lanka by the constitution 1972. This study will refer to the country as Lanka.
2. Like in any civil war, counting the civil causalities is a challenging and contested process. These are figures generally accepted as there has not been any verification yet.

international law." The "previous report"[3] mentioned in the resolution claimed that there was credible evidence that both belligerent parties had committed crimes against humanity, especially during the last stages of the war, which ended in May 2009 with the defeat of the LTTE. The British Channel Four has shown disturbing video evidence[4] of "killing fields" and eyewitnesses too have come forward to suggest that some 40,000 civilians died during the final days of the war (Weiss 2011).

How did Lanka—which prides herself on being the home of Theravāda Buddhism,[5] a philosophy known for its emphasis on non-violence—engage in this protracted war and deploy sinister terror and counter-insurgency military campaigns with scant regard for civilian lives? How did a country permeated by Theravāda Buddhist teachings become a "killing field"? This broad question has generated a considerable volume of literature. Lanka's post-independence political journey has been studied from a range of perspectives and by different scholarly disciplines ranging from anthropology to postcolonial and subaltern studies (Goodhand, Korf and Spencer 2010; Grant 2009; Imtiyaz and Stavis 2008; Spencer 1990a; Uyangoda 2011, 2007).[6] The literature tends to converge on three key factors that contributed to the violence in Lanka: (i) the ethno-national identity politics that have dominated the political arena in Lanka from the early twentieth century onwards, (ii) the dominance of Sinhala Buddhism in post-independence Ceylon, and (iii) the failure to accommodate the political demands of the Tamil minority.

This book will focus on a crucial segment of these complex developments: the powerful role of the Saṅgha Buddhist monks in the contem-

---

3. http://www.ohchr.org/en/NewsEvents/Pages/DisplayNews.aspx?NewsID=12001&LangID=E, Accessed 10 April 2012.

4. http://www.ohchr.org/en/NewsEvents/Pages/DisplayNews.aspx?NewsID=12001&LangID=E, Accessed 10 April 2012.

5. *Theravāda* (translated as "teaching of the elders") is the only surviving school of Buddhism within the *Hīnayāna* ("small vehicle") tradition. It is the dominant form of Buddhism in South-East Asia, and is therefore sometimes referred to as Southern Buddhism. This significance of Theravāda in the area is due to the missionary activities of Emperor Aśoka, who sent his *bhikkhu* son Mahinda to Lanka around 245 BC. Some scholars see Theravāda as one of four subdivisions of the *Vibhajyavādins* (Distinctionists), each flourishing in a different area, the other three being the *Mahīśāsakas* in the Deccan, the *Dharma-guptakas* in Central Asia, and the *Kāśyapīyas* in North India. The *Vibhajyavādins* were a continuation of the earliest school, the *Sthaviravādins* of the First Council: they were so named because they distinguished themselves from the heretical *Pudgalavādins* or Personalities, who asserted a kind of *Ātmavāda* doctrine (Gombrich 2006a).

6. For a wider bibliography on the conflict of Lanka see http://www.ices.lk/sl_database/ethnic_conflict/bibliography.shtml, accessed on 10 Aug 2011, and also http://www.safhr.org/index.php?option=com_docman&Itemid=350.

porary politics of war and peace in Lanka.[7] It is not a coincidence that the period from 1995 to 2010, which saw the political mobilization of the Saṅgha, also saw the violent rejection of various power-sharing proposals. It was the proposed power-sharing with the Tamils through some kind of federal arrangements that made the Saṅgha engage in violent political agitation. The same period witnessed an evolution from conflict, to peace negotiations, to ceasefire agreements, to international mediation, to constitutional proposals, and finally to the resumption of the war leading to a violent military climax.

As we explore the role of the Saṅgha in Lankan politics and society, we are especially interested in how and why they were hostile to peace proposals that involved elements of power-sharing and federalism.[8] Federalism is often recommended as an institutional/constitutional modality for solving intra-state conflicts based on identity features such as ethnicity, language, race, region or religion. Bangladesh, Ethiopia, India, Indonesia, Iraq and even the United Kingdom are contemporary states that have adopted varying degrees and forms of federal principles in order to resolve existing and potential internal conflicts, create, and sustain stability. Parallel to this, already established federal states such as Australia, Canada, Switzerland and the United States of America are intensifying their federal politics in an attempt to allow for greater democratic participation. In political science debates, federalism is generally accepted as a procedural arrangement that allows government to function effectively even where societies are divided or fragmented. Some societies, however, have resisted the federal solution. Lanka is one such a state.

Federalism has been debated in Lanka for more than ninety years. As we will show later in this introductory chapter, there are many good reasons why federalism appears to be a natural solution to Lanka's problems. Neighbouring states such as India and Malaysia adopted federal constitutions and have subsequently enjoyed political and economic development. The regional and international communities generally supported a federal "solution," and large sections of the Tamil and Muslim minorities were in favour as well. However, can federalism really work in Lanka as believed by these agents? If so, why was it rejected

---

7. The term Saṅgha (or also *Samgha*) originally referred to the total community of four types of faithful followers of the Buddhist community: (i) the ordained male-*bhikkhu*, (ii) the ordained female-*bhikkhuni*, (iii) laymen *Upāsaka* and (iv) lay women *Upāsikā*. However, as time passed, in Sinhala society, the ordained bhikkhus were referred to as the Saṅgha possibly due to the lead role they play in the Buddhist church. In this study, the term Saṅgha is used in both the singular, to denote a monk and plural, to denote large group of monks.

8. In this book, I use the term "federalism" to denote constitutionally agreed governance which includes elements of self-rule and collective shared rule (L. Anderson 2007a; Burgess and Pinder 2007; Elazar 1987; Seymour and Gagnon 2012; Watt 2008).

so violently? Nancy Bermeo has asked key questions at a more abstract level: "How can states avoid ethnic violence and best accommodate multiple ethnicities? ... Is adopting federalism the best way to cope with territorially based diversity? Simply, can we import federalism as an institution?" (2002, 96) In Lanka, these questions were answered firmly in the negative. Lanka rejected any form of federal constitution and instead adopted a military strategy, with huge human and material costs, to settle the protracted ethnic civil war and re-centralize the state. Among those who rejected federalism, the Saṅgha formed the most radical group, despite their position as the people who "embody" Theravāda Buddhism with its emphasis on non-violence.

In this book, we explore how the political élite of the Sinhala majority, and especially the powerful Saṅgha, responded to federalism. We will see that for the Saṅgha and similarly radical groups, federalism was not a proposal to be rejected politically. Rather, the very proposal itself—merely talking about power-sharing—fuelled the conflict it was meant to pacify. Élite attitudes towards federalism will thus provide us with a lens through which we can see in some detail the mind-set that determined Lanka's political course during the period under investigation.

Within the context of our investigation, our focus will be on the Saṅgha, as we identify them as the key actors in Lankan politics and society. In order to be able to understand the Saṅgha political influence, we will need to reconstruct how their political attitudes are shaped and how, in turn, they are able to shape political attitudes in the country. Moreover, as we look at the formation of their political attitudes, we must pay special attention to the manner in which they reconcile their views—especially their militant support of the war effort—with the normative Buddhist ethics that govern their lives. These investigations will then bring into sharper focus more general questions such as: Are modern political concepts such as federalism incompatible with the Saṅgha and hence the Sinhala worldview? Why, indeed, is the discourse of political justice and liberal peace repulsive to the majority of the Sinhalas?

In light of these questions, an interdisciplinary approach is essential as we explore the political significance of Sinhala Buddhism and the Saṅgha, who as the unelected agents of their religion managed to exert a key influence on state policies. In contrast to the conventional approaches usually taken by scholars of Buddhism and its institutions, we avoid focusing on Buddhist philosophy and the metaphysical dimension of the Theravāda school and its key texts, with the exception of some necessary references to selected Theravādin concepts and Pāli texts such as passages of the epic *Mahāvaṃsa*. Still, this is not a study of the religious life of the Saṅgha or their śāsana—the oldest surviving institution based on Buddha's life and teaching. A considerable amount of literature on the modern Sinhala Saṅgha fraternity is already available (Gombrich and Gupta 1986; Malalgoda 1976; Seneviratne 1999). We add to the existing literature by focusing specifically on the intersection of religion and politics. We aim to explore the Saṅgha self-understanding in a political context. How do the Saṅgha understand what it means to be a Sinhala Buddhist? Moreover, on that basis, how did they justify their response to the minority demands for greater political equality during the protracted ethnic war?

Following the years since the military defeat of the LTTE, scholars have proposed a range of explanations for the Lankan conflict. Among the more frequent explanations are (i) the aggressive ethnoreligious nationalism of the Sinhalas;[9] (ii) the ethnicity-based separatist terror politics of the Tamil Tigers; (iii) power contestation among the Sinhala élites; and (iv) the incompatibility of an over-internationalized peace process and the local/regional socio-political reaction. While all these theories contribute to our understanding of the war in Lanka and the failure of the peace efforts, this book will focus specifically on the role of the Sinhala Saṅgha in mobilizing the Sinhalas to pursue a military campaign rather than search for a power-sharing arrangement with the Tamil minority. Focusing on the Saṅgha, and specifically their hardline attitude towards power-sharing arrangements such as federalism, will help us appreciate the political nature of Sinhala Buddhism. The political dimension of Sinhala Buddhism becomes especially apparent during the period under investigation (1995–2010) because the international peace process and the principles of modern liberal democracy and federalism on which it drew tended to marginalize the Saṅgha, thus provoking a reaction. The broader and more general question which is at stake here is whether the "principled distance" (Bhargava 2009, 2007) between the secular state and religion[10] can indeed be maintained in traditional societies[11] such as Lanka, where Buddhism and the Saṅgha are the principal political, societal and cultural powers that inspire the majority of the population. Any process aiming to facilitate a transition towards a

9. I use the term "ethnoreligious" to indicate a group mobilization that combines a religious faith/practice with a given ethnic identity such as "Jewish" or "Sikh" (Marty and Appleby 1997; M. Thomas 2006; Winter 1996).

10. I use the concept of "religion" in its broadest sense. For example, "religion" does not necessarily involve belief that there is a God. As is well known, Buddhism does not advocate a concept of God. We understand "religion" as a set of beliefs and practices dealing with spiritual and sacred ideas (Beckford 1999).

11. The term "traditional society" is used to denote non-industrial societies and societies in transition from a rural agrarian to a market-based capital economy. We do not wish to imply, of course, that "traditional" societies are marked by backwardness; rather, we wish to indicate that these societies approach contemporary challenges in a particular manner in that their imagined or real past does not seem to correspond with the present or a projected future (Giddens 1994; Rostow 1959).

liberal, democratic peace in Lanka must appreciate the cultural dominance of Theravāda Buddhism and hence of the Saṅgha.

The wider research context

The Lankan case helps us to explore the limits of the modern practice of promoting liberal democratic peace in deeply divided states as an attempt to overcome the political and cultural problems associated with division. Western states or groups, who are often eager to implement some kind of federalist arrangement between the warring factions, encouraging them to become equal members in a collective political, economic and social bargaining process, generally mediate these peace efforts. Apart from the open advocacy of federalism, which as is often argued has deep Judeo-Christian roots, the very notion of peace that underlies these attempts is also defined by Western concepts of conflict resolution, reconciliation, minority rights and justice.

The kind of well-established "solutions" suggested and encouraged by external forces, even if they appear to be of universal appeal, do not always receive a favorable response. In Lanka, Tamil separatists as well as Sinhala nationalists rejected the idea of federalism because they had their own understanding of peace and justice based on centuries-old perceptions of "self" and "other." Moreover, they not only rejected proposals which many outside observers and commentators would have considered obvious solutions; they even interpreted such well-meaning proposals as provocations, so that the mere mention of federalism and power-sharing fuelled the conflict rather than contributed to its resolution. Western observers and politicians did not understand the dynamics of this situation.

We do not wish to dismiss the efforts of the global peace industry and the INGO-led conflict resolution campaigns simply because they were informed by Western models. Our analysis must go deeper. We must reconstruct how exactly the most obvious proposal turned out to be the most counter-productive. This is the area where we can learn much from the Lankan conflict. The Norway-led peace negotiation, the Scandinavian ceasefire monitoring, the US, EU and Japan-led reconstruction and development agenda, and India's good will diplomacy—all failed to appreciate the importance of making the Saṅgha an integral part of the various multi-track processes that were part of these efforts. They either willfully or ignorantly tried to replace the hegemony of the Saṅgha with a new, "modern" hegemony of Western ideas and practices. Even a cursory overview of the situation of the Saṅgha would have made it clear that this was an important group on the defensive. Given their classical self-understanding, their conceptualizing of Lanka as the guardian of true Buddhism in the world, and given their outlook on the general (especially the Western) secular world, it is clear that the Saṅgha viewed the war waged by the Tamil Tigers as a siege. To them, the war was not only a real and concrete danger, but it was also symbolic of the wider cosmic dangers that Buddhism faced in the modern world. The failure of successive governments to tame the Tigers politically or militarily directly threatened the self-understanding of the Saṅgha, who then proceeded to transmit their anxiety to the lay society. The war was undoubtedly the most serious internal challenge to the Saṅgha interpretation of Sinhala Buddhism and the state built upon it. In times of national crisis, Sinhala Buddhists will seek the leadership of Saṅgha. This study is interested in the political dimension of this leadership, and we will therefore focus on the Saṅgha politics and their influence during the period from 1995 to 2010.

The dominant understanding of the Saṅgha in the context of the Lankan crisis is that they were "spoilers" of the peace process (Brekke 2009; Goodhand and Korf 2010; Lewis 2010; Höglund 2005). This characterization of the Saṅgha as "spoilers" implies that they were a somewhat annoying disturbance rather than a central pillar of the process. They represented backward and outdated forces, which fought, it was assumed, a hopeless fight against modernity. This view, however, proved to be a costly mistake, not because it led to wrong theories but also because it informed external interventions, which ultimately made matters worse. Sinhala Saṅgha are not just "spoilers." As we shall explain in subsequent chapters, they define the spiritual and socio-political culture of the Sinhala nation. Consequently, attempts to introduce federalism without the support of the Saṅgha, or even against their will, were counterproductive.

The example of Lanka allows us to explore the current limits of the Western project to extend its modernity to other parts of the world. While academics in international relations observe a "return of religion" in the politics of the twenty-first century, the situation in Lanka demonstrates that religion never ceased to be a key influence on politics and society. It appears that academic observers, distracted by the ideological conflict of the Cold War, simply overlook how politics is made in large parts of the world. However, this "blind spot" is not just an academic problem; the peace efforts of the international community reveal an analogous blindness. The idea that one could encourage/force Lanka to adopt a federal system without including the Saṅgha in the negotiations displays a considerable degree of ignorance of how the society and politics of Lanka work. Predominant Western concepts still assume that ultimately religion is a backward force, to be relegated to the realm of private beliefs, where it may "spoil" and, at worst, slow down the inevitable advance of a Western, liberal-democratic rationality. Yet, it is precisely this attitude, which provoked a strong militant resistance, and not just among the Saṅgha. This study will explore the nature of this resistance.

Method and structure

This book will combine a number of separate but related approaches in order to reflect the richness and complexity of our subject. Much of our research is informed by a perspective, which we call "historical-reconstructivist" (Habermas 1979), because the important role of the Saṅgha in Lanka, especially their close relationship with the Lankan government, will need to be historically reconstructed in order to appreciate how key patterns were created in the early post-Buddha period. Thus, we do not take for granted existing patterns of political relations as "natural" or "normal" but instead explore how they emerged historically and how they evolved through time. In an approach, that draws inspiration from Michel Foucault's genealogical method (Foucault 1978); we emphasize the conditions of the emergence of patterns of relationships and the lasting effects of such patterns and their evolution through time.

Again drawing on Foucault's terminology, we are especially interested in how the Saṅgha, based on their historically evolved self-understanding and position within society, "problematized" (Foucault 1985) various developments and challenges within Lanka and from outside. As we shall see, the manner in which the Saṅgha problematized certain challenges to their self-understanding shaped the space of possible responses that the Lankan polity was able to give to those challenges. In this historical process, certain dynamics emerge which lead us to talk about "waves" of Saṅgha resistance. At various stages in the development of the Lanka polity, the Saṅgha articulated their resistance to proposals, which from their point of view threatened to undermine Lanka's unique position as the primary representative and protector of Theravāda Buddhism in the world. Through these waves of resistance, the Saṅgha situated themselves within the Lankan polity, culminating in the remarkable creation of a Saṅgha political party, the Jāthika Helà Urumaya (JHU), and in the support, they offered to the war effort.

We thus find both an underlying continuity in Saṅgha mobilization and radical changes in the manner in which the Saṅgha articulated and manifested their resistance. What remains constant throughout this history is the background of Sinhala Buddhism, and hence the Saṅgha have to refer to their selected Buddhist scriptures, texts and practices as the unshakable foundation of everything they do. As we noted previously, and as we have occasion to note throughout this study, the Sinhala Buddhist background forces the Saṅgha to rationalize and justify the ethical choices they make, especially when it comes to the use of violence. Changes in the Sinhala Saṅgha mindset can thus be traced by looking at the manner in which they rationalize their actions in relation to their Buddhist beliefs, historical texts and practices. We therefore will look at the lives of three key Saṅgha in order to explore how they navigated their renouncer beliefs and became political activists. The three Saṅgha leaders included in this part of the study are Venerable Walpola Rāhula, Venerable Gaṅgoḍawila Sōma, and Venerable Athuraliyē Rathana. Looking at how the historical dynamic referred to above unfolded in their lives, and how they in turn continued and shaped this dynamic, will allow us to conclude our historical reconstruction by looking in depth at the mindset of the recent and current generation of Saṅgha activists. Our accounts of the three Saṅgha obviously cannot aim to provide anything like full biographies, but at least we can try to establish how these activist-leaders made their ethical choices and how they managed to mobilize large sections of the Sinhala population to support their cause. The lives of the three Saṅgha thus become lenses through which we can trace the overall historical dynamics as under a microscope.

As explained previously, we use the Saṅgha response to federalism as a further focus in order to understand why exactly power-sharing proposals were considered so dangerous and unacceptable. We have already alluded to the wider significance of this question within the context of a world politics that continues to be dominated by Western concepts. For this purpose, we will reconstruct the history of the debate on federalism in Lanka, emphasizing key Saṅgha interventions. This part of our study will thus focus on the concrete fate of a theme—federalism—in Lanka rather than on the life of Saṅgha leaders. Both parts aim to give us a more detailed insight into the overall dynamics of the Lankan polity.

This research benefitted from fieldwork we were able to conduct in Lanka. Interviews were conducted with Venerable Athuraliyē Rathana, one of the leading Saṅgha; Disānayaka Mudiyanselage Jayaratne, Prime Minister of Lanka and Minister of Buddhist Affairs; Venerable Dr. Ittademaliye Indasara Thero, the Vice-Chancellor of the Buddhist University; Venerable Professor Mahinda Saṅgharakkitha, Chief Saṅgha at the historical Kälaṇiya Raja Maha Temple. Other interviews were conducted with officials in the Ministry of Buddhaśāsana, academics and activists concerned with Saṅgha politics. Throughout our research, we were able to draw on literature available in English, Sinhala and Tamil. The research was also informed by our own experience as a peace activist with key functions as a facilitator during the peace dialogues between the state of Lanka and the now defeated Tamil Tiger rebels.

In accordance with the aim of our research and the approach chosen, the book has the following structure: This introduction introduces some of the key themes of our analysis. In particular, we will briefly look at the puzzle that motivates our research. Given that many observers felt that there were in fact many good reasons to think that federalism was a possible and promising solution to the violence and crisis in Lanka, it is even more striking that the very proposal not only was not productive but also proved to be counter-productive. The first chapter provides a historical introduction to the Saṅgha community, their history, sources of inspiration, their self-understanding and their role in the Lankan society and polity. Special attention will be paid to the importance of the *Mahāvaṃsa* epic. Chapter two looks more specifically at the history of the political involvement of the Saṅgha by investigating the various waves of resistance they offered at key transition moments in the history of the Lankan polity and by looking at the lasting effects of this resistance. Chapter three offers the above-mentioned discussion of three key Saṅgha leaders in an attempt to understand in greater detail how they navigated the ethical choices they had to make in order to combine their roles as world renouncers and political activists. In chapter four, we will review the debate on federalism in Lanka and how it intersected with the history of the polity of the country. In this context, we will also compare the "spirit" of federalism with the political dimension of the Theravāda cosmology.

In the final section of the fourth chapter, we will look back at the book as a whole, provide a summary and draw our conclusions. What lessons can be learned from our analysis for both the Lankan context and the wider international context? This final chapter will also give us an opportunity to discuss what the future of the country may hold, in light of recent events—especially the defeat of the LTTE. Will the LTTE defeat confirm or end the historical dynamics our study has identified?

Only two years after the conclusion of the war, the Norwegian government published a report highlighting the main consequences of the war. According to the report, six major trends can be observed:

1. Sinhala nationalism is now firmly back at the center of power.
2. A new political dynasty (Rajapakse) has emerged, challenging the dominance of the English-speaking political families that traditionally held power or were close to the center of power in Colombo.
3. A shift from an essentially mainstream two-party dynamics to a more streamlined, unipolar system has occurred.
4. While in the past power-sharing proposals had placed the state under considerable pressure to adopt a course of reform, no such pressure existed following the defeat of the LTTE.
5. The end of the LTTE state-building project also meant the emergence of a new politico-military regime in the north east of the country.
6. The LTTE defeat also implied the redefinition of the state-minority relationship with the hegemony of the Rajapaksa-led SLFP,

> severely impairing the bargaining power of minorities and opposition groups.[12]

In our conclusion, we will be able to reflect on these trends and evaluate how they might affect the role and position of the Saṅgha and how in turn the future of the polity might be affected by the future development of the Saṅgha self-understanding.

The conflict in Lanka: The burden of the past

The complex, violent, political conflict in Lanka is the result of many factors including religion, nationalism, historical memories, post-colonial élite rivalry, ethnicity and economic oppression. More recently, the denial of minority rights, armed separatism, flawed mediation efforts, the rejection of federalism, and counter-insurgency warfare have also played a major role in the continued unrest. At a deeper level, however, the conflict is understood to be rooted in a historical process of incomplete state formation and post-colonial ethno-national politics (Uyangoda 2011; Jenkins 2008), stemming from the failure of the island's majoritarian democracy to become multi-ethnic and inclusive of those who are not Sinhala Buddhists.

Popular Sinhala nationalist rhetoric and the Sinhala historical memory, in the form of oral and written tradition, hold that Lanka primarily belongs to the Sinhalas (Roberts 2001a), but scholars argue that Lanka has been multi-ethnic and multi-cultural from ancient times (Gunawardana 1990, 1971; Intirapālā 2005). The power and influence of history when analyzing and interpreting a protracted ethno-national conflict is well established (Bandarage 2009; Brun and Jazeel 2009; Horowitz 1985; Liu and Hilton 2005; McGarry and O'Leary 1993; Philipson 2001; Sahadevan 2002; Thompson and Karayanni 2004; Varshney 2002). The past—whether retold through myth, constructed narrative, or an official record of events—has the power to reshape the dynamics of the "present." S. G. Smith argues that views of the past fuel socio-political attitudes and civic culture like no other factor:

> our commanding practical interest in how we share action with other actors is distinctively engaged by presumed information about past occurrences. We recognize that past occurrences have determined the conditions of action sharing, constraining our practice with regard to which actors we share practical reality with and which compounding actions we may or must join in progress. (2009, 1)

---

12. Published by the Norwegian development agency NORAD, see http://www.norad.no/en/tools-and-publications/publications/evaluations/publication?key=386346. Accessed on Nov. 10, 2011.

The ethno-national claims of many conflicting communities are frequently based on singular, often homogeneous and monolithic claims rooted in history (whether real or imagined), which contradict their modern pluralistic realities. Chabal and Daloz (2006) draw attention to the limits of modern political science to understand and present alternative discourses between mono-ethno-centrism and a globalized universalism. Regardless of whether it manifests itself in its primordial or modernistic version, nationalism takes many other non-dialectical positions (A. D. Smith 2001, 2000) and continues to create, shape and sustain "imagined communities" (B. R. Anderson 1983).

One of the most ingrained beliefs held by the Sinhalas in the construction of their national history is that Buddha himself envisioned the island as the future sanctuary of his teaching. According to this belief, the teacher entrusted the future ownership of Lanka to the Sinhalas as "guardians" of his teaching. This point of conviction planted in the social cognition of the majoritarian Sinhala Buddhist society generates the desire for a tighter grip on the socio-political structure, projecting a mono-Buddhist identity and constructing a Pan-Sinhala ethnicity in every sphere of the society. This Sinhala-Buddhist identity construction is further fuelled by the fact that Lanka is considered as the home of ancient Buddhism by the rest of the Theravāda Buddhist world, and that it is the only place on earth where the Sinhala language and culture are found. The Sinhalas are a population of merely 15 million (2010) on an island of only 65,000 square kilometres, while 70 million Tamils live a mere 30 kilometres away in Tamil Nadu, India, and a further 30 million live in other parts of the world. The senses of fragility and precariousness caused by these limitations of space and population have been deepened by repeated invasions from South India and by over four centuries of European colonization beginning in the sixteenth century. This situation together with its historical background is what Schaller and Abeysinghe term as the "structural context" that creates a political psychology of "double asymmetries" in power relations (2006, 616).

An imbalanced geo-demography often contributes to the construction of structural asymmetries. These asymmetries in turn produce reactionary and paradigmatic power relations in reference to other contestants in a given socio-political realm. Though the nearly 6 million Jews are the 76 per cent majority in Israel, they are in fact a diminutive minority compared to the surrounding Arab population or indeed the worldwide Muslim population (Peleg 2004). The resulting sense of insecurity tends to be reflected in militarization. This socio-political psychology operates within a cross-pollinating "interactive double minority" frame of reference, which further generates deep fear and distrust. This distrust and corroborating combative political events help each involved group to demonize the other (Eidelson and Eidelson 2003; Rouhana and Bar-Tal 1998; Rouhana and Fiske 1995; Schaller and Abeysinghe 2006).

Historical memories re-lived in the writings of a religious chronicle, archaeological evidence of repeated invasions, subjugation, loss of life style, and strongly demarcated geo-physical realities could have contributed to the construction of an ontological insecurity that is implanted in the collective political psyche of the Sinhalas. Such insecurity was vividly displayed in the collective struggle for independence from the 450 years of European rule during the early years of the twentieth century. In many ways the struggle for independence did not proceed as a struggle for freedom, secular civil liberty, or pluralistic democracy like in India under the Gandhi led Indian Congress (Sen 1993; Upadhyaya 1992); rather, it was to recover, repair, and restore an ancient version of the Sinhala-Buddhist civilization (Krishna 1999; Malalgoda 1976; Tambiah 1986). Sinhalas believe they are the original and only true owners of the island and mobilize their politics based on this self-understanding.

The Tamils: A different history

The Lankan native Tamils make up approximately 12% of the island's total population. They are largely Hindus and traditionally live in the northeast province of the island. A further 6% of the Lankan population, living in the central hills of the island, are Tamils of Indian origin, the descendants of Tamils who came from India for plantation work during the British rule. The native Tamils challenge the Sinhala version of history and have their own ownership claims to the island. They claim that ancient mythical King Rāvaṇa of the Rāmāyana epic was a Tamil Hindu (Pillai 2003; Zvelebil 1988). Tamils were the dark skinned inhabitants of the island encountered by Prince Vijaya—the father of Sinhalas according to the *Mahāvaṃsa*—as he accidentally landed on the northwest of the island. *Mahāvaṃsa* further narrates that Vijaya married Kuvaṇṇā, who according to Balasingham (2004) was Tamil, and established his kingdom. Satchi Ponnambalam (1983) claims the Sinhala language, (based on the Pāli of Theravāda text), became widespread in the island with the advent of Buddhism.

The act of "choosing" a past and relating it to the present has never been an easy task for the Tamils in Lanka. Viewing, interpreting and using history became part of the political process. Their preferred version of history significantly differs from those advocated by the Sinhalas, which not only deny the Tamils (co)inhabitancy in the ancient island, but also brand them as aliens, intruders or invaders. Tamils recognize the presence of the Sinhalas on the island from a very ancient time, but would add to the theory that the Sinhalas are part of a great Dravidian family, who have developed their own identity due to the influence of Buddhism and who are not a special Aryan group (Hellmann-Rajanayagam 1990).

One consequence of these conflicting claims is that several incompatible assumptions are taken very seriously. These assumptions dismiss common features that the two views share (Gunawardana 1979). Based on these ethno-nationalist interpretations, both sides have treated the other as an opponent ready to wage war. Sadly, some modern academics take the same line of argument (Dharmadasa 1989). In one extreme version of this narrative, the Venerable Walpola Rāhula, one of the most influential Saṅgha, maintained that the victory of Duṭṭhagāmiṇi over the Tamil King Elāra in 200 BC was the beginning of Sinhala nationalism: "it was a new race with healthy young blood" (Rāhula, 1959, 79). Anthropologists such as Obeyesekere dispute this:

> There were historically two major opposed ethnic identities, Tamils and Sinhalese.... The opposition stabilized the Sinhala-Buddhist identity.... The Sinhalese could be mobilized by their rulers to fight the invaders... the myth became often a rallying point for Sinhala nationalism.
>
> (Obeyesekere 1979, 282)

Because of these extreme and polarized positions, race, nationality and political territoriality are often distorted and confused. Anurādhapura and Polonnaruwa, two great ancient cities of Sinhala civilization, contain evidence of Tamil presence (Devendra 1959), while in Jaffna, the modern centre of the Tamil homeland, there is evidence of a Buddhist culture in places like Nāgadīpa and Kandaroodai (Shalk 2014). Coperahewa and Arunachalam (2002) suggests that at least 25 per cent of the modern Sinhala language comprises words that are Tamil in origin. This testifies to the fact that these groups lived side by side for centuries. However, post-independent popular nationalist literature often dismisses these common grounds and discredits the rare attempts by historians like Gunawardana (Gunawardana 1995, 1985, 1990) to create clarity on these questions (Goonewardena 2002; Goonewardena and Goonewardane 1992). From the mid-1980s to the current date, Sinhala nationalist intellectual debate has been dominated by the *Jāthika Chinthanaya* (national consciousness) movement, with Gunadasa Amarasēkara and Nalin De Silva as its key agitators. According to Nalin De Silva, "[t]here is a common culture in this country and we must seek our solutions to our problems within the framework of that common culture. The inherent common culture in this country is...best described in Buddhism" (1990, 34). Similarly, Gunadasa Amarasēkara claims:

> Our National Ideology is the Sinhala-Buddhist ideology that has evolved through a period of about two thousand years. The main assumption behind Jāthika Chinthanaya is that, although there are many ethnic groups in this country such as the Sinhalese, the Tamils, and the Muslims, all of them belong to basically the same culture; as such, they must be referred

> to as one nation. We believe that the people of this country, while belonging to different ethnicities, are bound by the same culture and are heirs to the same Jāthika Chinthanaya. What is racist about that? (1992, 23)

As a direct result of this "past-forwarding," the Sinhalas in the independent state of Lanka began to look into their mytho-historical past while actively denying the multinational reality of their present and future.

Drawing attention to the multinational history of the country is not to deny the fact that there were people with distinct differences, who fought for political power. However, these were more likely intra-dynastic conflicts with power centres moving between Tamils, Sinhalas or a mixture of both communities. The possibility that they were primarily inter-ethnic conflicts as portrayed in the post-independence nation state discourse is remote (Rogers 1994). Interpretations of history often supersede contemporary social and political debates in Lanka and tend to hide the political motivations fueling them. This process, in addition to many other adverse results, created clashes between nostalgia for the past and a disdain for the present, giving rise to confrontation based on ethnic identity and ideology. Both dominant ethnic identities became preoccupied with the search for legitimacy in their own history, and this search was pursued at the expense of the other's legitimacy.

The Sinhalas, because they were in control of the country's parliament for many years, had the advantage of being able to make serious structural and institutional amendments in order to undermine the Tamil history of Lanka and to reduce the Tamil socio-political space. Decades of such "majoritarian" impositions—including the disenfranchising of the Indian Tamils, the debate over the national flag and anthem, the overnight declaration of Sinhala as the official language, the state sponsored Sinhala settlements in predominant Tamil constituencies, and the neglect of the Tamil regions in national development programmes—led to the steady growth of frustration, alienation and political divorce.

At the same time, the Tamils were determined to restore their historical position and strength. Perhaps it was for this reason that the LTTE, the most articulate and militant Tamil national mobilization, adopted the name புலிகள் "Pulighal" (Tigers) and a proposed national flag featuring a raging tiger. A Bengali type tiger was the state symbol of the great Cōla dynasty from 310 BCE to 1250 CE (Sastri 1977, 1976). History is often politicized through the ethnic interpretations of archaeology, which provoke nationalism and the quest for a new identity that affects even the more globalized diaspora (Demmers 2002). The case of Eelam Tamil nationalism neatly fits into this analysis, even while its global growth is largely a reactionary political force in the context of a homeland democracy where Tamil concerns are deliberately ignored and suppressed.

The colonial impact

The first Europeans arrived in Lanka around 1505 (Bailey 1952; K. M. De Silva 2005; Peebles 2006) and the process of colonial subjugation was at its peak in 1815, when the British conquered Kandy, the last kingdom of Ceylon. Now completely under British control, the island was declared a single "unitary" political entity (Kumarasingham 2006), a move that had far-reaching consequences for future Lankan politics.

The British colonialists introduced a commercial economy, built up much-needed infrastructure for this purpose and introduced, among many other ideas, the ideology of nineteenth century liberal individualism. For them, these developments were part of the process of introducing "civilization." When confronted with the heterogeneity of identities and cultural practices on the island, they classified them as stemming from distinctly different "races." Along with the main Sinhala and Tamil races, the British carefully divided Ceylon into Up Country and Low Country Sinhalas, Indian and Ceylonese Tamils, Muslims and Moors, Veddhas, Malays, Dutch and Portuguese Burghers, and even sub-groups such as the Rodiyas, a nomadic gypsy group now largely assimilated into other identities (Rāghavan 1957; Rogers 2004). This drive for ethnic classification had direct political ramifications when, in 1833, the British developed a system of political representation based on racial identities (Nissan and Strirrat 1990). In 1833, when the common administration for the island was set up, three unofficial members were selected to represent Low Country Sinhalas, Burghers and Tamils. Later, in 1889, two more members were included in order to represent Kandyans and Moors, thus making the politics of the island dependent on racial representation (Nissan and Stirrat 1990). This race-based representation was in force for almost a century until the 1931 Donoughmore Commission,[13]

13. The Donoughmore Commission was appointed in 1927 by the colonial government to recommend self-rule for Ceylon. The commission replaced the ethnic based representation with a universal franchise including all women above 21 years of age. This made Ceylon the first non-European country to grant voting powers to women at a time when the UK voting age for women was 28 (Russell 2005). In Lanka as in India, the British created an educated class to provide administrative and professional services in the colony. By the late nineteenth century, most members of this emerging class were associated directly or indirectly with the government. Increased Lankan participation in government affairs demanded the creation of a legal profession; the need for state health services required a corps of medical professionals; and the spread of education provided an impetus to develop the teaching profession. In addition, the expansion of commercial plantations created a legion of new trades and occupations, landowners, planters, transport agents, contractors, and businesspersons. Certain Sinhala caste groups, such as the fishermen (*Karāve*) and cinnamon peelers (*Salāgama*), benefited from the emerging new economic order to the detriment of the traditional ruling cultivators (*Goyigama*).

which recommended a territory-based constitution (Barron 1988). By then Lanka had developed into a living paradox: on the one hand, all its citizens were equal before British rule, while on the other, they were separated by their racial and ethnic distinctions.

By the turn of the twentieth century, the southern Sinhala élites had become ambitious and influential through their trading partnership with the ruling British (Jayawardena 2002). Using their wealth and power, they mobilized a new national identity, largely defined by the Sinhala language and their Buddhist practices. Revivalists like Anagārika[14] Dharmapāla (1864–1933) spearheaded an emotional religious and ethnic awakening in the south coastal regions (Amunugama 1985; Deegalle 1997; Moor 1989; Seneviratne 1999; Tambiah 1992). This was in many ways a radical departure from the intellectual Buddhist discourse that was envisioned by Saṅgha such as Hikkaḍuvē Śrī Suṃaṅgala (Blackburn 2010). Anagārika was keen to restructure the society along ethno-nationalist lines while Suṃaṅgala was trying to systematize and restore religious learning. Externally, the revival of liberalism and objective oriental scholarship challenged the British rule (Bell and Bell 1993). As Gellner (1997) has argued, new realizations of ethnicity and nationalism emerged within the discourse of social reform movements because of the influence of western education, economic factors, improved media, as well as changes in class structure and political representation.

The printing of the *Mahāvaṃsa*, the most influential epic of Vaṃsa literature in Lanka, in 1837 and British sponsored archaeological discoveries in the ancient capital cities of Anurādhapura and Polonnaruwa provided solid textual support to the growing "newspaper nationalism" (Tennekoon 1990). However, each community, to serve their new political desires, interpreted these discoveries differently. For the Sinhalas, these provided historical evidence of the ethnic superiority of the Sinhalas (Kemper 1991, Nissan 1984). For the Tamils, these same discoveries provided a new source of pride in the glorious past of their *Saṅgam* era (Zvelebil 1994).[15] The emotional reaction to the discoveries of a "glorious past" was initially directed against the British, questioning their right to rule over such an advanced civilization. Lankan élites came to the

14. *Anagārika* means one who does not inhabit a house. Before and during the time of Buddha the term indicated those who had left home for a more ascetic life. This term was adapted by Dharmapāla, to intiate a new lay order (Guruge 1965). See ODB page 12.

15. Though the idea that early Tamil literature was fostered in ancient academies on a submerged landmass has been widely discredited, literary historians do still refer to Tamil literature from 200 BCE to 300 CE as Saṅgam literature. Saṅgam literature is the oldest known *Dravidian* literature, written in Tamil. In contrast to contemporary literary works in Sanskrit and Pāli, Saṅgam literature is surprisingly secular, dealing with day-to-day themes such as love, war, governance, trade, eloping, bereavement, and mourning in a unique South Indian context.

firm conclusion that the invading foreigner, (පර සුද්දා) "*para sudda*," or the alien whites had to leave in order to allow a free nation to regain its pride. After a prolonged period of reforms undertaken through the Colebrook Commission of 1832, the Donoughmore Commission of 1928 and the Soulbury Commission of 1946, British rule ended in 1948 (Mendis 1952).

Soon Lanka's post-independence English-speaking Sinhala élites maneuvered electoral politics by advocating the language, religion and culture of the Sinhala majority. Though partly a top-down, élite-driven process, Sinhala nationalist sentiments could not simply be "turned on" or "off" by the political class. Rather, these sentiments permeated society more broadly and were tied up with expectations of the state as the protector and benefactor of the Sinhala peasantry, a discourse infused with Sinhala Buddhist ideals of righteousness and moral regeneration. Nationalist ideology "provided a moral lens through which electoral politics and the actions of the state could be evaluated and imbued with legitimacy" (Venugopal 2011, 84).

Independent but divided

In February 1948, the British handed over administrative powers to a Sinhala-led government. Before long, the Tamils, who had for a considerable time argued for political power-sharing, began to be seen as the main challengers to a monolithic Sinhala-Buddhist political and cultural project. Tamils were portrayed as invaders, and were labelled පර දෙමළා "*para demalas*," the alien Tamils or the "dangerous other" in the nationalist political psychology and vocabulary (Kapfere 1988). One of the practical points that further justified the Sinhala agitation was that a disproportionate number of the Tamils held top professional and civil jobs as a consequence of the British missionary education in Tamil areas. The political and civil equality and democratization articulated and demanded by Tamil leaders further fuelled the Sinhala antagonism, until both ethnic groups treated the other as an enemy of their ambitions. In independent Lanka, this cross ethnic demonizing process (Mitchell 1991) became a political separator for Tamils and Sinhalas, who had already been divided based on their language and culture.

Two tragically regressive political acts in the modern history of Lanka were to prove disastrous for Sinhala-Tamil political relations. First, in 1936, a Pan-Sinhala Board of Ministers was formed. The exclusion of non-Sinhala members from the Board of Ministers through the manipulation of the Executive Committee system made cooperation among the Sinhala and Tamil élites even more difficult. This particular incident is a reminder that Donoughmore-type constitutional reforms do not by themselves provide for equitable representation and power-sharing

(A. J. Wilson 1974, 13). Then, in 1949, nearly one million Indian Tamils were disenfranchised in one of the very first decisions of the independent government of Lanka (Muthiah 2003). This disfranchisement was the result of a series of legislations in 1948–1949: the Citizenship Act No.18 of 1948, the Indian and Pakistani Residents (Citizenship) Act No. 3 of 1949 and the Ceylon Parliamentary Elections (Amendment) Act No. 48 of 1949. The three Acts in effect withdrew the voting rights of almost the entire Indian Tamil estate worker population. More than 72,230 of them had voted at the elections of 1947 (A. J. Wilson 1974, table 4.1). These acts of systemic manipulations of the political system to undermine and exclude the Tamils deeply hurt the Tamil élites as well as the rest of their community.

The governance of the newly free Lanka by the ruling United National Party (UNP), one of the oldest, largely Sinhala political organizations, was very similar to that of the colonial era. English was still the dominant language and many sectors, especially the Sinhala press, expressed the frustrations of those who had imagined a reinvigoration of the glorious past after independence. As a result, language became a crucial driving factor behind national identity. As Benedict Anderson (1983) has argued, "print capitalism" paved the way for a greater circulation of material in the vernacular language and helped to solidify an "imagined" nation. However, by 1956 their ethnic leaders, who were mere "*Kalu Suddas*"—dark white men, disappointed the average Sinhala villager. The 2500th anniversary of the death of Buddha and the landing of Prince Vijaya were commemorated in 1956. After 450 years of colonization, this was an ideal political and cultural opportunity for the more radical Buddhist nationalist and their monks to demand a Sinhala nationalist state order.

S. W. R. D. Bandaranaike,[16] (SWRD) frustrated after failing to gain the UNP leadership, broke rank with the party, claiming that it had failed to build a Sinhala state. SWRD was a skilled orator who agitated for an immediate introduction of a total "Sinhalaness" into the public and political sphere. An Oxford graduate and student union president, he used his influence to position himself as the alternative Sinhala national leader. In his march to power, SWRD adopted a nationalist transformation in attire as well as in ideology. Despite having argued for a federal solution for the island in 1926, he now appealed to the rural Sinhala Buddhist consciousness for support in creating a single national identity to construct a Sinhala majority hegemony (Clarance 2002; Manor 1989). His

16. Solomon West Ridgeway Dias Bandaranaike was the only son of Sir Solomon Bandaranaike Mahamudliya (chief government interpreter) who had become rich and powerful due to his services to the British rule. Son Bandaranaike gave up his high Anglican faith and embraced Buddhism to find political popularity. In this book, we will refer to him as SWRD.

already considerable influence amongst the powerful Saṅgha increased tremendously with this move and they vigorously supported his cause. As a combined result of these forces, the ruling UNP was replaced with the nationalist Mahājana Eksath Peramuna (MEP or People's United Front), which was an extension of the Sinhala Mahā Sabha (The Great Council of Sinhalas), which SWRD had created to propagate his nationalist ideologies. The MEP easily won the 1956 April election on a nationalist platform, and in contrast to the UNP government, no minority members were included in the cabinet, making the ruling government a Sinhala-only regime.

Sinhala élites had been using the language issue to promote their individual and cultural ambitions. It is noteworthy that J.R. Jayawardene as early as 1944 moved a resolution in the State Council to make Sinhalese the official language of Ceylon. He argued,

> I had the intention of proposing that only Sinhalese should be the official language of the Island; but it seems to me that the Tamil community and also the Muslim community, who speak Tamil, wish that Tamil should also be included on equal terms with Sinhalese. The great fear I had was that Sinhalese being a language spoken by only 3,000,000 people in the whole world would suffer, or may be entirely lost in time to come, if Tamil is also placed on an equal footing with it in this country...(State Council Debates, May 24, 1944). (Zackariya and Shanmugaratnam 1999, 81)

Within weeks, the new government of 1956, as promised during the election, introduced the "language bill," making Sinhala the only official language of the country and mandating that all state communication, including communication involving the courts, be conducted in Sinhala. Tamils now had either to learn Sinhala in a short period or lose their jobs in the state sector. Tamil leaders treated the bill as oppressive and protested against the restrictive legislation with Gandhi-style non-violence—"*satyagraha*"—outside parliament (DeVotta 2000; Kearney 1978). Even during the legislative deliberations of the bill, anti-Tamil riots broke out in Gal-Oya, a historically Tamil area that had been colonized by the Sinhalas under a new settlement and irrigation project (Manor 1989; Uphoff 1992). With the language bill, the new government used political power and its administrative/linguistic hegemony to the advantage of the Sinhalas. Eventually the country would witness an active state project of "Sinhalanizing" its general administration and socio-political space (Samaraweera 1981).

In 1958, violence broke out again across the country when the northern Tamil activists refused to follow the new government regulation to use the Sinhala "ශ්‍රී" (Sri, meaning "blessed") character instead of the English alphabets on all vehicle number plates. The Sinhala retaliation to this challenge to the Colombo administration resulted in some 400 assassinations, and left at least 12,000 homeless. Almost all the victims were Tamils (Vittachi 1962, 1958). Ethnic riots, sometimes encouraged or even sponsored by the state, occurred in 1956, 1958, 1970, 1972, 1977, and in 1978. Tamils who lived outside the Northeast, in Sinhala majority areas, were the main victims (Kauffmann 1996; Senaratne 1997; Tambiah 1986; Wickramasinghe 2006a). The MEP victory reconfigured power relations in post-colonial Lanka (Uyangoda 2010) as the newly formed coalition government rewarded their wide support base in Sinhala rural society by granting a new rural élite access to state power. Even as the social support base for the political élites broadened, ethnic representation in national politics narrowed and the state became openly Sinhalanized (Bastian *et al.* 2010). Discriminatory policies in the fields of language, university admission, state employment, and land ownership were institutionalized and further compounded by symbolically important measures related to Buddhism and the national flag (Chelvanayakam 2005; Jeganathan and Ismail 1995; Moore 1985; Richardson 2005; Spencer 2008; Tiruchelvam 2000; Uyangoda 2011, 2007).

The process of Sinhalanization continued under Sirimāvo Bandaranaike, SWRD's widow, who was in power under the banner of the Sri Lanka Freedom Party from 1960 to 1965 and from 1970 to 1977. On 22 May 1972, under a new constitution, the state Ceylon became a republic, and the name of the island was changed to ශ්‍රී ලංකා (Sri Lanka). This Buddhist term was loaded with symbolism: some twenty years previously, Tamils had protested against the extreme Buddhicizing of the public space. The new constitution provided a "foremost place" for Buddhism and made the head of state the custodian of the Buddhaśāsana, i.e. of the entire Buddhist church including all aspects of its religion, its teaching and its practices. What this meant in practice was that any prospective head of state had to be a Buddhist. It further diminished the prospect of any meaningful political bargaining or power-sharing by declaring Lanka to be a "unitary" state, a pre-emptive measure designed to block any Tamil claim to regional rule. This was an unprecedented move.[17] As many modern researchers on the constitutional transformation have shown, this was not based on Lanka's indigenous political history but on a construct left over from the British colonial policy (K. M. De Silva 2005; Edrisinha 1998; Marasinghe 2002; Mendis 1931).

Until the unification by the British, Lanka, throughout history, had been a state of collective kingdoms: the largest such kingdoms were originally called Rohana, Pihiti, Maya, and much later, there were the kingdoms of Jaffna, Kandy, Kotte and smaller kingdoms. Post-independent Sinhala ruling élites eagerly imported and installed the unitary

17. See 1972 Constitution of Lanka, Chapter 1 Article 2 and Chapter 2 Articles 6. at: http://www.tamilnation.org/srilankalaws/72constitution.htm. Accessed on 6 March 2009.

model in order to concentrate all present and future powers in their hands, giving them a political carte blanche. What was until then an institutional discrimination became constitutional in 1972. The new constitution removed the safeguard that the Soulbury constitution had provided minorities.[18]

The process above was carried out without any consultation with the civic body at large or with the affected population (K. M. De Silva 1996; A. J. Wilson 2000). Further developments in the Sinhala political and social marginalization and suppression of the Tamil population included the 1970 ban of Tamil media and the 1971 "standardization" of higher education, which required Tamil students to have higher, marks than the general population to enter universities (C. R. De Silva 1974; Olupeliyawa *et al.* 2007). The climax of this process was the 1978 constitution, which centralized power in the office of an executive presidency. The political landscape was further irreparably damaged in June 1981 when the state police was involved in the burning of the Jaffna library, considered the centre of Tamil scholarship. This confirmed for the Tamils that the time for coexistence had passed. The systematic ethnic marginalization of the Tamils and their politics deeply divided the national polity along ethnic identity lines while creating a permanent democratic deficit. Lanka was slowly but inexorably transforming into an ethnic state, negating her historical multi-nation existence.

In response to the concentration of power in the Sinhalas and the continuation of a system of social and political repression, Tamil nationalist politics began to take shape with the emergence of a demand for self-rule in the form of a separate state. In 1976, the Tamil polity reformed as the தமிழர் ஐக்கிய விடுதலை முன்னணி, the Tamil United Liberation Front (TULF), with a more radical and ethnic nationalist ideology. On 14 May 1976, at its first national convention in Vaddukoddai in the Northern Province, the party unanimously adopted a resolution demanding a separate state for the Tamils.[19] TULF, with its firm ethno-nationalist demand, enjoyed landslide victories in the Northeast at the 1977 general election and became the first Tamil party to function as the official opposition.[20] With mass support for an independent Tamil State, as had happened in East Pakistan and Malaysia, radical Tamil youth had begun

18. The 1948 Soulbury constitution's article 29.1–3 guaranteed equality for all religions and ethnicities. See http://www.nationalarchives.gov.uk/documentsonline/ceylonconstitution. Accessed on 5 March 2009.

19. See http://www.sangam.org/FB_HIST_DOCS/vaddukod.htm for the full text of the resolution, Accessed on 3 March 2009.

20. See the results of 1977 general election at http://www.slelections.gov.lk/pdf/General%20Election%201977.PDF, Department of Election Lanka, Accessed on 15 March 2009.

to dismiss traditional parliamentary politics and followed the ideology of an armed revolution against the Sinhala state. Various groups formed with Marxist-Leninist as well as ethno-nationalist ideologies and began to attack state symbols in the Northeast (Fair 2005; Shastri 1999; Narayan Swamy 1999). In July 1983, one such attack by the LTTE, killed 13 Sinhala soldiers in Jaffna, the biggest loss the army had suffered until that point. As part of the Sinhala retaliation, Tamils once again became the target of unparalleled state-orchestrated violence in the south and the hills. This pogrom, now known as "Black July," was a permanent turning point for democracy in Lanka, killing some 4000 Tamils and displacing 150,000. The violence produced two long-term consequences. Tamils disinherited from the state of Lanka began to support the cause of a separate state and to use violence as a means of political negotiation, and the state of Lanka began to view Tamils and their separatist politics as a permanent and deadly threat to the Sinhala-Buddhist nation. For the ultra-nationalists in the Sinhala south, the 1983 riots were a natural reaction of a nation threatened by a historical enemy.

By failing to recognize the need to create space for the national "other" within the structure, the Sinhala élites, in their eagerness to create a mono-ethnoreligious state, placed Lanka's post-independent politics on an illiberal trajectory, readily led by the cultural patriarch of the Saṅgha. The Saṅgha, in their eagerness to construct a mono-Sinhala social order, supported the nationalist power politics that dismantled the democratic principles and instead planted the seeds of one of the most protracted civil wars in South Asia. The ethnoreligious ideology of Saṅgha further re-fuelled the Tamil separatist nationalism and became the political midwife to the LTTE, arguably the world's most formidable separatist movement.

LTTE separatism and the war

The LTTE began as a small group of Tamil militants led by self-trained Veluppilai Prabhakaran. Due to its sheer discipline and with material support from Tamil Nadu, by the mid-1980s the LTTE had become a strong military force (Narayan Swamy 1995). With its highly sophisticated international operations, unmatched military skills and inspirational ethno-nationalism, the LTTE defied the traditional understanding of the role of non-state actors (Goodhand 2010; Stokke 2006; Woodhead 2011). By the year 2000, the movement had not only caught worldwide attention with its dramatic military operations and suicide missions but also managed to create and maintain a de-facto state of roughly 15,000 square kilometres in the greater parts of the north of the island—approximately 25% of the island and 90% of the northeast. The growth, operation and final defeat of the LTTE are now well-documented

(Hopgood 2005; Narayan Swamy 2010, 2005, 1999; Stokke 2006; Schalk 1994; Trawick 1997; Van de Voorde 2005).

If the LTTE was, as is sometimes claimed, the world's most effective guerrilla group, then by facing such a group and its terror politics for more than two decades and by finally defeating its military might comprehensively, the Lanka state, its army and the Sinhala Buddhists behind them have demonstrated the intransigent will of the Sinhalas to not share their sovereignty with the Tamil minority. Sinhalas have proven to the world that they will rather fight a bloody and prolonged war with the Tamils, sacrifice thousands of their young men and women, face economic and social stagnation and earn the antipathy of the international community, than agree to recognize the right of the Tamils for a shared-rule arrangement. Their chief desire is to create a majoritarian hegemony over the island and to continue to protect that. The Sinhala Buddhists of the island, through their successive governments over the last three decades, have fought one of the bloodiest civil wars in recent world history. The will and endurance of the Sinhala Buddhists, 45 per cent of whose population live with a daily income of less than two US dollars,[21] to mobilize their nationalist conviction is astonishing and challenges some widespread ideas about both Buddhism and ethno-nationalism.

Behind this, will power and determination of the Sinhalas are the Mahā Saṅgha who mobilizes the national psyche. Many indigenous and international observers argue that the Mahā Saṅgha's claim that Lanka is a land only for the Theravāda Sinhala Buddhists, and the violent reactions of the Tamils to this claims, are key components of this protracted ethno-national conflict. At this stage, the question is whether this ideologically charged impact of Buddhism on the state is an isolated development in the contemporary world. This work will argue that it is not.

During the period of this research (1995–2010), many observers considered the conflict a prime candidate for a federal solution as a compromise between a separate Tamil state and the existing centralized unitary Sinhala majoritarian system. The proposal of constitutional changes along federalist lines found support among moderate Sinhalas, and the international community. The LTTE too indicated a willingness to consider such a proposal. However, key Saṅgha activists and their nationalist followers adamantly rejected the federalist proposal, because the concept of federalism was directly opposed to the Saṅgha understanding of Lanka's "cosmic mission." Thus, federalism was unacceptable as a solution to the conflict and further fuelled the Saṅgha agitation. In order to be able to understand how federalism could have this perverse and

21. See World Bank and Asia Development Bank country reports on Lanka. http://data.worldbank.org/country/sri-lanka and http://www.adb.org/countries/sri-lanka/main, Accessed on 10 Aug 2011.

unintended effect, it is important to reconstruct the federal discourse in Lanka.

Federalism in Lanka

On July 2, 2009, a mere six weeks after the dramatic and comprehensive military victory that ended the 30-year civil war with the Tamil Tigers, President Mahinda Rajapakse declared:

> There is no way for federalism in this country. I am willing to search for a political solution and the TNA (Tamil National Alliance) must agree to this. They also must know that they can't get what they want.
>
> ("Federalism not possible" Rajapakse *The Island,* 7)[22]

With this statement, the victorious president concluded a ninety-year debate on federalism and reassured the Sinhala masses that the island would always remain a centralized unitary state with the Sinhala majority at the political epicentre. He reiterated the fact that the possibility of federalism or federal power-sharing in Lanka had ended.

President Mahinda Rajapakse enjoyed his highest-ever popularity ratings after winning the war against the separatist Tamil Tigers. In the statement above, the president was articulating not only his personal belief, but also the collective mind of the majority of Sinhalas, especially of the culturally powerful Saṅgha, who have historically and successfully opposed any power-sharing arrangements with the minorities. In recent years, the Saṅgha have violently opposed any proposed federal constitutional arrangements aiming to satisfy Lanka's Tamil demands and have concretized the idea of Lanka as a unitary state. The federal option failed in spite of multi-level and multi-actor efforts to promote federalism as the most viable solution to a long-running military conflict.

Both Tamil and Sinhala élites were central in the construction of the ethnically based political ideologies, which they supported with reference to archaeological discoveries, the interpretation of historical texts and the colonial legacy of race-based representation. These opposing mind-sets were instrumental in codifying the existing religious, ethnic, linguistic, and regional particularities of each identity, diminishing the possibility of a common civic bond. Post-independence, undemocratic, and majoritarian actions by the Sinhalas further widened these deep divisions (Stokke 1998).

While the ethno-nationalist ideologies in Lanka were contesting for hegemony in their respective spheres, in post-World War II conditions, other multi-ethnic states in the region such as India and Malaysia were

---

22. President Rajapakse's interview with the Indian newspaper, *The Hindu*, as reported on the front page of *The Island* of 7 July 2009, http://pdfs.island.lk/2009/07/07/p1.pdf, Accessed on 20 April 2011.

able to implement federalism as a solution to the challenge of multi-ethnic representation and participation. However, the political trajectory in Lanka was different.

In 1919, the Tamil and Sinhala élites began pre-independence negotiations on the nature of an independent Ceylon when Ponnambalam Ramanathan founded the Ceylon National Congress to demand the reform of British rule. Ramanathan, representing the Tamils, agreed with James Peiris and E. J. Samarawickrama, negotiating on behalf of the Sinhalas, to share power in the legislature, with a seat for the Western Province where the Tamil political élites resided. The next inter-ethnic arrangement was the Mahendra Pact, signed in June 1925 in Jaffna, which proposed future power-sharing, in which the Tamils would maintain one-third of the seats with Sinhala representatives holding two-thirds.

Debates on federalism have been central to any constitutional possibilities in the troubled modern history of Lanka. Ironically, in 1926, two decades before Lanka gained independence from the British rule, some Sinhala élites promoted federalism. SWRD argued in a series of political commentaries that "federalism provides the best democratic solution for Ceylon's internal and external challenges... Some form of federalism would be the only solution to our problem" (Rāghavan and Bauer 2006, 107). Bandaranaike argued for "liberty," which he defined as the transfer of political powers to individuals. He further believed a federation with India would be the best security arrangement for post-independence Ceylon (Manikkalingam and Ratnayake 1995). At that time, James Rutnam, who represented the Tamil polity paradoxically opposed federalism in a response to Bandaranaike (K. M. De Silva 1996).

The second prominent discussion on federalism came from the Kandyan Sinhalas, who appealed to the Donoughmore Commission to design a federal system along the lines of the U.S. model in order to preserve their cultural identity, distinct from the Sinhalas of the Low Country. The Kandyan National Assembly declared in a memorandum that:

> Ours is not a communal claim or a claim for the aggrandizement of a few: it is a claim of a nation to live its own life and realize its own destiny... A federal system...will enable the respective nationals of the several states to prevent further inroads into their territories and to build up their own nationality. (Wickremeratne 1928, 55)

These attempts were aborted because of pressure from the powerful, largely southern, Sinhala élites. The Donoughmore Commission of 1927—like the Soulbury Commission[23] under which Ceylon became

23. A commission sent by the British government to Ceylon (now Sri Lanka) in 1944 to examine a constitutional draft prepared by the Ceylonese ministers of government and to make recommendations for a new constitution. The Soulbury Commission called for

independent—did not pursue the federal option. One of the questions that remain unanswered is why the colonial British government (which actively promoted federalism in Australia and Canada, and proposed quasi-federalism for India under the India Act of 1935) did not consider the federal option for Ceylon, particularly as both the Tamils and Up Country Sinhalas had demanded such an arrangement. While there were some ethno-national biases in the above pacts, this élite exercise was largely guided by the nation-state concept. However, these early power-sharing agreements, like the subsequent Banda-Chelva Pact[24] of 1957 and the Dudley-Chelva Pact[25] of 1965, failed to become realities due to the partisan power struggles between the Sinhalas led by the Southern Saṅgha (Kearney 1964).

SLFP and UNP, the two major Sinhala political parties, from time to time made election promises that they would address and solve the Tamil issue. When in power their efforts were rather reluctant and lacked the necessary political will and flexibility. 1956, 1965 and 1987 saw three attempts to constitutionalize Tamil demands for greater autonomy.[26] However, in the face of violent opposition led by the Saṅgha, these projects were abandoned or allowed to become defunct. In response to this political insincerity, Tamil demand for greater autonomy from the late 1970s onwards were expressed in terms of concrete calls for federalism and later for total separatism.

The federal debate in Lanka has oscillated between the strong majoritarian unitary ideology of the Sinhalas and the equally strong desires for self-determination of the Tamils. Some have argued that these parties

---

the retention of universal adult suffrage and territorial rather than communal representation, as specified by the constitution of 1931, which was based on the recommendations of the Donoughmore Commission (1927). However, in order to ensure that minority groups would secure more seats, electorates were delimited in a new way.

24. On 25 July 1957, a power-sharing pact was signed between the Prime Minister Bandaranaike and the Tamil Federal Party Leader S. J. V. Chelvanayakam. This agreement came to be called the Banda-Chelva pact. See: http://www.satp.org/satporgtp/countries/shrilanka/document/actsandordinance/bandaranayake.htm, Accessed on 12 Sep 2010.

25. Another power-sharing agreement was signed on 24 March 1965 between Prime Minister Dudley Senanayake and Chelvanayakam, known as the Dudley-Chelva pact. See: http://www.satp.org/satporgtp/countries/shrilanka/document/actsandordinance/senanayake.htm accessed on 12 Sep. 2010. In 1987, the Indian Prime Minister Rajiv Gandhi in the style of a regional superpower forced the Lankan state to sign the Indo-Lanka accord, which made constitutional changes in order to create nine provinces. However the Lankan state did not implement the said accord with political honesty.

26. The 1956 Banda–Chelva Agreement, the 1965 Dudley–Chelva agreement, and the 1987 13th amendment to the constitution to create Provincial Councils.

neither understood nor genuinely agreed to the true ideal of federalism even when their representatives declared in Oslo as late as 2002 that

> the parties have agreed to explore a political solution founded on the principle of internal self-determination in areas of historical habitation of the Tamil-speaking peoples, based on a federal structure within a united Sri Lanka. (Oslo Communiqué 5 Dec 2002)[27]

During the various stages of the debates—interspersed by pacts, violence and peace talks—the power-sharing discourse had a distinct discursive trajectory. What started with specific issues such as fair representation and Tamil language rights became a much broader demand for greater political devolution and autonomy. The later debate tended to be about wider issues such as Tamil nationhood, (internal/external) self-determination and even the idea of a confederation. Typically the state response offered "too little, too late" and failed to guarantee the physical safety of the Tamils living in majority Sinhala areas. Even with all these drawbacks, the idea of a federalized Lanka still seemed to be relevant to the resolution of its political impasse for many reasons. The debate on federalism has continued within the constitutional and structural reforms of the state over the past decades and the question of why federalism was considered a favourable solution, yet violently rejected by the Saṅgha-led Sinhala nationalists, is the focus of the following section.

Indigenous factors supporting a federal solution

Lankan politics practised federalism in the past

Historically, Lanka has consisted of many coexisting kingdoms representing diverse ethnic, linguistic, cultural and territorial cleavages. Historian K. M. De Silva maintains that King Devānam Piyatissa, ruler of Lanka at the time of the arrival of Buddhism, after his association with Emperor Aśoka assumed the title Devānam Piyatissa "Mahārajā." However, his influence over the mountainous and southern part of the island was minimal. According to Silva, "...other rulers on the island did not readily acknowledge his sovereignty over the whole land" (K. M. De Silva 2005, 15). According to the *Mahāvaṃsa*, the Sinhala warrior king Duṭṭhagāmiṇi "united" the island only after defeating as many as 32 kings in the course of his 15 years of war against the Tamil king Elāra, who had ruled the central capital Anurādhapura for over 40 years. The success of Duṭṭhagāmiṇi could have been the first significant triumph of centripetalism over centrifugalism in the island's political power distri-

27. At the end of the third set of direct talks between the GOSL and the Tamil Tigers on October 22, 2002, both parties signed what is known as the Oslo Declaration/Communiqué see http://tamilnation.co/conflictresolution/tamileelam/norway/021205oslo-declaration.htm for the full text, Accessed on 10 Aug 2011.

bution. The list of 171 kings of Lanka from 480 BCE to 1518 CE shows the existence of simultaneous kingdoms in the island (Mendis 1932), and the unified Lanka of Duṭṭhagāmiṇi's legacy was soon fragmented by invasions and internal rivalries which re-created multiple kingdoms.

When the first European colonists arrived on the island Lanka, there were five separate kingdoms: Kandy, Kotte, Sithāwaka, Raigama and Yālpaanam (Jayasuriya 1999; Obeyesekere 1977). These five were further divided into sub-kingdoms and separate regions. Although scholars argue that the pre-colonial period is under-studied, there is enough evidence to confirm that the island had never been a unitary state until it was declared to be an administrative unit by the British in 1815 (Strathern 2004). On the contrary, there were multiple kingdoms within which a decentralized polity operated (Strathern 2002). It is therefore unsurprising that the notion of a unitary state and the very enforcing of such a notion was a colonial and post-colonial political project (Imtiyaz and Stavis 2008).

Minorities demand federalism[28]

Lankan minorities, including the Up Country Sinhalas, the Tamils and (to a lesser degree) Muslims, have demanded federalist concessions from Sinhala rulers since 1929 (Edrisinha 2005; Haniffa 2011; Oberst 1988; Thiruchelvam 2000).

In 1949, one year after independence, a nationalist Tamil political section formed the இலங்கை தமிழ் அரசு கட்சி — Ilañgai Thamil Arasa Katchī (ITAK) (Lanka Tamil State Party), which was also known as the Federal Party (FP). Its leader S. J. V. Chelvanayakam argued for a federated province for the Tamils in the Northeast, which the Tamil popula-

28. In this book, we follow the broad understanding of federalism advocated by Elazar: "The debate of defining federalism is varied and contested. Federalism, as we understand the concept—in its political form—is related to the problem of the concentration, diffusion and, most particularly, the sharing of power in political and social systems. Federal principles grow out of the idea that free men can freely enter into lasting yet limited political arrangements to achieve common ends and protect certain rights while preserving their respective integrities. As the ambiguity of the term "federal" reveals, federalism is concerned simultaneously with the diffusion of political power in the name of freedom and its concentration on behalf of energetic government. Institutionally, federalism is a form of political organization, which unites separate polities within an overarching political system so that all maintain their fundamental political integrity. It does so by distributing power among general and constituent governments in a manner designed to protect the existence and authority of all while enabling all to share in the system's decision-making and executing processes. In its most practical manifestations, the workings of federalism are reflected in the processes of intergovernmental relations and negotiated coordination among the general and constituent governments and the interests they represent." Daniel J. Elazar, "The Themes of a Journal of Federalism," *Publius*, 1971 1(1), p.3.

tion endorsed at repeated elections. Due to the support for this idea, the FP enjoyed success in the parliamentary elections of 1956, 1960, 1965, 1970 and 1975. On the strength of these victories, the FP entered power-sharing pacts with the ruling governments as in the Banda-Chelva Pact of 1957 and the Dudley-Chelva Pact of 1965. However, as noted above, these agreements failed to become a reality. By 1975, the Tamil polity was frustrated because the Sinhalas did not show any willingness to respond to their requests. Chelvanayakam summarized the disappointment as follows:

> it is regrettable fact that successive Sinhalese Governments have used the power that flows from independence to deny us our fundamental rights and reduce us to the position of a subject people....I wish to announce to my people and to the country that I consider that the Tamil Eelam nation should exercise the sovereignty already vested in the Tamil people and become free. (A. J. Wilson 1988, 88)

In response to a series of such disappointments, the FP was transformed and became the separatist இலங்கை தமிழ் அரச கட்சி: the *Tamil United Liberation Front* (TULF). The new party moved towards a separatist agenda and declared their separatist demands in the *Vaddukoddai Resolution* (A. J. Wilson 1988; Phadnis 1969).

The Vaddukoddai declaration for an independent state of Tamil Eelam (தமிழ் ஈழம்) culminated in the nationalist separatist demands on which the LTTE launched their military campaign. Although some question the sincerity of their claims, even the LTTE, throughout the war, publicly maintained their willingness to enter into a federal arrangement with Lanka if the latter was willing to grant them federal rights as e.g. in the Canada-Quebec arrangement. The LTTE's proposal for an Interim Self-Governing Authority (ISGA) for the areas under their control was a blue print for such an extended federation. This was an attempt to build on the successive but ultimately unsuccessful attempts to institute a federal system on the island.

The existing constitution already includes federal elements

After the 1987 Indo-Lanka peace accord, the thirteenth amendment to the Lanka constitution institutionalized a Provincial Council (PC) system and embedded a "two tier" governing structure (Premdas and Samarasinghe 1988; Hancocka 1999; Hennayake 1989). In practice, however, these Councils proved to be a structural and financial burden and their operation became counter-productive. Nevertheless, even in 2012, these constitutional mechanisms were still in place. The PC mechanism, which was modelled after the Indian model of power-sharing between centre and province, was too limited, however, to be considered a genuine federal system (Edrisinha 2005). The executive president at the centre was able to dissolve any province without giving reasons. While in theory, the provinces were meant to have their own police forces, land rights, taxation and educational policies, the full implementation of these provisions never happened. Furthermore, most of the fiscal and budgetary controls were with the centre. The three areas of governance that were divided as the Provincial List, the Reserved List and the Concurrent List never articulated in detail the separation of powers.[29] However, even with the above-mentioned limitations, if the Accord had been fully implemented, they just might have paved the way for the future development of federalism in Lanka. However, the Sinhala élites, pressured by the Saṅgha, did not favour the full implementation of the accord. The Saṅgha even during the signing of the Accord led a violent opposition, which included an attempt on the life of visiting Indian Prime Minister Rajiv Gandhi.

PCs, they argued, would further strengthen separatist demands and would benefit the LTTE's military helping them to fight Lanka. Such arguments proved to be lame excuses for the Sinhala élites and Saṅgha, because after the comprehensive defeat of the LTTE in May 2009, in a post-war state some 24 years after signing the accord, Lanka could have genuinely implemented the devolution and let the regional political bodies function semi-autonomously. However, such post-victory political magnanimity was not an option for Rajapakse or his powerful Saṅgha turned politicians (Höglund and Orjuela 2011).

Exogenous factors supporting a federal solution

Federalism is considered as the best option

Some form of federalism is frequently suggested as the best option for creating a stable, democratic, constitutional arrangement in divided societies especially where the divisions are based on ethnicity (Burgess 2006; Burgess and Pinder 2007; Gagnon and Tully 2001; Simeon 2009). Democratization scholars Linz and Stepan argue that ethnically constructed federal units within democratic states provide channels for ethnic groups to engage with the state system (1996). Other scholars have argued from both theoretical and empirical perspectives that federalism is the best solution available for the resolution of protracted intra-ethnic conflicts (e.g. Barnes 2001; He, Galligan and Inoguchi 2007; Hicks 2011; Horowitz 1993; Kincaid 2011; Lijphart 2004 and 1992; McGarry and O'Leary 1993, 2006; Roeder and Rothschild eds. 2005; Simeon 2009; Tillin 2007). This view is commonplace across a wide range of disciplines from conflict analysis to the study of multiculturalism (Burgess and Pinder 2007; Church and Dardanelli 2005; De Frantz 2008;

29. See the full text of the Accord and the lists at http://tamilnation.co/srilanka-laws/87thirteenthamendment.htm, Accessed on 30 March 2009.

Gagnon 2009; Kriesi and Trechsel 2008; Karmis and Maclure 2001; Kymlicka 2009, 2001, 1996; Kymlicka and Norman 2000; Mattes and Savun 2009; McRoberts 2001; Nolte 2002; Gagnon and Tully 2001; Rāghavan 2006, 2014).

Federalism is a constructive response to demands for separation made vis-à-vis unitary states. "Federalism offers a compromise between a unitary state and secession; it plays a prominent role in agreements on terminating civil wars between ethnically-defined parties to the conflict. ... It offers the possibility of a compromise between a unitary state and demands for separatism" (Gromes 2010, 354). Federalism helps consolidate democracy in situations where various nationalisms compete for hegemony and/or recognition in the political arena (Máiz and Requejo 2005), and it can provide an alternative to unilateral separatism as in the case of Quebec (L. Anderson 2007b). Federal states are also better equipped to manage fragmented, contested, and diverse identities as in the case of Ethiopia (Kefale 2013), India (Adeney 2014) and many other states such as South Africa, Nigeria and Switzerland (Moreno and Colino 2010). Furthermore, it can build and strengthen institutional capacity for advancing the process of democratization in homogenous states as demonstrated by the case of Austria (Karlhofer 2015). Federalism is not without criticism. Some have argued that federalism weakens state structure and causes fragility as in Belgium (De Winter and Baudewyns 2015). However, Alan Gagnon, echoing Heisler argued:

> I don't think federalism solves conflicts. I don't think it can avoid conflict. I think it ought to provide a context in which conflict can be approached, arbitrated and managed. Multinational federalism is a more refined model of federalism and it has added potential for state managers to come to terms with political issues confronting diverse societies. (2007, 28)

Burgess and Gagnon, scholars of comparative federalism, draw attention to the fact that at least in the classic federations, federalism and democracy have been mutually reinforcing:

> When we are reminded that previous scholarship in this area (federalism and democracy) has largely been occupied with modern classic federations, such as the USA, Switzerland, Canada and Australia, it becomes much clearer why contemporary scholars of federal studies should come to the general conclusion, as they do, that federalism and democracy—notwithstanding tensions between them—are ultimately mutually reinforcing. (Burgess and Gagnon 2010, xiii)

Canada, Spain, and Malaysia are further examples of how diverse cultural and political identities can co-exist within a federalist system.

Indian Influence

India, the regional superpower, had long advocated Tamil rights in Lanka (Hennayake 1989; Keethaponkalan 2011; Premdas and Samarasinghe 1988). India's regional policy and direct involvement and her costly and failed attempt to install federalism in Lanka are well-documented in the literature (Edrisinha 2005; Dixit 1998).

India played a major role in promoting and facilitating the idea of an armed Tamil rebellion from 1984–1989, and in advocating and enforcing a would-be form of federalism through the Indo-Lanka accord in 1989. Finally, they helped Lanka militarily to defeat the Tamil Tigers (Keethapongalan 2011). Throughout this chequered history, India, while arguing for the devolution of more political powers to the Tamils, had firmly discouraged the notion of a separate state in the northeast of Lanka; instead India promoted some form of federalism that would grant the Tamils a degree of autonomous self-rule.

The 1987 Accord amended the Lankan Constitution (13th amendment) and created a Provincial Council system with significant powers, and merged the Northern and Eastern Provinces, thus creating a contiguous area that roughly corresponded to the geographical idea of Tamil Eelam. The Accord mandated the deployment of an Indian Peacekeeping Force (IPKF) to monitor (and enforce) its implementation. India positioned herself to negotiate on behalf of the Tamils and used her political weight to extract a compromise from the Lankan government, but soon found there was limited willingness from both sides. The LTTE, not a signatory to the agreement, refused to disarm. The IPKF's attempt to force them into compliance sparked a bloody war with massive casualties on both sides. Among Sinhala nationalist constituencies, the perception of Indian infringement on Lankan sovereignty and fears that the unitary state was under threat spawned violent opposition. This culminated in the second JVP uprising in the south, in which marginalized Sinhala youth driven by a heady mixture of Maoism and nationalism staged an insurgency in 1987. The uprising was brutally crushed by the government in 1989 (Chandraperuma 1991; Moore 1993; Samaranayake 1999).

Meanwhile, opposition to India's intervention in the northeast continued. In a peculiar twist of history, there was a convergence in the interests of the Lankan government and the LTTE as both sought to force the withdrawal of the IPKF. In 1989 President Premadasa's government and the LTTE held two rounds of talks in Colombo in which both parties agreed that the IPKF should withdraw within a year. After the Indians withdrew in 1990, the pro-Indian Tamil groups, which India had used as allies or proxies, were crushed by a reinvigorated LTTE (Balasingham, 2004; K. M. De Silva 2005; Destradi 2012; DeVotta 2010; Dixit 2003; Krishna 1999; Loganathan 2006). Even today, after the military victory of

Lanka, India is actively promoting the idea of (some level of) federalism in Lanka (Bandarage 2012).

The international community supported a federal solution

The military victory in May 2009 came after one of the most internationalized, multi-actor, systematic, and thoroughly theorized peace processes in recent times (Spencer 2012). The Norwegians were invited as negotiation facilitators by President Chandrika Kumaratunge Bandaranaike (Bullion 2001). The ceasefire agreement was signed with a Scandinavian monitoring mission on the ground. Six rounds of direct talks between the Tamil Tigers and the Government of Lanka were held from 2002 to 2005. A team of experts from the EU, Japan and India were also acting as observers and advisors to the process (Höglund and Svensson 2009). For many enthusiastic actors, Lanka was promising to become a success story in conflict resolution. The peace process, from inter-party communication to humanitarian development, was dominated by international actors (Goodhand *et al.* 2005), a fact which some commentators in retrospect have criticized as a case of "over-internationalization" (Uyangoda 2010). All of the above actors supported, favoured and facilitated federalism in Lanka. However, as we know, not only was federalism rejected but the ideology of the unitary state model was also reconfirmed. Understanding this surprising process of rejection and the role of Saṅgha within it is the key aim of this research. Perhaps due in part to their positive experience as federal states, many members of the international community, including Australia, Canada, Germany, Switzerland and USA, were actively involved in the Lankan process and openly supported a federal solution.

Federalism rejected

In light of the many reasons why federalism appeared as a natural solution to the problems in Lanka, how do we explain its rejection in Lanka by the Sinhala majority? After ninety years of debate and deliberation, the federal option is still highly unpopular and widely rejected by the Sinhala political élites, most vehemently among the Saṅgha.

Will Kymlicka (2007) observed that over the past few decades there have been positive responses to federalism's policy of accommodating minority rights in North America and Western Europe on the one hand, and an opposite trend in Central Europe, Asia and Africa on the other. While multinational/multicultural states such as Belgium, Canada, Spain, Switzerland, and even the United Kingdom have actively searched for constitutional and institutional designs to incorporate politics of the peripheries, other states—particularly in Asia—have often violently refused to consider any such minority aspirations for political and cultural autonomy. Here a noteworthy aspect is that almost all the Theravādin states in Asia—Burma, Cambodia, Laos, Lanka and Thailand—have experienced bloody civil unrest due to their firm refusal to accommodate minority rights.

There are the key reasons given to justify an inflexible and undemocratic state response. They include the legacy of the past, the very political manner in which the past leaves traces in memory, colonial divisions and injustice, élite competition within the majority group, powerful religious/cultural actors, fear of other regional/external influence, and the argument that economic development rather than political power-sharing will fulfil minority aspirations. The federal discourse of the minority was considered an attempt to break the territorial integrity of the island, an internal and international conspiracy against the ethnic Sinhalas and their Theravāda Buddhist civilization. This interpretation justified the campaign for a comprehensive military solution. Defending the unitary status of Lanka with every means available to the state became a "just holy war" of Sinhala-Buddhism (Bartholomeusz 2002) led by the Saṅgha community. However, the Saṅgha community has failed, to date, to make a collective and authoritative case against federalism in Lanka. Judging from their actions and pronouncements, the federalist agenda has evoked a number of phobias in the minds of the Sinhala Saṅgha and their nationalist followers. Federalism, as understood by the Saṅgha, is an attempt to (i) make non-Sinhala Buddhists equal political owners of the island, which is unacceptable as Sinhalas are the only "nation" while others are mere communities. It is also an attempt to (ii) subdivide the island and undermine its present homogeneous Sinhala-Buddhist identity to incorporate other religious/ethnic identities, which will in turn undermine the *Dhammadīpa*,[30] the island of (Buddhist) dhamma. This belief is driven by the fear that Tamil demands for federalism are a pretext for establishing a Tamil state—a fear nurtured by historical precedents. Such a future Tamil-Hindu state carved out of the island would inevitably seek the destruction of Sinhala-Buddhist Lanka.

These deep-seated fears are reasons why the Saṅgha, as the agents of the Sinhala-Buddhist ideology empowered by an unbroken lineage and tradition, have violently opposed federalism. The reason for their stance cannot be understood without appreciating the role and influence of the Saṅgha, how they conceptualize Sinhala-Buddhism, interpret Lankan/global history and predict the future of Sinhala society and its polity.

---

30. *Dīpavaṃsa, Mahāvaṃsa* and the *Cūlavaṃsa* record that Buddha himself declared Lanka as Dhammadīpa—the island where his Buddhist doctrine will be preserved and propagated. See R. T. Clifford, "The Dhammadīpa tradition in Sri Lanka: three traditions within the chronicles," in B. L. Smith B. (ed.) *Religion and Legitimation of Power in Sri Lanka*, Anima Books, Chambersburg, PA, 1978.

The Saṅgha and Sinhala Buddhism[31]

Traditionally the majority of Buddhist studies have fallen into three main categories: the study of Buddhist doctrine, the anthropology of Buddhist societies and the study of the history of South Asia. However, there is also now an emerging focus on understanding the impact of Buddhism on state formation and democratic politics (Blackburn 2010; Borchert 2007; Braun 2009; I. C. Harris 2007; Keyes 2013). This interest in the political implication of Buddhism grew out of a desire to understand why in almost every Theravāda Buddhist state one can find high levels of protracted political unrest and violence. Burma (Schober 2011; South 2008), Cambodia (Kent and Chandler 2008; Lilja and Öjendal 2009), Laos (Abeysekara 2011; Evans 1998), Lanka, Thailand (Jerryson 2009; McCargo 2008a, 2009a, 2009b; Tamada 2009) are all Theravāda Buddhist states experiencing some form of protracted conflict relating to the definition of their statehood.

The scholarly literature suggests three main reasons why the political involvement of the Saṅgha contributed to the conflict in Lanka. First, scholars have argued that the Sinhala Saṅgha involvement is atypical. In other words, the Saṅgha have "betrayed" the true nature of Buddhism (Amunugama 1985, 1991a, 1991b; Seneviratne 1999; Tambiah 1987). Second, others have drawn attention to the specific features of Sinhala Buddhism, which make it state- and ethno-centric (Kemper 1991; B. L. Smith ed. 1978). Finally, scholars have pointed out that the democratic forces and the democratic political mechanisms failed to recognize and negotiate with Sinhala Buddhism (Abeysekara 2008, 2004; Malalgoda 1976).

The central point of understanding Sinhala politics is to appreciate the complex relationship between the Saṅgha and the legitimacy of the state. The Aśokan model shaped the śāsana in Lanka. This "traditional"[32] Sinhala heritage has been enshrined in a sacred history through the Vaṃsa volumes and other literature. In this tradition, the relationship between the Saṅgha and the state/ruler is one of immediate, unbroken, reciprocal legitimization (Bechert 1974, 1970; D. E. Smith 1974; B. L. Smith ed. 1978).

---

31. I use the term *Sinhala Buddhism* to identify the way Theravāda Buddhism is practiced amongst the Sinhalas. How the doctrine, the role of the Saṅgha and the practice of Buddhism in Lanka differs from other countries has been discussed by many scholars including, Bardwell Smith, Gananatha Obeysekara, H. L. Seneviratne, Richard Gombrich, Sarath Amunugama, Stanley Tambiah, Steven Berkwitz, Steven Kemper, and Mahinda Deegalle.

32. Heinz Bechert distinguished three phases in the development of Buddhism: 1) canonical (from the time of Buddha to the time the teachings circulated as texts), 2) traditional (from the time of the texts to the Buddhist exposure to western colonialism), 3) modern (from the time of colonization to the present) (Bechert 1974).

One cannot overestimate the impact of the colonial experience on the Saṅgha's self-understanding. Lanka had been a Buddhist kingdom for many centuries. Most of the non-Sinhala kings in the country either became Buddhists or accepted the responsibility to protect and promote Buddhism. As the rulers of a Buddhist kingdom, the rulers in Lanka were also expected to protect the Saṅgha and their institutions. In 1815, for the first time in its history, the whole island came under the rule of a non-Buddhist foreign colonial power. The experience of colonial domination dramatically changed the Saṅgha and their śāsana, shaping the Saṅgha attitudes towards early democracy in Lanka and towards non-Buddhist "others" around them, especially those with political power.

Theravāda canonical teaching does not directly conflicts with democracy (or federalism). Buddhism offers the opportunity of *Nirvāna*[33]—of reaching the final goal and "no-return" status of life in the cyclical journey of birth and rebirth—to everyone. Buddhism does not—in theory or literally—believe in any hierarchical class or caste system.[34] It also affirms the impact of karma[35] on everyone depending on his/her (in) actions. Taking these facts alone, the universality of democracy/federalism and Buddhism should complement each other in a constructive manner. However, when it comes to the organization of the Saṅgha and their śāsana, aimed at becoming enlightened or and then attaining nirvāna, we find a strict hierarchical order based on age, gender, knowledge and the *kuśala* (positive karmas). Thus, Theravāda as it is institutionalized among the Sinhalas can also provide points of friction between democracy and federalism (Clifford *et al.* 2003).

How exactly these conflicting dynamics between the canons and the practice influenced Sinhala society is largely a matter of context. Based on Theravāda interpretations, the relationship between the Saṅgha and the Sinhala polity has always favoured a centralized state-centric authority. The Saṅgha often found it difficult to accept and adopt democracy

33. The end goal of every Buddhist. Nirvāna is the end of cyclical birth through saṃsāra based on karma. See Oxford Dictionary of Buddhism (ODB 2004, 194).

34. In Sri Lanka, there are several caste and sub-caste identities in practice. Elections for power representations are often fought on this caste system (Jiggins 2010; Ryan 1953; Silva 1999) Lanka's Saṅgha are divided into three major Chapters based on caste 1) Amarapura (largely southerners of the Durāwa caste), 2) Rāmañña (largely from the Salāgama and lower country Goyigama caste), and 3) Siyam (for the Kandy/low country Goigama caste). The Siyam in turn is divided into two major temples as Malwathu and Asgiriya of Kandy (Jiggins 2010; Malaldoga 1976; Palaniappan 2008; Samuel 2007).

35. Karma (or *kamma*) is the ethical action that results in merit (*kusala*) or demerit (*akusala*). Based on such *(a)kusala*, one is born in the next birth. No one has the power to alter such merits (ODB,137).

as presented to them during the last 200 years of their encounter with colonialists. As we shall examine in later chapters, the Saṅgha attitudes towards democratic values entail many paradoxes.

The politics of the Saṅgha defends the sovereignty of the land, its *ethnie* and Theravāda faith, which in turn are best maintained and expressed by the unitary state. This thinking has produced a kind of "*Sinhalatva*"—an ideology or a consciousness (චින්තනය) like Savarkar's "Hindutva" (Savarkar 2009; Sarkar 1996)—that considers the Sinhalas as the only group with a political claim to the land. Through such ethnic hegemonizing and political centralization, Sinhala nationalism institutionalized a form of non-democratic if not indeed totalitarian politics.

This research will explore how the Sinhala Saṅgha have produced this religiosity using the *Mahāvaṃsa* and related Sinhala texts, and then used this religiosity to shape the politics of modern Lanka. The key contribution of the *Mahāvaṃsa* was to transform Pāli Buddhist ethics into Sinhala Buddhism (Harvey 2000; Reynolds 1979). In this ideologizing process, the Saṅgha have managed to declare the act of defending the island as a Sinhala Buddhist unitary state a religious duty, which justifies and could require the use of violence. Within this context, questioning or challenging the politics of Sinhala Buddhism amounted to a rejection of its core values and made the challenger an enemy of Sinhala ethnicity, their Buddhism and /or the unitary nature of the island. Because federalism argues for equal citizenship, equal political rights and the recognition of sub-state regional autonomy in Lanka, the federal discourse in Lanka became the ideology of an enemy. We cannot label the Sinhala Saṅgha as religious fundamentalists, for they do not refer to or adhere to an original religious text to justify their worldly action. Nevertheless, we may safely call them "political fundamentalists" because they idealize a certain version of society codified in the pages of the *Mahāvaṃsa*.

Theravāda ethics and political violence

The study of Buddhist ethics and their complex relationship to modern societies, especially to the issue of war and violence, has generated a considerable volume of literature (Hallisey and Hansen 1996; Hallisey 1992; Jones 1979; Keown 2001; Love 1965; Prebish 1996a; Reat 1980; Zimmerman *et al.* 2006).[36] The relationship to political violence as in Lanka complicated the matter even further. There are no readily agreed-upon

36. On the methodological, conceptual and interpretational complexity of Theravāda Buddhist ethics see the special issue of the *Journal of Religious Ethics*, Spring 1979, Vol. 7, No.1, especially the editorial at pages 1–10. Damien Keown states that "Buddhist ethics is aretaic: it rests upon the cultivation of personal virtue" (Keown 2001, 2). The view that Mahāyāna involves a kind of virtue ethics has been more extensively developed, especially given the claim that the Bodhisattva's compassion can override rules (Cooper and James 2005; James 2004).

methods of interpretation or analysis. Furthermore, the Theravāda canon distinguishes two different kinds of ethics depending on whether they have otherworldly connotations (*lokottara*) or not (*laukika*, of this world). The way ethical principles apply to the Saṅgha, whose primary objective in life is to endeavor nirvāna, and to the lay Buddhist are different. For example, a Saṅgha has 227 *pātimokkha*[37] rules to follow, which include celibacy, not using money etc.—but these rules do not apply to the lay Buddhist.

The primary objective of the teaching of Buddha is to understand the suffering—*duḥkha*—of this world and to train one's mind and life in order to overcome such suffering by overcoming the cycle of birth and re-birth that one is involved in as a result of one's own (in)action. *Duḥkha* is one of the four noble truths Buddha preached in his first sermon. In English, there is no single word to capture the essence of the Buddhist meaning of *duḥkha*. The rough translation as suffering is somewhat misleading. *Duḥkha* is the remorse that comes from the understanding of the impermanence of life and everything around it. There are three kinds of *duḥkha*: *duḥkhā-duḥkha*, which is the universal suffering in the world caused by illness, death, poverty, etc., *viparināma-duḥkha*, which is the suffering caused by change over which we have no control, and *saṃskāra-duḥkha*, which is the formation and deformation of consciousness and *anātman* (no self). In this process of overcoming *duhkha*, there are clear decisions to be made. Some practices and thoughts are to be avoided while others are to be embraced. Taking part in this process—being on the "path"—decides whether individuals, the people and society are "for" or "against" Buddhism.

Aided by the historical position they have occupied in Lankan society, the Saṅgha hegemonize the interpretive matrix according to which people, ideas and things stand for or against Buddhism. Selecting and popularizing ethics relating to war and peace is a largely contextualized process, and it is for this reason that the history of the Saṅgha in Lanka (and elsewhere) has produced such a variety of results and outcomes. Scholars now agree that the view of Buddhism as a global/translocal phenomenon based on some original canon cannot explain the function of contemporary Buddhism. Instead, modern Buddhism survives because of the process of "inculturalization" within the local setting as the key act of interpreting Buddhist values, attitudes, traditions and texts. Analyzing this "localizing" process, Erik Braun argues that

> Past scholars studying Buddhism, especially in Southeast Asia, often went so far as to celebrate the conception of a single translocal form of Buddhism as a worthier counterpart to seemingly more ephemeral and corrupted local expressions. But in recent years scholars have moved

37. *Patimokkha* (or *Pratimoksa*) are the code of conduct of Saṅgha discipline given in the Vinaya Piṭaka. See (Prebish 1974a).

> well past a simplistic division between a supposed translocal and authentic core of Buddhism opposed to local "corruptions," in favor of a view that sees meanings and values for forms of Buddhism—even translocal Buddhism's–emerging at local levels. Yet further refinement of this division is ongoing, especially concerning conceptions of Buddhism in the modern era. (2009, 936)

Karunā, maitrī and ahiṃsā are key virtues of Theravādins. Maitrī is to be understood as kindness, benevolence or goodwill, the first of the divine abidings. Karunā is absolute compassion, the second divine abiding. *Ahiṃsā* is the moral principle of non-violence towards fellow human beings, animals and plants. In Theravāda, the teaching of Buddha embodies universal kindness towards all living beings. Yet throughout history and in the present day there are examples of violence and war in states where Theravāda is the majority state religion. Almost all Theravādin states have experienced abysmal levels of violence against their own citizens in the recent decades. This obviously demands some explanations. What are the possible justifications of violence in the Pāli Canon, tales of Aśoka-the universal wheel-turning monarch (*cakkavatti*), post-canonical narratives such as the *Mahāvaṃsa*, as well as contemporary postcolonial Lankan Theravāda beliefs and practice? Theravādin canonical writings do not offer specific, detailed discussions on war or peace (Premasiri 2003; Bartholomeusz, 2002). Most modern Buddhist theology on the ethic of war and peace derives from Buddha's discourses on life and society or his encounters with kings and rulers (DN II 72–76; Panditha 2011; Rhys Davids 1972; Walshe 1995). In Lanka, we find at least three different schools of thought regarding the Theravādin ethic of violence:

1. Violence is a necessary element in the historical unfolding of the Theravādin narrative (Bartholomeusz 2002; Kapferer 2004, 2001, 1988, 1985, 1979; Kiblinger 2003; Obeysekere 2003, 2002, 1995; Tambiah 1993, 1992, 1986).
2. There is no evidence of support for violence within the Theravádian tradition (Deegalle 2006a, 2006b, 2003, 2004; Pandita 2001; Premasiri 2003).
3. Presenting violence as an ethical duty in the context of the Theravāda tradition is always a result of the power play by the Saṅgha and the state since the time of Emperor Aśoka (Amunugama 1985, 1991b; Gunawardena 1971, 1979; Spencer 1990a, 1990b).

The dominant voice in this debate on the ethics of peace and war in Lanka belongs to the Saṅgha, who appeal to two contradictory positions. On the one hand, the Saṅgha are the symbol of the teaching of Buddha and his doctrine. They subscribe to an extensive philosophy based on compassion and renouncing of this world. However, they also are the spiritual and cultural guardians of Theravāda and hence of Lanka. This dichotomy of "renouncing yet involved" rests on a fine and fragile balance in Sinhala history. The Saṅgha, who are the symbol of a renounced life dedicated to the search for the path to nirvāna, due to their intrinsic involvement are an inseparable part of the politics and governance of their society. They have also shaped the Sinhala worldview and thus the subsequent actions taken as a result of this worldview. Over the course of history, it is obvious that the Sinhala Saṅgha have both produced a violent political ideology as embedded in the *Mahāvaṃsa* and continued to represent Buddhism as a non-violent philosophy of renunciation.

The violent element of the Sinhala Buddhist ideology was strengthened during the colonial era. In order to generate and popularize it, the ethno-nationalism presented in the historical narrative of the *Mahāvaṃsa* supplied a scriptural justification. The *Mahāvaṃsa* even records violence between different monastic orders. In fact, in Lanka the canonical ethic on war and peace are often adjusted to the local and contemporary conditions; in other words, the canon can become secondary to localized political ideology. What matters is not what Buddha preached, but rather what his followers like Venerable Mahānāma of Mahāvihara—the legendary author of the *Mahāvaṃsa*—heard, understood, and interpreted at least some 1000 years Buddha's death. Such "sub-ethics" (Hallisey and Hansen 1996; Harpham 1992) drive socio-political moral life in Lanka. Narratives like the *Mahāvaṃsa* continue to prefigure, configure and refigure the politics of the Saṅgha and their society.

Buddhism has undoubtedly contributed to the prosperity of a great agrarian civilization since the era of Emperor Aśoka of India. Furthermore, Buddhism fostered a cultural and economic renaissance whose influence extended from Afghanistan to China, in the process transforming the social, political and spiritual philosophy of the populations it touched. However, within that process there was also evidence of regressive trends which contradicted the very teachings that Buddhism publicly stood for. One clear feature of Theravāda Buddhism is the direct, influential and intrinsic relationship it maintained with the ruling élites wherever it arrived, supporting them by protecting the state's centralized rule under a Buddhist ruler.

In Theravāda Buddhist states such as Lanka, instead of a secularization process, we find a deep "religionizing" during the formation of the state as a cohesive political identity developed. In the case of Lanka, ethnic and religious identity struggled for legitimacy and political power well before independence in 1948. Bond (1998), Malalgoda (1976), Tambiah (1992, 1986) and Seneviratne (1997) have documented this process in detail. Such a contest did not demand reforms of religious traditions. On the contrary, they opposed the ruling authorities and their secular models that attempted to distance religion from governance. The 1817, the Ūva Wellasa rebellion against the British colonists, which will be discussed later, was a militant challenge led by religious actors demanding the legitimacy of Buddhist governance in Lanka. In Lanka, the notion of independence did not come from secular forces but through an attempt to re-establish and re-assert the legitimacy of Buddhism and its chief-interpreters, the Saṅgha, eventually restoring them at the center of power. As Walpola Rāhula summarized in 1947, the Saṅgha demanded political freedom from all forces to reestablish their historical heritage and power. In Lanka, federalism had to negotiate with Buddhism—not the other way around. That is the fundamental reason why the fashionable thesis of the "return of religion" is unable to explain the war, the peace process or even the recent military victory, because religion *never* left the politics of Lanka.

— 2 —

The Social and Political Role of the Saṅgha in Lanka

> The social life of a Saṅgha is like a flight of a bird in the sky. You can see the bird but you will never be able to trace it.
>
> Venerable Khammai Dhammasami[1]

Introduction

What is the ideal life of a Saṅgha? This question challenges the entire recorded history of the Buddhaśāsana. No other question has, throughout history, generated such deep, divisive interpretations in the Buddhist kingdom, giving birth to many of its *Vādas* (doctrinal schools) and *Yānas* (traditions of practice). Just a few weeks after the *Mahāparinibbāna*[2] of Buddha, the Saṅgha, at their first council,[3] disagreed on a number of theological and religio-social aspects of their daily life (Hallisey 1992; Prebish 1996b, 1974b). For the *Bahusrutas* (the learned), the dhamma (the mastering of the teaching of Buddha and his philosophy) was important, while for the *Seeladharas* (the disciplinarians), salvation came through the stricter observation of the *Vinaya*[4]—the ascetic disciplines (Chatalian 1983; Findly 1992). These disagreements have not diminished after twenty-five centuries of discourse, and they promise to remain an issue of contestation in the Buddhist world.

---

1. Venerable Dr Khammai Dhammasami, Chief Incumbent Oxford Buddhist Vihāra, Oxford. Interview 10 July 2010.
2. In the Buddhist texts, the death of Buddha, his departure from life and journey to the nothingness of nirvāna ending the cycle of birth and re-birth, is referred to as *Mahāparinibbāna.*
3. The first meeting of nearly 500 Arahats was held at Rājagaha just a few weeks after the death of Buddha. Here, the senior monk Mahā Kassapa is said to have acted as the overall leader (ODB: 66).
4. Vinaya is the set of ascetic disciplines described in the Vinaya Piṭaka—one of the three key texts of Buddhism. A Theravādin ordained Saṅgha has to follow 227 of such rules.

The renouncer tradition of spirituality, whereby one seeks spiritual salvation through a radical departure from home and society, is not an exclusively Buddhist heritage (Silber 1981; Whitehouse and Laidlaw 2004). Asocial or even antisocial traditions of spirituality existed prior to the establishment of Buddhism as a key spiritual force in northeast India. There were several traditions of wandering mendicants such as the *Jaina*[5] (Bühler 1878; Flügel 2006, 2005; Osier 2007; Schubring and Beurlen 2000) and *Ājīvakas*[6] (Basham 1951), who left civilian life and lived on alms in search of spiritual enlightenment. It was from these traditions (collectively called the *śramanas*)[7] That the Buddha first gained spiritual directions. The Buddha's revolutionary contribution at the time was to present the *Madhyama Pratipatti*, the "middle path" between the Brahmans, who were preoccupied with their countless rituals, and the torturous ascetic practices of the ascetic *śramanas* (Bronkhorst 1998).

Buddha argued for the importance of two key factors: moving away from the repetition of the customary rituals of Brahmanism, and rejecting *śramanism*'s punitive focus on the body. He emphasized the importance of the mind as the key center of meditation yet he remained within the renouncer tradition. It appears, as far as the Pāli canons permit us to determine, that Buddha strategically avoided any abstract (and thus contested) attempts to re-define the forces of karma, instead taking karma as a given part of the status quo. His followers were encouraged to eliminate *tṛṣṇā*, or human desires and cravings, which are the basis of all *duḥkha* (the sufferings in human life). As De Jong (1972) shows, Buddha very clearly distinguished between parallel traditions in asceticism, Yoga, and *śramanism*. Although the prescriptions he gave to the Saṅgha were less punitive in comparison with the other śramanic traditions, the Vinaya rules he gave had their own restrictions, especially when compared to the modern Saṅgha community. The earliest Saṅgha were to follow these *nisraya—vrksha mūla*: sleeping at a root of a tree; *piṇḍapāta*: begging for meals; *pāṃsūkūla*: wearing rags found in cemeteries; *pūtimūtra-bhaisajya*: drinking cow urine as the only medicine—and to practice the 227 rules of the *Pātimokkha* (Vin. I: 28, 58). These practices constituted the inner and outward signs of the commitment of the Saṅgha (Gombrich 1992, 1988; Wijeyeratne 1983; E. L. Thomas 1933).

5. Jainism is an Indian religious order very similar to Buddhism and was propagated by Mahāvīra, a contemporary of Buddha. Jainism, unlike Buddhism, believes in a Jīva, an eternal soul, and follows a stricter form of *Ahiṃsā* (non-violence, extending to plants and unseen insects), (see the *Oxford Dictionary of World Religions* p.280).

6. A breakaway sect of Jainism founded by Makkhali Gosāla (ODB: 6)

7. Indic religions can be divided into two basic types: *Sramanas* (the unorthodox renouncer type) and Brahmanism (the orthodox, established and ritualistic type).

Buddha's advocacy of a peripatetic yet coenobitic alternative for the Saṅgha was initially a radical compromise challenging the social and political context and attracting a new generation of followers. However, the significant difference of the Buddha's teaching, compared to the traditions that preceded it, was the "middle-path" teaching. He encouraged homelessness, wandering without desire, and living a simple life, but never advocated the total rejection of, and withdrawal from, human society. Aspiring Saṅgha were to have two motivations: they had to live a life of "detachment" to find spiritual salvation, while remaining on the fringes of society, from where they could teach others how to find enlightenment. The Saṅgha were to remain meditative during the four-month rainy season (*vassāna*), travel and preach the dhamma during the remaining eight months. The modern Theravāda interpretation of these two guidelines creates a tension of "renouncing but re-engaging." The Saṅgha occupy the in-between space of renouncing and re-engaging; they are the mediators of the tension between these two poles of existence. This is what is meant by Venerable Khammai Dhammasami's dictum, chosen as a motto for this chapter, that it is possible to see a Saṅgha but impossible to ever "trace" his life.

It remains difficult to analyze the early Saṅgha socio-political behaviour and its impact on their contemporary polity because, after twenty-five centuries, the only means of doing so is to study the original texts and their narratives. Most of these narratives concern the inner dynamics of the individual and the collective dynamics of the Saṅgha community, and as a result, most research will involve re-reading and interpreting early Buddhist texts.

Richard Gombrich's account of early Saṅgha society deliberately attempted to bypass the sociology of religion, thereby challenging its two popular and hegemonic prisms: the Marxist narrative of material history and the Weberian school of economic order. To Gombrich, the rise of religions, especially the simultaneous growth of a number of Indian religious philosophies, took place independently of surplus production processes. He maintains that an argument based on a linear, progressive production process and the rise of a surplus economy was unable to explain the birth and growth of many religious discourses of the *śramana* traditions such as Jainism, Ājīvakas, or Buddhism. His understanding of renouncer religions also went against the dependency theory of the priestly class, which he considered to be "not very informative" (Gombrich 1988, 13).

Available historical evidence, including evidence concerning the growth of Western civilization, also calls into question the value of the economic "surplus" account of the birth and growth of religions. The birth and subsequent growth of the Christian faith did not occur under favorable economic conditions. In fact, the radical changes in the religious landscape inspired by the teachings of Jesus Christ took place against a backdrop of economic, social, political, and even military oppression. Marcus Borg's work (1998) highlights alternative methods by which the Jesus movement attracted its early followers against all odds. As Hopkins (1998) shows, during the first three hundred years of its existence the Jesus movement was a persecuted peripheral discourse, yet its adherents were unwilling to surrender their beliefs even in conditions of extreme socio-political oppression.

One may argue that the Jesus movement was entirely different in theology and practice from what we witness today in a post-Protestant Western context. Are economic theories better at explaining the rise of Protestantism? Is Protestantism the result of capitalism or vice versa? These questions lead us to Max Weber's analysis. Weber pioneered the sociological analysis of Indian religions including Buddhism. After publishing his *The Protestant Ethic and the Spirit of Capitalism* (1904) and *The Religion of China: Confucianism and Taoism* (1968 [1951]), Weber ventured to analyze the structure of Indian society and its relation to the two key religions in India: Hinduism and Buddhism. His *Religions of India* (2000 [1958]) remains a standard methodological matrix popularly used in Western academic circles for reading and understanding the religious sociology of the Indian sub-continent as a whole and Buddhism (and Hinduism) in particular. However, there is less appreciation for Weber's third thesis than for his previous work. It found more opposition than any of his other works, mainly from the Indologists. Classical Indologists argue that without first-hand knowledge of Sanskrit or Pāli, the most influential ancient languages, one cannot re-interpret the ancient society of India (Bayly 1983; O'Hanlon 1985). Sociologists on the other hand criticize Weber's argument because it approaches the complexity of Indian society by employing a predominantly Western economic conceptual framework (Appadurai 1996). As a result, the Weberian account is unable to explain the social dynamics that led to the emergence of not one but three distinct renouncer religions, namely Buddhism, Jainism, and Ājīvakas. Weber's framework is also limited in that it cannot explain why Buddhism emerged as the dominant religion in places where it arrived (rather than the place where it originated), while Jainism remained on the periphery and Ājīvakas disappeared. The contribution we can make to these specialist debates is naturally limited, but it is worth highlighting that historians and Buddhalogists alike have struggled to establish a precise explanation for the formation of a pioneer Saṅgha society that remained a marginal sect until it found favour with Emperor Aśoka two centuries later. In our view, the rationale and the objectives of the Saṅgha Samāja are best understood by revisiting the functional dynamics of their society as revealed in the *Vinaya Piṭaka*. Although it is difficult to reconstruct the details of the society of Buddha at the moment of its emergence, we will nevertheless try to compose a general picture that will work as our background for understanding the origin, development and the subsequent politicization of the Saṅgha community. While the Indian Saṅgha Samāja was the basis for the establishment of the Sinhala Saṅgha, this chapter will also aim to explain how the Sinhala Saṅgha emerged with an outlook that was very different from, if not opposed to, the outlook of the original Saṅgha.

Buddha, the Saṅgha and politics

It may be possible to argue that the Buddhist renouncer religion, whether by design or through the political maneuvers of the agents of power, became a structural tool of mass domestication. In a broader Marxist understanding, this means that the social discourse created by Buddha and the Saṅgha community indirectly supported and fortified the existing base of the socio-political order. However, if we are to test the validity of this hypothesis, the counter argument should also be considered. Could the radical renouncer religion advanced by Buddha in fact be a form of resistance to, and contestation of, the power structure of the polity, as has been argued by Silber (1981). Can non-engagement be a form of passive protest? Did Buddha aim to challenge the ruling powers through a kind of structured civil disobedience and by calling for an alternative social order and power distribution? Is this the kind of passive aggression that Gandhi adopted, centuries later, against the British colonial rule in India? With Gandhi, we have a classic example from recent history to illustrate the power that simplicity and renunciation still hold within Indian culture even some twenty-five centuries later. Further, it could be that Buddha, by emphasizing the other world as the only permanent state, may have subtly undermined the political powers of his time. Through his teaching, he seems to have challenged the two key contemporary political powers passively, yet with formidable force. He denounced the mytho-polytheistic, hierarchical and ritualistic Brahmin authorities, and he challenged the rulers through a radical form of civil disengagement.

Was he in fact mounting a Nietzschean challenge by denying the existence of any superior God or self (*anattā*), and instead promoting a rational sense of the inner man (Krummel 2005; Wallis 2008)? Some commentators suggest that Nietzsche was heavily influenced by early Buddhist thinking, even borrowing from it for his methods of philosophical deconstruction (Bilimoria 2008). This line of argument seems plausible because, in comparison to the contemporary *śramana* renouncers of his time, Buddha refused to surrender life to a total fatalistic nihilism.

Instead, he argued for an inward analysis of life and of the attachments that come from cravings and desires (*tṛṣṇā*). Buddha never entirely gave up on human life, even when it offered no meaning, as he believed it was the crucial stage of the "continuous flow" (saṃsāra) that would determine the direction of the journey of life. He preached the possibility of overcoming not just the *duḥkha* (suffering) of this life but also the entire trans-migratory cycle of birth-death-and-rebirth caused by karma. His middle path discourse, while recognizing the emptiness of civic life, nevertheless admitted that the path to spiritual liberation was (with rare exceptions) gradual and sequential. Until the point of spiritual liberation, the goal of life is to live within the guidance of the renouncer principles: the four noble truths.[8] It is in this context that the Buddha outlined a delicate, and controversial, lifestyle for his followers. This lifestyle was encapsulated in a series of principles to guide his lay followers and in a distinct way of life for the Saṅgha, his immediate disciples. Buddha permitted any layman to enter the Saṅgha-hood and any Saṅgha to return to the lay life at any time: a *modus vivendi* that has continued to operate throughout the entire history of Buddhism. This structure was a crucial element of dissent by passivity, in that it created an alternative and counter-cultural social structure through which the entire social fabric was re-defined in relation to Buddhism: everyone was either a member or a supporter of the Saṅgha class, which, standing on the fringes of society, had the potential to destabilize the established secular powers.

While scholarly opinion is divided on this, it is possible to argue that these arrangements represented a call for a parallel society, a different order of being initiated by following Buddha's renouncer ideology. However, like all other areas of Buddhist studies this is only an alternative analysis of what little history there is available. Twenty-five centuries have passed, during which already scarce information has been constructed and reconstructed through the lens of history. History may not be able to provide us with an authentic account of Buddha (Clark 1930). As we know, no history has the ability to totally escape the socio-political orientation of the narrator. With an appreciation of the limitations of our historical knowledge in mind, we will now turn to an investigation of the early Saṅgha movement.

8. Also known as the *Arya Catur Satya*: the four foundational concepts preached by Buddha in his very first sermon. *Duḥkha:* life/existence is full of suffering; *Samudaya:* suffering arises from craving desires, *Nirōdha* (in nirvāna all suffering ends) and *Arya Ashtanga Mārga*: the eightfold path is the way to nirvāna. The eightfold path incorporates *Samyag-dṛṣṭi* (the right view), *Samyag Samkalpa* (the right resolve), *Samyag Vācha* (right speech), *Samyag Karmānta* (right action), *Samyag Ājīva* (right livelihood), *Samyag Vyayāma* (right efforts), *Samyag Smṛti* (right mindfulness), *Samyag Samādhi* (right meditation).

The first Saṅgha: A social background

Understanding and interpreting the origin of Buddhism have always presented historical, archaeological, and sociological challenges. Many parts of Buddhism are highly contested by many scholars of different schools, in part because the Buddha did not record any of his teachings, and in part because of the many controversies and divisions within the different schools of Buddhism. Scholarship on early Buddhism is still at an early stage of development, without much progression from its beginnings in the 1800. Eugene Clark reflected on this condition seven decades ago, with his assertion that the discoveries at present have "not advanced our knowledge in any significant manner" (Clark 1930). Still, as J. W. De Jong, a scholar of early Buddhism, noted:

> It would be hypocritical to assert that nothing can be said about the doctrine of earliest Buddhism ... the basic ideas of Buddhism found in the canonical writings could very well have been proclaimed by him [the Buddha], transmitted and developed by his disciples and, finally, codified in fixed formulas. (De Jong 1993, 26)

We know, for example, that the Indian society in which Buddha lived, preached, and called his first Saṅgha disciples was anything but monolithic. Historians and Indologists agree that Buddha's society was multilingual, multiethnic, and multi-faith, and that it had multiple forms of governance (Schopen 2002; Stein 2010; Thapar 2004). However, Kapilavastu, where Siddhartha was born during the fifth or sixth century BCE,[9] was one of the city-states known as Janapadas, located in a remote area relatively free from the dominant influence of Brahmin socio-politics. The fact that Kapilavastu was separate from the Hindu Brahmin society facilitated the existence of a casteless structure,[10] and based on the

9. After nearly two centuries of debates, scholars have not been able to agree on the dates of Buddha's life. At a conference in Goettingen as recent as 1988 no less than 18 different theories were presented by scholars on the dates of Buddha (Bechert 1991). Most books available on Buddhism place the Buddha into the sixth century BCE with 563–483 as one of the most commonly quoted dates. However, recent scholarship is moving away from this theory, placing Buddha's life firmly within the fifth century BCE. As Nakamura noted, "[g]iven the poor state of early Indian chronology, one can appreciate one scholar's statement that it is quite remarkable to have a dating theory fall into such a limited difference of merely one century" (Nakamura1977, 12 ff, quoted in Dillon 2000, 525).

10. The caste system derives from Brahmanic Hinduism, which categorizes the society according to four Varna (Colors). In Lanka, the influence of caste is found amongst the Sinhalas, the Tamils and even the Muslims. The Sinhala caste system has at least 24 major and sub categories. Goyigama (famers), Durāve (tree climbers), Karāve (fishermen) and Salāgama (Cinnamon peelers) are the four major Sinhala castes (Jiggins 2010).

model of governance he later recommended to the Vajjins and his own followers, Buddha was probably influenced by a semi-democratic or, at least, oligopolitical structure (Dig II: 73–75). Buddha was born a member of the Śākya *ethnie*, and was often referred to as "*Sakyamuni*" (the sage of Sakya). His mother tongue is not known, but is suspected to have been a "non-Indo-Aryan dialect" (Gombrich 1988, 49) or similar to Magadhi (De Jong 1993), while Pāli, in which the canon were composed, is a later language preserved and promoted by the Theravādins.

There are two main schools of thought regarding the nature of the society of Buddha. Some argue that Buddha's society was in a state of permanent transition and plagued by socio-political tensions, while others maintain that his society was stable and prosperous, which enabled the development of an elitist discourse on society, life and death. After giving an extended account of various socio-economic and political aspects of Buddha's society, Darian argues:

> We must emphasize that while economic factors were important in the rise of Buddhism, the aspiring merchant was able to succeed financially under the Hindu caste system. And it is questionable whether he would have chosen Buddhism if not for other, irresolvable status dilemma.
>
> (Darian 1977, 226)

Still, while Buddhist literature does not reveal a "consciousness of a period of dramatic change having been traversed" (Bailey and Mabbett 2003, 3), it is fair to say that the time of Buddha was a period of change and that society was in transition (Darian 1977).

At Buddha's name-giving ceremony, many learned astrologers were said to have predicted that the princely boy would be a *Cakravattin* (an emperor) or a sage and leader of society. It is important to note that almost all accounts of the early life of Buddha present these two futures for the young boy. This represents an evolution in the outlook of the recorders of Buddhist history. While Buddha's attitude towards power and rule seems quite detached in Pāli Buddhist texts, put together at least a few centuries after his death, the conceptual identity of the Buddha (and later the Saṅgha) was replaced with that of an emperor. It is noteworthy that the king and the Saṅgha are both considered as occupying positions of influence and rule: one by power and the other by way of radical renunciation.

H. L. Seneviratne (1999) postulates that throughout the modern history of the Buddhist śāsana, the Saṅgha preferred to position themselves in one of two power positions, preferring either to *be* the kings or to be *beside* the kings. The conceptual approach to power and kingship found in the post-Buddha texts seem to gravitate around four central notions, as presented by Gokhale (1966):

1. A powerful centralized leader is inevitable in a world where the number of spiritual virtuosi is decreasing.
2. Kingship is a divine gift awarded for merits gained in a previous life.
3. Kings should have the knowledge and ability to maintain a balanced treasury and an effective standing army.
4. A king should be the compassionate father figure who rules the state with the virtues of dhamma.

The ruler king and the renouncer sage are two antithetical but deeply intertwined themes at the center of Buddhist theology. The relationship between the two positions is dialectical, not unlike the relationship between the concepts of nirvāna and karma. Nirvāna is the ultimate place of nothingness and bliss, which one can achieve with the power of *kusala*, (positive) karma (merits). Throughout the course of human life, one can accumulate all the necessary merits to guarantee the path to Nirvāna. These concepts represent two equal yet opposite poles of human life: one demand the act of merit collection here and now while the other forces humans to focus on Nirvāna. The first rule applies more to the lay world, while the latter applies to the Saṅgha. For this reason, the laity has five principles to follow while the Saṅgha follow 227 rules.[11] In the Theravādin tradition the Saṅgha are the key intermediary of merit collection for the lay world, and their first duty is to show the path of salvation to the lay world (Bechert 1973; Bond 2003; Malalasekara 1967; Rāhula 1956). These tensions between nirvāna and karma and between Saṅgha and layperson were present from the very early stages of the Buddhaśāsana.

Another key influence of the Buddha movement on political governance concerns the attitudes towards political power as they are described in Buddha's original teachings. His discourse advocated withdrawal from society and living on alms, but the Saṅgha were still considered a privileged group because it was their responsibility to share the dhamma with the rest of society. Furthermore, unlike the contemporary *Sramanas*, Buddha encouraged his followers to assist their community in whatever manner available. One can imagine that rulers may favor groups that cultivate attitudes that urge men to seek an otherworldly life rather than worldly political power. What appears to be an attitude of inwardness and quietude is also the complete opposite of the model used by the Brahmin, who survived on state and temple treasuries, who based their spiritual power based on the Vedas—which were written in

11. The five moral rules of Buddhism-*Pañca Sīla*—are: do not kill; do not rob; do not fornicate; do not lie; and do not become intoxicated (ODB, 210). For the 277 rules a Saṅgha is to follow in Theravāda Buddhism, see: http://www.accesstoinsight.org/tipitaka/vin/sv/bhikkhu-pati.html, Accessed on Aug 10, 2010.

Sanskrit, the language of the élite—and whose social and civic leadership always ran parallel to that of the king, thus competing with kingship. As Bailey and Mabbett argue:

> it was natural for the ruler to seek legitimacy in a new and universal ideology. ... it is therefore not surprising that rulers such as Aśoka should have expressed disapproval of trivial ceremonies but patronized lavishly the community of Sramanas. (2003, 175)

The key point of differentiation is that Buddha, whether by strategic choice or simply because of a difference in philosophical approaches, did not challenge the rulers in any open, direct manner. Instead, he provided a socio-political and economic alternative to the status quo, in which the rulers tried to preserve their power and counter wide-ranging societal changes while constantly being challenged by the Brahmin élites. The other-worldliness of Buddhism may have appealed to rulers as it seemed to divert attention from the concrete living conditions of the ruled to more abstract and transcendent ideals. Could this new movement be used to domesticate society and thus to consolidate existing power structures? It is possible that this is the reason why the rulers and élites during the time of Buddha and after were often eager to accept and patronize Buddhism politically. However, the possibility that Buddha's apolitical polity and his asocial or even antisocial engagement indirectly strengthened the existing power structures has not been sufficiently researched. Some scholars (S. Dutt 1984; Kosambi 1946, 1955, 1963; Kosambi and Kosala 1952; Thapar 1989) present this argument, and we believe that this proposal may help us understand the politics of Buddhism, especially the Theravāda version, through the lens of political science.

Buddhism revolutionized some parts of India. It transformed almost every aspect of the society and its peoples. However, it did not become what Hinduism to India. Even at its peak times, Buddhism was a second religion, where there was already an established and heavily institutionalized religious ideology (Hinduism). Nevertheless, Buddhism established itself as being capable of convincing the masses, who had little to no experience with a systematic religious philosophy. Buddhism in general and the Theravāda tradition in particular, seems to have been able to successfully use state power and strategic diplomacy to advance its path. Certainly, this is true in the case of the Post-Aśoka era in Lanka, Burma, and Thailand—all prominent Theravāda states in the modern world. This relationship between the Theravāda tradition and state power and hegemonic diplomacy is another area of Buddhist history for which there is only a very limited scholarship.

The rise of the Saṅgha

Responding to the uncertainty

Most scholars agree that Buddha lived in an era of major transformation. Thapar (1960) shows that many social structures, some centuries old, were changing rapidly. The four key kingdoms of ancient India—Avanti, Vatsa, Kosala, and Magadha—were thriving due to good weather, heavy monsoon rains, and surplus harvests, assisted by new irrigation techniques which improved output (Gokhale 1980, 1969; Thapar 1960). At the same time, major class divisions began to form based on occupation, influence and wealth. Within this class system, there were ruling élites, soldiers and administrators, and tenured or bonded labourers. Newly established rulers sought new land and opportunities for political expansion, often in competition with each other.

New cities and increased migration uprooted large numbers of people, changing traditional ways of life. Although they offered economic opportunities, new settlements were often ridden with parasites and insects, spreading illnesses such as malaria. From the Buddhist literature we learn that many lay people wanted to become Saṅgha as a way to adopt a simpler, more secure life (Vn. 1: 18; Thg. 55[12]). Brekke (2002) and Chakravarti (1987) outline a number of the socio-economic reasons why soldiers, thieves in hiding, criminals, debtors, bonded labourers, runaways, and former sex slaves joined the order. The marginalized members of society—those who had been disadvantaged by the rapid social changes, and thus those who felt they had very little to lose—were attracted by the idea of a radical renunciation as the foundation of an alternative way of life that promised peace.

The new way of life seemed appealing also because it did not rely on religious rituals, which were usually obligatory and often came with financial burdens. Instead, Buddha invited the masses to look at the meaning of life from within. Buddha proposed that one should approach duḥkha not by searching for a way to manage or overcome suffering, but by becoming aware that all experiences are *anicca* (impermanent).

> Buddhist psychology also states that all pleasurable experiences are fleeting and continually changing. Pleasure is therefore experienced as loss (suffering), which leads to new desires and the attempt to gain new pleasures to compensate for the loss. The view that a separate self exists perpetuates and is driven by desires in the endless cycle of becoming (co-dependent production). (Christensen 1999, 40)

12. Theragāthā means literally "the verses of the elders." It is the eighth book of the *Kuddhaka Nikāya* in the Sutta Piṭaka of the Tripiṭaka.

Accordingly, Buddha explained that most of the factors that influence human life come from within rather than from external forces or events. In many ways, this is a reductionist approach. It may have appealed to many who were dissatisfied with their immediate reality but unable to avoid or change it. In addition, this individualistic and inward-looking discourse ran counter to the rigid caste system due to its emphasis on equality, which may have been attractive especially to the middle and lower classes. Buddha consciously constructed a narrative against the hierarchy of the Hindu caste system. While he was born into a higher caste, he challenged a system that denied the potential of individuals and bonded them for the duration of their worldly lives, denying their nirvāna (Krishan 1998).

Responding to suffering and loss of meaning

From the standard biographical accounts of Buddha's life, we know that his decision to leave a civic life was based on the fact that he could not find happiness or meaning even while surrounded by luxuries. Buddha's father, advised by astrologers, kept the young prince away from anything that would disturb him emotionally. Yet on one of his rare journeys outside of his palace, the prince saw four disturbing signs of reality (*satara pera nimiti*): an old man, a sick person, a corpse, and a *śramana*. He witnessed the four points of suffering: *jāti* (birth), *jarā* (decay), *vyādhi* (sickness), and *marana* (death), causing him intense sorrow. The news that his son had been born, after thirteen years of marriage, only intensified his worries (Rāhula 1974, ix). He named the child Rāhula (fetter). In the aftermath, his servants tried to entertain him and his father arranged a magnificent party to celebrate the birth of a grandson, yet Siddhartha left home that night, disturbed by the emptiness and ugliness of all sensual entertainment. Prior to his final departure (the *mahā-nikhamana*), Siddhartha saw his son for the last time and vowed to return only after finding answers to his questions. This narrative illustrates the psychological tensions Buddha was trying to negotiate. He had entered into a mental state called *saṃvega* (the shock that leads to a renouncer life) (Coomaraswamy 1943). As explained in the *Anguttara Nikāya*[13] (3: 38),

13. *Aṅguttara Nikāya* is one of the five sections of the *Sutta Piṭaka*. The other four nikāyas are *Dīgha* (long), *Majjama* (middle), *Samyutta* (linked), and *Khuddaka* (short). The text records the discourse between Buddha and members of the Saṅgha and others. The *Dīgha Nikāya* contains 34 long suttas, the *Majjhima Nikāya* contains 152 suttas of middle length, the *Samyutta Nikāya* comprises 2889 suttas grouped together (*samyutta*) according to their contents in 56 *samyuttas*, and finally the *Aṅguttara Nikāya* is a collection of more than 2300 suttas arranged in eleven sections. Whereas the *suttas* in these four collections are for the most part in prose, the fifth collection, the *Khuddaka Nikāya*, comprises many famous texts in verse such as the Dhammapada, the Suttanipäta, the Theragāthā and the Therīgāthā. In the Theravā-

saṃvega carries a number of possible meanings; in this case, to tremble or start with fear. Johnston explains the term in the following way:

> *Saṃvega* as a religious term denotes the first step towards conversion, when the perturbation of mind is produced by something and leads to consideration of the inherent rottenness of the world and so to the adoption of the religious life. (Brekke 1999, 854)

Brekke adopts a controversial position in his analysis of *Buddhacaritam:*[14]

> The Buddha is essentially, what William James called the sick soul: Make the human being's sensitivity a little greater, carry him a little farther over the misery-threshold, and the good quality of the successful moments themselves when they occur is spoiled and vitiated. (1999, 856)

It is difficult to state firmly, in any conclusive sense, that the primary reason for Buddha's and the Saṅgha's renunciation was the impact of a deep-rooted cognitive dissonance. Brekke takes his cue from a Western notion of twentieth century psychological analysis to determine the mind-set of a religious movement from twenty-five centuries ago. Then he selects texts such as the *Buddhacharitam,* a poetic epic, composed by a non-Buddhist author, in a language used by the rivals of Buddha (the Brahmins). Furthermore, frustration, fear, disappointments, a deep cognitive dissonance, and similar negative energies alone could not have shaped the Buddha's character. Historians testify to the fact that Buddha had a great aptitude for critical analysis, even in front of his critics and enemies. Later, his ability to lead a successful social movement also bears witness to the fact that he had strong communication and public relations skills as well. The fact that he continued to live a renouncer lifestyle for another fifty years also indicates that Buddha had more than fear as a motivation. Brekke himself agrees that the "fear alone" thesis is too reductionist (1999, 862). Evidence of Buddha's dialectical discourse and the surrounding metaphysical arguments, as recorded in the Pāli canon, are witness to the sound intellectual capacity of Buddha's philosophy. If one is to try to argue that these theological philosophies are the works of other, later

---

da tradition the volumes Tripiṭaka (three baskets), comprising (i) the Abhidhamma Piṭaka, on metaphysics, (ii) the Sutta Piṭaka, on discourse, and (iii) the Vinaya Piṭaka, on discipline, are the most important texts. For details see http://www.accesstoinsight.org/ptf/buddha.html, a Pāli Text Society supported link, Accessed on 20 June 2010.

14. *Bhuddhacharitam* is a 2nd Century C.E. Sanskrit poetic epic composed by Aśvaghoṣa. For the most part that printed in The Buddhacarita or Life of Buddha by Aśvaghoṣa, which was edited and translated by Professor Edward B. Cowell (first published in 1894 [text] and 1895 [translation], reprinted together New Delhi, 1977). The readings and translation have been supplemented by E.H. Johnson's text and translation entitled Buddhacarita or Acts of the Buddha (first published in Lahore, 1936; reprinted Delhi, 1995).

followers, as in many established religions, consideration should be given to the fact that Buddha and his preaching could not have survived if it had failed to surpass the already well-established intellectual discourse of the Brahmins. However, Buddha's sensitivity and attention to detail, and the psychoanalytical impact of these traits, are key aspects of his decision to depart from a comfortable lifestyle in favour of renunciation.

Forming new identities

Forming a new social group identity through networking appears to have been a key phase in the first stages of the establishment of the Saṅgha Samāja, beginning with Buddha and his first disciples. One half of *Vinaya Piṭaka* record the first months of Buddha's life after the awakening (Vin. 1–4).[15] Although he initially decided to be silent, after persuasive requests from the god Brahma, he chose to go forth and become a teacher of the dhamma. Before doing so, Buddha contemplated whom he should teach first. He thought of his two former teachers Uddaka and Kālāma Rāmaputra and, realizing they both had died a few days before, decided to visit the five friends with whom he had practised ascetic meditation prior to choosing his "middle path." The men were over two hundred kilometers away, and Buddha walked to meet with them. The five (Koṅdañjña, Mahānāma, Assaji, Vappa, and Bhatia, former fellow seekers) became Buddha's first disciples.

In that part of the *Vinaya Piṭaka*, we find the story of Yasa, a rich merchant who had had a similar spiritual awakening. He was wandering without a home, and came to be a Saṅgha under Buddha, bringing his mother, his father, and his father's former wife to the faith. Yasa, as a Saṅgha, then called four and then fifty of his household members to the Saṅgha fold. The first Saṅgha community was established, now numbering sixty with the inclusion of these new converts. Research has highlighted the important role played by social networking for the survival and growth of micro-movements (Gokhale 1986; Stark and Bainbridge 1980). When society changes through rapid urbanization, the density of the average social bond is reduced. The opportunity to live closely and associate at a personal level, as in rural settings, is taken away. Urbanization causes community members to live in close proximity but without personal and individual contacts, sharing only geographic and physical, rather than emotional and spiritual, space. The social dynamic changes, and people begin to seek answers to their new challenges and opportunities in order to fill the vacuum of meaning created by the new realities. Often, finding likeminded people who follow the same ideology helps to manage this process, and hence it is rational to use contacts in order to

15. For the full English text, see http://www.ancient-buddhist-texts.net/Texts-and-Translations/Mahakhandhako/index.htm.

identify groups of people with similar mind-sets.

New members then introduce other contacts to the group, as part of a process of reconfirming their decision and increasing their level of comfort and their influence within the new movement. Gokhale has shown that for eighteen of the individuals included in his study of the early Buddhist converts the primary reason for conversion was the influence of relatives (Gokhale 1965, as cited in Brekke 1999). One of the key attractions of becoming a Saṅgha during Buddha's time is the fact that, unlike other contemporary religious movements, Buddha did not require any prequalification to become a Saṅgha. Further, the casteless and non-hierarchical structure that Buddha proposed for his movement was a huge attraction in a society where every decision was based on caste membership. A casteless organization created opportunities that had never before been available, attracting a greater and wider social network and prompting the creation of a new sense of identity-based belonging.

Counter-cultural resistance

One of the major points of confusion in interpreting and understanding Buddhism arises from the fact that Buddhism has a number of conflicting dynamics at its center. The popular question in the West is how Buddhist societies, such as Cambodia, Laos, Myanmar, and Lanka, could produce the level of violence and illiberalism that has been seen in the last half century. For many asking this question, there is only one Buddhism: the one experienced by Western powers during the nineteenth and twentieth century colonial era. The dominant understanding of Buddhism in the West is built on this version, which some have termed 'British Buddhism' (Almond 2007; Lopez 1999).

Buddhism as experienced by members of a Buddhist society stands in sharp contrast to this monolithic ideal. The lived experience of Buddhist countries reveals that Buddhism can mean many different things to many different people. Buddhism, wherever it arrived and flourished, evolved through at least three different processes. Building on the arguments advanced in the work of Gombrich (2009, 2006a, 1996, and 1988), I. C. Harris (1999b), Spiro (1996, 1982), and Tambiah (1996, 1992, 1986, 1984, 1976, 1970), we propose to distinguish three "types" of Buddhism:

1. Intellectual Buddhism, as described in the Pāli texts,
2. Institutionalized Buddhism, which defined a dialectical social relationship between the śāsana and the state, and
3. Indigenous Buddhism, which established the practice and promotion of the Buddhist beliefs in conjunction with, and often assimilating, indigenous folk spiritualities

The dominant contemporary understanding of, and approaches to, Buddhism are governed by the first and the third of these interpretations. Colonial officials and Western Indologists and anthropologists have produced a large quantity of analyses of intellectual and indigenous Buddhism. In retrospect, it appears that most of this analysis travelled on a rigid trajectory, perhaps governed by any number of historical motivations (including a colonial approach to studying Buddhism). Thus, there are a number of contesting sets of variables within Buddhism, including ruler vs. ruled, Western vs. oriental, developed vs. primordial, and rational scientific vs. emotional traditional. Understanding institutionalized Buddhism has either been ignored or, at best, considered a secondary priority. Early attempts at a sociological deconstruction of Buddhist societies largely suffered due to these limitations and their heavy dependency on the established interpretations of intellectual and indigenous Buddhism.

Attempts to understand the reality of institutionalized Buddhism by using Western concepts have not produced many noteworthy results. Fortunately, there is now a growing interest in understanding the dynamics that gave rise to some of the bloodiest political violence in postcolonial, post-cold war conditions in Buddhist states such as Cambodia (Broadhurst 2002), Laos, Myanmar (Bischoff 1995; Holliday 2007), Lanka, and Thailand (Jerryson 2009). The continuing social and political crises in these predominantly Theravāda states have come under the scrutiny of political anthropologists and conflict resolution practitioners, and increasing attention is being paid to the influence of institutional Buddhism on these conflicts. Yet it is a conceptual as well as an empirical challenge to move away from the existing paradigms. In order to understand the dynamics and working patterns of institutional Buddhism, a fresh reading of the politics of early Buddhism and the subsequent establishment of Buddhist politics becomes necessary. Reconstructing the institutionalization process of the early Buddhist order promises to help in this endeavor, despite the challenges, discussed above, involved in interpreting the canonized texts. At this point, we seek to map the institutionalization of the Buddhist order and the resultant political powers this process created. This is not to argue that this facet of Buddhism is more important or authentic than the others, because claims like this would only lead us into the dead end of debates on what Buddhism "is." For our purposes, it is sufficient to state that all these aspects of Buddhism travel as parallel and yet intertwined and mutually influencing social dynamics, but by highlighting the processes of institutional Buddhism we will be able to investigate whether early Buddhism outlined and effected an alternative power arrangement in society.

Scholars of Buddhism are divided on the attitude that Buddha held towards kings and their political power over both society as a whole and individual human lives. Tambiah claims that Thai society based its attitude towards royal and political power on Buddha's politics as articulated in his deliberations, supporting his 1976 work *World Conqueror and World Renouncer: A study of Buddhism and polity in Thailand* with references to canonical writings (1978). Spiro, on the other hand, argued that Buddha was apolitical or even anti-political (1978, 1977). Richard Gombrich, in an attempt to mediate between these positions, argued that both views could find support in the canonical texts. The canons were so broad that they left room for more than one interpretation. In fact, he pointed out that the canons may support contradictory and opposing views (1998).

From the key texts of the Tripiṭaka and other Buddhist literature such as the *Jātaka Kathā*, the *Buddhacarita* and the *Vaṃsa* literature, it is clear that Buddha regularly interacted with the kings of his time. The *Vessantara Jātaka*[16] is a popular story in which Buddha, in one of his previous births, was a prince—heir to the throne. While aspiring to become the future Buddha he gave away his right to be the king, family, and finally his own head as a gift so that the merits he collected would be great. During his lifetime, Buddha advised righteous kings as well as immoral and unjust kings. He also adhered to the requests of kings and accepted gifts and rewards from them. He intervened to settle wars, and at other times he ignored the ruling powers altogether. In the *Cakkavatti Sīhanāda Sutta*, Buddha presented the ideal model of a king (Dhammapada 129; *Dīgha Nikāya* 1: 7, 135; 3: 61, 80–98, 127–149; *Mahāvaṃsa* 1: 44–70 and 71–84; *Samyuththa Nikāya* 1: 75–76, 86; *Vinaya Piṭaka* 1:7, 122).

Contrary to the dominant Hindu tradition of the time, Buddha did not believe that kings were semi-gods or divinely appointed. The Buddha had an entirely different and more realistic concept of kings and kingship. In the *Aggañña Sutta,* he posited a social contract theory of monarchy. According to the Hindu myth, the first king of India was Mahāsammata, a name whose origin the Buddha reinterpreted as meaning "elected by the majority" (D.III, 93; Ja.II, 352). Thus according to the Buddhist theory, kings derived their legitimacy from general consent, i.e. from the people they ruled. However, several stories in the Jātaka implicitly suggest that people had a right to overthrow a king who was cruel, unjust or incompetent (Ja.I, 326; III, 513–514; VI, 156). It is clear that the texts support and uphold Buddha's multifaceted relationship with kings and their politics. One possible explanation for this relationship is that Buddha called for a

16. The Jātaka stories tell of the 547 previous births of Buddha, while he was aspiring to be the future Buddha. The 547th Jātaka narrates of a time when Buddha was king. The full story is available at http://www.sacred-texts.com/bud/j6/j6013.htm, Accessed on 20 June 2010.

radical renouncer life, and yet within such a life he found reasons for getting involved in the affairs of "this world," including the politics of the day—a model that provided the foundation for the Saṅgha community.

While the canons support both political involvement and an apolitical Buddha in an eschatological sense, it is evident that Buddha's primary influence on society was exercised in a more indirect manner. Rather than using direct social or political influence, Buddha undermined the contemporary order by living a different kind of life, and the retelling of his life story was the most effective teaching tool at his disposal as he aspired to become the Buddha in order to find the way of salvation for the entire living world. Buddha's life manifests his belief that intervention was both necessary and possible.

Thus Buddha, like many other religious founders, played the role of a prophetic teacher, who had found salvation and was willing to share his insights with others. In this role, he presented an alternative to the existing world order and, in the process, gained some of the authority that had been lost by the worldly authorities, who failed to relieve the masses of their suffering. Buddha never sought authority in this world; instead, he sought to create an alternative and superior order. By empowering individuals to place their faith in a moral and ethical authority, he helped them acquire some distance vis-à-vis worldly authorities, thereby evoking an alternative, "parallel" order in which people related to each other in a different manner. Moreover, Buddha advised his Saṅgha to adopt the very same alternative "mediator of power" role in their society by using their spiritual ability to lead their people to a condition: Nirvāna, far better than the one the king could offer. By placing himself in an in-between position, and by appealing to the significance of both this-worldly and otherworldly aspects of existence, the Buddha was able to appeal to a broad audience with different people responding to different aspects of his teachings. Some Saṅgha who followed him would have preferred the total renouncer life based on soteriological peripatetic notions. Others would have expected an eschatological reordering of society, while others still would have preferred the role of the "intermediary" agent between concrete questions of individual existence and abstract questions about cosmology. Buddha's teaching and example were able to traverse the entire range of philosophical questions, thereby providing a framework in which even the most minute issues and problems found their very own cosmic significance and place.

Experts agree that Buddhism's massive success and deep influence (especially when compared to competing *śramana* traditions) were largely due to the relationship it maintained with society and to the dual role played by the Saṅgha, who were both renouncers as well as spiritual leaders for the rest of society. The apolitical tone and casteless ideology was eagerly embraced by the new middle class trading societies, providing the structural support for the establishment of the Buddhist social ethos. Yet, even if the tone was apolitical, the result is still political: a new way of life that to some extent cultivated a greater distance from the political powers. From its inception, Buddhism allowed the Saṅgha to obtain a degree of autonomy from society and thereby inaugurated a Saṅgha-state relationship based on interdependency.

In a limited way, this argument supports Weber's observation that the Saṅgha community moved from its beginnings as an unstructured social movement to a property-owning and monastic order exploited by the rulers for domesticating the masses in later years (Weber 1958). This also may relate to what the literature calls "oriental despotism," a patrimonial structure of power based on a rigid bureaucracy preventing a Western-style state formation in "hydraulic societies" (Leach 1959; O'Leary 1989; Wittfogel 1957). However, as we have argued, these theories do not explain the institutionalized Buddhist politics of the early Saṅgha in Lanka. In fact, if we are to believe the theories, the Saṅgha were an agency *within* Lanka's socio-political structure. Our analysis suggests, in contrast, that the Saṅgha created a parallel—and to some extent autonomous—order within the existing socio-politics of the state. This is crucial if we want to understand the radical nature and effectiveness of the resistance they were to offer to proposals and trends that threatened to undermine their understanding of Lanka's unique position as the protector of Buddhism. Chapter three of this study will look at the lives of three Saṅgha—Venerable Walpola Rāhula, Venerable Gaṅgoḍawila Sōma, and Venerable Athuraliyē Rathana—who in more recent times used exactly this authority and autonomy traditionally claimed by the Saṅgha in order to mobilize the Saṅgha in Lanka, (and through them the Sinhalas) to engage in politics in a more open, radical and direct manner. We speak in this context of an attempted Buddhicization of politics, but it is important to point out that the activities of Rāhula, Sōma and Rathana drew on the potential that the Saṅgha role entailed from its very beginnings. During various "waves of resistance," the Saṅgha were able to actualize this potential according to the requirements of the situation. Modern Western scholars should not be surprised by the power, which the Saṅgha hold. During 'normal' times, this power remains latent; but when they feel they need to take action they can reliably use their position in Lankan society.

When the Saṅgha enter into Lanka's mainstream political activity, they do not shy away from endorsing political violence. They were supporters or even direct conspirators in plots and conspiracies to remove or assassinate kings; the fate of Kīirti Śrī Rājasiṃha is a prominent example. They opposed democratically elected governments, planned the assassination of a Prime Minister, and took part in armed rebellions in 1971 and 1988. They are, and have historically been, opposed to any power-sharing arrangement with the Tamil minority, whose demand for equal rights was overshadowed by the terror politics of the separatist LTTE. That the Saṅgha were able to act in this manner apparently without alienating the surrounding society is due to the fact that they occupy a unique position in-between the state and the laity. In this position, they are unchallenged. The fact that they can claim this authority is partially due to social and political dynamics initiated by Buddha. This heritage, however, did undergo an evolution whereby the dhamma conception promoted by Buddha within a multi-religious society became an exclusive claim defining a mono-ethnic and mono-religious society as proposed by the *Mahāvaṃsa* epic (see below).

There is an extensive body of literature available on the development, growth, establishment, and decline of religious sects (e.g. Barker 2006a, 2006b; Beckford 1976; Cornwell 2007; Crotty 1996; Freston 1994; C. E. King 1982; Shah and Toft 2006; Wilson and Martin 1981; B. R. Wilson 1970, 1961). Until recently, the greater portion of these studies concentrated on Christian sects, largely operating in the West. However, of late there has been a new focus on non-Western religions, beginning with variants of Islam as an after-effect of 9/11 (Cesari 2009; Lincoln 2006; Rabasa *et al.* 2004). Yet the historical context in which Buddhism developed went largely unnoticed among Western scholars. What little research is available is already some decades old and is limited in its ability to explain the Saṅgha-led politicization of Buddhism. This narrow research base makes it difficult to comprehend how and why the Saṅgha in modern Theravāda states are either bringing forth or renewing a militant brand of Buddhist engagement with their respective polities (Jerryson 2009; Joll 2010; Juergensmeyer 2010b, 1995; Kitiarsa 2009).

For these reasons, any attempt at reconstructing the nature of the original Saṅgha Samāja and the many schisms and splits that marked its subsequent history (Pandit 2005; Sujato 2008) is challenging, but that challenge confirms the legitimacy of the attempt. It may be necessary to examine multiple explanations, and to understand the original dynamics that drove able and intelligent men to renounce their ordinary lives and to embrace a radical sect. Areas of focus, if information is available, include the life and message of Buddha, the wider socio-economic conditions during his lifetime, and the demographic and psychosocial composition of his first group of followers.

The Buddhist community, the Saṅgha, and the dhamma are closely interrelated. There is no Buddhist community without the Saṅgha, who embody the faith and its life philosophy. There cannot be a Saṅgha without the dhamma, which includes an invitation to take the path of a Saṅgha. Finally, there cannot be a dhamma without the active preaching of Buddha, who taught the Saṅgha to memorize his teaching. The life, message, and impact of Buddha has fascinated scholars and philosophers for centuries and has established itself as an independent branch of learning in history, religious studies and sociology. Particularly after the British encounter with the Buddhist world during the nineteenth century and the early decades of the twentieth century, the academic study of Buddhist theology in English and other European languages was widespread (Almond 2007; Baumann 1995; Gombrich 2009, 1990a; E. Harris 2006).[17] While our study of the Saṅgha movement will draw on the modern understanding of the life and teaching of Buddha, it is important to stress that the goal of this work is not to study the literal or metaphysical interpretations of the dhamma. We wish to trace the transformation of the Saṅgha, within the historical context of Buddhist expansion, from being a peripheral sect to their ultimate position as king makers championing a renouncer state religion. What were the transformative influences that enabled the Theravāda version of Buddhism to flourish in a state like Lanka, and how did the Saṅgha help preserve Buddhism in the country in the face of internal and external threats to the faith?

Mahāvaṃsa and its impact

Everyone who ventures to understand the history and contemporary politics of Lanka discovers the influence of the narratives in the *Mahāvaṃsa*[18]

17. For a comprehensive bibliography on Buddhism in European languages, see http://www.globalbuddhism.org/bib-bud.html and http://www.buddhanet.net/e-learning/buddhism/bibliography.htm, both sites accessed on 15 June 2010.

18. *Mahāvaṃsa* means great genealogy or the story of the great race/clan. To date there are many translations of the original Pāli texts. The first English translation was prepared by George Turnour, *The Mahāvaṃsa in Roman Characters with the Translation Subjoined, and an Introductory Essay on Pāli Buddhistical Literature.* Vol. I, containing the first thirty-eight chapters, Cotto 1837, by the order of Arthur Hamilton Gordon, Governor of Ceylon. Original copies of this text are held at the Universities of Cambridge, Oxford, Edinburgh, and at the British Museum. A digital version of the second part of the book is available at the digital library of the University of California. The Saṅgha of Ceylon wrote not only on ecclesiastical matters but also on political history as they saw it. Dīpavaṃsa is the oldest known Pāli chronicle; the *Sāsanavaṃsadīpa* by Saṅgha Vimalasāra in 1929 is the latest one. In between these two, we have *Sumaṅgalavilāsini* by Buddhaghosa, a key Saṅgha commentator of Buddhist literature (fifth century CE), *Samantadīpikā, Mahābodhivaṃsa, Dīpavaṃsa, Vaṃsatthapakāsinī, Dhātuvaṃsa, Thūpavaṃsa, Cetiyavaṃsatkatha, Nalāadhathuvaṃsa* and *Saddhammasangraha. Mahāvaṃsa* is the most influential epic in Lankan religio-politics. *Cūlavaṃsa* is the last section of the *Mahāvaṃsa.* See: (Law 1947, 1994) for more discussion. Wilhelm Geiger's translation is the one most commonly used today. See *The Mahāvaṃsa or, The great chronicle of Ceylon,* translated into English by Wilhelm Geiger, assisted by Mabel Haynes Bode (1960 [1912]), under the patronage of the government of Ceylon. This research refers to the digital copies of both these translations.

epic (Mhv.) and their current political interpretation (C. S. Anderson 1999; De Silva and Bartholomeusz 2001; Spencer 1990a). While it is clear that ethnoreligious nationalism is a major framework for the Sinhala Saṅgha, we still need to identify its major sources. From school textbooks through to political debates and serious academic research, the impact of the *Mahāvaṃsa* on Sinhala society cannot be overestimated.

The approach to, and treatment of, the *Mahāvaṃsa* has been as controversial as the substantive issues its contents raise. It is generally agreed that the epic was compiled by Venerable Mahānāma of the influential Mahāvihara fraternity of Sinhala Buddhism in the six century AD, and was later continued by other monks. The *Mahāvaṃsa* is the key book in the Vaṃsa[19] literature (Strathern 2004; Walters 2000). The text and the narrative style are similar to, and borrow heavily from, the fourth century epic *Dīpavaṃsa.* Because the *Mahāvaṃsa* covers a timeline stretching nearly 25 centuries, the text is useful to diverse fields of study, including religion, history, archaeology, politics, and even anthropology. The epic was originally "compiled for the serene joy and emotion of the pious," an objective that is restated at the end of each new chapter.

The modern treatment and discussion of *Mahāvaṃsa* has led to diverse opinions, and the debate about the meaning and vision implied in the text continues to this day (Dharmadasa 1992, 1977; Gunawardane 1979, 1971; Mendis 1931).[20] Some have considered it a religious work of poetry that should be read with a sympathetic attitude (Bloss 1973; Collins 2003, 1998, 1992, 1990; Scheible 2006). Others interpret it as a political narrative that uses exaggerated metaphors and symbolism to justify the supremacy of Sinhala Buddhism (Bechert 1978; Kemper 1991; Spencer 1990a; B. L. Smith ed. 1978; Tambiah 1992). Some scholars see it as a valuable resource for studying the history of India and Buddhism (Berkwitz 2008a; Thapar 2007, 1981). A small number of scholars (Bartholomeusz 1994; DeVotta 2007)[21] have interpreted the *Mahāvaṃsa* as an ethnic interpretation of Sinhala supremacy over others in Lanka, thus informing the rise of what is known as "Protestant" Buddhism in the late nineteenth and early twentieth centuries as part of the struggle against colonial rule in what was then Ceylon (Baumann 1997; Bertelsen 1997; Gombrich 1995; Prothero 1995). The *Mahāvaṃsa* continues to influence the present political, religious, and ethnic mind-set of the Sinhala Buddhists. Berkwitz suspects that the *Mahāvaṃsa* in many ways "controls the modern

19. *Vaṃsa* is a generic term used to denote the chronology.

20. The 1970s and 1980s produced a large collection of literature chronicling the debate on the Mhv. between Dharmadasa and Gunawardana (1979), (See Tambiah 1997).

21. Is it beyond the scope of this research to provide an extensive discussion of Buddhist history as it is imagined and recorded in literature; however, an overview of Vaṃsa literature (especially as it relates to the Mhv.) can be found in Berkwitz 2004.

Sinhala psyche" (2003, 579).

A text is meaningless and fails to inspire life unless it is re-read, re-interpreted, and re-applied—and the *Mahāvaṃsa* text is no exception. For the purpose of this research, the contemporary readings and use of the text as "history" form our central focus. The purpose of these modern readings are twofold: first, to create an overarching Buddhist identity centered on Lanka as the "blessed land," visited by Buddha (Walters 2000); and second, to reinforce Sinhala hegemony through a narrative of the Sinhalas as the first "civilized" settlers and thus the legitimate rulers of the island. In our study, we will explore the historical use of the text as a tool by which the Theravāda Saṅgha community religionized the Sinhala race and their politics. Through the same method, the authors politicized the Buddhism of the Sinhalas.

Thus, while primarily written as a religious text of history, the *Mahāvaṃsa* nevertheless provides the foundation for an ethno-religious political ideology. In the words of Smith, "By this transformation, the basis was laid for the ideology of state-Saṅgha relations, which proved historically relevant. In this way, history was made by historians in early Ceylon" (B. L. Smith ed. 1978, 7).

As a reflection of the important link between the visits of Buddha (Chapter 1–3) and his prediction that the island would be the centre of his teaching, *Mahāvaṃsa* identifies Vijaya, the father of the Sinhala race, as the founder of a particular religious-political nexus, of which the Saṅgha became the "interpreters" as well as the agents. Further justifications for Sinhala dominance also come from the repeated references to Damilas, or Tamils, defeat at the hands of the warrior King Duṭṭhagāmiṇi (chapters 1, 24, 25, 27, 28, 29, 30–33).[22] With this background, the purpose of reading the epic *Mahāvaṃsa* becomes didactic and polemic in that it helps to Buddhicize Sinhala politics and rationalize ethnic Sinhala majoritarianism. From the nineteenth century onwards when the texts were made available to the public (ironically under colonial rule), the *Mahāvaṃsa* was taken as a reliable historical document (Walters 2000), re-creating a certain "*Mahāvaṃsa* mind-set." This reading has continued to define Sinhala politics, despite serious questions concerning the reliability of the *Mahāvaṃsa* as a historical source (Emmanuel 2000).

A full review of indigenous and western scholarship on the *Mahāvaṃsa* is beyond the scope of this research.[23] In order to understand the current

22. Duṭṭhagāmiṇi (161–137 BCE) is the hero warrior king of *Mahāvaṃsa*. According to *Mahāvaṃsa*, he did not like the Tamils' presence in the Sinhala-Buddhist land. His mother had dreams that her son would get rid of the Tamils, and when he became the king of Ruhuna, he waged an all-out 15-year war against the Tamil king Elāra of Anurādhapura, eventually uniting Lanka as a single entity under his rule.

23. See Kemper (1991) for a review of the importance of the chronicles for Sinhala culture.

justifications for a certain version of Sinhala Buddhism, largely based on the *Mahāvaṃsa* the epic and its texts will be analyzed only with a view to establishing how the Saṅgha, the general political community, and popular culture receive, interpret and promote the text. Buddhist histories in Lanka are produced and consumed primarily in order to provide reassurance of a spiritual, cultural, and (where possible) ethnic relationship to the Buddha. The writers of the *Mahāvaṃsa* intended to make the Sinhalas a unique people. In other words:

> Just as the Buddha had somehow taken possession of Lanka, so it was the destiny of the Sinhala kings to conquer and rule over the whole island. These rulers would prevail over a unified state and indeed a whole society that was dedicated to the preservation and cultivation of Buddhist ideals. (Strathern 2004, 193)

Tambiah commented:

> This constant strain to identify the religion with the state and the Buddhist state, in turn, with a Buddhist society creates perpetual internal cleavages of a sort that are absent in Hindu India (except when that society collides headlong with a militant, excluding religion like Islam).
> (Tambiah 1973, 59)

The earliest available record of the *Mahāvaṃsa* in modern times comes from an English translation of the original Pāli text by George Turnour, dated 1837. Turnour was a government agent in the Ratnapura province of Ceylon under the British Raj. The original text, until then known only to a few monks, was translated with the help of the commentary, '*Mahāvaṃsaīkā*' which was found in another ancient temple in Mulkirigala, in the deep south of Lanka. The translation, published by Oxford University Press for the Pāli Text Society of London, generated so much interest that the colonial government commissioned a search for all such historical texts in Lanka and India. This marked the beginning of a systematic archaeological exploration in modern South Asia. However, it was the German translation of the *Mahāvaṃsa* seven decades later by Wilhelm Geiger that prompted an analytical examination of the ancient text. The British government appointed Geiger to produce an English translation of the text, which was published in 1912. One can easily agree that if it had not been for the liberal efforts of the British colonists, the *Mahāvaṃsa* epic, which was to become a core reference for the ethnoreligious politics in Lanka for the last 100 years, might have remained the hidden, little-known text that it had been prior to the nineteenth century.

While these European translations created a renaissance among Modernist and Oriental schools in the West, who argued for a more liberal, non-colonial approach to understanding the social structure in Lanka, it had the opposite effect at home. The Sinhala élites, who for some time had been arguing for greater independence from the colonial administration, found a new and powerful legitimation for their claims and in the process created waves of nationalist passion based on nostalgia for the lost "golden era" glorified in the *Mahāvaṃsa*. Key religio-political revivalists of the early twentieth century, like Anagārika Dharmapāla, Venerable Walpola Rāhula, and others, based their demands for a Dhammadīpa and thus a pan-Buddhist identity on the *Mahāvaṃsa* version of the island's history and society (Seneviratne 1999).

Dharmapāla (1864–1933) was an important Buddhist reformist who agitated for a total Buddhist society in Lanka. He created the concept of '*Sinhala Bauddhayā*', a Sinhala who is essentially a Buddhist, which has become a key term in the modern ethno-national political lexicography of Lanka. The *Mahāvaṃsa* managed to inspire Sinhala nationalists including scholar monks (Rāhula 1956), cultural activists (Sirisena 1971),[24] academics (Dharmadasa 1992), and social critics (Amarasēkara 2003, 1992) like no other text. Yet the goal, the circumstances of its composition, and the religious orthodoxy of the authors of this great chronicle should make us question the purpose of the text (Mendis 1931). It was Geiger, two decades after his scholarly work on the chronicles, who maintained serious doubts regarding the impartiality of the narrative. The chronicles start with the record of three different visits of Tathāgata-Gautama the *Buddha* to the island of Lanka, thus making Lanka the only place outside India to be visited by the great teacher. In its opening chapter the *Mahāvaṃsa* describes in formal and venerating language the visit of Buddha, who blessed the island and prophesied that it would always remain Buddhist. Geiger, however, warned:

> There is a good number of fables, legends and tales of marvels in the *Mahāvaṃsa*, and we must in each particular case attempt to find out whether there is in the narrative an historical kernel of truth or not.
> (Geiger 1930, 208)

The three places that Buddha allegedly visited—*Mahiyangana* (in the east), *Nāgadīpa* (in the north), and *Kälaṇiya* (in the southwest)—are among the most venerated worship centres of modern Buddhism in Lanka. Worshipers have gathered at these vihāras for over one thousand years. However, modern scholarship based on archaeological findings has shed serious doubts on the significance of these places and events as narrated by the *Mahāvaṃsa* (Emmanuel 2000). One could argue that in a spiritual context, narrations of omnipresent ability, the super-powerful, and the divine abound. Therefore, these visits of the Buddha, even if they

24. Piyadasa Sirisena was an inspiring ethno-nationalist writer who produced popular volumes on the history of the Sinahala race based on the *Mahāvaṃsa*. See (Amunugama 1979) on Sirisena's new image of the "Sinhala Buddhist."

were mere inventions of the writer, need to be taken seriously for what they have managed to inspire, especially because this thesis is more concerned with the socio-political impact of the text and its wider narratives than with the authenticity or the theology of Sinhala Buddhism.

The contents, authorship and relevant periods of the various parts of the *Mahāvaṃsa* are assumed to be as follows:

1. *Mahāvaṃsa* Part I	Covering the time period from King Vijaya to Mahasen (from 563 BCE to 556 CE), composed by Ven. Mahathera Mahānāma around the fifth century CE
2. *Mahāvaṃsa* Part II	Covering the time period from King Mahasen to Parākramabāhu I (from 556 CE to 1150 CE), written by Ven. Mahathera Dhammakitti in the thirteenth century CE
3. *Mahāvaṃsa* Part III	Covering the time period from King Parākramabāhu I to Parākramabāhu II (1150 to 1200), written in the late sixteenth century by an unknown author
4. *Mahāvaṃsa* Part IV	Also referred to as Cūlavaṃsa, covers the time period from King Parākramabāhu II to Sri Vikrama Rājasiṅha (1273 to 1815), written in the late nineteenth century by various authors including Ven. Hikkaḍuvē Śrī Sumaṅgala

One of the most serious challenges to the accuracy of the *Mahāvaṃsa* account concerns the sixth chapter of the epic, which describes the arrival of prince Vijaya on the day of the *parinibbāna* (departure from life) of Buddha. Prince Vijaya claimed to be the grandson of a ferocious lion that terrorized the jungles near the kingdom of Lālapura in India. According to astrologers, the princess of Vanga country, near Lālapura, was to become the mother of a new and pure race. She wandered away from the palace, met and fell in love with the lion of the jungle, and bore him twin children. At the age of 16, Sinhabāhu, the son, escaped the caves and later killed his lion father for 3000 gold pieces. He settled near the kingdom of Lalapura. He took his twin sister as wife and had children. One of Sinhabāhu's sons, Vijaya, was evil and had become the oppressor of the people. Learning this, Sinhabāhu, put Vijaya and 700 of his followers on a ship and sent them upon the southern sea. The ship carrying Vijaya landed in Tambapaṇṇi ("place/beach of copper"), a northwestern port in Lanka (*Mahāvaṃsa* 1: 1–35). Vijaya, first through diplomatic marriage to the indigenous beauty Kuvaṇṇā, and later by bringing military support from his homeland India, conquered the indigenous rulers and established his kingdom to become the father of the Sinhalas (*Mahāvaṃsa* 7: 1–15). However, as Geiger points out, the oldest period of Sinhalese history from Vijaya to Muṭasiva (Mhv. Ch. 6–Ch. 11, 6) is rather obscure. The story of Vijaya's descent from a lion is a typical legend of totemistic character and explains his clan name *Sīhala* (1930, 210).

Apart from the totemism and incest that account for the mythical origin of Vijaya, the *Mahāvaṃsa* record is striking also because it appears to endorse the political intimidation, terror, and violence used to conquer the natives whom the *Mahāvaṃsa* terms *Yakṣas* (devils). In contrast to the lives of the evil natives, the rule of Vijaya is continuously presented as superior and justified. As Anthony Smith explained, this account reflects, "the construction of the core of a historical '*ethnie*' that lives in the myths, memories, values and symbols... and in the characteristic forms or styles and genre of a certain historical configuration of a given population" (1986, 15).

The writers of the *Mahāvaṃsa* may have felt that they needed to give a diachronic account of Buddhism and the Theravāda school in order to detach the evolution of Buddhism from the highly ritualistic structure of Brahmanic Hinduism (Eliot 1921; Coomaraswamy 1986, Coomaraswamy and Sister Nivedita 1967). Nevertheless, as argued by Obeysekere, Buddhism could neither detach itself totally from the Hindu social context nor preserve the original purity of a rational philosophy; rather, there was what we may call a "process of fusion" with Hindu practices and beliefs. In addition, at the time when the chronicle was composed, there were numerous internal controversies of a theological and practical nature amongst the Saṅgha. After the third Saṅgha council under Emperor Aśoka, the Theravādin tradition, which let down roots in Lanka, was divided into three monasteries: Mahā-vihāra, Abhayagiri-vihāra, and Jethavana-vihāra, This division was so deep that it took another 1000 years to achieve a form of reconciliation (Tambiah 1985). However, the narrative of the *Mahāvaṃsa*, which was composed as late as the sixth century CE, retrospectively records the totemistic origins and the "identity" creation of the Sinhalas, possibly moved by the emence threats to the capital of Anurādhapura (Harischandra 1998; Smither 2007). Anurādhapura is the one remaining symbol of a glorious Sinhala civilization, which had existed at least since about 500 BCE until the Cōla Kings, who were South Indian Dravidian Tamils, captured it. De Silva says the chronicles were the work of Saṅgha of a certain fraternity (Mhv. XV: 1–9) to advance a certain ideology: "the central theme of the later chapters of *Mahāvaṃsa* was an epoch-making confrontation between the Sinhalese and the Tamils, and extolled as a holy war fought in the interest of Buddhism" (K. M. De Silva 2005, 17).

It is remarkable that the *Mahāvaṃsa* chronicles, which record the influence of a humanist spiritual philosophy such as Buddhism, should advocate and promote a deeply divisive ethnocentric nationalism. What motivated the authors to present the Sinhala *ethnie* and its Buddhist affiliation as superior to the parallel "other," the Damilas? Even more astounding and sociologically important is the fact that the cardinal aim of the chronicle appears to be the desire to construct the racial supremacy of the Sinhalas and therefore to attempt to undermine some of the core virtues of Buddhism. In many ways the core of the *Mahāvaṃsa* teaching often appears to contradict the fundamental virtues of the Pāli teachings of Buddhism, such as *metta* ("love based on benevolence"), *karuṇā*, ("unreserved compassion"), *muditā* ("rejoicing in the good fortunes of another"), and *upekṣā* ("emotionally detached state of impartiality"). In contrast to these virtues, the *Mahāvaṃsa* constructs four fundamental ideological principles that guide modern Saṅgha politics:

1. *Mahāvaṃsa* asserts that the Buddha used fear and physical pain on *Yakṣas* (the original inhabitants of the island) in order to expel them before taking charge of the land. According to the *Mahāvaṃsa* the *Yakṣas* are sub-human beings, whose failure to understand the teachings of Buddha led to their expulsion (Gunawardana 1978; Bandyopadhya 2016).
2. *Mahāvaṃsa* also asserts that Vijaya, the founder of the Sinhala race, killed the *Yakṣas* and others and became king.
3. *Mahāvaṃsa* claims that throughout history the Saṅgha helped the kings to fight off non-Theravādins, with Duṭṭhagāmiṇi as the most remarkable example.
4. Directly and indirectly the *Mahāvaṃsa* account implies that the use of violence for the protection of Buddhism is appropriate and that such violence is a service to Buddhism and thus to Buddha himself.

The Sinhala Saṅgha

The relationship between the Saṅgha and the political sphere in Lanka has gone through at least three key periods of change: the inauguration of the Buddhaśāsana by Gautama Buddha in India and its transmission to Lanka around 300 BCE; the growth and development of a civilization with Buddhist identity in Lanka, and the rise of a "Protestant Buddhism"[25] that ran parallel to the Christian missionary movements during the colonial era.

The arrival of Buddhism and the subsequent establishment of the śāsana and its samāja in Lanka was a political as much as a spiritual project. Reliable records of early Buddhism in Lanka are largely found in the texts written to promote and protect the faith and activities of a

25. We use the term "Political Buddhism" to denote a process of instrumentalizing the Buddhist texts, ideals, values, and institutions in order to achieve a political goal. This we differentiate from "Pāli Buddhism," which is found in the canon, and "Popular Buddhism," which is what the Buddhist masses practice in Lanka. Buddhist Politics, which is the attempt by the Buddhist laity as well as Sangha community to influence the secular structural polity

select group of people. Biases and personal or group-oriented motivations are unavoidable in these texts, which include the Vaṃsa literature and related texts such as the Pūjāvaliya,[26] Stūpavaṃsa (Berkwitz 2006a), and *Nikāya Sangrahaya* (Kongasthanne 1989). Scholars have struggled to extract from these texts, which remain the most comprehensive narratives available on the subject, an accurate history of the developments. It is a strange fact indeed that India, where Buddhism began, should have lost most of its original texts either as a result of natural processes or because of struggles for dominance between rival religious groups. Out of these texts, the *Mahāvaṃsa* stands—with all its biases—as the only piece of record that can provide a continuous history. While the accuracy, reliability, and purpose of this text is questionable for many reasons (Emmanuel 2000), the text is used by scholars in many different fields to trace the trajectory of South Asian Buddhist history and its impact on the relevant societies.

According to the *Mahāvaṃsa*, the arrival and establishment of the Theravāda version of Buddhism in Lanka occurred during the rule of King Devānampiyatissa. Bhikkhu Mahinda—believed to be a son of Emperor Aśoka of India—was sent to convert the king, who would later establish the śāsana in Lanka.[27] Based on other historical markers, this event would have occurred during the latter part of the third century BCE. Emperor Aśoka, following his grandfather Emperor Chandragupta of the Maurya dynasty, expanded his monarchical rule uniting the greater part of the Indian subcontinent (Keay 2011, 2001; Seneviratne ed. 1997; Thapar *et al.* 2007). Aśoka crushed the rebellious Kaliṅga army, but the devastation and the human suffering caused by his ruthless army disturbed him and, in his mood of regret, he listened to a Buddhist Bhikkhu who explained to Aśoka the meaninglessness of the victories of this world and invited him to follow the path of dhamma. Aśoka not only converted to Theravāda Buddhism, but also arguably became the most influential figure in the history of Buddhism and its establishment as a world religion. Aśoka envisaged a new world order that was governed by dhamma and to that end sent missionaries into nine different directions covering key locations in the east and west. The *Mahāvaṃsa* records the arrival and the conversion of King Devānam in the island of Lanka (Geiger and Bode 1912, 92–96; Geiger 1960, 91–93, *Mahāvaṃsa* XIV: 1–23).

26. Pūjāvaliya was compiled by Saṅgha Mayurapada in the thirteenth century. See full text at http://enriqueta.man.ac.uk:8180/luna/servlet/detail/Manchester~91~1~104479~106049, accessed on 15 August 2010.

27. However, Kosambi (1969) and Thapar (2004) have both argued that outside the Sinhala chronicles, no other records can be found that would corroborate these historical developments.

The *Mahāvaṃsa* account very clearly records how a renouncer religion could become the epicentre and ideology of the state. It took nearly 300 years for Buddhism to become India's royal court religion after Buddha's Mahāparinibbana, but in Lanka, it became the state religion in just one day. Buddhism in Lanka was never (nor was it ever meant to be) a civil religion that permeated society from the bottom up. Instead, it arrived and was established because of what were initially a state-to-state and later a state-to-society process. Buddhism arrived, convinced the ruling élites, and then became the religion of the king's court before it reached the masses in any meaningful manner, in what was perhaps a process of first spiritualizing the ruling secular power and then domesticating the rest of the state. Religion and state are here not separated; on the contrary, the state is impregnated with religious ideology. This original configuration, which primarily involved the ruling élite and the Saṅgha in ancient Lanka, remains the historical model with far-reaching implications even for today's society in Lanka. The Saṅgha fraternity in Lanka, unlike their Indian initiators, did not build up a meaningful relationship with the ordinary society and its common citizens. Instead, there was a royal relationship involving political and economic power.

After the shock of 9/11, Western academics hurriedly returned to studying the complex relationship between religion and politics (Al Sayyad and Castells 2002; Appleby 2000; Bayes and Tawḥīdī 2001; Blank 2001; N. J. Brown and Hamzawy 2010; D. Brown 2000; Bunt 2002; Dark 2000; Gaus and Vallier 2009; Griffin 2004; Haynes 2010; Heyking 2000; Jenkins 2002; Juergensmeyer 2001; Lewis 2010; Macklem 2000; Sacks 2002; Stump 2000; Ungureanu 2008). This renewed interest, however, has not undermined the common modernist bias, which take religions seriously only as an obstacle to the inevitable unfolding of modernity. In Lanka, however, the inseparable relationship between Theravāda Buddhism and the state is a foundational political reality. The institutionalization of Buddhism in Lanka was the result of geo-political realities and international politics, especially the formation of a strategic alliance of regional powers with a super-power ideology. Throughout the history of Lanka, the formation of state power vis-à-vis the rest of the society has progressed only because of the interaction between Theravāda Buddhism and its Saṅgha, who were more than ready to act as the intermediaries of power.

The religious institutionalization of Buddhism in Lanka was instrumental in legitimizing the ruling élite, and in return, the kings endorsed Buddhism (as presented by the Sinhala Saṅgha). This reciprocal legitimization continued for centuries and constructed a religio-political reality that the society has come to accept. The role of the Saṅgha in explaining a new spiritual philosophy on life, suffering, and death was deeply attractive to a society that seems to have not had any organized religious discourses. Furthermore, as the history of Lanka shows, the benevolence of the king and ruling élite, to the extent that it was influenced by this new religion, could also have helped ensure that the people embraced the religion.

Modern archaeological findings confirm that the establishment of Buddhism in Lanka, nearly a century after it originated in India, had a different trajectory than in India (Chakrabarti 1995). In Lanka, Buddhism received state recognition and protection from the day it arrived. According to the account included in the *Mahāvaṃsa*, the king embraced the teachings, accepted the Saṅgha, and declared the island to be Buddhist within a six-hour period (Mhv. XV: 1–9).

In contrast to the original peripatetic Saṅgha life style, the Saṅgha in Lanka preferred to be *Grāma vāsin*, living near cities with direct state sponsorship in order to help their faithful followers. The wanderer tradition was secondary compared to the "settled" Saṅgha who received unlimited state sponsorship. This transition from a wandering preacher to a counsellor of a fixed abode is often cited as an example of a decline in the Saṅgha's spiritual orthodoxy. However, as Ivan Strenski (1983) and many others have argued, this change reflects a process of socialization, which was necessary even if it led to a more relaxed observation of the rigid Vinaya codes. Thus, some 100 odd years after Buddha, when Buddhism arrived in Lanka the Saṅgha established themselves as an order of stationary monks (Bechert 1978; B. L. Smith 1978). In addition, because the Saṅgha abandoned their itinerant tradition, it was easier for the laity to offer them alms and collect their good merits. It is this reciprocal exchange with the laity that eventually helped the Saṅgha to become proprietors with powerful economic interests. It is also for this reason that *Ārṇaya vāsi* and *Pāṃsūkūla,* the jungle dwelling and extreme ascetic orders, did not become as influential in Lankan society. While they were held in great esteem because of their self-denying spirituality, the secular civil laity was unable to benefit from their practices (Bechert 1992; Coningham 1995; O'Conner 1993; Yalman 1962).

The *Mahāvaṃsa* records that the King requested to live within the boundaries (*sīma*) of the Saṅgha command (Mhv. XV: 182–184), thus intensifying the Saṅgha-state nexus. Walpola Rāhula, one of the most influential recent Saṅgha activists, commented:

> From the 3rd Century BCE, to the end of Sinhalese rule in the 19th CE, only a Buddhist had the legitimate right to become the king of Ceylon. By about the 10th century, this belief had become so strong, that the king of Ceylon had not only to be a Buddhist but a Bodhisattva.
>
> (Rāhula 1956, 62–63)

The *Mahāvaṃsa* text reflects how the socio-political structure of the Saṅgha Samāja developed over the centuries. Three aspects of this structure are highlighted throughout: the Saṅgha positioned themselves between religion and society; and they were the unquestioned gatekeepers who could give access to spirituality and religion; they also positioned themselves as key advisors to the ruling élite; and in this position, they were held in the highest esteem by all segments of society.

Preserving this delicate position was not always straightforward. There were numerous occasions on which the state intervened to "clean" Saṅgha society (*śāsana śodhana*) by disrobing and expelling some of the wrongdoers. "Impurities" within the Saṅgha had occurred from the time of Aśoka, who expelled a large number of them at the third council for two main reasons: disregarding Vinaya discipline, and fighting between the different nikāyas. Lankan history shows that these internal fights were so intense that during the reign of Parākramabāhu I the king dismissed the Abayagiriya and Jetavana faculties, bringing all the Saṅgha on the island under one authority and supervising the ordination of any new Saṅgha (Mhv. LXXIII: 20–22; LXXVIII: 25–30).

It was during this era that the concept of Saṅgha Rāja—a supreme leader of the Saṅgha, elected from among their ranks—was considered, despite Buddha's opposition to the practice. Centralized state control of the politics of Saṅgha society continued until the fifteenth century. The arrival of, and long occupation by, white Christian colonial powers was a historical turning point, not just for the politics of Lanka but also for the way in which the Saṅgha related to Lankan society. The attitude of the Christian colonists towards Buddhism in general and the Saṅgha in particular fundamentally reshaped Saṅgha society. The sociological and political changes that occurred during these centuries have been well documented and analyzed (Bond 1992; Frost 2002; Gombrich 1998; I. C. Harris 2007, 2005; D. A. Scott 1992).

Under colonial rule, the Sinhala Saṅgha took on different political roles—some as collaborators; others remained indifferent to the colonial powers, and still others became rebels. The relationships they developed with each of the colonial masters (Portuguese, Dutch, and British) influenced their society, and the resulting changes from the sixteenth to the early twentieth century laid the foundation for the socio-political mind-set, which characterizes the Saṅgha in Lanka today. Analyzing this transformation, the social anthropologist Kitsiri Malalgoda went beyond the scholarship of Obeyesekere, Gombrich, and Tambiah by highlighting the political re-awakening of the Sinhala Saṅgha during that time, often provoked and manipulated by the colonists.

The British, who had the longest and most influential rule in Lanka, approached Buddhism with modernist values while also manifesting their colonial and missionary zeal. Most observers agree that the modern form of Saṅgha engagement with the Sinhala society was largely shaped as a protest against the systematic dismantling of the Saṅgha-state heritage and the social changes resulting from the state-sponsored promotion of Protestant Christianity. In order to counter the influence of the Protestants, the Saṅgha successfully copied their methods and transformed Buddhism into what Obeyesekere and Gombrich termed "Protestant Buddhism." The experience of colonial oppression thus affected the role of the Saṅgha and their psyche in important ways:

1. The British failed to keep their promise to preserve the important political role of the Saṅgha. As a result, the interdependence and mutual legitimization that marked the state-Saṅgha relationship were dissolved. The British systematically undermined the power and wealth of the Saṅgha by introducing land reforms and taxation laws.
2. As the Saṅgha lost their central influence, non-central Saṅgha associations were formed, largely dependent on the good will and support of local élites.
3. Locally and regionally, the identity and self-understanding of the Saṅgha was therefore more open to the influences of geography, caste, sub-caste, doctrine, and personality.
4. These changes were accompanied by the emergence of a "Protestant" consciousness among the Saṅgha, which was directly primarily against the Christian missionaries and the colonial rulers but could also be redirected against other groups and people perceived as posing threats.
5. Also in response to the broader forces of modernity and globalization, the Saṅgha redefined their role from being the "guide to the other world (and the other life)" to being more concretely the "protector of the *ethnie* and polity."

The Saṅgha under colonial rule

Ironically, the structure and strength of the contemporary Saṅgha community developed under colonial rule. As we review this evolution in the Saṅgha self-understanding, we note that the three different colonial powers dealt with the Saṅgha in three distinctly different ways. The Catholic Portuguese were particularly aggressive in their conversion attempts. By 1551, the king of Kotte, who had grown up under Portuguese Franciscan teachings, was baptized as a Catholic, thus becoming the only Christian ruler of Lanka. In comparison to the Portuguese, the Calvinist Dutch were more tolerant towards Buddhists and the Saṅgha, partly because their trade interests superseded religious considerations (Malalgoda 1976). The British however, had the most complex relationship with the Saṅgha in Lanka.

After 300 years of disarray, the Saṅgha society had lost its structure. The Tamil king Kīirti Śrī Rājasiṃha, in his efforts to consolidate his rule and find favour in the eyes of the élites and masses, became a reformer, supporter, and promoter of Buddhism and its Saṅgha. His strategy was to strengthen the Saṅgha and harness support through them. In 1753, he invited the Siam (Thailand) Saṅgha to help re-establish the order of the Saṅgha within the Theravādin tradition. The new order, named *Siyam Nikāya*, had two distinctive features: based in Kandy, they were the official custodians of the Tooth Relic, and they belonged to the Goyigama (also spelled Govigama) caste. The king then ordered all the Saṅgha, even those in the areas now controlled by the Dutch, to come under the leadership of Siyam. Based on a theological argument over whether the new chapter should be *Ārṇaya vāsi* (jungle dwelling and meditating) or *Vihāra vāsi* (living at the edge of the village where they could help the people), the Siyam chapter eventually split into two, with *Asgiriya* taking to the mountain range and *Malvatu* largely settling on the river banks.

After failing in their efforts to win over the king for a trade partnership, the Dutch promoted the higher ordination of southern, lower-caste men in order to weaken the king. Since the Siyam of Kandy would not accept this, the Dutch sent these men to Burma. The first southern member of the Karāve (fishing) caste to be ordained was Saṅgha Aṃgahapiṭiyē Ñāṇawimala in 1803. This order began as *Amarapura Nikāya*, named after the seventeenth/eighteenth century capital of Burma (Bischoff 1995; Buddhadatta 1965, 1952). By 1811, the Dutch had helped five such southern Sinhala groups to be ordained in Burma.

In 1861, a group of Siyam Saṅgha rebelled against caste rigidness and broke off to start the *Rāmañña Nikāya*, which officially disapproved of caste separation and invited all castes into monkhood. However, there is no record to indicate that they invited or permitted non-Sinhalas to become Saṅgha. The modern Saṅgha community in Lanka has roughly 40 different nikāya with differences based on customs, regions, lineage, or temple traditions. The three chapters described above remain key players, of which Siyam is the largest and most influential.

Gombrich (1971) argued that the nature of "colonial Buddhism" changed during the period of British rule. While the colonial period as a whole witnessed the growth of intolerant political agitation, the Portuguese and Dutch periods were still marked by "fluid boundaries," which allowed the Saṅgha to continue working with society. While the Portuguese (1505–1656) were aggressive in their conversion efforts and in the process engaged with the Saṅgha, the Dutch (1658–1786) actively promoted the establishment and growth of various Saṅgha fraternities for trade or political ends (Crane and Barrier 1981; Malalgoda 1976; Rogers 2004). In contrast, the English tried to exclude the Saṅgha and indeed Buddhism more generally from the management of the colony. According to Obeyesekere (1970), it was during this period that we saw the rise of "Protestant Buddhism," which was advanced by Anagārika

Dharmapāla (1864–1933) and his contemporaries.

The British approached the situation in Lanka in this manner for a number of reasons. First, notwithstanding the powerful church-state nexus in their own country, their modernist outlook may have suggested that state and religion were to be separate; second, they understood the colony as a missionary opportunity and accordingly proceeded to do what they could to undermine the validity of Buddhism in a territory now ruled by the British. For example, Methodist Missionary Rev. Spence H. Hardy argued that it would be illegal for the British government to protect Buddhism (Houtart 1974). Finally, the British may well have understood Buddhism's powerful influence on society. Undermining this influence would have strengthened the power of the colonial rulers. These considerations may have led the British administration to ignore the spirit of the 1815 treaty, where the British promised to respect the Buddhist faith in the country. Instead, they actively worked towards the exclusion of the Saṅgha from politics, and they replaced the *Pirivena* education with mission schools, which often benefited from state support (Houtart and Lemercinier 1976a, 1976b; 1977, 1978; Liston 2000). The *Pirivenas* were the bhikkhu schools of higher learning, which over centuries had allowed the Saṅgha to cement their cultural hegemony. By 1852, the British declared the total withdrawal of their support of Buddhism and actively promoted the construction of Anglican churches, including some just next to famous temples such as Kandy and Kälaṇiya. These developments had different effects in the Up Country, with largely Goyigama Saṅgha, and the Lower Country, with largely non-Goyigama (Durāve, Karāve, Salāgama, and others) caste Saṅgha orders. It is clear that their exclusion from the politics of the country implied for all Saṅgha a material and spiritual loss. Accordingly, regardless of their differences, anti-colonialism became the focus of resistance for the śāsana. The Sinhala Saṅgha interpreted colonialism and the spread of Christianity primarily as a threat to Buddhism and the Saṅgha community, which meant that the defensive lines that the Saṅgha drew between themselves and various "others" were drawn along ideological lines. Buddhism thereby provided the fundamental space where freedom was to be articulated, and the Saṅgha became the key agents for redefining the state.

When the British missionaries launched an aggressive conversion campaign, which directly and openly attacked Buddhism, it was primarily in southern Lanka that the Saṅgha led by prominent activists such as Hikkaḍuvē śrī Suṃangala, Mohoṭṭiwattē (or later Migeṭṭuvattē) Guṇānanda, and Ratmalāne Dhammāloka, opposed the missionaries with organized protests.[28]

28. A detailed discussion of the monks who actively promoted and participated in these protest movements is available in Malalgoda (1976); Seneviratne (2001); Tambiah (1986); N. Wickramasinghe (2006a).

The lower country Saṅgha, whose orders were initiated under the patronage of the Dutch, did not own or manage large properties and hence relied on the support they received from lay people. Wealthy business owners in the South had built large temples for the Saṅgha and in return expected the Saṅgha to support their businesses and political ambitions. As a result, the Saṅgha in these areas were particularly close to the lay people, and due to their mutual dependency, the Saṅgha had reasons to think that they were called to act on behalf of lay society against colonial oppression. Suddenly, they had become political leaders, and they found the support of lay people and even foreigners such as Rhys Davids and Henry Olcott (Snodgrass 2007). Ironically, the British attempt to separate state and Saṅgha in order to make Buddhism a "private" affair of believers backfired. The Saṅgha were not to be excluded; on the contrary, the very attempt to exclude and marginalize them provoked them to openly adopt the role of political leaders.

This creation of a political Buddhism was directly influenced by the discourses emerging from Vidyodaya[29] and Vidyālaṅkāra,[30] the two most prominent *Pirivenas*. As Jonathan Watts (2004) argued, the colonial administration promoted a secular nation-state identity and marginalized the traditional position enjoyed by the Saṅgha, moving them to the periphery and unintentionally launching a search for new forms of "engaged Buddhism." This process, now famously termed "Buddhism Betrayed" (Tambiah 1992), produced two distinct discourses: Vidyodaya promoted a Saṅgha re-entry into the power centers of politics, while Vidyālaṅkāra argued for a rational Buddhism of the type that was vigorously promoted by Dharmapāla. However, many contemporary commentators (Abeysekara 2002; Berkwitz 2003; Deegalle 2004; P. De Silva 2006; Seneviratne 1999) agree that it was the elitist interpretation of the role of the Saṅgha promoted by the Vidyodaya circle and prominent monks such as Venerable Walpola Rāhula that inflamed a new brand of postcolonial political Buddhism.

The role of the Saṅgha in politics in general and in peace-building in Lanka in particular has gained considerable academic attention (Abeysekara 2001; Berkwitz 2008b; Blackburn 2001; P. De Silva 2006; Deegalle 2006a; Jerryson and Juergensmeyer 2009). The Saṅgha are the third reality of the "*Trividha Ratna*," the triple gem of Buddhism,[31] and the Murade-

29. This was the first such institution to train Bhikkhus outside the temples. It later became a full university. See http://www.sjp.ac.lk/aboutus/history.html, Accessed on March 21, 2010.

30. Today Vidyālaṅkāra operates as a training centre for monks. See http://www.vidyalankara.com, Accessed on March 21, 2010.

31. Buddhists accept the Buddha, Dhamma (his teaching), and Saṅgha (his monks) as the "triple gems" that provides guidance and advice.

vatā, or the guiding deities of the land, the religion and its people. What was largely an elitist engagement in advisory politics appeared to take an explosive turn around the mid-nineteenth century. A few years after the defeat of the Kandyan kingdom, the last sovereignty in Ceylon, by colonial British troops, the masses were without an indigenous leadership. Among the pioneers who challenged British colonial rule was Ven. Kudapola Thera, who inspired a rebellion in 1848, a century before the British would grant independence. Wariyapola Sri Sumaṅgala, Giranagama Mahinda, Sikkim Mahinda are only a few of the prominent Bhikkhus who played a direct political role and whose memory can inspire nationalist mobilization even today. This intervention of the members of the Saṅgha Samājà in the politics of Lanka has never been reversed.

Anagārika Dharmapāla was one of the key leaders advocating a radical redefinition of the role of the Saṅgha (Amunugama 1991a, 1985). Venerable Walpola Rāhula's *Bhikshuwāgē Urumaya*—the *Heritage of a Bhikkhu* (1946)—articulates this radicalization in a powerful manner by presenting the call for a new Saṅgha self-understanding as a continuation of the Saṅgha tradition and heritage. The book was published in Sinhala two years before independence, and an English translation was published in 1974, three years after the 1971 insurgence of Janatā Vimukti Peramuna (JVP).[32] This re-engagement of the Saṅgha with society eventually led to the formation of an all-Saṅgha party, the Jāthika Helà Urumaya (JHU), which ensured that the Saṅgha would now also feature in the electoral politics in post-independence Lanka (Deegalle 2004; 2003). The JHU manifests the notion of the supremacy of the Sinhala ethnic religiosity and thus resonates with widespread nationalist sentiments. We will have occasions later in the book to discuss these developments in greater detail.

The Saṅgha and post-Protestant Buddhism

The scholarly analysis of the arrival, establishment, growth, institutionalization, relative decline and re-emergence of the Saṅgha and their politics in Lanka has so far tended to focus on two aspects. There is a body of literature which looks at the Saṅgha (and Buddhism) in Lanka as the result of the extension and expansion of the intellectual and social influence of Indian Buddhism (N. Dutt 2003, 1998, 1980, 1960 1945a, 1945b, 1941; Geiger and Becchert 1960; Geiger 1930; Gokhale 1986, 1965, Gombrich 2006b, 2005, 1996, 1992, 1990a, 1990b, 1984a, 1984b, 1975a, 1975b, 1966; Rāhula 1978, 1974, 1956; Tambiah 1992, 1984, 1977, 1976, 1973, 1970,

32. *Janathā Vimukthi Peramuna* is the Maoist/Marxist party that launched two anti-state armed rebellions in Lanka, in 1971 and 1988. JVP has fragmented since then. However, the largely southern Sinhala party is considered the third political force in Lanka after the main United National Party and the Sri Lanka Freedom Party.

1968). And there is also literature that looks at the establishment of Buddhism in Lanka as a political project with the Saṅgha as the most visible symbol and the most effective agent of this project (Abeysekara 2004, 2001, 2000, 1999; DeVotta 2009, 2008, 2004a, 2002, 2000; Gunawardana 2003, 1988, 1979).

Following independence, Lanka tried to adopt a "modern" approach by both recognizing the prerogative of Buddhism while accommodating the other three main religions—Christianity, Hinduism, and Islam. Article 6, Chapter 2 of the 1972 constitution states that "The Republic of Sri Lanka shall give to Buddhism the foremost place and accordingly it shall be the duty of the State to protect and foster Buddhism while assuring to all religions the rights granted by section 18 (1) (d)."[33] Every government since 1948 tried to manage this delicate balance of maintaining Buddhism as a superior yet equal religion on the island, but it is clear that even this "foremost but equal" balance runs counter to the state-religion relationship that is symbolized and actualized by the Saṅgha.

The Saṅgha community in Lanka develops many different features of Theravāda Buddhism and practices different aspects of its teaching. Beside the major three nikāya, which are largely a caste based formation, the Saṅgha in Lanka can be identified in at least three broad ways based on their political (in)activity: those who are politically active and able to mobilize the political consciousness of the Sinhala Buddhists; those who try to be apolitical even while sharing the same public space, and those who have totally withdrawn from the social space. As mentioned earlier, this study focuses on politically active Saṅgha and their impact on the modern democratization process of the island, taking into account the multi-ethnic (and multi-national) political reality of the state. The early twentieth century polemical rhetoric of Anagārika Dharmapāla, who campaigned for a laymen-led Buddhism, transformed into a search for a liberal and intellectual Buddhism that began immediately after independence and developed during the 1960s. The highly anglicized and urbanized middle class Sinhalas sought to reconcile the authoritative discourse of Buddhism with a more liberal framework. During this period, often referred to as the *Sanskruthika Navodaya* (era of cultural reawakening), a Sinhala civil intelligentsia promoted a re-reading of Buddhism and its influence in accordance with the changing self-understanding of the urban Sinhalas.

Martin Wickramasinghe, Lester James Peiris, Ediriweera Sarachchandra, Walpola Rāhula, Mahagama Sekara, and John De Silva were among the leading figures in this search for a redefinition of the Sinhala people and their culture as a whole (De Mel 2001). These members of the cultural élite tried to contextualize Lanka's past in order to construct a (some-

33. Refer to constitution of Sri Lanka. http://pact.lk/may-1972/.

what artificial) indigenous identity. In this process of "in-culturing", they were attempting to move away from the remaining influences of Indian cultural hegemony in Lankan social identity and its Pāli/Buddhism heritage. They encouraged a new dress code for Lankans, promoted the use of Sinhala in public discourse and declared the rural village a sanctified place of authenticity. However, these elitist projects were not drawn from the wider national or regional social dynamics, but were largely manufactured urban imaginations. Accordingly, they failed to have an impact on the Saṅgha community, their ideology, or on state policies, which had already taken an "ethnic turn." As a result, these projects contributed to the hegemonizing of Sinhala culture, imposing "Sinhalaness" on the whole of society. For the non-Sinhala Tamil, Muslim, Burgher, and Malay minorities, this "national" cultural construct was nothing but a systematic process of further marginalization and isolation.

Parallel to this process, minorities began to search for their own versions of state and society. The Burgers, who for two centuries had enjoyed the close patronage of the colonial state, found their future options limited. Most of them migrated to either Australia or the UK, searching for a better life, and the remaining Burgher population actively developed ways to assimilate into the mainstream society (Roberts 1994, 1993, 1979; Roberts *et al.* 1989).[34] The Muslims (Moors and Malays) also began to seek new legitimacy within the changing socio-political landscape. While economic and political survival may have been their primary reason for engaging in this search for legitimacy, the Muslim population did not interpret the societal changes as part of a process meant to undermine their ethnic or national identity. In contrast, the political psychology of the Tamil population was different.

The Tamils in the north had benefitted from prolonged missionary education projects and thus were able to secure respected and protected civil service positions as well as central professions in the active economy. Thus, as the major social and political changes began to take place and "Sinhala-ness" became the measure of things, they saw their own position undermined. Initially they questioned this Sinhalizing of the wider society but received no tangible response from the ruling Sinhala élites. With virtually no channels open for them to voice their concerns, the Tamil élites initiated a full-scale campaign proclaiming their own identity outside Lanka's sovereignty. Regional political changes, which included the formation of new states such as Singapore and Bangladesh during this time, may have ignited imaginations of an independent ethnic Tamil State in the north and east, where Tamils were the majority population.

34. Roberts himself is of Lanka Burger origin and thus analyzes the situation of Burgers in the country on the basis of his own experience. See http://thuppahi.wordpress.com/, Accessed on 15 June 2010.

After the assassination of SWRD by Saṅgha Thudawē Sōmārāma in 1959, the reputation of the Saṅgha suffered greatly (Manor 1989), preventing them from adopting an even more prominent role in public politics. Many leading Saṅgha activists became backbench supporters of one of the three major parties (UNP, SLFP, or the Leftists), and many others "took refuge" in cultural and traditional roles such as teaching, astrology, or native medicine. In fact, the period between the 1959 assassination and the 1971 revolt shows a relative withdrawal of the Saṅgha from politics, perhaps suggesting that Saṅgha political activism is largely possible when they are neither in a controlling nor in a marginalized position in the political system. At all other "normal" times, the Saṅgha are actively seeking to increase their political influence. The 1971 armed rebellion and the role that the (mostly young) Saṅgha played in that revolt stand as an early indicator of the changing nature of the Saṅgha activist involvement in society (Kodikara 1989; Moor 1993; Samaranayaka 1999).

In many ways, the turn towards activism of this kind could also be interpreted as a serious collapse of any effective Saṅgha leadership, leaving the Saṅgha without an alternative self-understanding and without a meaningful project. Leaders such as Walpola Rāhula had left the country due to the intensity of the political debates. The Saṅgha had many reasons to be disillusioned: a failing political system, an indifferent and immobile hierarchy, and an ever-growing threat to their culture and identity. The fact that the Saṅgha became again involved in a second armed rebellion in 1988, seventeen years later, indicates the degree of their frustration (Goodhand 1999b; Grobar and Gnanaselvam 1993; Matthews 1989; Pfaffenberger 1988).

By the late 1980s and mid-1990s, the Saṅgha had regained their political place in society. 1988 witnessed an unprecedented level of Saṅgha involvement in the second JVP revolt. The signing of the Indo-Lanka Peace Agreement in 1987 and the subsequent arrival of the Indian Army in the north were key developments causing this remobilization.[35] However, the government crushed the uprising, albeit with questionable methods (Abeysekara 2001; Keerawella and Samarajiva 1995; Singer 1991, 1992; Uyangoda 1989). Abeysekara argues that this was the first time since pre-colonial times that so many Saṅgha were arrested and killed in Lanka. As a result of these developments, the role of the Saṅgha and of the politicians had become blurred; even notions such as justice and violence had lost their precision in light of prolonged state and non-state terror politics, with some of the Saṅgha heavily involved.

The 1994 general election, after 17 years of UNP rule, was seen as a par-

35. The Indo-Lanka Peace Accord was signed in July 1987 but the LTTE opposed the Accord and continued to fight, which in 1988 led to the arrival of a 100,000-man strong Indian army in Lanka.

adigm shift in Lankan politics. The radical economic, social, political, and constitutional transformations on the island combined with the devastating impact of the war had created deep resentment across the party divisions. As a fresh hope for change, Chandrika Bandaranaike, daughter of former Prime Ministers SWRD and Sirimāvo Bandaranaike, returned from her exile and contested the election. A number of factors including her family ties and the fact that she was the widow of Vijaya Kumaratunga, a popular actor-turned-political activist, helped her victory. It is not uncommon in Asian politics for a female relative of a male political leader to assume power, as in India, Bangladesh, Philippines, Pakistan, and Lanka (Richter 1990, Thompson 2002). Yet the most important reasons for Chandrika's victory were her promises to introduce transparent government and to seek political reconciliation with the ethnic Tamils. Tessa Bartholomeusz commented:

> Kumaratunga's landslide victory in 1994 can be attributed to numerous factors, one of which is Kumaratunga's ability to respond to popular desire for political and ethnic reconciliation by configuring herself as the embodiment of Buddhist motherhood, a deeply felt and widely recognized metaphor for dependent co-arising (and therefore for compassion and cooperation). (1999b, 223)

Chandrika tried to use her popularity to transform political consciences in the wider society and to promote a power-sharing mechanism with the Tamils, accepting the LTTE as a legitimate partner in peace talks. Yet her support dwindled once it became clear that she was unable to fully appreciate the political nature of Buddhism in the country. Chandrika had been a member of the French student movement during her studies there in the 1960s, and thus may have been out of touch with the rituals of power that her new role required her to undergo. Her father and mother had used popular Buddhist customs and sentiments in order to construct devout Buddhist profiles for themselves. In contrast, to date there are no public images of Chandrika offering flowers at a Buddhist shrine, a customary picture that every political actor in Lanka, Buddhist or not, would have to produce in order to appear legitimate. Saṅgha groups were suspiciously monitoring the liberal agenda of the new government and their worst fears became a reality when, in 1995, just within a year of coming to power, Chandrika's government proposed a comprehensive power devolution as a political "package." This proposal suggested defining Lanka as a union of five regions with equal powers, out of which a central (federal) government would be formed. The UNP and JVP opposition interpreted the package as a destruction of the unitary nature of the island and thus as a betrayal of the land of Buddha.

The dormant Saṅgha forces united in their opposition to the package, once more attempting to convert their *de facto* political status to a *de jure* position. Opposing the package became a new beginning for a Saṅgha politics that was to change the destiny of Lankan politics in the few years that followed. The new radical Saṅgha aimed not just to change politics but also to become a political force itself by forming an all Saṅgha political party that was the first of its kind in the world. They were determined to contest the election. This new activism was a response to wider societal changes that threatened to deeply affect the Saṅgha samāja. As George Bond (2003, 1992) has shown, the Saṅgha, already faced with numerous challenges due to the rapidly changing economic, political, and social conditions, were further challenged by a growing movement of lay devotees.

A lower-middle class, semi-urban lay movement led by socially engaged Buddhist organizations like the Sarvodaya[36] was growing in numbers, displaying considerable activism and involvement. They engaged in meditation and other practices without the leadership of the Saṅgha, seeking an alternative interpretation of Buddhism within the Lankan context. The lay Buddhist movement was calling for a reform of the traditional, institutional and indigenous Buddhism, partially ignoring the Saṅgha leadership. However, this was not the first time that Lanka had seen a lay revival campaign. The biggest such movement was arguably the one led by Anagārika Dharmapāla, Olcott, and their supporters in the early twentieth century. In the past, however, the success of such lay reformists was largely based on the fact that they promoted a Sinhala Buddhism wrapped in an ethno-nationalist discourse. The creation of Buddhist Sinhala schools as an alternative to missionary education, demanding the Vesak holiday,[37] and designing and demanding the acceptance of a Buddhist flag, are key achievements of this lay movement, which often operated without any Saṅgha leadership (Prothero 1995; Roberts 2000). Yet even if they were able to function without Saṅgha leadership, it is likely that they were permitted to act in relative autonomy because their aims were not in direct conflict with the Saṅgha outlook.

Donald Swearer distinguished three types of lay Buddhist movements in Lanka: those that help the Saṅgha in their religious duties; those who collaborate with the Saṅgha to promote social welfare; and those who seek Saṅgha leadership/support for political reforms (Swearer 1970). We

36. Sarvodaya is the largest lay Buddhist organization campaigning for a society organized according to Buddhist values. See http://www.sarvodaya.org/activities/peace/recent-history, Accessed 3 May 2011.

37. Vesak is the month corresponding to April/May in the Western calendar. Vesak has become the most significant period in the Buddhist calendar because according to Theravādin belief, the birth, enlightenment, and death of Buddha all took place on the full moon day of this month.

can identify at least four major laity revivals in Lanka in recent history: first, Anagārika Dharmapāla, Olcott and their supporters campaigned for modernization, along the lines of Protestant Buddhism; second, Buddhism became the basis for a political/cultural awakening during the 1956 Buddha Jayanthi year; third, the meditational and disciplined life promoted by the Vinaya Vardhana and Sarvodaya movements explored Buddhism without direct Saṅgha involvement, and finally, Buddhism became a key reference point for lay activists within the context of the debates surrounding the war in Lanka. None of these movements aimed to question or challenge the Saṅgha, but rather to reform and redefine their role (Bond 1992; Matthew 1999; Seneviratne 1999; Tambiah 1993, 1992, 1986). Perhaps, as Michael Ames argued, the *Vinaya Vardhana* (discipline developers) was the only movement during the last 100 years that directly challenged the lifestyle and authority of the Saṅgha. The lay movement that argued for a negotiated peace based on Buddhist teachings challenged the Saṅgha position on this issue, but ultimately was unable to affect the deeply entrenched forces of ethno-nationalism represented and mobilized by the Saṅgha.

The Sinhala Saṅgha and the Tamils of Lanka

The relationship between the Saṅgha and the Tamils of Lanka is yet another un-researched area within Sinhala Buddhism. For centuries, there was a strong Buddhist influence amongst the Tamils of India and to some extent amongst the Tamils of Lanka. Monius has pointed out that the Tamils' mono-Hindu identity is a recent development. Accordingly, until the end of the *Saṅgam* era (second to fourth century CE) the Tamil literature was dominated by Buddhist and Jain themes composed by Buddhist and Jain authors. The later Chōlas and Pāndava kingdoms systematically prioritized the Hindu faith and turned Buddhism into the "other" religion (Monius 2001, 3–4). Scholars believe that the composition of the Tamil epic *Manimekalai*—the story of a Jain woman who converted to Buddhism—is a solid witness to the vibrant influence of Buddhism amongst the Tamils. Scholars suspect that great Buddhist writers of the fifth century CE like Buddhaghoṣa and Buddhadatta either were Tamils or were of Tamil origins (Barua 1945).

In Lanka, the ideological narrative of the *Mahāvaṃsa*, while confirming Buddha's visit to Nāgadīpa in the north of island, constructs the very opposite of this history. In the *Mahāvaṃsa*, the Tamils are invaders; they are unholy and illegitimate, even if they were righteous rulers such as King Eḷāra. The central hero of the *Mahāvaṃsa*, King Duṭṭhagāmiṇi, is praised for his war-like attitude towards the Tamils and for finally diminishing the Tamil kingdoms. දෙමළා (Demalā)—the Tamils—is a derogatory term in the *Mahāvaṃsa* narrative. Therefore, the account of the *Mahāvaṃsa* effectively constructs the Tamil identity as an enemy of Buddhism and hence by implication as an enemy of the Sinhalas.

Prior to the arrival of the European colonists, the strongest Sinhala kingdom in Kandy was for centuries ruled by kings of Tamil origin. Some of these kings, such as Kīrti Śrī Rājasimha, devoted extensive energy and material resources to the revival of Buddhism at a time when Buddhism seemed to become an institutionally moribund religious tradition (Holt 1996). In fact, the revival led by Kīrti Śrī in the eighteenth century succeeded in re-creating a Buddhism that was "revived and re-established in classical form, as it happened, for the last time in the history of Ceylon" (Malalgoda 1976, 258). Yet the communal identity of the Sinhala élites and their conviction that the Buddhist religion and its way of life were superior—a conviction that was sustained and cultivated by the Saṅgha—deeply marked the socio-political psyche of the Sinhalas.

During the British colonial period, the Tamils benefited from the education provided by missionaries and obtained influential positions within the colonial administration. As a result, the Sinhalas perceived the Tamils as traitors. The "Protestant Buddhist" revival under Henry Olcott and Anagārika Dharmapāla had a strong ethnic bias. Ignoring the historical contribution made by the Tamils to foster Buddhism, Anagārika's Buddhism was essentially and exclusively a Sinhala faith. He coined the term "Sinhala-Bauddhayā" in order to describe the close, essential relationship between the Sinhalas and Buddhism. By trying to turn Buddhism into an "ethnic faith," he further distanced the Tamils from Buddhist culture and thereby from the Saṅgha, who propagated such thinking.

While some Tamil élites such as Pollanampalam Arunachalam and Ponnampalam Ramanathan worked together with the Sinhalas during the struggle for independence, the subsequent Sinhala refusal to share power eventually convinced the Tamil leaders that they needed to create their own political parties along ethnic lines. As they began to demand equal rights, they angered the Saṅgha, who began to dismiss the Tamils and their politics as antithetical to the Sinhala-Buddhist state. Since the country became independent in 1948, no other group in Lanka has opposed the Tamil political demand for greater political and cultural autonomy in the northern and eastern regions more than the Sinhala Saṅgha. They have opposed and blocked every effort by moderate Sinhala leaders to look for compromises.

In the post-independence era, over the last sixty plus years, the relationship between the Saṅgha and the Tamils has broken down to such an extent that there are hardly any modern Sinhala Saṅgha who are able to preach the dhamma in Tamil. According to the Sinhala Saṅgha mind-set, the Tamils did not seem worthy of sharing the teaching of Buddha. After the end of the war in 2009, some Saṅgha have moved to the northern and eastern area, but the purpose of their travels is not spiritual. The Saṅgha willingly became a part of the further militarization of the conquered Tamil area, thereby provoking a renewed and hardened antipathy among the Tamils. From ordinary citizens to academic scholars like Stanley Tambiah, Tamils have responded by articulating their criticisms of the Saṅgha. An improved if not healed relationship between the Saṅgha and the Tamils is an essential condition for political peace and civil stability in Lanka.

Conclusion

Dramatic political transformations do not come easily within the Lankan Buddhist discourse. As with Chandrika in 1995, the lay movements in the 2000s were trying to plough a terrain that had hardened over twenty centuries of ideological conflict. The Saṅgha were not willing to have their influential position and powers curtailed. Instead, they turned inwards and developed a narrower notion of Buddhism that would soon show signs of becoming a "Sinhala Buddhist political fundamentalism"[38]. The Saṅgha looked at the vulnerable sections of the society and called for further radicalization. They appealed to the Sinhalas to embrace a total බෞද්ධකම (*Bauddhakama*) or "Buddhistness," like the *Hindutva* of Indian politics. The Saṅgha wanted the state to cease all negotiations and proposals that entailed the possibility of a power-sharing arrangement with the Tamils. For them the island belonged to Buddha and thus only to Buddhists. This position was non-negotiable: every village had to be Buddhist in culture and nature. No non-Buddhist centres of worship were permitted, and the Saṅgha did not hesitate to set fire to many churches, especially to the new evangelical churches.[39] They also demanded that a new law be enacted to prohibit conversions from Buddhism to other religions. Many suburban city centres were decorated with Buddha statues, flags, and other symbols, and all key roundabouts in the cities had a white Buddhist statue placed in them. In the morning and evening, the chanting of Pirith[40] was to be broadcast in public, and they demanded that the state media have more Buddhist centred programming. They demanded state banks to practice Buddhist economic principles and other Sinhala businesses at the national level to adopt an openly Buddhist identity. They urged the state to design state buildings

38. Richard Gombrich argued that the term "fundamentalism" could not be used for Sinhala Saṅgha as they do not borrow their ideology from any Buddhist text/scriptures (2006c). However, as we have demonstrated, Sinhala Saṅgha draw their ideology from passages of *Mahāvaṃsa*, which amounts to a socio-political fundamentalism.

39. See a list of such attacks at http://www.tchr.net/religion_churches2.htm, Accessed on Aug 10, 2010.

40. *Paritta* is Theravādin traditional chanting in Pāli for protection against evil. (ODB: 213)

reflecting Buddhist architecture. Schools were to have more scheduled classes to teach Buddhism. The Saṅgha appealed to the masses to think of their country as a Buddhist state, indeed as Buddha's state. Contrary to its intentions, the poorly planned liberal project of Chandrika provided the impetus for a new wave of ethnoreligious awakening amongst the Saṅgha. As they combined their religious awakening with a nationalist agenda, it was bound to resonate with a large spectrum of the Lankan society. The result was a new brand of militant Saṅgha willing to use intimidation and political power to advance their cause. In the struggle between traditional forces and forces of change, tradition not only prevailed but also outdid proponents of change in terms of radicalism (Brekke 2007; DeVotta 2004b; DeVotta and Stone 2008; Rowell 2009). In summary, the evolution of the self-understanding of the Saṅgha in Lanka went through four major phases:

1. From the Pāli Tripiṭaka teaching to the Mahāvaṃsic outlook (from 300 BCE to 500 CE),
2. from monastic worldview (Lokottara) to social worldview (Laukika) (500 CE to 1700),
3. from a universalistic, open outlook to an ethnic and caste orientation, (1700–1900), and finally
4. from being supporters of political groups and policies to direct political engagement (1900–2010).

During the transitions from one phase to another, key Saṅgha leaders made crucial contributions, as indicated in Table 1, opposite.

The militant Saṅgha opposition to a negotiated peace arrangement with the LTTE and their support for the military campaign and eventual victory over the Tamil Tigers was one of the most important moments in the unfolding of the contemporary Sinhala Saṅgha and their śāsana. Having introduced the historical formation of the Saṅgha as arguably the most influential agent of war and peace in Lanka in this chapter, we will now look in Chapter two in greater detail at the various "waves of resistance" that mark this evolution. We will see that the climax of this evolution—the Saṅgha agitation in favour of a military solution to the war against the LTTE—is the result of a historical dynamics in which the Saṅgha at key moments resisted developments and trends that threatened to undermine their status and self-understanding. These "waves of resistance," in turn, contributed to the very formation of this self-understanding. Chapter three will then complement this analysis by looking at the intellectual and spiritual formation of the latest three key activists in the above table: Walpola Rāhula, Gaṅgoḍawila Sōma, and Athuraliyē Rathana. This is in order to understand how they were able to make the crucial ethical choices, as Buddhists and as Saṅgha, which allowed them to actively engage in Lankan politics and to support a course of action that embraced the use of extreme degrees of violence.

Time	Key Saṅgha	Contribution
1698–1779	Välivița Saraṇaṃkara	Re-established the Upasampadā Argued for non-Goyigama caste members to be ordained, leading to the establishment of Amarapura, Rāmañña and other sub chapters
1827–1911	Hikkaḍuvē Śrī Sumaṅgala	Re-established the Saṅgha as learned advisors in society Reformed Saṅgha education, encouraging Saṅgha to study in secular institutions
1864–1933	Anagārika Dharmapāla	Argued against the traditional Saṅgha monastic orientation, urging the Saṅgha to get engaged and involved in reforming lay society Argued that those of Buddhist and Sinhala ethnicity are the owners of Lanka
1907–1997	Walpola Rāhula	Constructed a "Saṅgha heritage" Provided the academic/intellectual support for Saṅgha involvement in society including party politics
1948–2003	Gaṅgoḍawila Sōma	Argued for a Sinhala Buddhist re-ordering of modern Sinhala society
1966–	Athuraliyē Rathana	Campaigned for a military victory against the Tamil Tigers and against political power-sharing Argued for a Sinhala Buddhist political system to create a *Dharma Samājà* (righteous society)

— 3 —

An Army in Yellow Robes: Saṅgha Political Resistance 1815–2010

> In order to guarantee the success of the war effort, we will always help our war heroes through action.
>
> Ven. Elle Gunawansa Thero (July 2000)

Introduction

The arrival, establishment, growth and defense of Buddhism in Lanka occurred under the leadership of the Saṅgha. Once introduced by the Indian Theravādin Saṅgha, the śāsana was placed under the leadership and protection of the Sinhala Saṅgha. Throughout their 2300-year history, the Sinhala Saṅgha have performed two fundamental functions: first, they are to defend, protect and promote Sinhala Buddhism; second, they are to fight those they perceive to be threats to their faith. The epic writings of the *Mahāvaṃsa* are thought to be the historical record of the heroic efforts of the Saṅgha and of the kings who helped them fulfill their role.

In accordance with their self-understanding, we can identify various "waves" of Saṅgha activism throughout their history. Starting from the mid-eighteenth Century, seven major waves can be identified (see Table 1).

Even a cursory survey as provided by the table above shows that the key features of these waves of political activism all relate not just to the purity of Buddhist teaching but also to the political status of Buddhism: from reforming Sinhala Buddhism (1750–1815), to defending the same (1860–1900), to making Buddhism an essential feature of a united and independent state (1930–1972), and finally to fighting perceived threats (1995–2010). This trajectory of political involvement changes as it proceeds from reviving the Buddhism of the Sinhalas to waging a war—both spiritually and literally—in order to cement and protect the Sinhala claims to the right to rule over the entire island and its culture. The uniqueness of the Sinhala *ethnie*, and their legitimacy as rulers of the

Figure 1. Venerable Elle Gunawansa pictured preparing the newly appointed Army Commander Lieutenant-General Jagath Jayasuriya the blessings of the Triple Gem.

blessed land of Lanka: these are the recurring key themes, re-ideologized with each wave of political involvement, of the Mahā Saṅgha.

A study of the recent colonial history and its impact on the modern politics of Lanka cannot escape the issues of ethnoreligious nationalism referred to above. Any study of Lanka's present political condition requires us to adopt a historical perspective particularly with respect to the tradition of ethnoreligious nationalism that shaped the present situation of the Lankan polity. Studying present day Lanka is to step into her past because her political present, as we shall see, unfolds with remarkable continuity from her past (Clements 1992; Kemper 1991; Roberts 1993; Phadnis 1976). Stephen Berkwitz, a scholar of modern Sinhala Buddhist nationalism, captures this continuity when he argues: "The Sinhala *Vaṃsa* that describe how the Buddha's relics were brought to Lanka illustrate that emotions can be cultural products that are instilled by historical narratives to accomplish a variety of ethical, social, and soteriological ends" (Berkwitz 2003, 579). Similarly, Steven Kemper summarized that in Lanka, the present is always the "presence of the past."

> The author of *Mahāvaṃsa* had every reason to look for continuity in the past. When Mahānāma compiled the first *Mahāvaṃsa,* he tried to make two connections—first with the Buddha himself, making the Theravāda monkhood, to which Mahānāma belonged, the guardians of orthodox belief; the second with the Sri Lanka monarchy, drawing a connection between religion, state and what was to become the Sinhala people.
>
> (Kemper 1991, 2)

Time period	Key leaders of political activism	Purpose of political involvement
1750–1770	Kīrti Śrī Rājasiṃha Saṅgha Välivița Saraṇaṃkara	Reestablishing the proper Saṅgha ordination after some 300 years
1800–1815	Dutch Rulers Saṅgha Aṃgahapiṭiyē Ñanawimala	Helping the Lower Caste Saṅgha Beginning of the *Amarapura* fraternity
1860–1875	Wesleyan Missionaries Rev. Daniel John Gogerly Rev. Spencer Hardy Saṅgha Mohoṭṭivattē Guṇānanda Saṅgha Hikkaḍuvē Śrī Sumaṅgala	Defending Sinhala Buddhism against Christian missionaries 5 great public debates: *Pānadura vādaya*
1885–1900	Arrival of the Theosophists Col. Henry Olcott Anagārika Dharmapāla	Establishing a "Protestant' version of lay Buddhism Buddhist schools Buddhist flag
1930–1945	D.S. Senanayake Saṅgha Walpola Rāhula	Saṅgha initiative to support the struggle for independence
1956–1972	SWRD Bandaranaike Saṅgha Māpiṭigama Buddhàrakkhita Saṅgha Walpola Rāhula	Constitutionalizing Buddhism as the state religion Making Sinhala the official state language Proclaiming Lanka a unitary state
1995–2010	Chandrika Kumaratunge Velupillai Prapaharan Mahinda Rajapakse Saṅgha Gaṅgoḍawila Sōma Saṅgha Athuraliyē Rathana	Urging the Sinhalas to return to their Buddhism Advocating a Buddhist Government led by the Saṅgha Justifying the war against the Tamil Tigers Rejecting the federalist proposals

Table 1. "Waves" of Saṅgha activism in recent history.

In Lanka, one can see that the continuous unfolding of the Theravāda Buddhist tradition and its concomitant politics has only changed in response to outside—often-forceful—intervention (K. M. De Silva 2001; Amunugama 1991a; Keyes 1978; Swearer 1970). A sizable body of literature is available on the historical nature of ethnoreligious nationalism and its violent conflicts that generated the present political conditions in

Lanka. These analyses are generated from within a variety of disciplines including history (K. M. De Silva 1997; Malalgoda 1976; Phadnis 1976; Roberts 2003), postcolonial studies (DeVotta 2007, 2005, 2004b; Krishna 1999), religious anthropology (Bartholomeusz 2002; Bartholomeusz and Chandra Richard D. Silva 1998a; Bond 1992; Deegalle 1996; Gombrich 1992; Spence 1990), and conflict analysis (Fox 2006, 2005, 2004a; 2004b; 2004c, 2003; 2001; 2000; 1999). Most of these analyses are provided from the political standpoint of liberal democracy and incorporate—sometimes explicitly, sometimes implicitly—the assumptions of modern, Western liberal culture. In other words, they tend to argue that the current crisis in Lanka is primarily caused by the country's failure to implement the principles of modern, Western democracies. Accordingly, the argument goes, the Sinhala Buddhist nationalist claim to exclusive "ownership" of the island and its governance denies the multi-ethnic reality of Lankan society, thereby marginalizing and frustrating the aspirations of non-Sinhala and non-Buddhist groups. The response from the margins in turn fueled further ethno-nationalist measures taken by the Sinhala élites. DeVotta, for example, spells out this argument:

> The Lankan case makes clear that outbidding and ethnocentrism can become embedded and path dependent. Indeed, many Sinhalese benefited from the ethnocentric practices successive governments pursued and they now protest against any proposal that promotes devolution or dispassionate governance. The fact, however, is that while these ethnocentric practices have benefited the majority community, they have led to an illiberal democracy and influenced the principal minority community to seek a separate state. (2005, 154)

Five years later, following the end of the war, he further argued:

> Nearly all these terms could be applied to Sri Lanka as well and the island has been branded a "control democracy," "illiberal democracy, "ethnocentric democracy," and "ethnocracy." That noted, during the Mahinda Rajapakse era it is authoritarianism and nepotism that have, in the main, ruled the day. For instance, under the Mahinda Rajapakse government, no criticism of the military and its leaders has been tolerated and those who have reported on crimes perpetrated by military figures or corruption within the military have been abducted, assaulted, imprisoned, murdered, and disappeared. (2010, 336)

While there is considerable truth in such claims, they fail to explain exactly why the Lankan political culture refuses to embrace "liberal" values and practices. This limitation also applies to studies that specifically explored the rejection of federalism by the Sinhalas (Horawitz 1993, 1990; Oberts 1998; A. J. Wilson 2000; Thirutchelvam 2000; Uyangoda 2007). For example, Uyangoda, a well-noted political scientist of Lanka, defending federalism wrote:

> At a time when a fairly serious attempt is being made to find a political settlement to Sri Lanka's ethnic conflict, it is important to defend the idea of federalism, notwithstanding the fact that the present negotiation process between the UNF government and the LTTE has its own drawbacks.... Firstly, the framework of co-existence is usually a constitutional model that should have the capacity to provide adequate flexibility to determine modes of power-sharing between the center and the periphery as well as among ethnic communities.... Secondly, the post-conflict political reform exercise should be understood. A project of state remaking in Sri Lanka presupposes a radical shift from the unitary state model as well as the legacy of majoritarian democracy. The present emphasis on federalism represents a significant conceptual shift.... Thirdly, federalism should not be understood as a mere exercise in devolving power to the periphery. It presupposes that the ethnic communities are equals and deserve equal worth and recognition. A discursive shift towards equality among communities is useful to enrich our political imagination at a time when transition from war to peace requires a great deal of creativity in constitutionalism. (2003, 10)

In conclusion, Uyangoda firmly argued:

> However, as I pointed out in this paper, resolving Sri Lanka's ethnic conflict requires addressing some fundamentals of politics in a polity that has been torn apart by violence and war. Sri Lanka's state needs to be rebuilt on pluralized ethnic foundations while structures of power-sharing should be created at state, sub-state and local levels. A program of deep federalization should define ethnic relations in regional units of federalism as well. (2003, 11)

These observations and suggestions are not atypical. While the argument for federalism in Lanka as a means to solve the bloody ethnic crisis was logical and sensible, very rarely did analysts attempt to unpack the Sinhala Buddhist objections to federalism. This inability to address the core objections mainly from the Saṅgha reflects a "political blind-spot" of cultural hegemony. If the majoritarian ethnoreligious nationalism of the Sinhalas should be the key reason for the failure of the Lankan democracy, then would it not be obvious to explore the very foundations of such nationalism? Why have the Saṅgha refused liberal democracy in general and federalism in particular? What exactly is the reason for the apparent incompatibility of these different sets of beliefs and principles? It is not enough, we argue, to treat the Sinhala and Saṅgha position as "independent variables." Buddhist societies are often studied through the western analytical lenses of "democracy" and "nation" rather than from the perspective of the relevant society and its historical and present socio-political anxieties. Fortunately, some recent approaches combining politics with anthropology—as e.g. in Crosby (2008b)—appear to move beyond the limitations of conventional studies. Our study too aims to contribute to removing a "blind spot" of cultural hegemony.

The aim of this chapter is to provide an overview of the continuous unfolding of ethnoreligious nationalism as promoted by the politically mobilized Sinhala Saṅgha, covering a period from 1815, when the British colonial rulers united the three historical kingdoms in Lanka into one administrative unit (Duncan 1994), to the present. We argue that this unfolding took place in a series of "waves," with new waves often being sparked as a response to perceived threats to the Lankan religious polity and the hegemony of the Buddhist Saṅgha. We will focus on key events that sparked renewed Saṅgha agitation, which then continued and often deepened the Buddhist identity politics that was informed by the *Mahāvaṃsa* ideology ever since its conception. The mytho-historical narratives of the *Mahāvaṃsa*—such as the origin of Vijaya (Strathern 2009a, 2009b), positioning the Sinhalas above and against other, inferior ethnicities (Scheible 2006), and making the Saṅgha and their interpretation of Buddhism the cornerstone for the definition of Sinhala society and its polity (Gunawardana 1995)—never failed to energize these historical waves of resistance.

Following brief remarks on the restoration of Buddhism in Lanka during the eighteenth century, our analysis will divide history into two sections. First, we will look at the period from 1815 to 1948, a period during which the colonial office incrementally introduced initiatives of limited participation for the local élites, which in turn initiated the restructuring of local politics along ethnic lines. The same period also witnessed the emergence of a "Protestant Buddhism" and the renewal of a vision of a classical Theravāda Society in Lanka. The second period, from 1948 to 2009, can also again be divided into two major periods. The period from 1948 to 1983 witnessed the emergence and consolidation of the Sinhala Buddhist hegemony and of politically sanctioned violence against minorities, culminating in the ethnic pogrom against the Tamils living in the South. These events in turn led to the birth of the ultra-militant Tamil separatist movement, the Liberation Tigers of Tamil Eelam (LTTE). The period from 1983 to 2009 thus sees the military struggle between the Lankan army and the LTTE. Throughout this time, as we shall see, the Saṅgha were advocating and supporting a military "solution" to the problem, thus demanding nothing less than the military defeat and annihilation of the LTTE. This was achieved in May 2009, marking another key moment in the history of belligerent Sinhala Buddhism.

We will emphasize the historical dynamics that unfolded from the various waves of Saṅgha resistance and politics. Moments of Saṅgha involvement were not isolated events, but were connected, giving rise to a political dynamics culminating in a violent crisis. There are some studies on Saṅgha resistance during the relevant period (Stirrat 1992;

Wickramasinghe 2006a, 2006b), but they fail to highlight the political dimension and long-term consequences of the Saṅgha interventions.

The revival of the Saṅgha community and the renewal of its political influence occurred during the reign of king Kīrti Śrī (1734–1784). The king's attempts to restore the śāsana and its administration by repairing and reorganizing a large number of temples in the district of Kandy and other parts of the island is well documented (Coomaraswamy 1908; Malalgoda 1976; Sivasundaram 2010, 2007a 2007b). Chapters of the Cūlavaṃsa (100, 133–136) praise the King for his work. Yet despite such praise, the king encountered opposition from both the nobles and the Saṅgha. The élites held his ethnicity against him, while the Saṅgha did not trust him as he had been of Saivite faith before he embraced Buddhism as his adopted religion. In spite of his considerable contribution to the restoration of Buddhism in the country, the Saṅgha considered him a non-Buddhist, and a non-Buddhist cannot be king of the Dhammadīpa. Samannakoḍi Disāwē and Moladaṇḍe Batvaḍana, two regional rulers, planned to have the king assassinated and to appoint the visiting Siam (Thai) prince as their ruler (Malalgoda 1976, 66). The plan found the support of Tibboṭuwāvē Siddhārtha Buddharakkhita and Välivița Saraṇaṃkara—the Bhikkhu whom the king had appointed as Saṅgha-*rāja*, i.e. as the chief of all Saṅgha. In modern times, these events set the scene for the subsequent Saṅgha involvement in power politics.

Saṅgha and Śāsana in Lanka

There is no other historical force that has influenced and shaped the very fundamentals of Sinhala society more than Theravāda Buddhism. Nearly twenty-three centuries since its recorded arrival, Theravāda faith has been the cornerstone of Sinhala culture, society and politics (Gombrich 2006a, 1988; E. J. Harris 2006; Rāhula 1956). The continuous influence and socio-political power that Buddhism and its Saṅgha enjoyed in Lanka could be compared only to a few other cases such as the Orthodox Jewish priesthood in Israel (Lustick 2005) or the Shiv Sēnā of India (Hansen 2005, 2001). Malalgoda observed that the notions of a "chosen people" were "observable no less among specific Buddhist communities like the Sinhalese and the Burmese than among the Jews" (1970, 424). Modern research has proven that unlike many similar historic civilizations, the Sinhala civilization was constructed around a conceptual theocratic social order where the Saṅgha played the most decisive role not just in the religious affairs but also in the socio-economic sphere and very importantly in the politics of the society (Coningham *et al.* 2007; Fleming 2006; Shaw 2004).

In the Buddhist trinity, the *Buddha* (person), the dhamma (his teaching) and the Saṅgha (the monks) are placed in a hierarchical order. Within this hierarchy, the person of Buddha and his dhamma are considered above the Saṅgha in a comparative sense, yet in practice, especially in Theravāda societies, the Saṅgha is treated as the embodiment of Buddha and his dhamma and accordingly has grown to be the most influential aspect of the three. Wherever the Theravāda school arrived and became established, it is the structure and social interaction of the Saṅgha, the priesthood, which finally shaped both the present and the future of the faith. This is true in almost all states, including Cambodia, Laos, Myanmar and Thailand, where Theravāda Buddhism is established as the foundation of social structure. The Saṅgha-state nexus is thus the key historical dynamic that shapes contemporary Sinhala politics, and it holds the key to decoding the current complexity.

It is intriguing that the Saṅgha, as the renouncers of the secular world order, in the process of doing so have become the guardians and guides of the same world and society in which they are symbols of spiritual withdrawal. This tension is inevitable because the Saṅgha are the bridge between the Buddhist faith and the world within which it operates. The Saṅgha engage in the search for their own nirvāna, marking the end of the cosmic journey of life in *samsāra*. This is the status that every Buddhist aims to attend. However, the Saṅgha are also the teachers for the rest of the secular world to find the path to nirvāna. The Saṅgha, in this in-between position are only becoming the true followers of Buddha, who himself struggled with these two conflicting responsibilities. The balancing act of withdrawing in order to search for spirituality and yet also of staying involved so that the dhamma will spread, recruiting believers and disciples, is an inherent tension in the life of a Saṅgha. The *Vinaya Piṭaka*—the canonical code of conduct in Buddhism—expects every Saṅgha to endure and live this duality (Vin. I: 21, I: 40). This then becomes the core philosophy of the Theravādins and their way of life. While the renouncers are expected to live a very basic and simple life dependent on the offerings of the believers, the act of teaching to a wider audience necessitates an institutional order. In the same framework, when a Saṅgha harbors an encompassing compassion towards his whole society, he needs the support of the king or the state and its governing mechanism (Bartholomeusz 1994; Burnouf 2010). Thus, the Saṅgha in Lanka are not merely spiritual teachers but are also the key protectors and guides of their society and every aspect of it, including politics.

This socio-political embeddedness of Theravāda ethics (Froese *et al.* 2008) forms the most formidable political force in Lanka's history and present. The complexity of this inside out (detachment) and then outside–in (re-engaging) movement of the Saṅgha meant that the politics of Sinhala society have always been subjected to the religious and "cosmic" nature of the Saṅgha project. While the state and its politics eventually (and often reluctantly) accepted the role of the Saṅgha in redefining the society, the Saṅgha in turn established themselves as the most important influence in forming and defining the state. The exchange of merit-collecting (*puñña kriyā*) became the operational principle for this Saṅgha-state contract (Bechert 1992; Egge 2002; Gombrich 1971a; Keyes and Daniel 1983; Samuels 2008).

Merit collecting is the aim of every believing Buddhist. S/he collects merits in order to be born in a better status that would lead to eventual nirvāna. There is no better way of colleting merit than to support the Saṅgha and Śāsana. While lay Buddhists benefit from such merit collecting by supporting the Saṅgha, the Saṅgha in turn direct the lay people on the path to nirvāna. Theorizing the Saṅgha-state structure, Tambiah argues that dialectical tensions are central to this contract:

> [O]ur thesis has been that canonical and postcanonical doctrines, the commentaries and the verbalizations of the believers, the structures embedded in their myths and rites, the patterns of their actions—which together reveal the coupling of Buddhism and the polity—are ridden with dialectical tensions, paradoxes, and ambiguities, which occur as parameters. By parameter, I mean that a constant component of the mix can vary in different cases and the variations—which are impelled by circumstances and are responses to situations—constitute the set or family of occurrences. Thus, the ideological armature can show pulsation between modalities. (Tambiah 1976, 516)

According to Tambiah, the Saṅgha and the political leaders of the state are the key pillars of the cosmic order, and the relationship between these two forces is thus the crucial source of order in the Theravāda states:

> According to the Buddhist scheme of things relating to the world, there are two foremost or superior beings, the bhikkhu and the king, but the former is superior. The king is the mediator between social disorder and the social order; the bhikkhu is the mediator between home and homelessness, between a world of fetters and a free state of deliverance, between the Buddha and the Cakkavatti as the two wheels of the Dhamma, between the Saṅgha and the polity and society in which it is located, between this-worldly and other-worldly pursuits. It is this totality that also makes Buddhism a world religion and not merely the pursuit of a few virtuosi. (Tambiah 1976, 12)

Recent scholarship on the Saṅgha-state relationship has in some ways departed from Tambiah's classical analysis (Abeysekara 2008; Crosby 2008a; C. R. De Silva 2006; Goh 2007; MacKinnon 2004; Rambukwella 2008; Wijeyeratne 2003). For example, Ananda Abeysekara demands that the traditional "Buddhism-Betrayed" lenses be widened in order to conceptualize the terms "religion," "politics" and "religious-violence" from within a "post-secular" order:

> Rather the questions, terms, and parameters defining which persons, practices, and knowledge can and cannot count as religion or violence, civilization or terror are produced, battled out, and subverted in minute contingent conjunctures. Put differently, they are authorized to come into (central) view and fade from view, to emerge and submerge, to become centered and decentered within a microspace of competing authoritative "native" debates and discourses. (Abeysekara 2001, 1)

Thus, the question of how religion and politics relate to each other needs to be approached from within the relevant society and political system. According to Abeysekara, our ethical-liberal political parameters always turn religion into a "problem" whereas we may have to accept that the only appropriate way to approach religion is to consider it an "apriority," i.e. an unavoidable social reality. Abeysekara demands a new kind of "un-inheriting" that will reinterpret history away from essentialist, binary positions:

> So if we are to understand, religion, violence, and culture, as nonessential, "historical" ideas, that is, as discursive traditions, or as "embodied arguments," we must, then, explore those micro spaces in which categories like religion and violence come to be invested with, and divested of, making authoritative meanings. The failure to do so, in my view, leads to the uncritical reproduction of native knowledge about such categories.
> (Abeysekara 2001, 42)

Kate Crosby, similarly, showed that traditional readings of Theravāda societies had always suffered from outsider hegemony.

> Social anthropological studies, on the other hand, have continued to focus on socio-political and socio-economic power structures, taking the nation-state as their true object of study. The parameters of this study are set by the concerns of western societal analysis rather than the priorities and authorities of the traditions and people under scrutiny. Pioneering attempts to assess modern Theravāda in relation to its own authorities combined these flaws, dismissing the validity of priorities, beliefs and practices that fail to match their outsiders' decocted essence of the very partial canon that these same outsiders had selected as authoritative, and ignoring the vast wealth of texts, both written and otherwise, transmitted within different forms of Theravāda. (2008b, 2)

Many of these more recent analyses stress that the Saṅgha-state nexus has to be understood from within the local political context, from an "insider" perspective (Schober 2008). This is especially true for the Saṅgha in Lanka (and other Theravāda states), who have quite deliberately and purposefully politicized Buddhism even by means of propagating the use of violence. The situation in Lanka is thus different from the situation in Japan, Taiwan and Tibet, where the Saṅgha generally adhere to principles of non-violence, discouraging violent political mobilization (Ardley 2003). In these societies, the tradition is not Theravādin. However, it can be argued that the activities and the political involvement of the Sinhala Saṅgha violates fundamental Theravāda beliefs and rituals—especially the notion *ahiṃsā*—as described in the canonical writings (Aung-Thwin 2008). The ideology of the *Mahāvaṃsa*, which presents Sinhala Buddhism as the purest manifestation of the teachings of the Buddha (based on his three visits) and the island of Lanka as the blessed (Sri) abode of that teaching, appears to sanction the very violation of these teachings in order to protect them.

Allan Clements, a Saṅgha turned dhamma activist, has, in his ethnographical account *Instinct for Freedom* (2006), recorded the brutal ethnic war in the jungles of Burma involving the soldiers of the military junta and bhikkhus who had given up their robes so that they could join the war. Clements juxtaposes two extreme attitudes among the bhikkhus: some would completely adhere to *ahiṃsā* principles even when confronted with brutal and violent oppression; and others would take up arms and kill if required in order to protect the followers of Buddha. As Clement's analysis shows, while some understand the noble qualities of Buddhism (*metta, muditā, karunā*, and *upekṣā*) as implying, *ahiṃsā* others understand them as a call to protect the faith community with extreme measures if necessary. The tension between these two attitudes exists also in the individual life of each Saṅgha, especially if the political context suggests that his religion, state, or *ethnie* are threatened. The Saṅgha thus assume that they are the ones who have to distinguish between what is a danger to their community and what is a blessing. They become the "gatekeepers" in charge of preserving the purity of their community.

Because of this tension, which unfolds from a quest for purity and authenticity, we often find a contradiction between the *Adhigama Dharma*, the experiential dimension of Buddhism, and the *Āgama Dharma*, the scriptural and doctrinal level of Buddhism, within Saṅgha practice. In light of these contradictions the question arises of how a Buddhist ethic operates in practice—how, in other words, the Saṅgha empirically rationalize their actions in relation to scriptural and traditional authority. How do they concretely and individually justify their involvement in violent politics? Even more recent scholarship, while acknowledging the urgency of the question, has struggled to find a suitable framework for an analysis of this evident contradiction (Abeysekara 2008; Berkwitz 2008b; Cosby 2008; C. R. De Silva 2006; E. J. Harris 2001; Jerryson 2009; Roberts 2001a; McCargo 2008b; McGranahan 2005; Samuels 2004; Wijeyeratne 2003, 2013). In our study, we propose to approach the question empirically by examining in some detail the mindset of key Saṅgha who over the years have advocated the political involvement of their community. The examination and analysis of their biographies, including their intellectual and spiritual trajectory, will form a central part of our study. As we shall see, however, their own formation was informed by the very history of this political involvement. Over the centuries, Saṅgha political agitation established itself as a tradition, which would operate in the background until actualized in waves of mobilization, usually in response to perceived threats to the religious polity. In order to be able to understand the mindset of key Saṅgha activists, it is important to be able to understand this historical dynamics, which is fuelled by "waves" of political resistance and activism.

Restoration of Śāsana 1750–1815

1750–1770: Upasampadā and the Kandy Saṅgha Authority

The Sinhala kings traditionally married south Indian royalty for political, military and caste reasons. This was also the custom of Vijaya, the first Sinhala king (Mhv. VII: 69–74). These marriage arrangements brought the *Nāyakkar* family of south India into the ruling circles of the Kandyan kingdom. In 1750, the sudden death of the childless king Vijaya Rājasimha made Kīrti Śrī Rājasimha (KSR), the king's first brother-in-law, the ruler. As a way of consolidating his rule and reversing the unfavorable attitude amongst the Saṅgha towards his Hindu identity, the king distanced himself from the Dutch occupying the south coast. KSR promoted and expanded Buddhist institutions appealing to the Sinhala masses through various popular projects. There were three basic reasons for his evangelical Buddhist activities. First, KSR tried to present himself as the defender of the faith protecting Sinhala interests against the political and military threat posed by the Dutch East India Company. Second, KSR was clearly struggling against the internal élites—even escaping assassination attempts—and thus felt the need to establish himself as a legitimate ruler hiding his Tamil-Hindu background. Lastly, due to these threats and his precarious situation he may have genuinely desired the comfort of the religion and the advice of its Saṅgha whom he knew so well (Holt 1996).

The impact of KSR's work resulted in one of the greatest revivals of Buddhism in modern Lanka. His support not only expanded the faith but also reestablished the Śāsana, which by this time had become nothing but a remote institution amongst the élite Goyigama and Raḍdala caste of Kandy. This revival was possible largely due to the initiatives of a single Saṅgha: Välivița Saraṇaṃkara (1698–1778). Saraṇaṃkara developed an alternative way of life guided by the *Vinaya* and became popular amongst the laity. His attempts to bring monks from Siam (Thailand)

and re-establish the higher ordination failed twice under king Vijaya Rājasimha. KSR, capitalizing on the situation, broke with tradition and asked for help from the Dutch to facilitate the sea voyage of Thai monks to Kandy, thus allowing for the reestablishment of the higher ordination process for the first time in 300 years. KSR, under the advice of Välivița, established Asgiriya and Malvatte, two new Saṅgha communities, and assigned "vast amounts of land to them" (Malalgoda 1976, 60–65). "There is hardly a Vihāra of any importance in the Kandy district," wrote Coomaraswamy, "which was not restored or newly built by him" (1956, 12). By 1765, Kandy Saṅgha exerted such influence over the entire island, by royal command, that all monks were instructed to visit Kandy in order to be interviewed and in order to have their ordination approved. Thus, the revival of the faith facilitated the re-establishment of centralized Saṅgha control in all matters concerning Buddhism and its relation to society.

1770–1815: The Southern Saṅgha Rebellion

The central control exerted by the higher (*Goyigama)* caste Saṅgha in Kandy was unacceptable to the lower caste coastal region Saṅgha, and hence they sought to undermine this control. As an act of protest, dissatisfied southern Saṅgha had their very first *Upasampadā* in 1772 at Toṭagamu Vihāra, followed by another in Tangalle in 1798, both being disapproved of by the Saṅgha in Kandy.

The political and military contest between the foreign colonialists and the Kandyan kingdom was at an impasse as well. With the tension between the Kandy and the southern Saṅgha in the background, it was evident that the key to gaining control was not just military might but also the ability to influence and change the delicate social-cultural balance. The Dutch had tried to do exactly this by attempting to assassinate king Vijaya Rājasimha with the help of Saṅgha Suriyagoda Rajasundara, Välivița's teacher (Malalgoda 1976, 58–59). The political division forced the Saṅgha to take sides and to show their political loyalty as they were looking for royal patronage and recognition. They decided to seek support from their own caste's Dutch trading partners, who were willing to sponsor their temples and life. In 1799, Holjoti Dines De Silva Jayatilaka Sriwardhana, a leading Salāgama caste merchant with strong ties with the Dutch company, helped finance a journey of southern Saṅgha to Burma for a higher ordination ritual and recognition. On their return in 1803, the Burmese monks who travelled with them helped create a new chapter for those who had been refused recognition by the Kandyan Saṅgha. This was the beginning of the *Amarapura* chapter in (southern) Lanka, named after what was then the Burmese capital. Amarapura granted higher ordination to lower caste Saṅgha and thus stood as a direct challenge to the *Siyam Nikāya* of Kandy. This was to have major consequences later as most of the revivalist Saṅgha of the nineteenth and twentieth century in Lanka were to come from Amarapura. Aṃgahapiṭiyē Ñaṇavimala, a dissatisfied Siyam member of the Goyigama caste of southern origin, became the first chief Saṅgha of the Amarapura chapter. However, after just a few years other castes such as Durāve and Karāve also desired to have their own chapters with Saṅgha ordained from their own caste. In 1807, Attudāvē Dhammarakkhita, who again received large financial and social support from Sinhala traders with Dutch connections, returned from Burma to start the *Rāmañña* chapter. Thus, the Saṅgha fragmented and yet thereby gained new momentum in an attempt to gain influence on the shifting political and financial powers in the country (Kemper 1980).

Redeeming the Sinhala Land 1815–1948

Many Theravāda states have histories of Saṅgha political involvement and resistance. Burma, Cambodia, Laos, Lanka and Thailand have a political history deeply colored by the saffron robe and its power politics, often including violent conflicts with the state. The Saṅgha's main concern is to influence and possibly control political power in such a way that the supremacy of the Theravāda faith and its ethnic and religious hegemony is guaranteed. Accordingly, Saṅgha resistance springs into action whenever changes are proposed to undermine this supremacy. Religious political resistance has received considerable attention in the literature (Almond, Appleby and Sivan 2003; Appleby 2000; Juergensmeyer 2010a, 1993; Jerryson and Juergensmeyer 2009; and Nussbaum 2007). Still, the case of Lanka is special as it combines the ethics of *ahiṃsā* with violent politics, thus requiring the Saṅgha to "reinvent" their Buddhism in the face of anything they perceive as "*parà*," i.e. as foreign to the land and faith (D. A. Scott 1994, 1992, 1985; Scott and Geertz 1990). These waves of appropriation of the Buddhist tradition stretch like an historical arc from the Mahāvaṃsic text to the political manifesto of the *Jātika Hela Urumaya* (JHU), the political party of the Buddhist monks, which was founded in 2002 and won nine parliamentary seats at the 2004 general election. Even at the time of writing (September 2012) this book, the JHU remains a strong defender and coalition partner of the Rajapakse government.

The period from 1815 to 1948 records a significant trend in Saṅgha politics. 1815 was the year in which Lanka fully surrendered to the British colonists, and 1948 was the year in which the country gained administrative independence. On 8 March 1815, largely due to internal rivalry and betrayal, resulting from the eccentric rule of the king Sri Vickrama Rājasimha, the chief ministers (Adigars) signed the *Kandyan Convention* surrendering the Kandyan Kingdom, the last indigenous rule of the

Sinhalas. Until then Kandy had been in many ways the center of Buddhism on the island. The subsequent capture and banishment of king Rājasimha, an ethnic Tamil and the last king of Lanka, by the British troops ushered in a radical period of politics and governance in the Buddhist land. The original text and much of the background of the Kandyan Convention are missing, thus making it difficult to reconstruct the circumstances. However, according to available primary texts, the Kandyan chiefs, advised by the Saṅgha, were not only concerned with their welfare, but with the protection of the Buddhaśāsana in Ceylon. Even at the point of surrender, they compelled the British to undertake the protection and promotion of not just the religion of Buddha but also of its bhikkhus and their inherited properties as places of worship. A few historical texts reproduced from the 14-point agreement demonstrate the seriousness of this commitment:

> (5th) The religion of Buddha, professed by the chiefs and inhabitants of these provinces is declared inviolable, and its rites, ministers, and places of worship are to be maintained and protected.[1]

The British accepted the condition that the Saṅgha and Buddhism be protected. For the Saṅgha this was the essential, minimum condition they would place on their surrender to British rule. They were drawing on a historical precedent set by the Tamil Hindu Náyakkar kings, who had ruled the island under similar agreements. It was not the ethnic background but the hope and promise to have, in a sense, a "Buddhist ruler" that was paramount. However, under British rule such hopes were short-lived.

1817: The Ūva-Wellassa Rebellion

The expectation and promise that the Buddhaśāsana was to be protected was the core of the compromise between the Chiefs of Kandy and the British administration. However, the promise was not kept. The British administration deliberately but subtly sabotaged the promise in two premeditated ways: by marginalizing the Saṅgha and keeping them away from the routine governance of the colony and by formulating decrees to acquire a vast amount of profitable agricultural land formerly belonging to the Saṅgha. By 1817, such measures had further undermined the Saṅgha confidence and self-understanding as the protectors and guarantors of the faith and the land. The 1817 rebellion in the remote districts of Ūva and Wellassa in the Kandy region took the British rulers by surprise. The citizens of the region were suffering economic hardship,

1. Captain De Brussche L., Lettres on Ceylon, 1817, Appendix Proclamation II, page 151; similarly in Marshall H, Ceylon, 1837, the convention IX, page 274, and Enclosure to Despatch, Brownriggs to Bathurst, November 5, 1816, C.O. 54/61. British Library archives.

which contributed to the unrest. The Saṅgha played a key role in initiating the protest, as De Silva explains:

> This was Vibävé, an ex-bhikkhu posing as Doraisámi, a member of the deposed royal family. The pretender claiming to be a Näyakkar prince is the point worth noting, both as evidence of Näyakkar dynasty's popularity amongst the Kandyans and as an acknowledgement as indigenous rulers. Vibävé made his entry at the shrine (dedicated to a Hindu god) of Katharagama in July 1817 soon after the annual festival there had been brought to a close. He made a declaration that he had been chosen by the god Katharagama to be the king. A population that was disconnected with the British rule was very receptive to his appeal. The rebellion that broke out in September 1817 took the British by surprise. (K. M. De Silva 2005, 303)

The Saṅgha-king identity suggested in these actions is intriguing and revealing, as it shows the Saṅgha attitude regarding the rightful rulers of the land. The monk Vibävé was exchanging his Sinhala identity with the identity of a Tamil prince, who was considered legitimate by the populace. Furthermore, it is significant that he chose a Hindu deity—Kataragama—to give legitimacy for the restoration of the association between Buddhism and government. Tradition records that the deity Kataragama was assigned the duty of protecting Buddhism in Lanka (Obeyesekere 1977, 1978; Pfaffenberger 1979). There were two turning points in the otherwise successful guerrilla-style rebellion. One was the capture of the Tooth Relic by the British forces, an event of great symbolic significance. The *Mahāvaṃsa* records how a tooth relic of Buddha was brought to Lanka, the Danta Dhātu, which is considered the most important relic of all as it was associated with the words spoken by Buddha (Yalman 1962, 321). In the Theravāda tradition, the one who owns the Dantha will rule the Buddhist world (Berkwitz 2006b; Trainor 1997). The other was the revelation of the real identity of the monk Vibāvë. Possession of the tooth relic legitimized the British as the true rulers of the Buddhist Island. The rebellion provoked such nationalist fever amongst the Sinhalas that the episode is still a "living memory" in school texts and popular culture, and modern Saṅgha still refer to their leadership during the rebellion as a true example of their vocation.

The British crushed the rebellion ruthlessly and increased the separation between the Saṅgha and the state. In 1832, they dismissed the special treatment given to the Kandy region and annexed it to the island creating one unitary state. The Colebrook-Cameron reform commission provided the legal framework for unifying British Ceylon as one single political and economic administration. The British were not interested in running a loss-making colony. They tried everything possible to extract profit from the island. First cinnamon, then coffee, and finally tea plantations were introduced to interior farmlands. By 1840, the rulers had introduced the Crown Land Encroachment Act (Moore 1989), which vested rights with the colonists to take over any land deemed wasted or underutilized. Traditionally the Sinhala peasants had no record or deeds for most of their land because it had been handed down from generation to generation. The authority of interpretation to decide to whom the land belonged was always with the British government agent. Accordingly, the Sinhala farmers lost a large proportion of their traditional land. The Saṅgha were especially affected, because they were looking after large and often idle stretches of land belonging to their temples. Acquiring land was an act of profit making, yet unknowingly the British rulers had stepped on the sensitive fabric of Saṅgha politics by dismantling the link between the Saṅgha and their villages (Evers and Siddique 1993; Evers 1969, 1968, 1967), visibly distancing the Saṅgha from the royal courts and undermining their economic strength.

1848: The Mātalē Rebellion

Because of the confiscation of land and the introduction of new taxes, a new Saṅgha led rebellion followed in 1848 (Warren 2004; Kostal 2005). Unlike other rebellions, the Mātalē Rebellion initially unfolded without élite support. The temple, which represented religious and moral authority, and the Saṅgha, who were the agents of that authority, had been marginalized and excluded from the daily governance of the island. Two of the key leaders of the rebellion, Sinchia Fernando and Hennadige Francisco Fernando, were from the coastal regions of Kälaṇiya and Moratuwa near the port city of Colombo. Possibly, in an attempt to hide their non-Buddhist background, they adopted the names Gongalēgoda Bandā and Puran Appu respectively. The two leaders gathered support from the peasants of Mātalē. The political revolt clearly also had a socio-economic background (Warren 2004).

The 1848 rebellion was a grassroots revolt against the oppressive colonialism. The movement gained momentum as Saṅgha leaders based in historical Mahiyangana got involved; Ven. Giranagama of the Daṃbulla cave temples also supported the revolt. Giranagama became the rebellion's ideologue, accepted by the peasants as their Buddhist leader. Following the traditional custom, he crowned Gongalgoda Banda as the new king and Puran Appu as the chief commander of a new Buddhist government. The rebellion thus aimed to restore the ancient social and political order in which a king guided by the Saṅgha ruled the Buddhist land. However, the revolt was no match for a well-equipped and trained British army. The rebellion was quickly crushed although the rebels were able to inflict considerable damage on their British enemies (De Mills 2012; Warren 2004).

The dismal failure of the Mātalē rebellion left deep scars in the nationalist psyche of the Sinhalas across the island. In response to the anti-colonial Buddhist nationalism that was gaining strength, the Colonial Office began an initiative to restore the place of Buddhism in the public eye, partly in order to contain the growing anger and frustration amongst the natives. While there was no intention of restoring the Saṅgha to their former prominence, a gesture was required to safeguard economic and social stability. In the face of much criticism from the missionary lobby, which by then had arrived in the Buddhist island in numbers and strength to convert the heathens, Governor George Anderson opened some remarkable avenues for Saṅgha to become re-involved in state affairs. While this gesture of reconciliation was meant to calm the disappointed Saṅgha, in fact some radical Saṅgha exploited the moment as an opportunity to mobilize and agitate further against the British. After the failed rebellion, the Saṅgha (almost) never again took any part in armed confrontation with the colonists. Instead, they tried to position themselves as closely as possible to the center of power and to advance their interests in a more indirect manner. Two further waves of resistance in 1883 and 1915 saw the Saṅgha aim at other enemies using different tactics. Instead of agitating against the colonists, whom they know they could not defeat, the Saṅgha turned their attention to those who were seen as collaborating with the regime: the Catholics, Muslims and Tamils.

While the damage caused by the loss of land was material, the Saṅgha would soon have to confront what was, from their point of view, an even greater threat. The England based missionary agencies with their overt evangelical zeal appeared to the Saṅgha as the "spiritual dimension" of the colonial threat. Malalgoda argued that it was a struggle for "recognition" that involved the Saṅgha in interdenominational competitions (Malalgoda 1973). The Saṅgha, who were not strong enough to organize a rebellion against the colonial regime, were at least able to respond to the challenge posed by the missionaries by organizing protests against the encroachment on the Buddhaśāsana. This configuration of forces allowed the Saṅgha to engage in political mobilization while appearing to remain a spiritual force. Saṅgha mobilization against the missionaries focused on three areas of activity: preaching, printed propaganda, and public education (Young and Jebanesan 1995; Young and Somarathna 1996). By agitating against the missionaries, the Saṅgha were able to utilize "religion" as a "nineteenth century term for ethnonationalism" (Da Silva 1998). Sirimalwatte (2009), drawing on Spencer (2008), maintains that later political protests and violence were a direct consequence of the ethnoreligious nationalism that was nurtured in key Saṅgha temples as a result of their agitation against the missionaries.

1860–1875: Defeating the Wesleyan Missionaries

The missionaries in Lanka used traditional methods such as education, preaching, and distributing printed material to advance their cause. Missionaries from the London Mission Society arrived in Lanka in 1805. The subsequent arrival of the Baptists (1812), Wesleyans (1814) and Church of England missionaries (1818) resulted in multiple missionary activities in many regions, especially after the British gained control over the entire island in 1815. Education programs supported by missions as well as church-sponsored newspapers and other publications often questioned or condemned the Buddhist faith, irritating the Saṅgha. Isolated, individual Saṅgha responses to these provocations took a decisive turn when Reverend Spencer Hardy authored and published "Kristiyani Prajgnapthi" (KP) "Christian Doctrines" in 1849. KP, which went through several editions, presented a more direct challenge to Buddhist doctrines. These attacks and challenges united the Saṅgha who had otherwise fragmented on issues of caste, region, and order.

It is a Buddhist tradition to defend doctrine and recruit new believers through public discourse. With colonialist confidence, British missionaries challenged the Buddhist monks to take part in public debates to explain and defend their faith. Five public debates, one of them later called *Pānadura Vādaya*, took place between 1850 and 1870. As an unintended consequence of this challenge, the missionaries provoked Saṅgha leaders, such as Migeṭṭuvattē Guṇānanda, who until that point was preoccupied with his literary work but suddenly embraced a new kind of militancy. De Silva described the effects of these debates as follows:

> Of the five debates, the first and second at Baddegama and Varagoda (both in 1865) were conducted in writing. The Udanvita (1866), Gaṃpola (1871) and Pānadura (1873) controversies were public debates. The Pānadura debate was the most notable of them all. There the Venerable Migeṭṭuvattē Guṇānanda proved himself a debater of a very high order, mettlesome, witty and eloquent if not especially erudite. The emotions generated by this debate had lasting effects on the next generation of Buddhist activists. The Anagārika Dharmapāla, for instance, came to view the Pānadura debate as "the great historical controversy between the Christian missionaries and the Buddhist yellow robed monks [where] the Christian party [was] ignominiously defeated. This was the first moral conquest which the Buddhists had gained against the Christians since the latter came to Ceylon." (K. M. De Silva 1981, 340–341)

The Saṅgha felt that they had "won" the Pānadura debates. Accordingly, the period from 1860 to 1875 saw an unprecedented unity and willingness amongst the Saṅgha to take their faith beyond the temple and defend it publicly. The Pānadura "victory" seemed to suggest to the

Saṅgha that they could fight back the missionaries and colonists on their own terms (Kloppenborg 2004; Malalgoda 1973).

1883: Buddhist-Catholic Riots

The violent riots of 1883 and the Saṅgha activities that sustained them were a manifestation of the growing militant Buddhism among the Saṅgha, especially among those in the South-West regions of the island. These regions had repeatedly suffered colonial oppression since the sixteenth century, first by the Portuguese and then by the Dutch. Both colonial masters did their utmost not only to establish their versions of the Christian faith but also to destroy the indigenous faith and its places of worship. Available historical records show the ruthlessness of this colonial practice. However, British missionaries went beyond their Dutch counterparts and became confrontational and openly aggressive in their missionary work. This was largely due to inter-denominational competition and thus to their eagerness to establish their "brand" of congregations and to receive state patronage. By this time, inevitably, the missionaries provoked the Saṅgha and their *dāyakas*.

In 1883, the political temperature reached an explosive level. With the arrival of Colonel Olcott (Proch 2009; Prothero 1993; Swearer 1970), an American Buddhist Theosophist (Trevithick 2008), to organize and support the Buddhist cause, Saṅgha political engagement became ever more mobile, strategic, and militant. Colonel Henry Steel Olcott was a Civil War veteran who had read about the Pānadura Debate, and upon his arrival, he proceeded to support the Buddhist revivalist cause by adopting the same techniques that were available to the Christian missionaries: the printed press, public education and political lobbying.

On the Easter Sunday of 1883, Migeṭṭuvattē Guṇānanda conducted a mass rally and procession in Kotahena, a Catholic stronghold near Colombo. The Catholics had suffered under the Anglican administration and were not in the mood to give in to further intimidation, even if it originated with the Buddhists rather than the Anglicans (Bartholomeusz 1998). They attacked the procession, thereby provoking an island-wide violent response by the Buddhists. The riots were led by the Saṅgha and their followers, resulting in death and destruction. The events reflected the changing nature of the Saṅgha resistance and its politics. In fact, the violent riots in Kotahena were only a surface phenomenon. Saṅgha agitation regarding the Buddhist identity of the people and the land had gone much further and prepared the people for further, more radical acts of resistance (Rogers 1987a, 1987b; Stirrat 1999, 1992; Sumathipala 1969).

The history of Saṅgha mobilization challenges Benedict Anderson's "imagined communities" thesis (1983), which presents a "big bang" genesis of ethno-nationalism that depended on the rise of print capitalism.

Anderson's account does not provide a valid framework for understanding the historic realities of ethnoreligious nationalism as it emerged among the Sinhala Buddhists. Ethnoreligious nationalism among the Sinhalas as constructed in the pages of *Mahāvaṃsa* predates the modern concept of nation and nationalism. However, Anderson's thesis provides some help as we try to understand the emergence of a nationalist identity among the Catholics in Lanka. The Dutch and the British colonists repeatedly marginalized the nearly three centuries old Catholic church in Lanka. The largely coastal community of Sinhalas who converted to Catholicism during the Portuguese period was never accepted as a legitimate "identity" by the mainland Buddhists. Their "alien" faith, culture, lifestyle and political loyalty marked them as an "enemy within." The Catholics, in turn, used the print media to promote their cause. *The Messenger,* a weekly tabloid, became the official organ through which the church developed and promoted her socio-politics. Catholics used their well-preserved school system to accentuate a national identity. Those efforts were directed against both the British and the Buddhists.

Rogers summarizes the novelty of the 1883 riots:

> Religious revival created a sense of solidarity that rioters could tap for wider support; such a unifying force had been lacking since the Kandyan Kingdom's loss of legitimacy. The other instances when rioting spread beyond one locality in the 19th century, the tax protests of 1848 and the grain riots of 1866, were collections of local protests, not unified responses based on alternative visions of social order. The religious riots of the late 19th and early 20th centuries were motivated by an ideology that could provoke outrage in localities not directly affected by the issue in question. (Rogers 1987c, 591)

As a consequence of the 1883 riots, the state prohibited all open-air religious activities—a harsh treatment for the practice of Theravāda Buddhism. Nevertheless, the Saṅgha, now better organized and internationalized, had gained new momentum to continue their revivalist activities with a great infusion of ethnoreligious nationalism. The Saṅgha demanded that *Vesak*, the birthday of Buddha, be declared a national holiday and that the newly designed Buddhist flag be recognized. Olcott gave moral, legal and material support for this wave of agitations.

Growing international anti-colonial sentiments, supported by the liberalist approach of the colonial civil administrators, helped to strengthen the Buddhist nationalist cause. As noted previously, the 1837 publication of the *Mahāvaṃsa* in English was part of a revival of the mytho-narrative of Sinhala supremacy and helped reconstruct the glorious socio-political heritage of the Saṅgha. The revival and its underlying ethnoreligious nationalism were nurtured under the careful leadership of key Saṅgha such as Guṇānanda and Hikkaḍuvē Śrī Sumaṅgala. The year 1915 was of great symbolic significance, as a century before the Sinhalas had lost their last kingdom, and the British, who had promised to protect Buddhism, had failed to deliver their promise (Frost 2002).

1915 Buddhist-Muslim Riots

The toxic political and socio-economic conditions that led to the 1915 riots are well-documented (Ali 1981, 1984; Blackton 1970; Dep 2001; P. T. M. Fernando 1969, 1970; Jayawardena 1970; Kannangara 1984; Kearney 1970). A century after the 1815 Ceylon surrender to the British rule, frustration and anger caused by the marginalization of the Buddhist faith were mounting. The entire socio-politics of the Sinhala society had been transformed in a manner unimaginable to the Saṅgha (Jayasuriya 1977; Mendis 1932).

On 28 May 1915, the Buddhists in Gampola—an ancient capital of Ceylon in the Kandy district—were conducting a religious procession very near to a mosque. Enraged Muslims challenged the Buddhists and accused them of deliberately disturbing and provoking the Muslim community. This "minor" incident soon spread violence and confrontation to other parts of the island, leading to statewide communal riots and violent conflict between Muslims and Buddhists. The riots provided the Buddhist communities with an outlet for their anger, thus provoking extreme degrees of violence.

The general politics of the island had undergone many changes since 1883. The colonial administration had started to realize the need to work with the local elités in the governance of the island. Most of the Colebrook-Cameron commission recommendations to indigenize the administration had been in place, yet the Saṅgha's hopes for genuine power-sharing if not governmental control in daily politics were continuously frustrated. Their demands, supported by well-organized campaigns, received a lukewarm reception. As Ali (1981) points out, there were divergent political currents at a crossroads. The Muslims in Ceylon were looking to their Indian brothers in a search for a pan-Asian Islamic brotherhood, while the Buddhists in Ceylon were trying to protect the unique ownership and leadership they claimed to have over the island. The colonial rulers were far too insensitive to feel the subterranean developments in the nationalist politics of the Saṅgha. They treated the riots as a rebellion against their rule, reacted by imposing martial law, and introduced orders to shoot on sight. After 10 days, state troops had killed at least 63 people and imprisoned some key Saṅgha and political figures, including the future Prime Minister D. S. Senanayake (P. T. M. Fernando 1969).

By the end of the riots, the colonial office had committed one of its worst blunders in mishandling the fast growing frustration in the Saṅgha ranks. The decision to ignore the signs opened the gates to a radicalized and indigenized path for politically motivated Saṅgha. After his victory in the public debates, Mohoṭṭivattē Guṇānanda had become the natural leader. He established the *Vidyodaya Pirivena* (schools) for young monks. By this time Hikkaḍuvē Śrī Sumaṅgala, the trusted commander of the campaign, Väligama Sri Sumaṅgala, another activist monk and Colonel Olcott, the key driving forces of the Buddhist awakening, had all died and the Buddhist nationalist movement and its aspirations were waiting for a public space to be redefined.

Anagārika Dharmapāla, by far the most influential Sinhala Buddhist nationalist in the recent history of Ceylon and hardened disciple of the theosophical movement and protégé of Olcott, turned out to be that iconic revivalist figure that the movement was waiting for. This wealthy, English-speaking campaigner was a vibrant speaker, educated at a leading missionary school, and a writer who had published his own *Sinhala Bauddhayā* (The Sinhala Buddhist) newspaper. Meanwhile, Piyadasa Sirisena, a prominent ethno-national novelist, edited the *Sinhala Jāthiya* (The Sinhala Race). The epicenter of these divergent forces was Vidyodaya, which would become one of the core Buddhist nationalist schools for key Saṅgha who would actively reshape the political destiny of Lanka.

In the self-understanding of the Saṅgha, their involvement in the riots of 1915 marked a significant milestone in Saṅgha politics, challenging the destiny of the island and its political culture. The two decades leading to the administrative independence of Ceylon were tarnished by deep intra-group rivalries amongst the Sinhalas based on region and caste backgrounds. These complications only aggravated the differences and for some time made it impossible for any unity to unfold amongst the Sinhala elités as they confronted Tamil political activists. Still, by the end of WW II, in the changed global order, when the British had decided to leave the Indian sub-continent, the Saṅgha in Lanka were well positioned to permanently reshape the politics of the island. When Ceylon was ready to be de-colonized, the Saṅgha fraternity had succeeded in implanting a new and dynamic definition of their role in society. Anagārika eloquently summarized the new definition:

> Buddhism (no longer) should be regarded as "other worldly." ... For Buddha desired "the evolution of social order which aims at the perfection of mankind and doing full justice to the rights of man." ... The Buddha was a "social revolutionary," who urged his disciples to adopt a "socialistic way of life"; indeed, he was a staunch "democrat." ... Marxism was a leaf taken from the Buddhist books. The early Saṅgha were "real communists" and theirs was a classless community. If Buddhism is to have a new birth, it must become a social religion, a synthesis of the Buddhist tradition and progressive humanism. (Guruge 1965, 547)

Based on these ideas, Saṅgha politics was widening the boundaries of a "Protestant Buddhist" ideology. The ethno-nationalism promoted by the Sinhala Saṅgha made non-violence and other virtues of Pāli Buddhism look artificial and restrictive, and the primordial ethnic affiliation became the most natural and centrifugal force for their social engagement. They thereby continued to replace the present with the past. They aimed to infuse the present social order with the ancient political model in which the Saṅgha, rather than the society, were at the center of political power. The extraordinary interest in Orientalism and remarkable archaeological findings at the time, supported by the modernist nature of the Victorian British rule, only helped to foster such thinking and furthered its structural political mobilization (Almond 2007; Blackburn 2010).

Encouraged by the charismatic leadership of Anagārika, Walpola Rāhula, a bhikkhu from an upper middle class family in the deep south of Lanka, entered the intellectual discourse on the role of the Saṅgha in the changing context. He is considered to be one of the most influential, academically able and intellectually profound Saṅgha in modern Ceylon. Being the first Lankan monk to enter a secular university and earn a foreign degree, he was well suited to the role of theologizing the modern role of Saṅgha. Rāhula, who we will discuss in detail in the next chapter, in many senses intellectualized the modern Saṅgha social conduct. His 1947 paradigmatic analysis, *Bhikṣuvage Urumaya* (later published as *The Heritage of the Bhikkhu: A Short History of the Bhikkhu in Educational, Cultural, Social, and Political Life* in 1974), became the textbook for the future Saṅgha political agenda. Rāhula gave leadership in drafting and formulating historical political documents such as the *Vidyālaṅkāra Declaration of Bhikkhus and Politics,* and the *Kälaṇiya Declaration of Independence*—a manifesto demanding total independence from the British. Through the collective impact of these developments, by the middle of the 1940s, the Saṅgha had once again positioned themselves as the most important actors in the realpolitik of Lanka.

Saṅgha political mobilization had one primary goal: to reinstall the *Mahāvaṃsa* glory of Theravāda Buddhism and to restore the role of the Saṅgha as the politically dominant force. They sought to revert to the pre-colonial social order in an attempt to organize the social structure along the lines of the Theravādin cosmic order in which the Saṅgha occupied the epicenter. The removal of colonial rule was seen as a precondition for such a return. The Saṅgha who initiated and guided such mobilization now had the support of a growing class of élites who had once been "nobodies," but who after a century of commercial dealings with the colonialists and after benefitting from the open education system created by the missionaries, had become "somebodies" (Jayawardena 2002). By 1948, the ethnoreligious nationalism of the Sinhalas had become a socio-political force that extended beyond the walls of the Saṅgha temples. The new form of ethno-nationalism in Sinhala politics was prominently led by the lay élites. During this second period of resistance, the Saṅgha exchanged their avant-garde role for a secondary position as advisors to organized political parties and their leaders. This era witnessed serious splits based on caste and chapters in the already divided Saṅgha community. They tended to support either the growing leftist movement or one of the Sinhala majoritarian parties, largely depending on their regional or caste affiliations (Jayawardena 1972; Matthews 1989).

Defining the Sinhala Nation 1948–1983

1948: Ethnicizing the elections

After decades of repeated attempts at constitutional reforms, the Colombo élites accepted the Soulbury Commission report and its proposal as the constitution for an independent Ceylon (Edrisinha and Selvakumaran 2000). The Soulbury Commission was the third colonial commission to review the transfer of power in Ceylon and to recommend a mode of self-rule. For the British, the stable and smooth transfer of power must have been a comforting achievement in comparison with the turmoil they faced in India and Burma. The Colombo élites, while divided in their ethnic political ambitions and agendas, nevertheless managed to find unity in their support of the leadership of D. S. Senanayake (DSS). DSS, a key leader of the *Temperance Movement* and loyal supporter of the Buddhist cause, was an agricultural entrepreneur with deep nationalist and western values (T. Fernando 1973a, 1973b; Senanayake 1985). He was sympathetic to minority concerns and was able to provide strong leadership to the divided Sinhalas and managed to reach out to extremely determined individuals like nationalist SWRD of the *Sinhala Mahā Sabah,* and G.G. Ponnambalam of *Ceylon Tamil Congress.* DSS may have hoped that the élites would honor the constitutional guarantees and lead the island towards a working democracy.

The independent government formed on 4 February 1948 reflected the political demography and stood as a symbol of fragile hope. However, beneath the overt signs of unity, the political foundations had developed deep cracks along ethnic, linguistic, and religious lines. Ethnically motivated political activism such as SWRD's Sinhala Maha Sabah and the Tamil Congress slowly eroded the fragile unity, while the ever-influential radical section of the Saṅgha emerged with a new political agenda supported by theological justification. The first government of Ceylon, however, was unwilling to address these issues. It feared the growing popularity of the leftist parties among the urban working class and the immigrant Indian laborers in the plantations. The pro-western United National Party (UNP) led by DSS—a wealthy planter himself—eventually introduced the Citizenship Act in an attempt to both neutralize the leftist power among the economically crucial plantation section and consolidate the rural (largely Sinhala) conservative vote. The Citizenship Act disenfranchised nearly 600,000 Indian Tamil workers and their seven constituencies in the Assembly. Amitha Sashtri noted:

> Thus, Senanayake's partisan and shortsighted efforts to consolidate an advantageous coalition with Kandyan élite at the expense of the Estate Tamil immigrant workers had the long-term consequence of increasing the importance of and resort to racism in the political rhetoric and mobilization in the following period. (Shastri 1999, 84)

A section of the educated Saṅgha developed a keen interest in leftist movements and trade union politics. As shown by Jayawardena (1974, 1972), the leftist movement, trying to lead the national awakening onto a Leninist path, was still managed by nationalists who were thinking along ethnic lines as they were looking into the future. The Lanka Sama Samāja Party (LSSP) (the Equal Society Party) was an upper middle class socialist outfit. In 1935, sons of wealthy merchants had undertaken graduate studies at prominent universities in the UK. They embraced the changes in Europe and tried to replicate them in their native country. N. M. Perera, who did his PhD research on the German constitution and the possibility of a greater Europe, was an effective LSSP leader (Moor 2007; Woodword 1962). Later in 1948, a breakaway group formed the Communist Party (CP). These two pioneer groups, like their numerous factions in later years, romanticized the concept of an equal society, but their deeply rooted religious and ethnic background never permitted them to break away from their Sinhala nationalism. Thus Ceylon, during the early years of independence, was struggling with two types of nationalism: an ethnoreligious nationalism with a rural mass following driven by a nostalgic vision of a mythical past, and a socialist nationalism that was pursuing ideas of a revolutionary future. On both fronts, the Saṅgha made their powerful cultural contribution. H. L. Seneviratne summarizes the developments:

> A group of monks who followed Dharmapāla to Calcutta (India) and had been exposed to Indian nationalism there later made Vidyalaṅkara (the Saṅgha University) the center of their intellectual and political activities. These monks continued to talk about socialism, but this has to be distinguished from the international socialism of the Marxists. Theirs was rather a "Buddhist Socialism." Increasingly it became more "Buddhist" than socialist did, and by the mid-1950s, it turned into a hegemonic Sinhala Buddhist chauvinism. (Seneviratne 1999, 131)

It was during this transition and due to the deep factions amongst the Saṅgha that the Ven. Walpola Rāhula gained considerable influence on Saṅgha politics. In 1947, Rāhula authored and published *Bhikṣuvage Urumaya,* the text that cemented his status as a Buddhist leader. Rāhula inspired a large number of powerful Saṅgha including Yakkaduwē Pragngārāma, Kotahene Paññakitti, Kallallē Anandasāgara, and Nāttandiyē Pangngankara, who all became extreme ethno-nationalists.

In 1952, just four years into his rule, DSS, the first Prime Minister and the iconic rallying point of Sinhala politics, died in a horse-riding accident. His United National Party went into disarray as they searched for a new leader. After many internal struggles Dudley Senanayake, son of DSS, was asked to lead the party and the island. Dudley was a reluctant activist. His Buddhist beliefs and behavior were far more innocent than the politics of the time (Jennings 1954). The falling demand for tea and rubber, the island's key exports, and the food demands of a rapidly growing population were having an adverse impact on the rural areas. The rural masses were disappointed and angry that they had to suffer more hardship under self-rule than under colonial oppression. 1956, an election year, provided the ideal context for the masses to vent their social frustrations and the opportunist political parties were more than happy to harvest the results.

1956: Ethnoreligious nationalism institutionalized

SWRD Bandaranaike was the only son of Mahā Mudliyar (chief interpreter to the government) Sir Solomon Dias Bandaranaike, an Anglican by faith of the Horagolle estate in Aththagalla near Colombo. Young SWRD was educated in the Christian culture and faith at St Thomas' College, the pre-eminent missionary school. Later at Oxford, he studied local government and federalism and became the student union president. On his return Bandaranaike took to politics and became the minister for Local Government in the first Cabinet headed by DSS. Yet SWRD was, in the words of Manor:

> A utopian idealist and ardent opportunist, a progressive and parochialist, an egalitarian and an imperious snob. He was a rationalist with fascination for the paranormal, an occasionally radical free thinker who helped to conserve many central elements of the existing order. He was vain and often shameless in pursuit of power. (Manor 1989, 1)

In contrast with his earlier idealist suggestions that Ceylon should adopt a Swiss style federal model combined with a greater political and military affiliation with India, SWRD pursued an ethno-Sinhala vision of the future of Lanka. He could not wait for the normal process of party politics to endow him with the leadership he desired. In 1951, he broke ranks with DSS and formed his own Lanka Freedom Party (SLFP). For this he used the basic network of contacts that he had cultivated among the rural masses and the Saṅgha through his Sinhala Mahā Sabha

(The great assembly of the Sinhalas), a movement which he formed in the late 1930s arguing for the supremacy of the Sinhala ruling powers. Through the effective use of power politics, Bandaranaike introduced two key ideas into the public consciousness: the ethnic superiority of the Sinhalas and the privileged and blessed nature of Lanka as the place where Buddha once walked. SWRD was perhaps the third personification of the Sinhala Buddhist consciousness of modern Ceylon. The first was the Anagārika, who called for a spiritual recovery; Rāhula then provided the intellectual and theoretical context for the revival, and Bandaranaike capitalized on these contributions in order to mobilize political power and institutionalize it for the long term. At the 1952 election, his new party was able to secure nine out of ninety-five seats in the assembly and became a strong opponent to UNP rule.

The 1956 election could not have escaped these wider realities. It was the 2500th anniversary of Buddha's birth. Bandaranaike launched his election campaign calling on the Sinhalas to rediscover and return to their heritage. He urged the Saṅgha, native doctors, schoolteachers, farmers and laborers (සඟ වෙද ගුරු ගොවි කම්කරු) to form the new five forces (Pañcha Mahā Bala Vēga) to rebuild a nation based on Buddhist values. He gained leftist support by promising a new national economic and foreign policy. In rural Ceylon, he argued for the urgent need to re-establish the lost culture of the Sinhalas, led by their language and Theravāda Buddhism, and promised to restore, once in power, the *Mahāvaṃsa* prestige of the Saṅgha. As a result of these promises, in April 1956 SWRD won a landslide victory and became the country's Prime Minister. With a prime minister who stood for Sinhala Buddhist nationalism, the institutionalization of ethnoreligious nationalism in Lanka proceeded at great pace. The Saṅgha and their politics were to change their trajectories permanently after 1956.

The politics of Venerable Māpitigama Buddharakkhita (VMB)

VMB, the chief Saṅgha of the historic Kälaṇiya temple, played a role second to none in the personal and political life of SWRD. In the early part of 1956, using his extremely powerful position, VMB formed the *Eksath Bhikṣhu Peramuna* (the United Saṅgha Front), which campaigned for the official status of the Sinhala language, supporting SWRD's candidacy. He was also a key member of the commission formed to investigate the status of Buddhism in Ceylon at the time. In a strategic move prior to the elections, the commission released its report, *Betrayal of Buddhism*. It argued for the restoration of the Buddhaśāsana, which had been betrayed by the British and their colonial collaborators, and demanded a new Buddhist government.

Figure 2. Venerable Buddharakkhita handcuffed and led away from the courts.

VMB, using his cultural position and influence over the SLFP party and the newly formed government in 1956, became a kingmaker in every sense. He was as powerful as an unofficial cabinet minister of the SWRD government. He used his Saṅgha *Front* in order to mobilize rural monks for political rallies and agitations. His association with the temple of Kälaṇiya and its wealth allowed him to become an effective power broker, and he used his position to acquire considerable wealth for himself and others. It was predictable, therefore, that his support for SWRD would fade. Various events and developments turned VMB and SWRD into political rivals. VMB's repeated requests for business contracts on behalf of his powerful friends, SWRD's proposal for paddy land reform as a result of which the Kälaṇiya temple would lose a large amount of idle land (Manor 1989, 277–279), as well as VMBs alleged sexual relationship with Health Minister Mrs. Wimalā Wijewardene, a widow activist with extreme nationalist views, were just some of the events that triggered a deterioration in the relationship between VMB and SWRD. Eventually VMB moved to openly oppose his political leader and initiated country-wide riots on at least two occasions: first, in response to the Tamils' refusal to use the Sinhala "Sri" prefix and, second, in response to SWRD's proposal to share power with the Tamil political leader C. J. Chelvanayakam. These riots turned VMB into the leader of a movement that unleashed violence against Tamil civilians across the island, discrediting SWRD (Manor 1989, 302; Vittachi 1958; Wriggins 1960). It is suspected that VMB was also implicated in a failed coup to poison SWRD in early 1959 as well as in the latter's assassination by Venerable Talduwē Somarathana, one of VMB's Saṅgha affiliates, on September 25, 1959.

In Lanka, the radicalization of Theravāda Buddhism under the influence of political Saṅgha continued during almost every transition period as witnessed in 1956, 1965, 1971, 1977, 1988, 1994 and 2000 (DeVotta 2007). However, most of these involvements were indirect and conformist until the Saṅgha participated in the 1971 and 1988 revolts led by the *Janathā Vimukti Peramuna* (People's Liberation Front), the nationalist Maoist party of rural Sinhala youth. These events marked another key threshold in the unfolding of ethnoreligious nationalism.

1971: The Saṅgha and the armed rebellion

The first ten years of post-independence rule in Lanka were primarily driven by élites and failed to reflect the common aspirations of the people. The 1956 government came to power on an ethno-nationalist promise, but soon faced difficult global conditions for Lanka's export economy. These difficult conditions combined with a rapidly growing population, which put pressure on the country's welfare system, meant that by 1970 the Lankan government had to borrow money at commercial rates from the IMF just in order to keep its daily operations going.[2]

In May 1970, a new government headed by Sirimāvo Bandaranaike, the widow of SWRD, was elected for the second time on a socialist and nationalist platform. *Janathā Vimukti Peramuna* JVP (People's Liberation Front) was one of the several leftist groups within and outside the parliament that supported the new government. It was led by Rōhana Wijevēra, a medical faculty dropout from the University of Lumumba in Moscow. There is a large volume of literature on the socio-political conditions that paved the way for the birth and growth of the JVP as a radical political mobilization of youth leading to the insurgency of 1971 (Baharati 1976; Kearney 1978; Kearney and Jiggins 1975; Moore 1989; Obeyesekere 1974; Samaranayake 1999, 1997; Warnapala 1975).

On 5 April 1971, JVP led a coordinated attack on over 100 police stations and brought parts of the country under its control (Arasarathnam 1972; Kearney and Jiggins 1975). As a founding and indeed leading member of the Non-aligned Movement, Lanka appealed to a wide range of countries to provide help in what seemed a desperate situation. The US,

2. For a detailed account of the island's financial liabilities, see the Budget Speech [1970–1971] by the Hon. Dr. N. M. Perera, M.P. Minister of Finance, Colombo on October 25, 1970.

Britain, Russia, India and Pakistan responded to the government's plea and supplied weapons and material. The Sirimāvo government eventually crushed the revolt and arrested the JVP leaders. Up to that point, the JVP rebellion was the largest example of civic unrest in the modern history of Lanka. The rebellion is the subject of many studies (Moore 1989; Samaranayake 2008; Venugopal 2010). These studies offer a wide range of explanations for the revolt, with one of the more popular theories arguing that the revolt was driven by educated but unemployed rural youth led by leftist ideologies; another suggestion is that the revolt was part of a Cold War conspiracy against the Lankan government. However, it was later established that 94% of the insurgents were Sinhala Buddhists and another 4% were Sinhala Catholics. The majority of the groups sustaining the revolt came from the Goyigama and Karāve castes of the southern region, indicating that the revolt was also a revolutionary Sinhala-Buddhist movement.

In fact, one of the remarkable features of the 1971 revolt was the extent of direct Saṅgha participation in the rebellion, resulting in the largest number of Saṅgha to face violent death in modern Lanka until the second revolt of the JVP in 1989. Economic, caste and class aspects notwithstanding, the Saṅgha involvement suggests that the revolt intended to restore a more radical Sinhala-Buddhist social order and that indeed successive governments in Lanka had not been radical enough in working towards such an order. The influence of Sinhala Buddhist nationalism within the JVP clearly overshadowed its socialist ideologies, thus setting a pattern that would continue until the 1989 revolt and beyond as the JVP opposed any power-sharing with the Tamils.

Sinhala Saṅgha politics have often rallied around key written texts and manifestos. In the post-colonial context, two booklets especially ignited the ethnic imagination of the Saṅgha and informed their political involvement. The first is *Bhikṣuvage Urumaya* by Walpola Rāhula, published in 1947, and the second is *The Revolt in the Temple*, published in 1953 by Don Charles Wijewardene, a member of the powerful Wijewardene family of historic Kälaṇiya, to commemorate "2500 years of the land, the race and the faith." While the former provided justification for the political activism of the Saṅgha, the latter called for a rediscovery of Sinhala ethnic supremacy against the competing minorities, especially the Tamils. Jonathan Walter characterized the 700-page volume as follows: "It constitutes a blunt statement that the Tamils are a threat to that historic mission and lays out Wijewardene's blue-print for a post-independence Sinhala Buddhist state which has gradually become a reality" (Walter 1996, 82).

As Amunugama has shown (1991a, 1991b, 1985), the link between the Sinhala Saṅgha and their counterparts in Calcutta prior to independence created a socialist ethos. Politically active Saṅgha in fact were seen supporting the UNP, the SLFP as well as the socialist parties in the first decades of independence. Because of their disappointment with the mainstream UNP and SLFP parties, more rural and young Saṅgha were attracted to radical leftist politics by the end of the 1960s. The socialist/ Trotskyite parties in Ceylon denounced the parliamentary system and romanticized an armed revolution. It is in this context that the book *Revolt in the Temple* and the political thesis that it projected intensified ethno-nationalism among the Saṅgha. Difficult economic conditions contributed to the desire for a new government and in fact possibly for a new political system. This attitude was far more common amongst the educated youth. The national foreign debt, which was 200 million rupees in 1955, had rocketed to 1235 million rupees by 1970, and around 700,000 people were unemployed, i.e. nearly 25% of the workforce (Gordon and Rankaduwa 1992; Lim 1968).

The full extent of Saṅgha involvement in the revolt was revealed only after the revolt, when the victorious government arrested and interrogated many of the rebels. It appears that rural young monks, who were more educated in a secular sense than their seniors, willingly offered themselves for the armed cause. They borrowed the JVP line of argument that in order to be a true Buddhist (monk), one had to defend the Buddhist land of Lanka even at the risk of death. The emotionally appealing *Maubima Nätinam Maranaya* (Motherland or Death) doctrine assigned to the Saṅgha the responsibility to shape the politics of this world, so that the *dāyakas* may live in a better world, in which they could live in accordance with the principles published in the key works. Young monks used their temples as nodal points in a network of cell groups in order to plan and propagate the JVP ideology. Though no member of the Saṅgha was tried as a leader of the failed revolution, moderate estimates suggest that between 2000–3000 killed and another 3000[3] monks were either arrested during the period because of their direct involvement. The JVP revolt of 1971 showed how the yellow robes could be used for violent politicization, and it demonstrated the Saṅgha readiness to act in an organized manner and to take up arms if necessary to protect religion, race, and land. The year 1971 thus became a turning point in at least three senses: first, it made it obvious to everyone that the Saṅgha—who until then had mainly been members of a few loosely arranged "patriotic" organizations—were ready to become radical political activists. Second, it highlighted the state-Saṅgha relationship as a key problem for any present or future government; and finally, it permanently altered the relationship between the laity and the Saṅgha. From now on, the Theravāda Saṅgha

3. Such numbers are very difficult to be accurate. The records show that at least 4000 monks underwent state sponsored "rehabilitation."

could be both otherworldly guides to nirvāna and armed defenders of their land and ethnic group (Abeysekara 2001; Jeganathan 1997).

1983: The Saṅgha and the ethnic pogrom

Some commentators have called the 1983 ethnic pogrom against the Tamils in Lanka a "genocide." The event clearly marked another turning point in the country's fragile democracy. The 1977 general elections brought the UNP back to power with an absolute majority, winning 140 out of 168 seats.[4] J.R. Jayawardene (JRJ), a pre-independence Ceylon National Congress activist and the author of the 1944 proposal to adopt the Sinhala language, became Prime Minister. JRJ was known for his pro-Sinhala stance and extreme conservative and pro-western economic policies. With a clear majority, he was able to change the election system from a first-past-the-post to a preferential representation vote. He then proceeded to appoint himself as the first US-style president consolidating extreme power in the executive (K. M. De Silva 1979; Warnapala 1979). The Tamil United Liberation Front (TULF), which had campaigned on a nationalist platform, won 18 seats and became the official opposition. JRJ tried to gain the TULF's support for his pro-western economic policies but failed. His frustration grew when the northern Tamil political demands provoked sporadic outbreaks of violence. The TULF was highly critical of JRJ's UK/IMF-funded mega projects such as the Mahāväli River diversion because they resulted in the Sinhala colonization of traditional Tamil areas.

During the District Development Council elections in 1981, UNP-led security forces burnt the historic library in Jaffna, which was considered a home for ancient Tamil literature. In 1982, JRJ extended his government through a referendum, evading an election; he also intensified the militarization of the Tamil areas. In response, Tamil armed youth mounted several attacks on the state security forces. In July 1983, one such attack killed thirteen Sinhala soldiers. The news of the killings sparked an emotional and violent riot against the Tamils living in the south.

The riots consisted almost entirely of attacks on the Tamil minority by the majority Sinhalese. While the scale of the violence may not warrant the use of the term "genocide," the attacks almost certainly exceeded the 1958 and 1977 anti-Tamil riots. The destruction of Tamil property vastly exceeded anything seen before, with, for example, at least seventy factories in the Colombo area wrecked and 70 to 90 per cent of Tamil shops and homes looted and burned in many areas. At least 135,000 Tamils living in Sinhalese areas fled to refugee camps while tens of thousands more hid elsewhere. The government's figure of just under 400 deaths is a serious

4. See Election Dept. http://www.slelections.gov.lk/pdf/General%20Election%20 1977.PDF, Accessed on 30 March 2009.

underestimate.[5] This was only possible because far more of the violence was organized than on previous occasions. In qualitative terms, the summer's "violence represents one of the nine or ten worst spells of face-to-face viciousness (without technology to provide distance) to occur anywhere since the Second World War." Extreme acts of sadism and mutilation were far from un-common at the height of the troubles. (Manor 1983, 450)

At least three different factors are often considered as the reason for such unprecedented Sinhala violence. First, it is argued that the violence was a spontaneous over reaction by a section of the Sinhala population who were particularly affected by the Tamil attacks. Second, some commentators hold the view that the violence was an opportunist exploitation of the criminal elements in the south, providing an excuse for the pogrom. Finally, it has been suggested that the violence was a carefully organized and state sponsored anti-Tamil campaign in order to tame the nationalist Tamil polity. It seems obvious that the island-wide pogrom against the unarmed Tamils could not have happened without the encouragement of the state or sections of it. One key feature during the riots was the leadership given by the Saṅgha. Traditionally when Saṅgha lead a procession of whatever kind or purpose, no one—not even the security forces—tries to intervene. UNP leadership with the help of the Saṅgha cleverly diverted the initial anti-government anger so that it turned into hostility towards the Tamil civilians. While the direct involvement of the Saṅgha was not on the scale of the 1971 JVP revolt, the sizable Saṅgha group that was involved still managed to cause damage that the island had not witnessed before. While the direct participation may have been limited, the silent endorsement of the campaign by the greater portion of Saṅgha once again confirmed their sympathy for Sinhala hegemony; it also showed that they were willing to at least tolerate violence as a means by which such dominance could be achieved.

Following the experience of the 1971 revolt, the radicalized Saṅgha had found a new reason for joining the political forefront: to fight the Tamil separatists. By mid-1982, a large number of young Saṅgha had gathered under the JVP banner in order to safeguard the motherland. Venerable Palipanē Chandānanda—a well-known critic of the UNP and its policies headed the Asgiriya branch of *Siyam Nikāya*. Key individuals like Venerable Maduluwawē Sōbitha of the Kotte Temple and Muriththettuwe Ānandá occupied prominent roles. In mobilizing the Saṅgha these actors now had two targets rather than just one: the pro-western government and the armed Tamil separatists. The 1983 anti-Tamil riots showed the intensity of the Sinhala violence as it was led by both pro-UNP and anti-UNP Saṅgha. It was evident that the Sinhalas were willing to take part in actions that

5. While to-date there is no official investigation into these riots, it is estimated that 4000 Tamils were assassinated during the two weeks of violence.

directly contradicted their Buddhist doctrine in order to protect the Sinhala *ethnie* and Lanka. They preferred to be "Bhumi-Putra" instead of Buddha-Putra: sons of the soil, not sons of Buddha (Amunugama 1991b).

1988: Armed Saṅgha and the second JVP revolt

The ethnic riots of 1983 changed modern politics in Lanka permanently. From among the many militant groups operating in the country, the Liberation Tigers of Tamil Eelam (LTTE) emerged as the most violent and most committed to a separate Tamil state. With the support of the Tamil Nadu and Indian governments, the Tigers became equal to or more powerful than the Lankan forces in some areas of the country. By 1987, the Tigers managed to bring 90% of the North and East (roughly 1/3 of the island) under their military rule. Yet due to the influx of Tamil refugees to India, the pressure from the Tamil Nadu state government, the demands of the Lankan Tamil political élites and, finally yet importantly, India's own regional power interests, the Indian Prime Minister Rajiv Gandhi virtually forced Jayawardene to sign the Indo-Lanka peace accord on July 29, 1987. The "Accord" aimed to create nine provincial councils to devolve political and administrative power to the regions with a special focus on the Tamil area. The accord also included a process for disarming the Tigers, which they refused to sign. The main opposition including the JVP vehemently opposed the accord. A reluctant JRJ also let his cabinet members openly oppose the accord, some promoting street violence, which led to an attack on the visiting Gandhi by a naval guard. The Saṅgha once again marched on the streets advocating violence against the state, looting, and burning state properties. In the process, some Tamil/Indian properties and personas came under attack. The accord failed to achieve its aims except for the arrival of 80,000 Indian troops in the Tamil area to disarm the Tigers, leading to a bloody Indian-LTTE clash (Bullion 1994; Cooper and Berdal 1993; Dixit 1998; Rao 1988).

In December 1988, at the end of JRJ's term, the UNP candidate Ranasinghe Premadasa (1924–1993) won the presidency by a narrow margin. Premadasa, who was of humble beginnings with a lower caste background, pursued an ambiguous approach to the Tigers. A strong opponent of the accord, he tried to negotiate with the Tigers while their terror politics of suicide missions and city bombings continued. The dual failure of the government to win the war and to undermine the Indian sympathy for the Tamil demands, and finally the change of the "unitary" constitution paving the way for the introduction of Provincial Councils provided strong rallying points for a new JVP campaign. In late 1988 and early 1989, the JVP mounted its second revolt, one that was even more violent and bloodier than the 1971 revolt.

In 1988–1989, the violent involvement of the Saṅgha in the second JVP revolt went even further than in 1971 (Pfaffenberger 1988; Uyangoda 1989, 2000, 2010, 2011; Venugopal 2010). Long before the second armed struggle, in 1972, the more ethno-nationalist Saṅgha had forced the Sirimāvo government to declare Buddhism the state religion, to establish Sinhala as the supreme language, and to change the official name of the country from Ceylon to "Sri" Lanka. The 1972 republican constitution, introduced without a referendum or a debate, largely followed a Westminster model with an executive prime minister, but with the judiciary subordinated to the parliament. This provision would enable the Sinhala parties, who always had the majority, to overpower any minority opposition (C. R. De Silva 1979). It further removed articles 29 (1) and (2) of the Soulbury constitution which guaranteed minority rights (Edrisinha 1999; Edrisinha and Welika 2008). These developments were justified as a response to the mounting pressure from the Tamils, who were increasingly resorting to violence as a means of forcing political negotiations on the issue of shared rule.

In this shifting context—constitutional changes, and a hardening of the JVP stance against India, against any power-sharing with the Tamils, against the LTTE, and against the UNP government—the Saṅgha found a new space for political involvement and recognition as mainstream politics moved towards their brand of ethno-nationalism. More than any other party in the country, the JVP systematically exploited and fueled violent Saṅgha mobilization. The JVP had more members from the rural youth than any other similar organization and exerted great influence among university students. JVP is pro-Buddhist, pro-Sinhala, and pro-poor rhetoric attracted young Saṅgha, who in turn organized themselves in a cross-nikāya network in association with JVP branches outside of their temple orders. An important side effect of these activities was the revival of many old Saṅgha organizations and the creation of many new ones.[6] Among these organizations, the *Mawbima Surakeemy*

6. Examples include the All Ceylon Buddhist Congress *(Samasta Lanka Bauddha Maha Sammelanaya)*; the Buddhist Theosophical Society; the Young Monks' Patriotic Organization (*Deshapremi Tharuna Bhikhsu Peramuna)*; the Organization of Patriotic Sinhalese Youth (*Deshapremi Sinhala Tharuna Peramuna);* the Young People's Patriotic Project *(Deshapremi Tharuna Viyaparaya)*; the Students' Patriotic Organization (*Deshapremi Sishya Peramuna)*; the Sinhalese Buddhist Organization *(Sinhala Bauddha Sanvidhanaya)*; the Sinhalese People's Organization (Sinhala Janatha Peramuna); the Sinhalese Progress of Women Organization (*Sinhala Kanthabhivrudhi Sanvidhanaya*); the Monks' Organization for Humanity (*Manavahithavadi Bhikhsu Sanvidhanaya*); the New Buddhist Revolutionary Group (*Nutana Viplawakari Bauddha Kandayama*); the People's Organization to Fight (*Janatha Satan Peramuna*); the Up-country Monks' Three Nikāya Organization (*Kandurata Trinikayika Bhikhsu Sangamaya*); the Monk's Three Nikāya Group (*Trinikāya Bhikhsu Balamandalaya*); the People's United Lanka Front (*Eksath Lanka Mahajana*

Viyapara (MSV) and *Deshapremi Janathā Vyaparaya* (DJV), which were largely led by young Saṅgha, became the most violent agents of terror. Young Saṅgha in these movements opposed their senior monks and accused them of betrayal if they failed to support the mobilization of the people against the security forces and the government. Many records published later revealed that young monks became informants and indeed even collaborators in the assassination of their senior monks by DJV members (Gunasekara 1999; Manoharan 2006; Tambiah 1992).

It is correct, of course, that the Saṅgha had rebelled before. However, the 1988/89 revolt was a novelty in the recent history of Lanka because of the level of destruction and violence committed. While there are no official figures available, it is estimated that some 5000 Saṅgha were killed during the revolt. Saṅgha who had previously taken vows of non-violence and renunciation took up guns and murdered even their own peers. The same jungle that was once their meditational abode had turned into a violent training camp. The Saṅgha, who are to lead their laity towards nirvāna, had become an anti-state army. While JVP may have provided the platform for such a drastic transformation, the 1988/89 revolt and the Saṅgha involvement show the Saṅgha as an active political force engaged in another historical wave of resistance against what they perceive as dangerous threats to their *ethnie* and island.

Conclusion

From this cursory survey of key moments in Saṅgha mobilization, we can observe that in each wave of resistance, the Saṅgha were able to claim societal, cultural and political space to promote their agenda, and this agenda acquired sharper contours as their ethnoreligious nationalist project took shape.

It is intriguing that until the mid-1900s—in spite of the *Mahāvaṃsa* account of the Tamil-Sinhala relationship—ethnicity was not the key issue underlying Saṅgha resistance. In fact, in the early nineteenth century during the Vellassa Rebellion, leaders such as Venerable Wilbāwe aimed to mobilize both Sinhalas and Tamils against the colonial rule. Furthermore, the Mātalē Rebellion was led by two Catholics from coastal regions. It could be argued that modern power relations took an ethnic turn at some point between the administrative reforms following the Colebrooke Cameron and Donoughmore Commissions. The McCallum (Jayawardena 1970; A. J. Wilson 1988) and Manning (Rajasingham-Senanayake 2001) reports introduced ethnicity as a fundamental principle of political representation, thus linking ethnic identity and political power.

Sabha); the Sri Lanka Buddhist Greater Congress (*Sri Lanka Bauddha Mahasammelanaya*); the Sri Lanka Sinhalese Buddhist Congress (*Sri Lanka Sinhala Bauddha Sammelanaya*); the Movement for the Defence of the Motherland (*Mawbima Surekeemy Viyapara*).

Internal Factor	Era	Nature	External Factor
Theravāda Hegemony	Before 1505	Protectionist Buddhism	Vādas/ Hinduism
Loss of Political power	1506–1832	Patriotic Buddhism	Catholicism/ Calvinism
Theosophical / Olcott	1832–1948	Protestant Buddhism	Christian Missionaries
Minority Demands	1948–1995	Predominant Buddhism	Power-sharing ideas
Political Humiliation	1995–2009	Pugnacious Buddhism	LTTE terror

The Saṅgha, as non-state actors, have used resistance politics throughout the recorded history of the island. The history of this resistance has been analyzed from a variety of perspectives. The approaches from the classical sociology of religion, inspired by thinkers such as Weber and Durkheim, have generated a considerable volume of literature (Malalgoda 1976; Orryu and Wang 1992; B. L. Smith, ed. 1978). However, many of these studies struggle to free themselves from the colonial heritage. Oriental anthropology for some time found itself to be a key interpreter of the Saṅgha-society dialectic. Yet most of these "outsider" observations seem to fail to appreciate the political dimension of Saṅgha activities (Ortner 1995). Critical post-colonial analyses have also tried to decode the resistance of the Saṅgha, yet they struggle to understand the continuity underlying the recurrent waves of resistance. Moreover, how and why do these waves energize a primordial ideology within a modernist context?

The political resistance of the Sinhala Saṅgha also shows facets of indigenous protest by a regional minority against the decomposing effects of a cultural globalization in which they seem to lose their traditional power bases and cultural hegemony. Still, the empirical evidence shows that the resistance itself makes use of the modern democratic social space. Furthermore, the rapid adaptation of, and preference for, a modern lifestyle with its new forms of technological and social forms of knowledge and power among the political Saṅgha to some extent embraces global trends. This ambiguous complexity is also reflected in the fact that Sinhala Saṅgha resistance does not seem to fit into Appleby's typology of traditional or national religious resistance (Appleby 2000).

I suggest that it is beneficial to look at the social psychology of Saṅgha resistance from a political science perspective (Wald, Silverman and Fridy 2005). Saṅgha resistance unfolded within the context of an exclusive claim to power by the Sinhalas against the democratic demands of power-sharing by a minority (Berkwitz 2003; E. J. Harris 2001; Sivasundaram 2010). The mytho-history accepted by the majority of Buddhists legitimates the violent Sinhalization of the land. It further justifies the Buddhicization of the island, even by violent means. These key paradigms of Sinhala Buddhist ideology are about power politics and concomitant claims to "ownership" of the island even though during the period under consideration the issue at stake was the governance of a multicultural if not multinational island involving a process of democratization and its failure. However, even with the tools of political science, it remains impossible to find a singular all-encompassing framework for the analysis of Saṅgha resistance because, as discussed, key behavioral determinants are extraneous to the political system.

Decoding Saṅgha resistance is difficult also because it operates on at least two different levels within the dominant politics. First, at the conceptual level, the Pāli canon of Sinhala Buddhism intellectualizes their cause. Secondly, at a societal level, the resistance is articulated in collective protests, often involving violence. At a conceptual level, the Pāli literature of Sinhala Theravādin Buddhism supports both a total pacifism—as embedded in the notion of—as well as a limited "just war thesis" leaving room for the militarization of the Saṅgha as for example during the time of King Gamini and in modern Thailand (Bartholomeusz 2002; Jerryson 2009; Mhv. XXII: 13–30). The canons also support the co-existence of other religious traditions as equals. However, as we have argued previously, the influential moral rationale for Saṅgha resistance in Lanka is drawn from the Vaṃsa literature. The *Mahāvaṃsa* and its colonial translations represent the crucial Vaṃsa text. As we noted, the *Mahāvaṃsa* both in its structure and as a narrative, justifies Sinhala Buddhist supremacy and presents Lanka as a land owned by (or at least bestowed to) the Buddhists (Mhv. XXI; Rambukkwella 2008; Scheible 2006; Sirimalwatte 2007). The political engagement of the Saṅgha in Lanka is implied and encouraged by the texts of the *Mahāvaṃsa* as the key instrument for the creation of a collective bond of a "chosen people" (Crosby 1999).

The complexity underlying waves of Saṅgha resistance refers to various dimensions of social and political struggle and is historically conditioned. Saṅgha-state relations can switch quickly from interdependency to mutual exploitation depending on the various interests at stake. Saṅgha resistance also refers to a struggle for leadership between the South and Kandy and entails a dimension of caste struggle. There is an economic aspect, especially for the laity who supports these Saṅgha. Resistance has often come from a semi-urbanite, lower middle-class Saṅgha section from *Siyam Nikāya* (of the south) and Amarapura, populated by the Durāve and Karāve caste. These dimensions are part of the socio-anthropological background of the political problems we are investigating.

The Theravāda school of Buddhism claims to hold the salvific *abhidharma* for the nirvāna of the individual. It differs from the other branches of Mahāyāna and Vajrayāna philosophies of Buddhism (Gombrich 1995, 1998; Trainor 1997) and is considered the earliest and most conservative school. The *Mahāvaṃsa* narrative, framing the identity and social space of the Sinhalas, stresses this exclusive soteriological position. Throughout their history, the Sinhala Saṅgha have positioned themselves as the protectors of the "chosen people," their faith, and their "promised land" ideology. Whenever the chosen people and their claims are challenged, the Saṅgha offered resistance. In the earliest times, they resisted different interpretations of the texts within their own school (Bechert 1970), later they resisted the teachings of different schools (Chandawimala 2007). *Mahāvaṃsa* is the record of kings who were either supported or opposed by the Saṅgha. The Saṅgha resisted the invading Hindu kings of India; they resisted the Sinhala kings who failed to maintain the close association of state and temples. Then the Saṅgha resisted the colonial invasions and occupations.

In the post-colonial period, Saṅgha resisted Western values as well as the life-style of their indigenous rulers. From 1956 onwards, they resisted attempts to undermine the supremacy of the Sinhala language and culture. During the 1960s, their resistance targeted attempts to design and implement mechanisms of power-sharing with the country's minorities. In 1971, the Saṅgha took up arms against a state perceived to be betraying the "Sinhalaness" of the land. In the 1980s, their violent acts of resistance were justified against the background of the separatist terror politics of the LTTE. In the 2000s, they resisted the efforts of the international community to broker a liberal peace agenda. In the first decade of this century, their resistance manifested itself in the support they gave to the "military solution" to defeat the LTTE, which was comprehensively achieved by mid-2009. The eschatological nature of the Saṅgha resistance did not stop with victory. In the post-LTTE era from 2010 onwards, the Saṅgha have mounted their resistance against the UN, INGOs and their local partners who have demanded an investigation of alleged war crimes.

In recent years, Lanka has witnessed the continuing political mobilization of the Saṅgha, who were pursuing two objectives: first, they mobilized society in order to support the military effort against the separatist rebels and their political demands and, second, they were looking for new and more effective ways of institutionalizing their ethnoreligious nationalism. By mid-2010, the fraternity of the Sinhala Saṅgha seems to have successfully achieved these ends. In May 2009, the Lankan army pulverized the entire leadership of the Tamil Tigers, using methods that international observers have described as "war crimes." Notwithstanding such accusations, the Sinhala Saṅgha have given their unconditional support to the war effort and its post-LTTE triumphalism. While to the wider non-Buddhist observing world this may appear as a contradiction, those familiar with the Saṅgha outlook understand that for the Saṅgha, their commitment to their *ethnie*, its royalty, and the land will always supersede in importance the commitment to the canonical Pāli texts.

Nationalism and its ethnoreligious interpretation is not an "imagined" phenomenon in the Saṅgha-led society of Lanka. Instead, it is a historical, institutional, and operational dynamic interwoven with the structures as well as the agencies of the wider society. Ethnoreligious nationalism has historically rejected not only the Western model of civic nationalism, but also the centuries old plurinational nature of the island. History in Lanka is seen only from an ethnoreligious nationalistic perspective. There is no other history than the one offered (and accepted) by the texts of the *Mahāvaṃsa.* It is a history written by the Sinhala Saṅgha for Sinhala Buddhists, justifying Saṅgha politics even if they demand violence. In this construction, the past was glorious, prosperous, and righteous because it was essentially Sinhala and Buddhist. The present is evil because its identity is impure, contaminated by non-Sinhala, non-Buddhist elements. Therefore, effort is needed to revert the present to the past, a specific version of the past in which Sinhala Buddhism was the unquestionable and exclusive source of meaning. The Saṅgha have given practical and ideological leadership to this quest for a "return" to the purity of the past. The fact that this quest has provoked a violent response—from the non-Buddhist "others" has not in any way shaken Saṅgha determination. On the contrary, the resistance provoked by the Saṅgha only confirmed the seriousness and righteousness of the Saṅgha cause, which in turn led to an intensification of the conflict.

The texts of the *Mahāvaṃsa* are very clear on this point. According to the *Mahāvaṃsa*, the conqueror King Duṭṭhagāmiṇi considered the "ගොළු මුහුද" (dumb Indian Ocean) and "හැඩි දෙමළා" (Gruesome Tamils) an ever present threat to his land, race and faith (Mhv. XXII: 80–90). Duṭṭhagāmiṇi's lamentation is not so much an attempt to acquire land or space; in other words, the problem is not just one of defending a country in the world of concrete political and military action. Rather, the historic "*Dhammadīpa*" refers to the rightful home of the Buddhist faith and the Sinhala race—the principles evoked refer to eternity rather than the next battle. The vision is one of cosmic proportions rather than political practicality. Similarly, King Duṭṭhagāmiṇi justified the war against the Tamil king Elāra, who was a just ruler, not just as a conquest within the realm of power politics but as an attempt to reclaim the land that was once Buddhist (Mhv. XXI: 10–38). This was the land where Buddha walked. This is the only *Dhammadīpa* of the Sinhalas and sharing this eternal "breathing space" was simply not negotiable.

By mid-2010, after the military victory, this framework has become part of the state agenda, directly dismissing the many nuances of liberal democratic rule. Sinhala Saṅgha politics in this form has challenged many of the predominantly Western assumptions that modernity would put an end to ethnoreligious nationalism. While recently Western scholars have come to appreciate the reality of religion in politics, Saṅgha ideology itself has remained a historical constant. The cosmic vision of the *Mahāvaṃsa* remains the key foundation of Saṅgha politics. The challenges faced by the Saṅgha—in the form of external conquest, internal plurality, relativizing democracy, and diffusing globalization—have not led them to depart from their way of perceiving history and the world; on the contrary, the Saṅgha outlook operates in such a manner that it expects to be challenged.

The fact that it finds itself "under siege," attacked from a range of forces—some concrete, some abstract—only confirms the necessity of the struggle. If we fail to understand the peculiar logic of this dynamics, we also fail to understand that commonsense power-sharing proposals—federalism—will be perceived as a threat and provoke Saṅgha resistance regardless of how well meaning these proposals are. The proposal of peace itself may intensify the conflict. As a "global minority," the Sinhalas—with a language that is not used anywhere else, and with a 70 million strong Tamil/Hindu population just 24 kilometers across the sea who traditionally have sympathies for Lanka Tamils—have developed a "triple minority mindset," clinging on to faith, race and land. Even after the ruthless victory over the equally ruthless—and once thought to be invincible—forces of the LTTE, the Saṅgha refuse to "rest." The military victory is just one moment in the ongoing and continuing cosmic struggle. They continue to try to influence and shape Lanka's polity in accordance with their vision, and for that, they are ready to face the next challenge.

— 4 —

Three Saṅgha Activists and Their Politics

Introduction

The possibility that a system of faith and its agents could influence intra- and inter-state relations is alien within the realist framework in political science, which privileges a narrow definition of power. However, the potential influences of "theopolitics" (Hoffman 1994) should urge us to rearrange our focus. A reconsideration of the role of faith within political systems is an important and urgent task.

For the Lankan context, much of the literature on Buddhism and its relation to the ethnic conflict may be classified as either theological essentialism or ethnic reductionism, both of which have serious limitations. Theological essentialism takes religious doctrine as its point of departure, whereas ethnic reductionism sees religion as a static aspect of ethnic identity (Brekke 2009). The previous chapter explored how the Saṅgha have enjoyed the hegemony of interpreting the past and shaping the present through their political activism. Yet the contemporary Saṅgha community and its influence on the politics of Lanka have not received the attention they deserve from a political science perspective. Traditionally most research done on the Sinhala Saṅgha falls into two key categories: first, there are a number of ethnographical studies of single village laity-Saṅgha and their monasteries (Bunnag 1973; Evers 1967; Swearer 1976, 1970). The second category of works analyses the Saṅgha in terms of their relation to society and the state (Bond 1992; Gombrich and Obeyesekere 1988; Mendelson 1975; Malalgoda 1976; Schober 1995; Seneviratne 1999; Tambiah 1976). Only a few studies on the Sinhala Saṅgha and their political role are available (Abeysekara 2008, 2006; 2004; Bechert 1970, 1973; Carringer 1979; Deegalle 2004; Frydenlund 2005). Even here, the theoretical templates used are not able to explain the phomenominological process of Lanka.

In order to understand Lankan political dynamics it is essential to study the way in which the Saṅgha provide the social, political, and cultural memories and interpretations and, in return, how the masses make the Saṅgha a symbol of political authenticity, stability and continuity. The aim of this chapter is to trace the cross-fertilizing dynamics between Sinhala Buddhist ethnoreligious nationalism and the worldview of three selected Saṅgha activists as they affected the local politics between 1990 and 2010. The chapter will reconstruct their worldview and perception towards the minority political demands in Lanka and the "unitary" ideology they advanced.

Sinhala Saṅgha Activists

Returning to the canons to re-purify religious practice is a Theravādin tradition. However, returning to the *Mahāvaṃsa* (and other Vaṃsa literature) text to re-energize their ethnoreligious polity is a specifically Sinhala Saṅgha tradition (Bond 1992; Tambiah 1989). The Sinhala Saṅgha have constructed and textualized an ethnoreligious nationalist politics, which, as presented in the pages of the *Mahāvaṃsa*, gravitates around three key dynamics: Sinhala Buddhism, Sinhala *ethnie*, and the unitary status of the island.

The exact number of total Saṅgha and *sāmaṇera*[1] presently living in Lanka is unknown.[2] The island does not have systematic data on such matters as robing or disrobing ordination is a private and spiritual affair of each temple and nikāya, but estimates put the number between sixty and seventy thousand.[3] The majority of Saṅgha do not engage in secular politics and are for the most part indifferent to, or silent on, the role of the political Saṅgha. As we will see later, a section of the largely urbanite southern Saṅgha dominate the political mobilization of the monks. Most of these southern Saṅgha, unlike their Kandyan counterparts, are deeply dependent on their lay supporters, who in return patronize the Saṅgha for their caste affiliation and political motives. The Saṅgha society at present is structured as follows:[4]

Chapter/Region	**Siyam/Kandy**	**Amarapura/South**	**Rāmañña/South**
Main Caste	Goyigama Malvatu Branch Asgiriya Branch	Karāve and Durāve	mixed region/ mixed but mainly Salāgama caste
Strength	35,000 Saṅgha 5,000 temples (M) 700 temples (A)	18,000 Saṅgha 2,000 temples	7,000 Saṅgha 1,000 temples

1. *Śrāmanera* is a novice monk who has not been fully ordained through the Upasampada ceremony.
2. Author's interview with the Ministry of Buddhaśāsana.
3. Interview with Ministry of Buddhaśāsana, 10 June 2011. Numbers are only approximate.
4. Interview with a number of Saṅgha in Colombo, Kandy, and Mātara.

Splits among the Saṅgha—based on caste and sub-caste affiliations continues (Kemper 1980). Today there are approximately fifty different sub-chapters, with most of them appointing their own chief Saṅgha (Hemasiri 1990).[5] Tambiah (1992) and Obeysekere (1974) Kearney and Jiggins (1975) argued that caste, in addition to nationalist ideology, was an important factor in the Saṅgha participation in the 1971 and 1988 armed rebellions. Jeffrey Samuels, after extensive field research conducted as recently as 2007, shows that caste is a key factor through which the Sinhala Buddhists experience their religiosity (2007).[6] A noble birth—to a mother who is a paragon of virtue, into a high caste, in a blessed place—is an integral part of Theravādin teaching on personal worth, as based on conditions extracted from Buddha's life and teachings.[7]

It is noticeable that the Saṅgha of *Siyam* and *Amarapura Nikāya* have taken a more proactive role in politics in comparison to the Rāmañña. Age, seniority, caste, wealth, family background, political connections, and the ability to mobilize wealthy members of the lay population are key factors within the śāsana structure. Only very rarely, will a Saṅgha break all these barriers and become influential purely based on his spiritual abilities. For example, the revivalist Gaṅgoḍawila Sōma was of the Durāve caste and his popularity remained restricted to the southern region. Saṅgha Pānadure Ariyadhamma of the 1980s was considered the last monk who was accepted across the divide. He too was a *goyigama* and was from the *Siyam Nikāya.*

Within this complex system, in order to be influential and able to mobilize opinion (whether spiritual or socio-political), one had to be strategic in appealing to the wider community. The majority of lay Sinhala Buddhists agree that the primary role of a Saṅgha is a spiritual one. Nevertheless, they appreciate and follow those Saṅgha who advance political ideologies to protect their *Rata* (country), *Jāthiya* (*ethnie*) *and Āgama* (religion). This is the basic nature of Sinhala Buddhist practice: to put country and ethnicity before religious ethics. It is historically embedded in the Sinhala socio-political psyche that the island belongs to Buddha and thus only to Buddhists. *Pūjāvaliya*, a thirteenth century Sinhala classic by Saṅgha Mayurapāda, states "මගේ ලංකාද්වීපය බුදුන්ගේ මහා තුනුරුවන් භාණ්ඩාගාරයක් වැන්න" (This Lanka is like the treasure

5. Also see ලංකාවේ නිකායන් පිළිබඳ තොරතුරු, (Details of Nikāya in Lanka), Department of Buddhist Affairs, Colombo, 1984.

6. For further discussion on the impact of caste amongst the Sinhala Saṅgha see Malalgoda 1976, 106–161; Roberts 1982; Dissanayake and McConatha 2011; Rogers 2004, 52–77.

7. The Nidāna-kathā is the lengthy introduction to the Jātaka book that narrates 550 previous births of Buddha. See Jātaka vol.1 p.48 (http://www.sacred-texts.com/bud/j1/index.htm), Accessed on March 10 2010.

house of Buddha's triple gem) and again "බුදුන් සතු ලක් දිවයින" (from Lanka owned by Buddha) (Thera 2000). Furthermore, the legitimacy of rulers is closely linked to the ruler's Buddhist identity. Bhikkhu Mahinda Deegalle, citing Don Martino de Zilva Wickremasinghe says: "Before the Pūjāvaliya, the tenth century Jetavanarama slab-inscription (No. 2) of [King] Mahinda IV (956–972 C.E.) vividly expressed this idea that 'none but the Bodhisattvas would become kings of prosperous Lanka'" (1999, 344).

This chapter will focus on three Saṅgha who continued the tradition of these interpretations in that they opposed power-sharing, advocated military victory and fundamentally redirected the politics of Lanka during the period of our study. This is not to argue that there were no Saṅgha activists who worked for political peace and social justice.[8] However, those who argued in favour of peace and justice often lacked the essential connection to the rural masses for two reasons. First, their appeal to follow the principles of Buddhist ethics was dismissed on the basis of the raging emotional and nationalist temper and, second, many Saṅgha who argued for such a position were urbanite liberals, often educated outside the island, and could not marshal a temple/caste/nikāya network. These Saṅgha lacked emotional and traditional militancy and thus their impact remained negligible.

Within the scope of political science, understanding the processes of accessing and using power, individually or collectively, requires us to study those who aspire to alter the course of their society and thus create and use these processes. The social dynamics activated and sustained in modern Lanka by the politically active Saṅgha activists cannot be analyzed without learning about their lives and the primary motivations underlying their political engagement. How did these politically active Saṅgha square the circle and advocate violence on the basis of Buddha's teachings? In order to be able to trace the self-understanding of the Saṅgha, this chapter will provide detailed studies of the lives of three key Saṅgha who were in many ways responsible for changing the broader political paradigms and the outcome of the war/peace process during the period from 1995 to 2010.

As the forces of globalization shook the foundations of traditional social securities of societies like Lanka, these Saṅgha, following their heritage, found a new and more energized moral authority to venture

8. In recent times Venerable Baddegama Samitha, who took a liberal view of the peace process, was the first Saṅgha to be elected to the parliament on a People's Alliance ticket in 2001, though as an individual candidate. The Venerable Mādampāgama Assaji of the Inter-Religious Peace Foundation (IRPF) and Scholar monk Mahinda Deegalle of Bath Spa University, UK are two other Saṅgha who argued for the ethics of positive peace in Lanka.

beyond the sacred and intervened in the secular. Within this context, the political order was failing, largely due to the protracted ethnic war. While the greater portion of the Saṅgha community watched the development with passivity or did nothing beyond wishing for an immediate dramatic change, a section of Saṅgha choose the route of direct political intervention. This mobilization produced a few key actors who emerged as "*yugapurusha*"—individuals who could symbolize a particular moment in time and synthesize the forces that were struggling for articulation. As the separatist war continued to dominate the affairs of the country, and as the political authority failed to find a new direction, these Saṅgha became the natural focal points for public life.

The three Saṅgha to be considered in this chapter and their periods of influence are as follows:

Venerable Walpola Rāhula	1995–1997
Venerable Gaṅgoḍawila Sōma	2000–2003
Venerable Athuraliyē Rathana	2004–2010

These three Saṅgha were selected for a number of reasons, which we will explain as we introduce them on the following pages. The analysis of their self-understanding in our selective biographies will help us understand why federalism, instead of providing a solution, fuelled Saṅgha hostility and agitation.

Venerable Walpola Rāhula (1907–1997)

Throughout the 2300 years of their history, the Sinhala Saṅgha performed two fundamental functions: protecting and promoting Sinhala Buddhism and fighting those who were a threat to their faith/practice. During the period from 1995 to 2010, as in earlier periods of history, many members of the Saṅgha came forward to interpret, influence, and redirect the politics and ultimately the state of Lanka.

For a number of reasons, I have selected the work of Venerable Walpola Rāhula to explain this political phenomenon. He deeply influenced the politics of Saṅgha society prior to the period under study, de-contextualized the *Mahāvaṃsa* ideology and managed to use its interpretation for political agitation and mobilization. He also gave leadership to oppose the peace process. My aim is to uncover the key motives of this learned Saṅgha who had renounced this world and yet returned not just to the world but also more specifically to the world of politics, thus preparing the contemporary path for the political engagement of the Saṅgha.

Rāhula was always referred to as a monk, and we follow this tradition, but it is interesting to note that he was a very unusual monk. He did not take the *Upasampadā* until very late in his life. He spent almost all

Figure 3. Venerable Walpola Rāhula.

his life as an *sāmaṇera*, with only the lower ordination. Living as a novice granted him more freedom, allowing him to move around and live where he pleased. An sāmaṇera receives the lower ordination—*pabbajjā*—so it is not wrong to say that he was ordained (Bowden 1893).

Rāhula's society

In many states, the last few decades of the twentieth century saw the beginning of a rapid but systematic de-secularization of the public space. The process could be violent—with 9/11 as an extreme manifestation—but the phenomenon had deeper transformative effects within as well as between states. Some have labelled this a "new cold war" (Juegensmeyer 1994) or an apolitical "de-secularization" (Beyer 1999) generated within a particular religious discourse (Haynes 2001). However, on closer inspection, dialectical negotiation between sovereign state power on the one hand and non-state spiritual power centres on the other is neither new nor restricted to a particular faith or state. Almost all major religions, whether western or eastern, renouncer or redeemer, monotheist or polytheist, have sought sovereignty, even before the idea of a state came into existence. The church/king association as well as the idea *of ummah* or *dharmaraj* are well documented in the annals of political history. Yet, while the politics of religion has received the attention of a growing number of comparative political scientists, the great majority have focused on global or regional trends (such as globalization, transnational diasporas, international religious terrorism, etc.), at the cost of ignoring the micro-dynamics of this process of de-secularization. The power of religious individuals to shape and direct the mind-set of a society is largely ignored, or at best marginalized.

By the middle of the 1940s the British Raj, whose contribution to the Allied cause in Europe had come at a high cost, was forced to rethink its colonial politics. This was especially the case in Asia, where Russia and China had emerged as new and permanent power blocks (Duara 2004; Elbaum and Lazonick 1984). Holding on to nineteenth century colonial politics was bound to bring more harm than benefit. This realization prompted a change in post-war foreign policy, compelling the British Government to draw up plans to withdraw from India and Ceylon almost simultaneously. By this time, Mohandas Karamji Gandhi's tactics had ignited the struggle for freedom in India, and the confluence of many factors with Gandhi's new non-violent political agitation made India's political independence inevitable by the late 1940s.

Lanka stood to benefit from this major regional realignment, even in the absence of any similar charismatic leadership or mass agitation for independence among the Lankan political élites (Manor 1989; Manor and Segal 1998, 1985, 1979). Instead, the political class, which had largely benefited from the trade and plantation sector of the British administration, sought only a comfortable compromise with the colonists. The exclusive and inter-related families at the top of the power structure in Lanka preferred to continue most, if not all, forms of colonial ties, which conferred immediate benefits on them as a ruling class (Jayawardena 2002; Moore 1989). At the same time, as has often happened in the country's history, the politically motivated, often urbanized, middle-class sections of the Saṅgha saw an opportunity to become involved and to regain their historic influence. However, Lanka's politics was never determined by laymen alone. It was the Saṅgha who first embraced the radical spirit of the Indian freedom movement. Two Saṅgha academic centres in the island by then had produced many influential monks who were positioning themselves as key social authorities. Anthropologist H. L. Seneviratne (1999) has vividly documented the social transformation of these monks, as they exchanged their *lokuttara* (supramundane) spiritual responsibilities for *laukika* (worldly) secular power politics. Anne Blackburn (1999) traced the influence of individual Saṅgha such as Hikkaḍuvē Sri Sumaṅgala in this transition. They moved from guiding society spiritually to political agitation for a specific world order. This was a natural extension of the pioneering work of the lay Buddhist revivalists Anagārika Dharmapāla and Henry Olcott. The Dharmapalites who travelled to India for Buddhist missionary work had witnessed the radical political transformation sweeping that land. They had also experienced the transforming role of the religious authorities in shaping the politics of the country towards becoming an independent state. These mobilized Sinhala Saṅgha were keen to generate a similar level of social activism and impact in Lanka. The faculty of Vidyālaṅkāra[9] was arguing for the formation of a more radical opposition, aiming to transform the immediate political future of the island. Among them, Walpola Rāhula was a powerful orator and writer.

Life and early work

The work of the Venerable Walpola Rāhula aligns with the process of Saṅgha politicization outlined in Chapter 2. The deep influence he exerted prior to the period under examination on the politics of Sinhala society as well as on the Saṅgha community was due in part to the manner in which he used the *Mahāvaṃsa* as a sacred history, giving rise to an activist ideology, which inspired him, and, through him, his fellow Saṅgha fraternity.

Rāhula was born in the Walpola area of the Mātara district, in the deep south of Lanka, on 9 May 1907. For many historical reasons, southern Lankan Buddhism had always been the radical stronghold of an agitating Protestant Buddhism (Kemper 1980; Malalgoda 1976; Rāghavan 2011).[10] Rāhula's social background reflected this, as it was steeped in the long and proud history of radical reformist Buddhist political engagement. Rāhula entered a temple school as a boy and was ordained as a novice by the age of fifteen. A promising student, he continued with Buddhist studies alongside his secular curriculum, including mathematics and English literature. The fact that Rāhula entered a secular university—what was then Ceylon University—may have caused suspicion among his contemporaries. The opportunity to read and study secular literature caused Rāhula to challenge some of the basic popular notions and practices of the Saṅgha of his time, and the young monk soon became popular for his critical engagement with the traditional establishment of the temple and it's social (in)activity. Rāhula took to reformist preaching—calling on the institutionalized Saṅgha to rediscover their lost heritage.

9. Vidyālaṅkāra (in Peliyagoda, north of Colombo) is a key Pirivena-Saṅgha training-center started by Venerable Ratmalānē Dhammāloka in 1875. The other Bhikhu pirivena is Vidyodaya, started by Venerable Hikkaḍuvē Śrī Sumaṅgala in 1873. These pirivenas were the centers of Saṅgha reform during the twentieth century revival.

10. Anagārika Dharmapāla, Hikkaḍuvē Śrī Suṃangala and Mohoṭṭivattē Guṇānanda are three examples of southern Buddhist reformists who advocated radical political changes in modern Sinhala Buddhism.

Rāhula disseminated his calls for reform through a series of pamphlets published in 1933–1934 under the title සත්‍යෝදය පත්‍රිකා *Satyodaya Patrikā* (Truth-revealing papers). Learning from the success of Christian missionaries, who used printed material to support their evangelical efforts, Rāhula found the free distribution of his printed views on Buddhism, Saṅgha, and Sinhala society to be a far more effective method of social engagement than the limited alternative of preaching at temples to those who were willing to gather there. In hindsight, Rāhula was keen to use whatever medium available to advance his argument in favour of redefining the role of the Saṅgha in society towards a more active political involvement.

In the early 1940s, Rāhula became an active participant in protests fighting for fair wages and improved working conditions organized by workers from major plantations and trading companies—whose owners were often British investors. As a young, articulate monk, he was a natural leader in protest activities. Rāhula's radicalism and his support for the Marxist-Leninist parties threatened to undermine the established order. In late 1946, Rāhula was imprisoned for a while with key leftists like N. M. Perera and Phillip Gunawardana for his active role in organizing labour strikes. As often happens when a radical leader is imprisoned, the experience only made him a more determined social reformer (Cuthberston 2004; Rodriguez 2006). After his release, Rāhula issued a more serious reformist appeal, first to the Saṅgha Samāja and then to the broader Sinhala society, including lay Buddhists and their political leaders. He gained popular support for his criticism of established, property-owning senior Saṅgha, for their abject failure to lead Sinhala society to its full potential. At this stage Rāhula's social agitation was based on the universal compassion inherent in Theravāda theology, which seeks first spiritual liberation and happiness for all.

Rāhula by now fully comprehended the potential of the written word, and in late 1947, he published a manifesto for the future in the form of a small yet well-articulated book. "භික්ෂුවගේ උරුමය" *Bhikṣuvagē Urumaya*[11] (*The Heritage of the Bhikkhu*) was in many ways an answer to the traditionalist critics. The book eventually became the manual for contemporary Saṅgha politics in Lanka. Published two years before the British left Lanka, Rāhula's comparatively short yet strategic and well-formulated intervention laid the foundation for a redefinition of the role of the Saṅgha in an independent Buddhist state after 438 years of European colonial occupation. All modern Saṅgha activists, irrespective of their affiliation or ideology, have used this book and its core argument as their

---

11. *Bhikshuvage Urumaya* was first published in 1946 in Colombo and its 34th edition was published in 2010, by S Godage Publishers, Colombo. Its English translation by Venerable Walpola Rāhula was published in 1974.

justification for secular political activism. As of 2010, the work is in its thirty-fourth edition and thousands of copies were distributed to almost every functioning temple library in the island. *Urumaya* in many ways permanently altered the traditional understanding of the dialectical relationship between the Sinhala Saṅgha and the society in which they live.

Bhikṣuvagē Urumaya

Bhikṣuvagē Urumaya, a work that "has influenced the monkhood more than any other in the recent history of Lankan Theravāda Buddhism" (Seneviratne 1999, 135), retains historical importance for at least two reasons when analyzing modern Saṅgha politics in Lanka. First, the Urumaya represented the collective articulation of a pre-independence discourse of the activist Saṅgha. Second, it laid the ideological foundation for the post-independence Saṅgha politics. Largely middle-class and urbanized, with above average education and exposure to European or regional societies, these élite monks were eager to construct a social order where the once glorified positions of power held by the Saṅgha would be re-established in independent Lanka. The Vidyālaṅkāra faculty, which envisaged a modern Lanka defined only by her Buddhist past, led the discourse and acted as the bridge-builders between a past—as envisioned in the *Mahāvaṃsa*—and an imagined future, in which the Saṅgha would take centre stage in the social and political order of Sinhala society.

Urumaya was not an isolated work. At least two previous texts paved the way for Rāhula's publication. One, the "*Declaration of Vidyālaṅkāra,*" was published on 13 February 1946, when the entire faculty of Vidyālaṅkāra unanimously put forward a text that called for a radical re-establishment of the powers of the Saṅgha in the political system. In concluding their Declaration, the faculty claimed:

> The divorce of religion from the nation was an idea introduced into the minds of the Sinhalese by invaders from the West, who belonged to an alien faith. It was a convenient instrument of astute policy to enable them to keep the people in subjugation in order to rule the country as they pleased... (Rāhula 1974, 133)

As Vesna Wallace has recently shown (2010) that, in arguing for a new social order, the Saṅgha at Vidyālaṅkāra borrowed from the past and re-introduced the principle of "integrated governance" of Buddhism and Sinhala ethnicity. From this perspective, a truly indigenous polity would have the Saṅgha at the centre of authority even though they are not elected in any democratic sense and are only representing the Sinhala Buddhists. This perspective was significant, springing from a Sinhala Buddhist ideology where violence, if needed, was justified within the context of a "just war" thesis (Bartholomeousz 2002, 2001).

The second text that informed an important part of the *Urumaya* context was the *Kälaṇiya Declaration of Political Independence*. On the strategically important and culturally charged full moon day of 6 January 1947, at an elaborate ceremony led by the chief monk of the temple, which, according to *Mahāvaṃsa* was built on the land where Buddha himself had preached,[12] a group of monks gave what in modern terms may be termed a Unilateral Declaration of Independence (UDI). They declared Lanka a sovereign, independent state with full rights to self-determination without foreign domination, and denounced all foreign occupations as illegal and immoral. After tracing the historical glory of the land, a brief statement declared:

> We therefore, the Saṅgha of Lanka, the Guardians of Life and Liberty and Sponsors of the Wellbeing and Happiness of the people of this island, assembled on this hallowed spot sanctified by the touch of the feet of the Master, do hereby declare and publish on behalf of the people, that Lanka claims its right to be a Free and Independent Sovereign State.
> (Rāhula 1974, 136)

The declaration did not come in isolation, as discussions surrounding the transfer of power were already underway. However, by making a declaration that pre-empted the public recognition of independence, the Saṅgha captured the strategic political position they desired and presented themselves as champions of the struggle for political freedom. This was another example of how the monks succeeded in contextualizing the *Mahāvaṃsa* ideological stance, which presents the Saṅgha as the political liberators of the Sinhalas. The Saṅgha efforts rested on the fact that they had established a genealogy of socio-political authority that led from Buddha to them. This is a clear process of framing an ethnicized Sinhala Buddhism to be the legitimate political force in independent Lanka, superimposing Sinhala ethnoreligious nationalism on the core values of Theravādin Buddhist ethics and hegemonizing Sinhala rule over the entire multi-ethnic island. The narrative style, the words chosen, and the dating of the declaration all showed the determination of the Saṅgha to return to their heritage after some four and a half centuries of colonial rule.

This declaration inspired the political élites and other nationalist forces in the country. The historical religious forces embodied by the Saṅgha gave them the impetus to reformulate their contemporary socio-political order. Rāhula included both these texts in his Urumaya,

12. The *Mahāvaṃsa* records that in his third and final visit to Lanka, Buddha, on the invitation of king Maniakkhika, preached the dhamma at Kälaṇiya. (Mhv. Chapter I, 34–37).

which instantly became a reference for political activism amongst the Saṅgha, who by now were determined to win what they considered as their rightful position of power.

Urumaya is rooted in the vision of Anagārika and Olcott, who saw the Saṅgha and its supporters at the centre of Sinhala society and politics rather than at the neglected periphery. The organic enthusiasm it generated among the Saṅgha across the island worried some members of the political élite, including DSS, the agriculture minister in the last pro-colonist government. DSS was a champion of the Buddhist cause, and he was expected to be the first Prime Minister of an independent Lanka. Yet he feared the power of Saṅgha nationalism, which the *Urumaya* had successfully mobilized. He tried to win over key members of the Vidyālaṅkāra, but instead the monks of this new social force organized themselves under the civil banner of the *Lanka Eksath Bhikṣhu Mandalaya* (LEBM), or the United Bhikshu Organization of Lanka. This was the first such organization in modern Lanka: a para-political social phenomenon that would have a deep impact in the decades to come (DeVotta 2007; Frydenlund 2004; Gamage 2009; I. C. Harris 1999a; Kent 2010a, 2010b; Wickramsinghe 2006). While an early attempt at forming a civil organization among the Saṅgha was made in 1938 as the Lanka Bhikshu Sammēlanaya (Bhikshu Conference of Lanka), it could not mobilize the same forces as the LEBM.

It was in this context of the early years of the independence movement in Lanka that the Urumaya became a textbook for Saṅgha politics. In this booklet, Rāhula provided the theological and theoretical justification for a new brand of "*Deshapalana Bhikshuwa*" (political Saṅgha) or "*Bhikkshu Deshapalanaya*" (Saṅgha politics), as he would name them (Rāhula 1947, xiii).

To date, there has been no systematic academic analysis of the text and the social impact of the *Urumaya* from a comparative political science perspective. However, the continued popularity of the text and the authority and legitimacy its use confer shows how widely accepted the text continues to be. Rāhula predicted the success of his own polemic. In the introduction to the second edition, he declared that the text provided a new justification for the political activism of the Saṅgha. It is evident that Rāhula foresaw that the Saṅgha fraternity of Lanka would eventually embrace and obtain the political role he envisioned for them, and he provided the ideological justifications that would shape the future governance of the state.

Structure and narrative of the Urumaya

Urumaya can be divided into five basic sections as follows:

1. The historical development of Buddhism and the Saṅgha in Lanka (chapters 1–5),

2. the role of the Saṅgha in developing a unique Sinhala culture (chapters 6–10),
3. the three European invasions and the role of the Saṅgha in the fight for independence (chapters 11–14),
4. British/Christian strategies for destroying Buddhism and the Saṅgha in Lanka (chapters 15–19),
5. the essential need for a new revival (chapter 20).

Out of the vast body of canonical texts, Rāhula selectively focuses on comparatively minor themes of Theravāda Buddhism in order to advance his political discourse. He employs at the outset a very liberal and extremely selective interpretation of the Theravādin scriptures, wilfully ignoring in his highly focused hermeneutics the holistic approach that underlies the teachings of the *Tripiṭaka.*[13] He wrote

> On careful reading of the *Vinaya Piṭakaya*, one may clearly see that the Rules of Discipline were introduced, changed or modified in accordance with the changing economic and social conditions to suit times and places. (Rāhula 1947, 11)

By this Rāhula assigned the interpretative authority of the most important codes to "time and place." His statement, which was part of his call for "political" engagement, anticipates what later came to be conceptualized as "socially engaged" Buddhism (S. B. King 2009; Queen 2000). For centuries, historians, anthropologists, theologians, and social scientists have analyzed the radical renouncer nature of Buddhist teaching in a large body of literature. In Lanka, Theravāda Buddhism championed a stricter form of social withdrawal in every ideological and conceptual sense. Rāhula himself, later, during his time at the Sorbonne, would defend the Theravāda school against its Mahāyāna competitors through his work *What the Buddha Taught* (Rāhula 1959) and *Zen and the Taming the Bull* (Rāhula 1978). However, in *Urumaya*, his mission seems to be openly political and narrowly nationalist as he focuses on the strong link between the Sinhala Saṅgha and society, using Buddhist canonical texts to justify his advocacy.

In the opening chapter of the book, Rāhula uses the ambiguous conceptual discourse of Theravāda and "social service," opening his text with the statement "Buddhism is based on service to others." This phrasing is no accident. His aim is to build a broad-based audience around a widely accepted and respected common currency. There can be no opposition to the call for service to society, which Rāhula supports with the story of

13. Tripiṭaka (Three Baskets) is the collective body of the three sections of Buddhist teaching: Sutta Piṭaka (discourse), The Vinaya Piṭaka (discipline) and Abhidharma Piṭaka (philosophy), (ODB: 309).

hermit Sumehda[14] during an earlier life of the Buddha, who gives up the opportunity to enter Nirvāna for the service of others. "He [Sumedha] renounced nirvāna as suffering in saṃsāra and took upon himself suffering in saṃsāra for others as nirvāna. A true Buddhist should have the strength to sacrifice his own nirvāna for the sake of others" (Rāhula 1974, 3).

He continues to construct a chronological history of the Saṅgha, situating the Mahāvaṃsic ideal of the hegemonic relationship of the Sinhala Saṅgha vis-a-vis the state in a modern context, while beginning with the birth of the Buddha, thus locating the origin and authority of the Saṅgha in the founder of the faith himself. After briefly presenting selected highlights of key events in the history of the establishment of the Saṅgha fraternity in India and Lanka, Rāhula gives an account of an ancient Lanka, in which the Saṅgha were a religious, social, and political force. His narration is primarily based on the *Mahāvaṃsa*, but also interwoven with strategic references to incidents, events, and context that support his ideological claims.

Seneviratne, an unreserved critic of Rāhula, maintains that the latter's use of the phrase "service to others" was nothing but a pretext:

> The Vidyālaṅkāra idea that the monk's vocation is social service was revolutionary, in that it has provided monks with an unprecedented excuse to seek profit and other secular goals. It has opened the floodgates and given rise to a new monkhood that many thoughtful members of the culture view with alarm. (Seneviratne 1999, 195)

Elsewhere he writes,

> The main reason why these new monks, who claimed their work is community service, have failed to live up to the standards of service envisaged for them by Dhammapada [and other key Buddhist texts] is that they have never intended any such [community service] in the first place. What they meant by community service was a licence for themselves to have greater involvement with secular society, beginning with politics. (Seneviratne 1999, 338)

Seneviratne also argues that the actual impact of Rāhula's intervention was contrary to the true nature of the Theravāda monkhood and that it misled the Saṅgha and their collective morality.

> The true and clear commitment of the monk is to the otherworldly goal, and when that is taken away, the monkhood is freed of its basis and monks can engage in any activity. ... However, when the floodgates are opened, as when knowledge is elevated over practice, there is no

14. For the full story see- http://arahan.tripod.com/story_sumedha.html, accessed on 10 March 2012, See also ODB pp. 282.

> inner way to control the activities of monks, whereas such control is the essence of the renouncer's commitment. (Seneviratne 1999, 172)

Later he writes:

> In the Urumaya and in the History [of Buddhism in Ceylon] it suits Rāhula to be an advocate of a Buddhism that glorifies social intercourse with lay society. ...the receipt of salaries and other forms of material remuneration; ethnic exclusivism and Sinhala Buddhist hegemony; militancy in politics; and violence, war and the spilling of blood in the name of "preserving the religion." (Seneviratne 1999, 186)

Seneviratne was prescient: many of his theses have been corroborated by the manner in which Saṅgha political influence unfolded. Yet if we look at the *Urumaya* from a more detached perspective, we need to acknowledge that Rāhula very cleverly built on what was already there, and his writing influenced both the Sinhala Saṅgha social psyche and the wider society. It may not be close to the Pāli canonical writings and their intended message, but one cannot deny the fact that Sinhala Buddhism, over the course of 2000 years, has evolved a different set of norms and values and mutated Sinhala Buddhism into a "protestant" form. As summarized by Tilakarathne:

> Throughout the history of Buddhism, there seem to have been two categories of monks, or rather, monks with two different slants. The best example of this division is the two great elders of the time of the Buddha, namely, Maha Kassapa and Ananda. The former was the epitome of relentless ascetic practice and austerity characterized by living in the forest, dislike for women, etc., clearly even more austere than the Buddha himself was. Ānandá was the exact opposite: city-dwelling, active, busy, a perfect private secretary, co-ordinator and champion of the liberation of women, visiting and meeting people. The texts say that Ananada could not attain arahanthood, the perfection of the path, until the Buddha attained parinibbana. Categories such as *gantha-dhura* and *vipassana-dhura, dhamma-kathita* and *pansukulika*, and *gama-vasi* and *aranna-vasi* that became important in the subsequent history of Buddhism may be traced back to the two elders. (Tilakarathne 2003, 177)

In the case of Lanka, the delicate balance between this world and the other may have tilted towards historical and socio-political engagement and away from doctrinal practices oriented towards the other world. However, the paradoxical tensions between the two paths are real and create opportunities, which Rāhula was able to exploit at a critical time.

Urumaya as an ideology

Rāhula borrowed from the argument developed by Anagārika Dharmapāla. Yet the "service to others" Rāhula had in mind is far from the kind of service the average rural Buddhist was familiar with. Rāhula's project was to exploit the existing tradition of community service for a mass mobilization in order to recapture the politically influential positions that the Saṅgha had historically enjoyed. This vision, based on the *Mahāvaṃsa*, targeted the future independent state of Lanka and its governing structure. *Urumaya* appeared in conditions that were ideal for channeling the existing social moods and forces towards a new political vision. As a monk with enough secular education and exposure to regional (especially Indian), political development, Rāhula aimed his text at the waiting generation of younger monks who had benefitted from a liberal education under the colonial administration. The new community of Saṅgha who were able to travel, meet more freely than their teachers, and read and understand secular sciences, were energized by Rāhula's arguments and the intellectual debate he provoked. To many younger Saṅgha, who desired a liberated monastic order, Rāhula had provided a blueprint for action. They had been waiting to receive a calling from a respectable voice. Rāhula's writing inspired them to develop Sinhala Buddhism and the role of the Saṅgha into a new direction that would alter both their own destiny and the political fate of the island.

With the self-appointed authority stemming from the success and the acceptance of *Urumaya*, Rāhula took to task the relaxed, rural Saṅgha leadership, challenging the ritualistic lifestyle of the average senior monk in Lanka. He even sarcastically stigmatized the fundamental rituals of the Saṅgha, which were mainly limited to the preaching of *banà*, officiating at Buddhist funerals and conducting the annual festivals of the temples. Rāhula's calculated attack on the rural Saṅgha attracted urban monks who were searching for new ways of criticizing the detachment of the monkhood from the life of the average Buddhist. Rāhula provided a moral justification for the many urban monks who were more keen to associate themselves with the political powers of the cities than to serve in the difficult and challenging rural temples. It was also a perfect springboard for those monks who had become fascinated by the socialist political ideologies flourishing in the political landscape. It was this section of Saṅgha that the pioneering socialist movements of Lanka targeted in the hope of recruiting them as collaborators. As Kumari Jayawardena noted

> These strikes were led by petty-bourgeoisie, which included Buddhist revivalists, the unorthodox fringe of the Ceylonese bourgeoisie and Theosophists, social reformers, temperance workers, and the more politically conscious nationalists who first gave the urban workers an element of trade union and class-consciousness. (1974, 6)

There were a number of circumstances that helped the *Urumaya* to mobilize politically motivated Saṅgha. Rāhula's historical contribution planted an ideological seed that was later to grow into one of the most significant political forces in Lanka. The role of the contemporary Saṅgha in justifying the war against the Tamil Tigers is now well recorded. Among the circumstances facilitating *Urumaya's* impact are the following:

1. the idea and possibly the expectation that a Sinhala Saṅgha should provide political leadership,
2. frustration caused by the diminished influence of the Saṅgha over centuries of foreign rule,
3. widespread disappointment with the traditional Saṅgha leadership,
4. a period of political uncertainty and transition, and
5. the personal values and beliefs of key leaders

Opposition to power-sharing

Rāhula remained committed to his ideology of the societal role of the monkhood until his death. In the mid-1990s, towards the end of his life, he again came to the political forefront. In 1995 and 1997, he led the opposition to the peace process and the constitutional changes proposed by President Chandrika Kumaratunge (CBK) to accommodate the demands of the Tamil ethnic minority. In 1995, CBK proposed a constitutional amendment, based on the federal model, aimed to address the root causes of Tamil political grievances. These were well received by most moderates, intellectuals, and most academics, who were keen to support a historical process that promised a democratic solution to the political crisis and a negotiated solution to end the war. Yet the attempts of the CBK government failed due to the formidable forces of the Saṅgha who opposed the process for various reasons, but largely on grounds of Sinhala Buddhist hegemony. At that particular time, the monks were able to point to the brutality of the Tamil Tigers' terrorism as a valid reason for their opposition. Rāhula vigorously campaigned against the proposal. His presence on the political front mobilized a large section of younger monks and nationalists against the peace process resulting in the defeat of the proposal. Rāhula not only urged others to rediscover the role of Saṅgha but also, through his own example, empirically redefined it. Weeks before his death Rāhula was firm in his ideology.

> (Being the season of Vesak, I asked the Ven. Rahula whether one should not think of maitrī and peace and could not a dialogue be held with the LTTE. His voice was strong and loud. The Ven. Rahula was agitated as he said,) "you are talking of peace and maitrī. What maitrī and peace is there when the terrorists in the North and East are trying to divide our country asking for Eelam." The Ven. Rāhula thundered, "our country is so small that four times our country could be accommodated in just one

> Indian State." I recall how he said, "get this straight and quote me, Sri Lanka is a Buddhist country. Let no one make a mistake. 70% of the country consists of Buddhist and Sinhala people. And make it clear that Sri Lanka is the only Sinhala Buddhist country in the world."
>
> (Rāhula cited in Peiris 1997, 12)[15]

In light of Rāhula's influence, we need to ask why it is that the Sinhala society was—and continues to be—more influenced by political Saṅgha than by the eremitic and ascetic monks who propagate a canonical Theravāda Buddhism. How is it possible for a politically motivated monk to radically reshape the ideology of the state? It is a historical fact that socio-politics, rather than Buddhist canons, had become the key reference point for Sinhala Saṅgha. In the public square, the Saṅgha initiated and cultivated a tradition in which they were more *bhumiputras*, or sons of the soil, than *Buddhaputras,* or sons of the Buddha. For these Saṅgha, Buddha himself was the example of dialectical socio-politics. He advised kings on war and peace and encouraged the Saṅgha to remain close to the royal courts. Finally, in the Cakkavatti Sīihanāda Sutta, which teaches the fundamentals of a just social and political order, he predicted a just king ruling in the shadow of the future Buddha (Wijerathna 2007a; Malalgoda 1970). The Sinhala Saṅgha justified their political involvement in terms of these and similar scriptures.

Rāhula, through his well-timed intervention in the form of the *Urumaya*, may have achieved two distinct but convergent aims. He legitimized the secularization of the modern Saṅgha and its interpretation of Buddhism as exclusively Sinhala, and he de-legitimized the "other," opposing voices not in support of this work. At a time when the political future of the island was more uncertain than ever, Rāhula's arguments became a rallying point for Sinhala nationalism, the ancient force that had once lost its direction but was now re-conceptualized by the articulate scholarship of the Saṅgha. The ethnic politics of later years were the natural extension of this inclusive and exclusive process. Here, as Derrida has pointed out, the "other" becomes the historical rogue against whom society needs to be reconfigured and secured (2005). In Lanka, in the Sinhala Buddhist narrative, there has always been an "other" who is often a "rogue" in every political and social sense. This is how society, the state and even the future are defined: it is not an exceptional state but rather the norm. Once the "otherness" is constructed and established, it justifies the punitive political order, which is often a centralized mechanism of exclusion and inclusion. At the dawn of independence in the late 1940s, when Rāhula presented his *Urumaya* thesis, it was the colonial administration

15. Roshan Peiris "Ven Rahula: learned and forthright," *Sunday Times*, 21 September 1997, page 12, http://sundaytimes.lk/970921/news2.html, Accessed on Aug 20, 2011.

and everything associated with it that was perceived and presented as the "rogue." As we have seen, it did not take long for the ethnoreligious nationalism of Sinhala Buddhism to designate the non-Buddhists, who shared the island, to be the new "rogues" in the post-independence era.

The identification of "rogues" within a system demands action whereby every citizen is mobilized to cleanse the societal space and order of the "rogues." The necessity of action legitimizes a punitive system of exclusion, which silences voices looking for alternatives. The excluded, in return, will react in a manner that further justifies their political status of "otherness," as "rogues." The Tamil Tigers, during their three-decade campaign of political terrorism, did just that. The LTTE's terror campaign reinforced the dreadful imaginations within the majority Sinhala mind, reproducing a whole social psychology that justified a war within a Sinhala Buddhist discourse. Athuraliyē Rathana, the current leader of the Jāthika Helà Urumaya (JHU) in Lanka's parliament, echoed the essence of this discourse:

> There are two central concepts of Buddhism: compassion and wisdom. If compassion were a necessary and sufficient condition, then the Buddha would not have elaborated on wisdom or prajna. Hitler could not have been overcome by maitriya alone. Today there is a discourse about peace in Lanka. It is an extremely artificial exercise and one that is clearly being orchestrated under the threat of terrorist attack. Our responsibility is to ensure that the jathika sammuti is given voice and the lie of the conflict sammuti is exposed. (Rathana, 2003)[16]

This process is the result of a deep ontological insecurity by which a violent anxiety is generated internally. Modern observers of Lanka's polity have testified that it has repeatedly reproduced this social dynamic, which follows a sensitive political trajectory, often led by the cultural élite: the Saṅgha. In 1915, 1930, 1947, 1956, 1978, 1983, 1988, and during the war from 1983–2009, the Saṅgha were among the instigators of upheavals. Walpola Rāhula was only one of those who, at a critical point in the modern history of Lanka, permanently reshaped the polity of the island.

Rāhula single-handedly answered those critics and scholars who lamented that brands of Buddhism were contradicting, or at least diverging from, the traditional teachings of the Theravāda canon and tradition (Gombrich 1998; Ling 1983; Obeysekere 1995; B. L. Smith 1972). Rāhula's vision had a decisive impact on modern Lanka. Fractured along caste, regional and party lines, the Saṅgha community had often operated as the most decisive non-state political force at the disposal of the ruling Sinhala élites. Walpola Rāhula through his ideology, work, and

16. From the paper presented by Rathana at the Bath Conference on Buddhism and Violence in Sri Lanka, 2003, as cited in (Deegalle 2006b, 20).

especially through his writing, re-focused the historical role of a Sinhala Saṅgha by re-contextualizing and intellectualizing the *Rata, Jāthiya* and *Āgama*—the unitary ownership of the island, the supremacy of the Sinhala ethnicity, and the institutionalizing of Sinhala Buddhism, in that order of priority. Thus, between 1950 and 2010, if the Sinhala Saṅgha agreed on any single issue, it was the determined and violent opposition to the proposal of political power-sharing with non-Sinhala minorities, which they interpreted as the death of the two fundamental features defining Lanka: Sinhala ethnicity and Sinhala Buddhism.

In reviewing Rāhula's impact, we conclude that it may be misleading to think of the relationship between the Sinhala nation and Sinhala Buddhism as an enduring phenomenon; instead, we must pay attention to the specific and contingent ways in which such notions as "Buddhist" and "nation" are defined. By examining particular native debates over what can and cannot count as "Buddhist," we may have to recast Buddhist nationalism "as a shifting configuration of discourse wherein competing interests struggle for rhetorical and political advantage" (Abeysekara 2002, 30).

Venerable Gaṅgoḍawila Sōma (1948–2003)

Global and national context

The 1994 general election promised to deliver change after 17 years of rule by the right-wing United National Party. The open economy, the demand that Lanka adjust to a pro-western culture, a protracted war and the abysmal human rights violations of the UNP regime had generated angry political reactions calling for a total transformation. Leading the opposition, Chandrika Kumaratunga, the widow of popular actor and activist Vijaya Kumaratunga, came forward as the symbol for change. Her readily marketable political family name generated formidable support in a country where élite names matter so much in politics. Her father was SWRD, assassinated by a Saṅgha in 1958 while serving as Prime Minister, and her mother was the world's first female Prime Minister in 1960. Left-of-centre liberal policies and her belief in a comprehensive political solution to the ethnic war earned her a comfortable victory. The hope of democratic recovery was so high that analysts claimed her victory as a new social transformation (Bartholomeusz 1999b; C. R. De Silva 1995; Sáez 2001; Schaffer 1995; Whall 1999; Zompetti 1997).

However, the island's deep-rooted political crisis was not easy to manage or resolve in a manner that would bring a sustainable and acceptable solution within any short period. Instead, Chandrika, like many of her predecessors, was caught between the nationalist south, led by vociferous opportunist political oppositions, and the terror campaign of the LTTE in the north. The Tigers walked away from the peace talks, which

Figure 4. Venerable Gaṅgoḍawila Sōma in Sakman meditation.

had been initiated with much hope, and had begun to mount dramatic military attacks not just in the war zone but also in the commercial-civil heart of the capital city and its environs. A failing economy due largely to the inexperience and mismanagement by the newcomers in the Chandrika camp added to the frustration. A president who had never held a political post at any level was confronted by multiple and varied challenges, both internally and externally, diminishing the popularity that her charisma had secured (Schaffer 1995; Zompetti 1997). Following an assassination attempt by the Tamil Tigers in 1999, Chandrika lost vision in her right eye. While her administration was able to respond to many of these new pressures with limited success, her ultimate failure was caused by the traditional Saṅgha resistance to her commitment to constitutional change. Chandrika either ignored the Saṅgha or dismissed them as irrelevant, yet this political ignorance and her disregard for the Saṅgha turned out to be a political disaster she could not survive.

By the year 2000, every socio-economic index of the island was trending downward. The Sinhala south was desperate for social–political, or spiritual alternatives. The subsequent entry (and the dramatic departure) of a charismatic, photogenic preacher, who knew the power of the mass media, could not have come at a better time for the advancement of Saṅgha politics in the recent history of Lanka.

Early life

Gaṅgoḍawila, who is often given the honorary title Sōma *hāmuduruvo* සෝම හාමුදුරුවෝ in Sinhala, was born in 1948 in Gaṅgoḍawila—a semi-urban area near the capital city of Colombo (Perera 2001). His parents were struggling to make ends meet with four children. Sōma, being the eldest of the family, offered to go to work and contribute to the family income at an early age. He managed the family-run grocery store. Gaṅgoḍawila is near Maharagama, where the influential Vajirārāma Temple and the Bhikshu Training Centre were situated. Young Sōma became a frequent visitor and a close associate of the Temple and its activities. The temple was headed by the respected Saṅgha Mäḍhē Pagññāsīha, who later became the chief Saṅgha of *Amarapura Nikāya*.

His strong association and involvement with the temple gave Sōma a new social identity and purpose, granting him far more respect than his previous grocery-keeper identity. After years of trying, Sōma eventually convinced his parents to permit him to enter the order of Saṅgha as a member of the the same chapter, which he did in July 1975. For obvious reasons his choice was to join the Vajirārāma Temple and have Mäḍhē as his teacher and instructor. With Mäḍhē as his teacher, the young Sōma managed within a short period to bring many modern elements to a temple, which was otherwise trapped, in tradition and ritual. One of these new elements was an initiative to develop a youth organization that would engage in Buddhist evangelism. This initiative became a major turning point for him and the temple. Sōma analyzed the reasons why the temple was unpopular with the youth, drawing on years of experience as a lay associate of the temple. His realization that there remained a gap between the expectation of the youth and what the temple could offer soon drove him into action. He started a dialogue centre intending to answer the contemporary questions faced by the youth within a popular Buddhist discourse. Deploying an unconventional, dialogical preaching style, Sōma attracted many followers. He adopted innovative and non-traditional methods of addressing the laity. Traditionally a Sinhala Saṅgha refers to the laity as "පින්වතුණී", Pinwathunī, (those who are collecting merit), yet Sōma would address lay people as "ඔය ඇත්තෝ" *oya äththō*, which is a term usually used by a Saṅgha when addressing another Saṅgha, or by a wife respectfully addressing her husband. The young followers who enjoyed his teaching encouraged Sōma to make his teaching available to a wider audience outside the temple walls. Thus, Sōma felt encouraged to take this new form of preaching to the street, a practice unseen in

Lanka for many years. Sōma would gather office and factory workers at a crowded bus stop on a weekday evening and start a dialogue on life and society in light of Buddhist concepts. The semi-urban low-income workers, who were burdened with existential questions, would eagerly listen and participate in this form of "street Buddhist dialogue," often until late evening. Sōma used what at the time were modern instruments of communication such as a megaphone, tape recorders and even music tapes to enrich his presentations, a practice not known within the tradition of Buddhist preaching in Theravāda societies (Deegalle 2007, 1997).

These were the early signs of a Saṅgha who was determined to both critically engage with modern society and benefit from the same modernity. The "critical customer" approach that we find in the life and work of Sōma, especially in his use of electronic media in later years, symbolizes a new brand of Saṅgha who, although more modern than their predecessors, were at the same time vociferously critical of almost all features of modern society. This paradox was a fundamental force supporting Sōma and the political psychology he helped to create (Clifford *et al.* 2003; Mensing 2010).

He would frequently ask a series of questions, always beginning with "Why is there suffering in Lankan society?" followed by "Who is a true Buddhist?" The first was an open inquiry in a society where war, political uncertainty and the failing economy had created social anxieties without the prospect of any clear solution, while the second allowed him to present his own analysis. Through these two dialectical and critical discursive questions, Sōma provided an alternative perspective, especially for people at the fringe of a society, which had turned inwards without hope or direction. Sōma in many ways embodied the ideal of the homeless street preacher, offering simple solutions to intrinsically complex questions. This was an image that the traditional Buddhist society could relate to: a wandering preacher explaining the meaning of life in both individual and collective terms. By adopting these practices, Sōma captured the attention of the semi-urban population who were hoping to find answers to modern social struggles through the (re)interpretation of popular Buddhist concepts. Nikki Keddie (1998) has shown that modern religious nationalism is essentially a semi-urban phenomenon (Gooptu 1997; Simpson 2006).

Sōma's popularity grew. As we shall see later, these two simple and popular questions—why Lankans suffer and how Sinhalas Buddhism could provide answers to the suffering—became the future social and political conceptual framework within which Sōma would campaign to reorganize the contemporary Lankan society and its polity.

After a period of ten years, Sōma had established himself as the field marshal of the new form of preaching and temple management. This was not without costs, as popularity and relentless demand for change made him many enemies among those who preferred that traditions continue unchanged. At this stage, Sōma began to address a strategic section of the temple supporters who were in many ways a microcosm of the wider Lankan society: the middle-aged employed and homemaking women. Throughout his subsequent career, Sōma appealed to Lankan women, referring directly to their experiences as he cited single motherhood, abuse and neglect at home, suffering caused by husbands struggling with alcoholism, the increasing costs of living, and the fear of war as evidence of growing social problems. Sōma's appeal to reorganize Lankan society according to the moral principles of popular Buddhism[17] (Kitiarsa 2005) had earned him a loyal audience amongst the middle aged and elderly female population of the country (52% of the population). Women, who traditionally suffer more than any other section of society during social crisis, had withstood the worst of the painful reality of the war in Lanka for decades (Argenti-Pillen 2002; De Mel 2003; De Alwis 2002; Somasundaram and Sivayokan 1994). Most families in southern Lanka had lost at least one member, often the breadwinner, to the war: mostly men from poor families who had joined the army or others who had died from LTTE attacks. Thus, the traditional role of women in family and society had changed, forcing them to face new social and psychological anxieties. Many were witnessing the moral decay of their husbands and sons now addicted to gambling and to a new culture of pubs, bars, and karaoke centres, which flourished in the new liberalized economic system.[18] These women needed solace, and Sōma answered these needs with his preaching, emphasizing the historical culture of Lanka and popular Buddhism. Seventy four per cent of the population accepts that Buddhism provides the ultimate answers to questions regarding the very meaning of life. In such a context, Sōma's teaching found resonance.

In response to criticisms about the appropriateness of a Saṅgha advocating the cause of women, Sōma authored a book on Yaśodharā, the wife of Buddha and mother of Rāhula. Yaśodharā is the paradigmatic female role model in Buddhist hagiographical texts. Yaśodharā bore the eternal anguish of personal and social loss when Buddha left her with the infant Rāhula, and when some nine years later Rāhula followed the steps of his father into monkhood. By entitling the book යශෝදරා රාහුල මාතා—*Yaśodharā: Rāhula Māta* (*Yaśodharā: mother of Rāhula*)—Sōma targeted both the young wives who had lost their husbands and the mothers who had lost their sons. By presenting an image of the ideal woman in stark contrast

17. I distinguish three types of Buddhism: 1. Pāli Buddhism (canonical writings in the Pāli language), 2. Popular Buddhism (what is sought after as Buddhism in Asian and Western societies), and 3. Political Buddhism (the use of Buddhism for political purposes).

18. An unregulated karaoke culture emerged in Lanka during this time. Often these centres were known for their links with the sex and drugs trade.

to the morally decaying male, who was dominating society and fighting a cruel war, Sōma touched the feminine psychology in at least two ways: as a monk who was willing to understand the suffering of millions of Buddhist women and, even more subtly, as a kind of masculine role model, whom these women never had in their lives. Sōma's empathy, identification and defence of suffering woman made him a venerated household hero.

Through his empathy with women, Sōma challenged the traditional temple culture including his guru and guide, Mäḍhē Pagññāsīha, in an innovative and creative manner. This is because in Sinhala Buddhism the Saṅgha have a very reserved attitude towards women, even refusing to accept female Buddhist ordination (Bartholomeusz 1994; Keyes 1984). As a direct influence of *Rāhula Māta,* many young women of key families closely connected to the temple followed Yaśhodharā's example and took the ultimate decision to overcome present and future suffering by seeking to be ordained as female monks or *Bhikkhunī*—a tradition that the majority Theravāda societies had barred for two millennia.

The exclusivity of the ordination of men and the rejection of the ordination of women, in contradiction of Buddha's teaching, is a core ideological position of modern Theravāda Buddhism (Bartholomeusz 1994; Bhikkhu Bodhi 2010; DeVido 2007; Tomalin 2009; Slone and Mort 2005; Jonathan 1994; Salgado 2004). Accordingly, by calling women to the higher life of Buddhism, Sōma angered some of the most influential members of the Saṅgha fraternity. As he noticed how his interpretations and activities troubled the traditional hierarchy, and following Saṅgha traditions, Sōma decided to go into exile. He left the *grāma vihāra vāsi* (living by the village) life and became an *āraṇya vāsi* (living in the jungle). Despite this gesture, Sōma was not a traditionalist. All his life he had rebelled against tradition by borrowing modern concepts while criticizing modernity and its impact. He recorded his thinking on tape, addressing wider issues that led to the crisis in the temple and explaining that the fundamental issues of the temple were connected to the core character of contemporary Sinhala Buddhist society and its hopeless polity. He pleaded with the dāyakas and the Saṅgha to unite in order to address and remedy these conditions. One core tactic in the preacher's arsenal was to create a discourse of "modern-ness" in order to analyze his surrounding "modernity." He pursued two interrelated and converging projects: first, the renewal of the spirituality and culture of contemporary Sinhala Buddhists and, second, the initiation of a new type of Saṅgha power politics. The core of both projects was the encounter and emerging relationship between the Sinhala polity and its Buddhism on the one hand and modernity on the other. As Lawrence Grossberg (2006) has argued, it is possible to have multiple modernities; however, the political and structural ontology of Sinhala Buddhism is stubbornly non-modern.

Sōma's voluntary departure from a comfortable urban temple to an extremely remote, rural village reinstated his status as true Saṅgha, reaffirming the respect he enjoyed at the temple and within the Saṅgha community at large. He took residence in Degamadulle near the Mahaoya River. His choice again was strategic. His new residence at the edge of the jungle was in the area of Mahiyaṅgana, which, according to *Mahāvaṃsa*, was the first place Buddha visited in Lanka and where he used his supernatural powers to tame the unbelieving native *Yakṣas* (Mhv. 1: 1–46).[19] Sōma, in his attempts to present himself as a prototypical Buddhist mendicant, decided to cover long distances by foot, *piṇḍapāta* (begging for his meals), and spending the night at the area's temples, meditating under trees or even by the side of the road. During these long walks, according to his biographer, Sōma covered "over 1000 miles or one third of the Sinhala Buddhist area of the country" (Perera 2001, 106). During these long marches, Sōma critically engaged with the popular practices among Buddhists, such as patronizing Dēvala-shrines dedicated to Hindu deities, attending healing meetings conducted by Pentecostal Christians, and following other Indian gurus such as Sai Bāba. He created controversies as he even condemned the worship of a Buddha statue or the worship of the Bō tree, which both had become integrated and demonstrative parts of modern Theravāda Buddhism. He represented a "puritan" version of Buddhism and presented himself as a reformer who aimed to revert the Sinhalas to the Buddhist texts. Such calls for reforms are often mere rhetoric devices serving political ends because Sinhala Buddhism had always intermingled with Hindu and other indigenous religious beliefs and practices (Gombrich and Obeyesekere 1988).

During this period of withdrawal and renunciation, Sōma kept his connections with his supporters and followers. He made sure that the news about his "protest and reformist walk" was known to his critics and to the masses. Through his commitment to revive the forgotten conventions of the Theravāda texts, Sōma became more popular especially amongst the urban middle-class Buddhists and particularly with the transnational diaspora, who preserved a nostalgia for their culture and traditions. Sōma soon became a politically charged, spiritual attraction to the visiting members of the Sinhala diaspora.

Modern scholarship nationalism has argued that in a globalized context of trans-nationalist social dynamics of contemporary diaspora communities are eager to adhere to and reproduce their homeland a nationalism that is founded on a religious interpretation of their iden-

19. In Buddhist literature, Yakṣas are flesh-eating spirits with dark powers (ODB p. 338). How the *Mahāvaṃsa* constructs the pre-Buddhist natives of Laṅka as Yakṣas is a question worthy of further study. According to the *Mahāvaṃsa*, Kuvaṇṇā, the first wife of Vijaya, the founder of the Sinhala race, was a Yakṣani (Mah.7: 5–40).

tity (Adamson 2008; Biswas 2010; Sageman 2004; Shain and Barth 2003). Consequently, unlike the previous waves of nationalism that grew on territorial, linguistic, or ethnic identities, within multicultural and modernistic discourse, religion has replaced many other forces of identity construction and social bonding. As a way of managing the new realities surrounding them in their adopted homelands, diasporas often embraced anti-secular and absolutist orientations. These often hybridized versions of homeland cultural practices are constructed around non-Western religious beliefs (Adamson and Demetriou 2007; Brinkerhoff 2008).

Identities are more taken than given in a postmodern context; they are taken by individuals and communities to suit a particular sociopolitical or even economic reality (Faist 2000; Martiniello and Lafleur 2008). This process of embracing "identities of convenience" produces a counter-dynamic when an outsider/other attempts to impose an identity that is different from that which is desired (Biswas 2004; Kapur 2010; Lyons 2007). This process of embracing and imposing identity and its political discourse has followed different trajectories among the diaspora of many states. In Lanka, the Sinhalas historically and politically wanted to adopt the identity of the "owners" of the land and accordingly tried to impose the identity of "visitors," "latecomers," "tenants," and "invaders," on other non-Sinhala communities despite historical evidence to the contrary. In this context, the Tamil diaspora tried to establish itself as a hardworking but oppressed minority nation with the legal and political right to self-determination. In opposition to this narrative, the Sinhala diaspora have projected themselves as an ethnic minority in the regional and global sense that has suffered centuries of colonization from India and the West. As Dibyesh Anand argued:

> A discursive approach does not deny any act of communal political activism. It only reveals it as contingent, as strategic rather than something unambiguously natural. Identification should be seen, not as an artefact or an outcome, but as a construction, a process never completed. Identities are increasingly fragmented and fractured; never singular but multiply constructed across different, often intersecting and antagonistic, discourses, practices and positions. (2000, 273)

At a time when the diasporic ethnic nationalism of the Lankan Tamils was at its peak, and when the armed resistance of the Tamil Tigers was considered a modern, effective, textbook guerrilla struggle, the Sinhala diaspora suffered humiliation in the liberal West for the illiberal governments of their motherland. The average Sinhala living in the diaspora was caught between the asymmetrical forces of centrifugal Sinhala nationalism and centripetal Tamil nationalism (Lyons 2006; Martiniello and Lafleur 2008; Orjuela 2008). A section of the Sinhala diaspora was more than willing to embrace Sōma and his Theravāda religious repositioning project as a force offering a new identity that could construct legitimacy and provide answers to their socio-political anxieties. Within a short time, Sōma was preaching on a worldwide stage, travelling to the parts of the world where the Sinhalas were a struggling diaspora. His international "missions" gained influence in Europe, North America, and key centres of East Asia. The culmination of such overseas "*dharma cārikās*" (missionary trips) was the invitation to establish a new Theravāda temple in Melbourne, Australia. Sōma moved to Australia, spending his time building an international network.

There is presently no detailed study available of Sōma's work and impact in Australia. All we know is that he was successful in establishing two new Buddhist temples, which became the central symbol of the new religious nationalism among the Sinhalas in Australia. The important issue for this discussion is not so much the new nationalist impetus Sōma created among the Sinhalas in Australia, and the administrative controversies surrounding them (Perera 2001, 158), but his return to Lanka after ten years of absence, now with well-developed networks in Australia and the rest of the world. He returned at the end of Chandrika's first term, at a time when Lankan society had lost its hope of a return to peace and prosperity—a time when the Sinhalas were looking for a political and cultural redeemer.

අඳුරෙන් එළියට — *Aṅduren Eliyaṭa: From darkness to light*

In the 1990s, academic debates on the growth of Sinhala nationalism had a profound impact on Lankan politics. Anticipating attempts in the political realm to find an acceptable and sustainable solution to the ethnic war, academics tried to define or defend the various political perspectives on offer. R. A. L H. Gunawardana and K. N. O. Dharmadasa, both from Pērādeniya University, led the two camps. For Gunawardana, the ethnic nationalism of the Sinhalas was a recent colonial construct (1971, 1979, 1995, 1990), whereas for Dharmadasa, Sinhala ethnic nationalism was an indigenous identity-based project that had begun much earlier with the introduction of the Sinhala script and language in the fifth century CE (1992). It is noteworthy that Dharmadasa's argument, in structure and content, was based on the Vaṃsa literature. Like many debates about the origins of nationhood, this debate too eventually entered a deadlock.

However, new scholarship suggests that it might be possible to move beyond the question of the timing of the origin of Sinhala nationalism, and to understand how and why such an ideology became a dominant force in reshaping the history and modern politics of Lanka (Abeysekara 2002; Bartholomeusz 2002; Deegalle 2006b; C. R. De Silva 2006; De Silva and Bartholomeusz 2001; DeVotta 2007, 2005, 2004a; Indrapala 2005; Obeysekere 2006; Premasiri 2006)

This scholarship finds common ground in the assertion that the conceptual understanding and the implementation of Sinhala nationalism are fundamentally contextual. At different times and in different conditions, different factors have generated or sustained nationalist forces that allowed the *jāthiya* and the *āgama* of Sinhala Buddhism to construct the same power structures. Often the literature draws on two different sets of explanations in order to account for the rise of a religiously inspired nationalism. First, there are the explanations informed by Marxism, according to which religion is to be understood as the "opiate of the masses," as an instrument of power. Because of the status of religion in society, governments who appeal to religious belief are often granted a higher authority and legitimacy, even by secular groups within these societies (Williams 1994). Evoking the power of God as a foundation of secular power often justifies the use of violence (Fox 2006; Little 2006).

A second explanation of the prominent role of religion in politics refers to the failure of modern secular governments to answer the ontological anxieties that plague societies today (Appleby 2000; Bader 2007; Bhargava 2007; Esposito 2007; Ignatieff 2001; Habermas 2006; Haynes 2010, 2008, 2007, 2004, 2001; Juergensmeyer 2008, 2006, 2005, 2004a, 2004b, 2002a, 2002b; Kukathas 2003; Levey 2008; Levey *et al.* 2008, 2006; Monshipouri and Welch 2001; Marty and Appleby 2004a, 2004b; Modood 2007; Sen 2005; Tibi 2002; Turner 2001; Van der Veer 2001). The secular principles and projects of modern governments have failed and often brought misery to the masses, justifying the regeneration of religious forces in politics to either edify or criticize the current social order. Thus, where governments fail to provide social, economic and cultural justice for the greater sections of the population, where modern secularism is seen as standing in the same tradition as colonialism, and where Western influence is seen as a continuation of colonial oppression, religion can become a voice of protest and resistance. These factors were certainly present at the time of Sōma's return.

Almost immediately after his return, Sōma resumed his previously successful style of dialogical preaching, but instead of gathering people in the urban city centres, as he had done previously, Sōma utilized electronic mass media for his latest mission. *Aṅduren Eliyaṭa* (from darkness to light) was the title of his weekly televised preaching, which became an instant success and a "must have" item in the competitive profit-seeking media market. Sōma soon became one of the most watched individuals on all the main channels. Many new FM radio stations had him speak regularly on a variety of topics. Through these efforts, Sōma in many ways created a new "social space" for the debate on Sinhala Buddhism, and this new social space also reflected a new emphasis within this debate. Whereas he had previously promoted Pāli Buddhism, Sōma now aimed to articulate a political vision through the lens of Sinhala Buddhist ethnic ideology. Dhamma, which was traditionally preached in temples and at funerals thereby found new modern and "secular" means and spaces to "Buddhisize" the socio-political consciousness. Sōma ensured that his new methods of repositioning popular Sinhala Buddhism would address and provide answers to some of the urgent, contemporary, political uncertainties of the Sinhala social psyche. As Yves Lambert (1999) has argued, Sōma succeeded in making an "Axial age" connection between the current political crisis and the secular pluralism that treated Buddhists and non-Buddhists as equal citizens. For him, however, this pluralism was simply not acceptable within the Dhammadīpa, the island that belongs to Buddha and his followers. Sōma, like his predecessors, argued that modernity and most of its products, including colonialism (Perera 2001, 17–24), Christianity (Perera 2001, 71–80), a multi-party parliament (Perera 2001, 32–43), multi-cultural democratic Lanka (Perera 2001, 44–70, 107–135), an open economy, a secular university education (Perera 2001, 141–155), and a judiciary system based on English law were all institutionalized Western/foreign influences and therefore enemies of නිර්මල බුදු දහම "*nirmala budhu dahama*" (pure Buddhism) (Sōma 2001, 2002).

While his presentations were often factually and conceptually full of errors, Sōma's rhetoric, available to Lankans in the comfort of their home or place of work, resonated with the majority. His appeal to the Sinhalas to be "සැබෑ බෞද්ධයන්" *säbä bauddhayan*—true Buddhists—through "බෞද්ධ සාරධර්ම" *bauddha sāradharma*—Buddhist morality—in order to shun immorality and to reconstruct the true "බෞද්ධ දේශයක්" *buddha deshayak*—the Buddhist state, captured the imagination of the largely urban and semi-urban middle class Sinhalas (Jayakody 2002). Adopting the methods of conventional advertising campaigns, Sōma developed a tagline for his mission: "සදාචාරය ජාතියක සෞභාග්‍යය උදා කරයි" "*sādacāraya—jātiyaka saubhāgya udakarai*"—Righteousness Enhances the Prosperity of a Nation. With this phrase, Sōma reassured large sections of urbanized Sinhalas that by embracing Buddhist righteousness they were not undermining their economic welfare; on the contrary, Buddhism was the answer to the fragile economic situation of the country.

The commonplace question, often asked in Western circles, of what Buddhism in Lanka means often provokes answers informed by anthropological studies and based on binary oppositions such as "worldly vs. spiritual," "rural vs. urban," "modern vs. pre-modern," or "orthodoxy vs. new age." The work of leading scholars such as Obeysekere, Seneviratne and Tambiah follows similar lines. Sōma's activities demonstrate, however, that these dichotomies are misleading. His success was due precisely to the fact that his message seemed to overcome these binary oppositions. More recent scholarship on the anthropology of Sinhala Buddhism has shown that the actual dynamics of Sinhala Buddhism transcends the binary oppositions referred to above (P. De Silva 2006; P. De Silva and Ishigaki 2002; D. A. Scott 1996). Moreover, as Premakumar De Silva maintains, those who continue to assume that such dichotomies are meaningful are unable to appreciate the real impact of Buddhism on Sinhala society (P. De Silva 2006, 169).

Sōma, in contrast to his pre-Australian life as a mendicant, embraced modern means of reaching the population. He also now lived a modern life in an urban environment, and yet he propagated the thesis that modern-ness and modernity were both enemies of Sinhala Buddhism. Sōma utilized his international network, especially the US-based Buddhist publisher Dayawansa Jayakody, to publish his speeches and preaching. He formed the "Jana Vijaya"—the People's Victory foundation—in order to promote his work throughout the Sinhala-speaking world. By this time, his discourse had moved very openly from a spiritual debate to social and political issues. As he continued to preach, Sōma constructed a particular version and interpretation of Buddhism that was adaptable to, but not consumed by, the "immoral" forces of modernity and globalization. By this, as Abeyasekara argues, he constructed "specific debates that rendered possible and centrally visible differing demarcations between what can and cannot count as Sinhala Buddhism" (2002, 31). He portrayed "*saubhāgya*" (prosperity), towards which middle class Sinhala society was tirelessly working, as the long-term goal for a Buddhist Sinhala state. It may be possible to argue that Sōma was thereby constructing a Buddhist charismatic movement with an in-built "prosperity theology." Sōma may have learned here from the success of Pentecostal Christianity, which recruited many converts in rural Sinhala villages. These movements presented material prosperity as one of God's blessings bestowed on the righteous, and they created their own communities and welfare structures—"mini-states" within the state.

It is now clear that, although he spearheaded the anti-conversion bill in Lanka (DeVotta 2002; Frydenlind 2005),[20] Sōma borrowed many theoretical and practical applications from these evangelical groups in order to contextualize Buddhism and to provide a challenge to the growth of Christianity amongst the rural Sinhala villages (Hresko 2006, 123). In this sense, Sōma's efforts paralleled Anagārika's, who constructed a "Protestant" Buddhism (Bertelsen 1997; Yang and Ebaugh 2001;

20. On 22 Aug 2004, the Lankan parliament, proposed by the JHU, debated a bill to any ban conversions to Christianity. See Bruce Matthews, Christian Evangelical Conversions and the Politics of Sri Lanka, *Pacific Affairs*, 2007, 80(3): 455–472 for a background discussion on this.

Gombrich and Obeyesekere 1988; Mellor 1991) against the influence of the "Protestant" missionaries. The most active and growing sections of Christianity in Lanka today are the health-and wealth-oriented, faith-based, charismatic movements. These movements, which have by now become a global trend, tend to provide a new negotiating power to the individuals and communities who have suffered the aggressive effects of globalization, which has undermined their local identities and subsistence (Coleman 2003, 2002; Hunt 2000). These church movements often have their own welfare systems providing basic needs such as health care, education, and micro-finance. By competing with them, Sōma may have contributed to the construction of a "neo-Pentecostal Prosperity Sinhala Buddhism" in Lanka: a phenomenon, which could be an indigenous Sinhala Buddhist response to a changing world order under the weight of globalization. The Buddhist social and political order he envisioned clearly also had an economic dimension. This is further clarified by his desire to enter power politics as a means to reconstruct a Buddhist socio-political and economic order. Sōma's phrase "*Sadācharaya Saubhāgya genadeyi*" (morality will bring prosperity) justified Buddhism in economic terms. If the people were willing to become සැබෑ බෞද්ධයන් (true Buddhists) he would lead them towards the desired prosperity.

In his discursive strategy, Sōma projected a bi-polar structure onto Sinhala society. Buddhist righteousness was opposed to the immorality of modernity, and he was the one who would lead the fight of the former against the latter. On the one side, he positioned Buddhism, the Sinhalas, their culture, family values and superior history. On the other side he found the open economy, consumerism, multi-party democracy, election systems, political corruption, Christianity, the LTTE, Muslim traders, Hindu sects (such as Sai Baba) and the I/NGO debate on human and minority rights. Sōma called on the Sinhalas to arm themselves with Buddhist ethics in order to fight against the immoral elements of contemporary society. The struggle of the Sinhala people was the righteous struggle against the eternal Western and foreign conspiracy. The Sinhalas had to live up to their assigned role as the custodians of the faith.

As an immediate step towards the recovery of the "උරුමය" (heritage) of the Sinhalas, Sōma asked citizens not to vote for the then government of Chandrika claiming that "its leadership had failed" (Sōma 2002, 33). He often confronted the urban Buddhists with the contradictions in their lives—how they compromised their Buddhism by participating in an unjust political, social, and economic order—and thereby appealed to the "shame culture" that prevailed on the island (Lu 2008). As an alternative to the existing system, Sōma advocated the urgent need to restructure the Lankan polity according to Buddhist values under the leadership of the Saṅgha, suggesting that he could be a superior leader to govern the country. The Saṅgha were superior leaders, he argued; because the true Saṅgha had no children, no family, and no attachments, allowing them to selflessly serve the country and its people (Sōma 2002, 42).

A universal Sinhala Buddhism (?)

Sōma's agenda mirrored a broader global trend within religion and politics. Modern scholarship on culture, religion and politics has argued that there are two main types of reactions to the tension between the demands of theo-politics and the demands for a secular order. One type of reaction rejects the globalizing forces and asks the faithful to return to their religious roots; the other type of response wants to see globalization read into the relevant religion through new interpretations of the canonical texts (Appadurai 1996; Giddens 1991; Kinnvall 2006, 2004; Levitt and Avillae 2004; Whitehouse 2002). The Sinhalas were faced with internal challenges, such as the raging war, and external challenges, such as immigration and the free flow of capital and information, with both kinds of challenges forcing radical transformations and uprooting the traditional security they had felt for centuries. As Kinnvall has summarized:

> My argument is that nationalism and religion supply particularly powerful stories and beliefs (discourses) through their ability to convey a picture of security, of a "home" safe from intruders. They do this by being portrayed as resting on solid ground, as being *true*, thus creating a sense that the world really is what it appears to be. (2004, 776)

Sōma, through his preaching and debates, capitalized on this power of religion with a call to action focused on two key political issues. First, he vocally raised suspicions about the Norway-led peace process that had started without the involvement of the Saṅgha fraternity and, second, he criticized proposals for political power-sharing arrangements with the LTTE-led Tamil nationalists. Many Sinhala nationalists, even those who disagreed with Sōma on his interpretation of Buddhist texts, now found a new platform on which to criticize the peace talks, calling the Sinhalas to (re)discover a Sinhala Buddhist ruling system led by the Mahā Saṅgha. Sōma openly expressed his intentions to form a political party for monks and asked his followers for support. There was speculation, never denied, that he was willing to contest the presidential election.

Sōma changed his contemporary Sinhala society in at least three ways. Firstly, he built a critical consciousness amongst the Sinhalas towards modernity and the relentless forces of globalization. While his criticisms were often based on sentiment and rhetoric rather than political analysis, he managed to capture the Sinhala imagination. Secondly, he mobilized grass root agitation against the Norway-lead peace process, which he understood as a symbol of inappropriate influence of Western and foreign powers on Lankan affairs. Thirdly, as a remedy for these social disorders, he proposed a new form of political, Saṅgha-led governance.

Venerable Gaṅgoḍawila Sōma, at the heights of his popularity, died suddenly on 12 December 2003 in a hospital in Moscow, while visiting to receive an honorary doctorate. His unexpected death fuelled suspicions that he had become the victim of the very international conspiracy he had warned against. While local and international forensic experts declared that Sōma died of a heart attack, for which he had undergone treatment earlier, his followers, admirers and funders would not let the matter rest. His funeral procession was a state affair and the cremation was accordingly performed on the national independence square. After his death, Sōma was declared අපේ කාලයේ බුදු හාමුදුරුවෝ—the Buddha of our time—by his followers. Sōma—his life, his work, even his death—influenced politics in Lanka for years to come. Some commentators would consider his thinking as a reaction to the effects of globalization, which undermine the indigenous space and identity (Friedland 1994). According to Stephen Berkwitz:

> As such, his work crucially recognizes that religious nationalisms today are developed as refuges of autonomous spaces, in opposition to a vast global system that is stripping nations of the ability to control their own religious, economic, political, and cultural spheres. (2008b, 76)

For us Sōma's work is not primarily reactionary; on the contrary, it stands in a line of continuity with the past. It is the continuation and re-awakening of a particular ethnoreligious Sinhala ideology. Globalization, largely a Western model of economic development, may have created a special role for Sōma, and it may have influenced the design of his campaign—but globalization did not create Sōma. As we noted previously, Sinhala Buddhist ethnoreligious nationalism was strong well before the modern world order came into being. Sōma's discourse was another attempt to preserve the hegemonic position of Sinhala Buddhism over the state of Lanka. His intervention was timely in light of actual (the LTTE) and perceived (globalization, the Norwegians, Federalist proposals, and the INGOs) threats. The key difference between Sōma and other Saṅgha activists was that instead of seeking state or political party sponsorship he created his own network of support. Instead of becoming "part of the ruling," Sōma desired to become "ruler" himself. Unlike many previous Saṅgha activists, Sōma did not have a team of people working with him but preferred to work alone, and presented himself as a self-proclaimed pedagogue, making his very person the agenda and agency of change. Venerable Gaṅgoḍawila Sōma symbolized the continuing contestation between worlds that is rapidly changing according to the logic of the market-based liberal democracy and between the inherently hegemonic ethnoreligious nationalism of the Sinhalas.

Venerable Athuraliyē Rathana (1966–)

Early life and activism

The 1983 ethnic pogrom against Tamils living in southern Lanka, believed to have been state-sponsored, produced at least two mutually reinforcing results. First, the Tamils came to believe that the state of Lanka was not only unwilling to protect their lives and property but would also use any opportunity to unleash terror against them. With this belief came the conviction that the only route to safety was to support the separatist LTTE and its armed struggle. Second, the majority of Sinhalas, especially in the South, and especially those with influence on state policies, came to believe that Tamil political demands had become a serious threat to be defeated at any cost, including heavy military action. The Muslims and the Tamils of Indian origin were caught in the middle of the dispute, often forced to take sides without much free will. While there was a minority of moderates on both sides of the divide, they either had too little influence or remained silent. In 1983, Venerable Athuraliyē Rathana was a student monk whose university entrance exam had been delayed due to the unrest in the country.

Rathana was born to a working class family in which his mother was the breadwinner (Abesekara 2010). His upbringing meant that he was aware of social inequality from childhood onward. Athuraliya is one of the poorest villages in the southern Mātara district, an area saturated with both the nationalist Maoism of the JVP and the traditional leftist politics led by the Communist Party (CP) of Lanka. One reason for this extra influence could be the fact that the founder and leader of the CP, medical doctor S. A. Wickramasinghe, was born in Athuraliya. It appears that poverty, the desire to collect merit and the caste basis of the Amarapura sect, were key factors in Rathana's decision to enter the Saṅgha. His keen interest in philosophy and reading won him a place at the Perādenya, the most respected university in Lanka.

Unlike Rāhula and Sōma, who were drawn into politics by their social contexts, Rathana established himself as a political activist early in his university career. By 1985, the effects of the government's liberal restructuring of the economy provoked protests, with Lanka's universities and higher education centres serving as bases of protest (DeVotta 1998; Oberst 1985; Shastri 2009; Warnapala 1979). The student body, especially in Pērādeniya, was divided into two key factions: one that was more internationalist in nature and that supported or was sympathetic to the separatist Tamil nationalism, and another composed of Sinhala national-

Figure 5. Venerable Athuraliyē Rathana.

ists controlled by the JVP. Due to his upbringing in Athuraliya and his own experiences at university, Rathana was initially closer to the former. During this time, he became friendly with a number of Tamil graduates who while not LTTE supporters argued for a Tamil socialism in the north and Sinhala socialism in the south. Rathana had adopted a middle ground on these political issues, leaving him in the position of being a trusted member of many groups who were otherwise opposed to each other. Yet the increasing level of LTTE violence by the end of the eighties and the equally bloody second JVP uprising in 1988–1989 forced Rathana and his contemporaries to pursue alternatives. During this time, Champika Ranawaka, an engineering graduate from the University of Moratuwa, "had become a close friend and political associate to Rathana." Ranawaka ultimately emerged as an extreme Sinhala ethno-nationalist and had a deep influence on Rathana's political life (Abesekara 2010, 33).

ජනතා මිතුරෝ—*Janathā Mithuro: Friends of the People*

By the end of the 1980s, after a decade of harsh experiments with massive social and structural adjustments, it became clear that the policy of liberal market-based development had failed in Lanka (DeVotta 2002; Moore 1990; Stokke 1997). The traditional argument that liberal economic policies with authoritarian rule will bring social and economic prosperity in a short span of time and a stable democracy was proven wrong in Lanka. Extended development projects such as the Mahāväli Irrigation followed a liberal economic model, largely based on Thatcherism, and did not benefit Lanka. The militaristic approach to the challenge posed by the LTTE in the north, the forced Indo-Lanka Accord, and the subsequent arrival of the Indian Peace Keeping Force all alienated the Sinhala masses, creating a complex political situation that could not find any immediate resolution within the available political discourses. Observers agree that this was a crucial era for Lanka's modern polity (Dunham and Jayasuriya 2001; Goodhand, Korf and Spencer 2010; Goodhand and Gunasinghe 2004). The uncertainty created a vacuum within Sinhala society, providing an opportunity for Sinhala Buddhist ethnoreligious nationalism to offer itself as an answer.

Rathana and Ranawaka invented a program that capitalized on the volatility of the socio-political situation. They gained some grassroots experience by working with local and international human rights groups such as the *Mauvarungē Peramuna: Mothers Front*[21] and Amnesty International. Realizing the limitations of these attempts and looking for a method to appeal to a wider audience, they launched "ජනතා මිතුරෝ" *Janathā Miturō*—JM or Friends of the People—a new political organization for university students to become activists and messengers amongst the rural citizens and initiate a new discussion on indigenous democracy. By this time, an intense discussion on the need to develop an indigenous democracy was on-going among the urban élites thanks to the work of neo-Sinhala nationalists such as Professor Nalin De Silva and linguistic activist Gunadasa Amarasēkara. Their "ජාතික චින්තනය" *Jāthika Chinthanaya*—National Cognizance Forum—propagated a search for a localized yet modern ethno-nationalist identity in politics and culture (Bastian 2009; DeVotta 2007; Edrisinha 2005; Hennayake 2006). Rathana, with the help of Ranawaka, captured the imagination of the Saṅgha reformists and developed it in an original way by taking the political discourse to the rural masses.

Rathana, like his predecessors, exploited the traditional Saṅgha method of barefooted mendicancy in order to galvanize his followers and popularize his motives. He travelled in rural villages addressing crowds including unemployed youth without higher education. These rural communities had never experienced this kind of top-down recognition and appreciation expressed by a learned, graduate Saṅgha who was visiting their humble dwellings in order to teach them. This was in total contrast to the experience of contemporary power politics in most of rural

21. *Mothers Front* was a project supported by international human rights groups in order to encourage and empower the mothers of victims of the 1988–1989 JVP uprising (De Alwis 2002; Goodhand, Hulme and Lewer 2000).

Lanka. Rathana was imitating Buddha's methods and the Theravādin tradition of reciprocal dependency and benefit but with a radical difference: Instead of the otherworldly dhamma, Rathana's message was very much of this world, based on his ethnicity, his Sinhala Buddhism, and of course the need to protect the land of Buddha. Within a very short period, the JM was challenging the hegemony held by the JVP in rural politics, especially in the deep south of the Mātara district, Rathana's home base. The growth of this movement was such that it managed to publish a monthly tabloid, *Asipatha*—The sword blade. Rathana projected himself as the key public figure of JM while Ranawaka was the ideologue and the editor of the newspaper. JM soon registered as a political party in Lanka, giving clear signals of the movement's interest in widening the existing power politics. The political landscape in Lanka until then had witnessed all kinds of divisions based on class, territory, language, ethnicity and caste, but JM reflected the beginning of a new force: an aggressive and exclusive form of Sinhala Buddhist ethnoreligious nationalism organized in the shape of a recognized political party led by a Saṅgha.

From Janathā Mithuro to සිහල උරුමය *(Sihala Urumaya)*

JM changed over time, adopting various names such as *Sinhala Weeravidhana* (SW)—Heroes Front of Sinhalas, *Sinala Urumaya* (SU)—Heritage of the Sinhalas, and finally the present *Jātika Hela Urumaya* (JHU) (Abeysekara 2004; Bastin 2009). The last transformation towards the current JHU reflected an ideological transition from a combination of nationalism and socialism to ethno-nationalism. Of course, Sinhala politics had always been defined and fought in terms of identities and ideologies. However, the JM gained a strategic advantage by building their political platform on the concept of an "indigenous democracy." In the absence of any major financial, social and ideological capital, JM turned towards Sinhala Buddhist doctrine and at least in its public discourse argued that adopting a Theravādin morality was the only way of improving society. Chandrika Bandaranaike came to power in 1994 on the promise of liberalism and peacebuilding and thereby changed the social context within which JM was operating. Most of the activists and nationalist elements that had supported JM as an act of protest now rallied around a new government that promised a negotiated peace settlement with the LTTE. For the general citizenry these years marked a period of hope (Bartholomeusz 1999b; Samarasinghe 1994; Schaffer 1995). However, as noted earlier, the peace promise failed by April 1995, nine months after it was made. The actions of the LTTE created fear and frustration among rural people who were hoping for a quick peace settlement. With the committed leadership of Rathana and Ranawaka, the previously scattered elements of JM launched their politics under a new party banner:

සිහල උරුමය *Sihala Urumaya* (SU), Heritage of Sinhalas, in order to attract those who were disappointed by the failure of the peace process. SU essentially became a political alternative for the ultra-Sinhalas. Many opposition groups, fearing that Chandrika would make constitutional changes paving the way for power-sharing arrangements with the Tamils, began to rally around and support the SU. With growing strength, the SU organized numerous protest rallies and very significantly made inroads in the greater Saṅgha fraternity, mobilizing the support of respected Saṅgha for their political agenda. It was in this context that influential Saṅgha such as Walpola Rāhula, Paravaherē Paññānanda (vice chancellor of Southern Ruhuna university), and Palipāne Chandananda, (the Saṅgha chief of the powerful Asgiriya chapter), emerged as leaders who challenged the power-sharing proposal, nicknamed as "the package."

The 1999 LTTE attack on the highly fortified strategic Elephant Pass led to the highest death toll in a single battle; the LTTE also captured some heavy weaponry from the SLA, creating a dramatic sense of fear and insecurity in the south (Murthy 2000; Oberst 1992). The LTTE were relentless in their bloody campaign and used a suicide bomber in an attempt to assassinate CBK during her campaign for a second term. She survived but lost sight in one eye, and won the election with a reduced majority. Her weakened position enabled the SU to promote their agenda, demanding a full military solution to the war. Rāhula and Sōma, in contrast, did not—at least not in public—propose the total annihilation of the LTTE as a final solution to the crisis, but Rathana used his protest marches to openly demand a "military solution." In one such protest, he managed to organize a "fast unto death" by Venerable Hädigalle Vimalasāra under the famous Bo tree in the centre of the commercial area of Pettah. Vimalasāra was a respected senior monk, and the public fast soon turned into a very emotional campaign against Chandrika's rule.

With these demonstrations, Rathana clearly moved beyond his mendicant life and internationalist ideologies. Instead, he became the new symbol of a militant form of ethnoreligious nationalism. The emotional and extremely nationalist opposition mounted by the SU eroded the image of the already weakened Chandrika government. Nevertheless, in the parliamentary election of 2000, SU only won a single seat, based on less than 2% of the national vote. The continued mismanagement of the economy, the micro-management style of the president, and the military successes of the LTTE, at huge material and human cost to the Lanka Army, continued to weaken the government from within. At the height of the internal political disagreements regarding the question of how the LTTE should be approached, the Lanka Muslim Congress, which for a considerable time had been demanding that their political issues be addressed, broke off from the ruling alliance, forcing the president to dissolve parliament and call a new election less than eight months after the previous one. As expected, the ruling UPFA then lost to the UNP opposition. In a complex outcome, SU did not win a single seat, gaining less than 55,000 votes. The election was marred by violent incidents. The victory of the UNP was attributed to the promise that it would negotiate a peace settlement with the LTTE and thereby establish the preconditions for an economic recovery. The UNP's programme was a "Business for Peace" model similar to projects operating in South Africa and Northern Ireland. Many minority parties, including the Muslim Congress, backed the UNP. The rather poor performance by SU was largely due to the island-wide "camping for peace" campaign launched by a group of civic organizations, of which many received funding by international non-governmental organizations (Höglund and Piyarathne 2009; EU 2002).[22] This campaign destabilized the popular support the SU had enjoyed for some time.

The UNP immediately launched an aggressive privatization program, which was perceived as favouring a small Colombo-based business community who traditionally supported the UNP (Bastian 2011; Venugopal 2008), provoking hostile reactions in the rural areas of the country. Moreover, the promised "peace dividend" did not materialize. Instead, with the help of the Norwegians, the government hurriedly signed a Ceasefire Agreement (CFA), which was widely perceived to be in favour of the LTTE.

These developments disturbed the Sinhalas, particularly the armed forces and the Saṅgha community. Soon the UNP became unpopular amidst a sense that Christian white foreigners led by the Norwegians controlled politics in Lanka and that the international involvement somehow gave legitimacy to the separatist LTTE. This was exactly the situation Sōma had warned against. The ruling UNP could not justify its soft attitude towards the LTTE, which was openly violating the CFA. The continued fear that the LTTE was using the CFA to collect more arms and the hope that she could gain more support in a new election led Chandrika to dismiss the parliament in 2004. The 2004 election gave Rathana and his SU a new opportunity to promote their cause. Rathana and Ranawaka campaigned under a different name—ජාතික හෙළ උරුමය (JHU)—and were determined to become the kingmakers of the island and to alter the existing power structures. Unlike many other Saṅgha activists, who let the context shape their agendas, Rathana became an agenda setter. In this sense, Rathana may symbolize the ultimate product of the kind of "Saṅgha heritage" defended by Rāhula. He became the embodiment of the political Saṅgha that Rāhula and Sōma had envisioned.

22. See the full report by the EU Election Monitoring Team: http://www.eueomsrilanka.org/FR2001.pdf. Accessed on 15 March 2010.

Rathana and ජාතික හෙළ උරුමය*—Jāthika Helà Urumaya (JHU)*

The 2004 election was a historic event: for the first time in history, an all-Buddhist-monk party nominated 200 monks for 225 seats. The subsequent election of nine Saṅgha as full-time politicians was of great symbolic significance for the entire Theravāda Buddhist culture in South and Southeast Asian states. The election was fought over the failed peace process, over proposals for changing the constitution towards a more federal arrangement, and most dramatically, over the possibility of establishing a *dharmarājya* (a righteous state) through a "Buddhist Democracy." Rathana was one of the key JHU members, and articulated the JHU vision better than anyone else in the Saṅgha fraternity.

Of course, this was not the first time that a Saṅgha stood for an election in Lanka. Venerable Migeṭṭuvattē Jinananda, a contemporary of Rāhula, was a candidate for the Colombo Municipal Council in 1943, five years before independence, but was not elected. In 1957, Wëlletoṭa Paññadassi contested for a village council position in the Mātara District and became Lanka's first elected Saṅgha in any governing political body. However, these elections were mostly symbolic and ultimately did not empower the Saṅgha community; they were primarily local events. After the 1971 JVP uprising and subsequent power struggles, the Saṅgha became more ambitious in setting themselves political goals. In 1977 Venerable Pinikahane Saddhatissa was the first Saṅgha to contest for a seat in parliament for Karandeniya but he too was unsuccessful.

In 1992, Venerable Baddegama Samitha, who like Saddhatissa was from the Galle district and an active member of the LSSP (socialists), contested for the Baddegama village council and won easily. He was one of the very rare Saṅgha to argue continuously argue for a more humane, compassionate approach to the ethnic conflict in the country; he also supported the idea of power-sharing. In 2001, he successfully won a seat in parliament and became the first Saṅgha Member of Parliament. He was part of Chandrika's coalition government and supported the peace process with conviction and compassion. However, the continued terror attacks by the LTTE diminished the credibility of advocates of moderate policies. Furthermore, the JVP/JHU anti-peace campaign in the south of Lanka was effective in leading voters towards a more ethno-centric position. Accordingly, in 2004, Samitha was defeated.

A few months prior to the April 2004 election, the Sihala Urumaya went through a series of internal conflicts. The key issue in these debates was the extent to which the Saṅgha should be participating directly in politics. Rathana and Ranawaka were uncompromising in that they wanted the Saṅgha involved in every political campaign; they wanted the Saṅgha to stand for election, to be elected, and then to use the political process to advance their cause. In light of such internal disagreements, the party eventually had to be dissolved, leading to the creation of the new "ජාතික හෙළ උරුමය" JHU party. The JHU was based on a radical, even more ethnicized version of Rāhula's Urumaya ideology, advancing Rāhula's ideas to their radical conclusions and thus adopting an openly anti-peace and racist rhetoric. Rathana and Ranawaka's campaign exploited every known Buddhist cultural practice, from using Buddhist vocabulary to organizing temple *pujās.* They claimed their effort was a "පාරමිතා පෙරහැර" (a demonstration of Buddhist virtues), "අධිෂ්ඨාන පූජාව" (an offering of determined efforts), "ධාර්මික පෙළහර" (a demonstration of righteousness) and finally all this was to achieve a "ධර්මිෂ්ඨ රාජ්‍යය" (a righteous state). Compared to some of the newer Saṅgha like Omaple Sōbitha, Ellawala Medhalankara and the charismatic Uduvë Dhammāloka, Rathana did not take on a prominent role in public rallies. He was the national strategist who designed the campaign. Until the 2004 elections, it was common for political parties in the south to use the Saṅgha for purposes of propaganda and mobilization, but for the first time in 2004 the Saṅgha themselves were mobilizing every aspect of popular Buddhism to enhance their popularity through the promise of creating a righteous land. They started every public meeting with a long period of *"pirith"* chanting. On the nomination and registration day at the national election commission office, they performed a *Bodhi Pūjā.* During their propaganda rallies, they arranged for the elderly, especially the Upāsikās, to chant "Sādhu, Sādhu, and Sādhu" as Buddhists would do in a temple.

Through these public demonstrations of popular Buddhist practices, Rathana initiated a process of "Buddhicizing the election atmosphere." Given that this process was initiated by the Saṅgha, it conquered political life with unquestionable authority. Under the JHU banner, the Saṅgha were using their ceremonial knowledge to mobilize the voters—a practice that was not used by the SU. The SU was primarily reacting to the LTTE separatist threat, whereas the JHU's agitation was more comprehensively directed towards gaining power. Among its targets were also both the established and the new Christian churches. Their anti-Christian position was coupled with a strong anti-Western rhetoric. Unsurprisingly, these anti-Christian agitations reached their climax after the sudden death of Sōma, which the SU and pre-JHU elements presented as the result of an international Christian conspiracy.

Moreover, the SU and the JHU can also be distinguished in terms of the caste backgrounds of both the supporting laity and the key Saṅgha. While key leaders of the SU were from a high caste, Rathana, it is believed, belonged to the Vananthannē (jewellery-making) caste, considered to be one of the lowest. Rathana's activities showed that he had no inhibition against using Buddhist ceremonial rituals for mobilizing voters and using the status of the Saṅgha to impose his political agenda on the ruling élites.

The JHU won seven seats in the 2004 election and obtained two additional seats due to the fact that they received 552,724 votes (5.97% of the national vote). The votes represented a tenfold increase over the SU's 2001 election result. The JHU acted as an independent opposition party in the parliament for a while, contributing to some intense verbal and at times even physical clashes with the others parties represented in parliament. Eventually the JHU joined the ruling party for the 2005 presidential election in order to support the hardliner Mahinda Rajapakse, who campaigned on an ultra-nationalist platform promising to defeat the LTTE militarily.

Analysts are divided on the role and influence of Rathana's JHU. For example, Mahinda Deegalle commented:

> I began writing this paper with reservations about the JHU's political ambitions and real intentions of entering into the Sri Lankan Parliament. Once I read their literature and reflected upon the current political crisis in Sri Lanka, I can see their importance and value in democratic politics at a crucial juncture of Sri Lankan history. On the one hand, as a minority party, the JHU can raise issues dealing with religion in Parliament to safeguard Buddhist and Sinhala interests; on the other, their activities in the legislature with vested interest on the Sinhala and Buddhist communities can be perceived by others in future as an inhibiting force for peace in Sri Lanka. Although the members of the JHU are portrayed in overseas media as nationalists and extremists, their current standing as a nationalist voice has also to be interpreted in the current volatile ethno-politics in Sri Lanka. (2004, 99)

However, these assessments, according to which the JHU had the potential to become a force for peace and a voice of the Sinhala nation turned out to be self-delusions. The JHU unreservedly supported the military campaign against the LTTE even when the huge civilian costs became obvious. Rathana, as the leader of JHU, became the most hardened supporter in parliament for the military campaign. He explained his position as follows: "Day by day we are weakening them [the LTTE] with our military force. Talk can come later."(*The Economist* 2007, 26) The ideology of the JHU and its support for the military campaign concretized the *Mahāvaṃsa* thinking that killing Tamils was an acceptable price for the protection of the Dhammadīpa. Rathana became the symbol of a neo-nationalist "*Buddhatvā,*" similar to the *Hinduttvā* of the Indian Sadhus, i.e. an ethnoreligious nationalism that seeks to become the conceptual framework for redefining the state and its subjects (Sarkar 1996). Rathana continues to contribute to the construction of this *Sinhalattvā* and defends it as the core of the Lankan identity.

Democracy vs. moral authority

In 2004, after ten years of Chandrika/UPFA leadership, the island had seen more LTTE violence than at any other time in history, provoking the Sinhala south to look for new political options. Already the SU was keen to exploit this political context, but it was the remarkable transformation of the SU into the JHU—an all Buddhist monks' party—that was decisive not only for the development of Sinhala nationalist politics but also for the wider context. According to Mahinda Deegalle

> the most recent radical development that occurred in Lankan Theravāda monasticism in the year 2004 [was the] the historic event of nine Buddhist monks becoming professional politicians in the Lankan Parliament. By any standard, 2004 is the watershed in the entire history of the Theravāda Buddhist monastic world in South and Southeast Asia. For the first time, a newly formed Buddhist monk political party identified as the JHU (National Sinhala Heritage Party) fielded over 200 Buddhist monk candidates for the parliamentary election held on 2 April 2004 to elect 225 Members of Parliament. (2004, 83)

Among the key factors that inspired the imagination of the largely semi-urban Sinhalas and helped them embrace the idea of a Saṅgha-led political order was the strength of Rathana's "morality" argument, which he underlined by incorporating Buddhist rituals into the political campaign. Sinhala history from the days of the *Mahāvaṃsa* onwards showed how the Saṅgha exercised leadership by using Theravādin norms, rituals, and traditions in order to legitimize or de-legitimize the state rulers. Under the leadership of Sorbonne-educated Chandrika and her outwardly secular "liberality," the state had deliberately failed to continue the tradition of recognizing the Saṅgha and giving them a kind of political legitimacy. In what we may call the Lankan "cultural consciousness," Chandrika was not the official and demonstrative "patron" of the Saṅgha, thus provoking Rathana and his team to deploy a strategy of "ritual displacement." As defined by Anagnost, the "politics of ritual displacement involve the contestation of ritual space with the aim of controlling this space and of undermining the moral credibility of the opponent" (1994, 221). Rathana challenged the state authority with the ultimate goal of transferring power back to the central religious authority in the country—the Saṅgha.

The 2004 elections were fought over a number of issues, such as peace, liberal democracy, economic recovery, and the future of the Sinhalas. Yet all these debates were secondary to the "culture gap" articulated and manifested by the JHU, who gained the political advantage by promoting a traditional yet extreme interpretation of Buddhist ethno-nationalism. Despite the state controlled media, the highly organized JVP (then a partner of the ruling party) failed to win the sub-urban nationalist mind to the extent that the JHU did. Nothing quite compared to the images, broadcast on an almost daily basis, of a group of 300–400 Saṅgha walking silently in the heavy rain and burning sun towards their meeting places.

How could Rathana inspire a country that had seen the decay of the Saṅgha, the defeat of the military and the repeated failures of political élites? In general, in the analysis of Western political science, democratic authority is always a contested notion. The ability to acquire and maintain power through democratic support and access to resources becomes the "art of government," but contemporary Western political science is limited in explaining the role of religion in this process. In Lanka, governance is historically legitimized by moral and socio-religious forces often defined by the hegemony of the majoritarian mindset. Scholars such as Rodney Hall (1999) and Muthiah Alagappa (1995) have demonstrated that this was the case also in feudal Europe, where the legitimacy of the secular rule was defined in a framework revolving around the notion of "faith."

As we have already argued, by introducing a cosmological order superior to the secular social and political order, the Buddha created a system in which these parallel processes were to be recognized and harmonized. There is a cosmic order that ultimately governs human society and its politics, and in Theravādin tradition, this cosmological order must be concretized by human action. Thus, these two orders can be harmonized only when the "this-worldly" order is arranged and organized in accordance with the "other-worldly" order. The epicentre of a Theravādin theory of governance is Buddha (or his relic), with the king/ruler, as the protector, next in line, followed by the rest of the powers, including minor gods, their deities and the devotees in hierarchical order. Roshan Wijeyeratne has explained in detail this "galactic" Theravādin cosmology, which provides an infrastructure for power politics in Lanka (2013, 2004, 2003, 2000, 1998). In light of this analysis, it is not surprising that even within the last kingdom of the Sinhalas in Kandy, its kings, regional rulers, and other officials were arranged in this order around the Tooth Relic of Buddha.

In Theravāda Buddhism the Bodhisattva, who is the one on the journey towards becoming the next Buddha, could be incarnated as a king or ruler. It is for this reason that in Theravāda states religion, rule, and ritual establish a relationship between rulers and the Saṅgha, and it is this nexus that had broken in recent years in Lanka for at least two reasons. First, Chandrika, as mentioned, failed to recognize the role and authority of the Saṅgha; and second, the ever-present separatist threat to the Sinhala state as well as Chandrika's failure to defeat it. The government seemed to have broken the traditional bond between rulers and Saṅgha, thus allowing Rathana to denounce the government as decadent and illegitimate. In her ideological stubbornness, Chandrika ignored the fact that while political authority in Lanka comes directly from the citizenry, the survival and legitimacy of authority are directly dependent on the endorsement granted by the Saṅgha. Rathana did not fail to remind his society of the ancient code of conduct followed even by non-Buddhist kings (including the Christian British rulers), which exhorted those in power to look after the "religion of Buddha, Saṅgha and its people." Until Chandrika, every political leader of Lanka had, though at times unwillingly, played this role of the protector of the "religion of Buddha, Saṅgha and its people" in order to have his/her authority legitimized.

Rathana and the war against the LTTE

There was nothing ambiguous about Rathana's political aims and ambitions. He explained: "the Saṅgha have entered the arena of politics in order to ensure the protection of the Buddhist heritage and values, which have been undermined for centuries."[23] Prior to the elections, he campaigned unceasingly for four objectives:

1. Chandrika's proposal to share power with the LTTE-led Tamil polity was clearly one of his primary targets. For Rathana, the land of the Sinhalas belongs to the Sinhalas, who had been treated unfairly for the last seven centuries. He argued that giving equal rights to the non-Sinhalas, who constituted less than twenty-four per cent of the population, was in fact an injustice to the Sinhala majority.
2. He promoted the idea of the total defeat and destruction of the LTTE by military means. In his worldview, the LTTE epitomized the ancient rivalry of Hindu Brahmanism against Buddhism, now made even more intense because the Buddhist enemies were influenced by the Western ruthlessness towards Buddhist people and their culture. Therefore, there simply could not be any negotiations while the LTTE existed.
3. Rathana, building on Sōma's legacy, also wanted to reverse the growth of the evangelical churches in Lanka. He argued that evangelizing rural Buddhist villages would be a step towards the destruction of the Sinhala Buddhist culture. The norms and habits of the Christian West were a direct threat to the existence of Buddhism and its culture. In response to this threat, he mobilized—often very violently—the rural Saṅgha in whose areas new churches were being built.
4. To a lesser degree and priority, Rathana demanded that the national economy be restructured in order to comply with the requirements of an indigenous, nationalist economic policy: a Lanka model of *Bhūmi Putra*[24]—giving priority to the local capital of Sinhala Buddhist investors.

With the 2004 victory, Rathana became a firm part of the contempo-

23. *Daily Mirror,* 19 February 2004; and Spotlight on Lanka, 8(25), 20 February 2004, at http://xi.pair.com/isweb3/spot/c0825.html. Accessed on March 23, 2011.

24. Article 153 of the Malaysian constitution guarantees special privileges to the ethnic Malays in providing quotas, special discounts and higher marks at exams—an affirmative action favoring the ethnic Malays, who are referred to as Bhūmiputra or Sons of the Soil.

rary politics of Lanka. Once in Parliament he proceeded to implement his goals. He was most persistent in developing a political justification for the total war against the LTTE. In May 2009, less than five years after the JHU had entered parliament, Lanka totally defeated the LTTE, killing all its top ranking officers, including its elusive leader Prabhakaran, who for the past thirty years had humiliated the Sinhalas. This victory was imagined, campaigned for, supported, and achieved by the JHU, a fact that elevated Rathana into the rank of a contemporary Sinhala Saṅgha who had lived, preached, and used his Buddhist identity and position to defend, at all costs, Sinhala Theravādian ethno-nationalist politics. He reaffirmed that in Lanka, peace and order could only come from the historical process whereby the Saṅgha and the Lankan polity legitimize each other. Furthermore, Rathana and his generation of JHU Saṅgha once again disproved the Western-colonial construct of Buddhism and war as mutually exclusive phenomena.

Rathana was often referred as the "war monk of Lanka" in the Western media, a title that accurately reflected his advocacy of a total military solution to the conflict with the Tamils. He was included in a list of the "world's worst religious leaders" compiled by the journal *Foreign Policy*.[25] Undoubtedly influential in cultivating the military mind-set in the present Sinhala society, he has no regrets that his "victory" may have come at too great a cost. He wanted to achieve the "total destruction of the LTTE", and given the priority of the goal, "civilian causalities should be considered unavoidable collateral damage and a necessary cost."[26]

Conclusion

The Saṅgha-led political protest in Lanka grows from a long-standing tradition with pre-modern roots. As we have seen in Chapter 2, changing contexts and themes have generated successive waves of Saṅgha resistance. Contemporary Saṅgha activists have exclusively come from southern Lanka, from different caste backgrounds, patronized by different political parties and caste conscious nationalist laity. What started as a protest against the Kandy, Goyigama-caste Saṅgha hegemony, eventually turned against the non-Buddhists and non-Sinhalas.

All these waves have been driven by two primary ideological notions. The first is that the Sinhalas are the custodians of pure Buddhism and that the island of Lanka belongs to the Buddhists and cannot be shared. The second derives from the first in that it considers all interventions—from the inside or from the outside—that appear to threaten the above foundations of the Saṅgha self-understanding as hostile enemy actions that call into question

25. See http://www.foreignpolicy.com/articles/2008/04/06/the_list_the_worlds_worst_religious_leaders.

26. Interview with the author, 23 June 2011, at his *Sadaham Sevana Vihāra*, in Colombo 8.

the eternal future of pure Buddhism and the Sinhala race in this world.

Every intervention—regardless of how minor or well meaning—is thus bound to be perceived as an existential threat. The Saṅgha self-understanding responds to the outside world by raising the stakes as high as possible. Every outside influence becomes a matter of life and death—and not just the life and death of individuals, or of a people, but of a cosmology, of life itself. This uncompromising attitude will inevitably turn into a self-fulfilling prophecy in which the very opposition it encounters confirms the essentially hostile approach it takes to "otherness." This is the reason why for the Saṅgha mind-set, the federal proposal was not at all a mere "political" proposal. It was a direct attack on their way of life. Well-meaning Westerners eager to bring "peace" to the country have failed to understand why their proposals were not only ineffective but also fuelled the conflict. To offer "federalism" to the Saṅgha as a "solution" was like pouring oil on fire. The dynamics of the Saṅgha self-understanding, worldview, and the historical dynamics of the wave, in which it manifested itself throughout millennia, are the reasons for the failure of federalism in Lanka. Thus, Lanka is an important case to consider as scholars and practitioners of contemporary politics continue to suggest federalism as a solution to problems of fragmentation and conflict in societies throughout the world (Iff 2013; Mehretu 2012; Seymour and Gagnon 2012).

Walpola Rāhula, Gaṅgoḍawila Sōma and Athuraliyē Rathana are only three contemporary Saṅgha who interpreted, lived and disseminated Sinhala Buddhist themes in their own context based on their individual experience and worldview. Both Rāhula and Sōma constructed and left behind a legacy of their own, while Rathana's lasting influence is yet to be seen. The three Saṅgha considered in this chapter in many ways continued the tradition of the elders (Theravāda) in Sinhala Buddhism and the ideological genealogy of their Saṅgha fraternity. From the point of view of secularization theories, the Saṅgha influence appears as an outdated outlier, as a phenomenon not to be taken seriously, an unfortunate remnant of the past. However, in a society such as Lanka, the Saṅgha influence and power is real. As we have seen, ignoring this reality—even if with good intentions—will lead to more violence, more hatred, and more bloodshed. It would be extremely important to explore to what extent the frequently reported "revival" of religion in other parts of the globe may be informed by a similarly deep-rooted dynamics.

The comparative political science frameworks are limited because they are marked by a large conceptual "blind spot" regarding the peculiar dynamics of the ideology of the Saṅgha and its concrete historical and contemporary manifestations. One of the main reasons for this oversight is that the underlying assumptions of Western political science are implicitly and sometimes explicitly normative. The focus is on the recognition of minority rights, liberal democratization, and multi-cultural universalism. From this perspective, the Saṅgha are simply overlooked and yet the Lankan polity co-evolves with them. The Saṅgha did not disappear with the advent of modernity, they have embraced some features of modernity and used them as tools for their agitation—e.g. mass communication media, globalized diaspora—but they were used in order to fight the very principles of modernity. The need to understand forces as if the Saṅgha is not just an academic exercise, but is also and most importantly a political need. The Western/outside world will not be able to meaningfully interact with these societies unless they understand and in some sense recognize the existence of these forces.

Popular Western scholarship tends to observe societies in terms of dichotomies and binary oppositions such as e.g. religious/secular, traditional/modern, and authoritarian/democratic etc. However, the Saṅgha are a good example of a political force that does not fit into these categories. They bridge the past and the present; they are religious but operate in the secular, and their role is not questioned by the majority of the populace. Because the political tools that Westerners use are modelled on such flawed dichotomies, they remain not only ineffective but also indeed counterproductive. It will thus be instructive to look at one of these concepts and tools—federalism—in order to see how exactly it failed to respond to the political reality in Lanka and how, if at all, it can be adjusted and possibly re-defined in order to become more sensitive to the religious, social and political reality of Lanka.

— 5 —

Federalism and Sinhala Buddhist Nationalism

Introduction

The previous chapters reconstructed the Sinhala Saṅgha mind-set in order to understand the Saṅgha as key actors within the Lankan polity. We noted how they not only rejected federalism as a solution to the separatist war in Lanka but also interpreted it as a threat undermining Lanka's unique position as the designated home of Buddhism, just as the war itself threatened the territorial integrity of island. The Saṅgha fought against federalism with the same motives that made them engage in and support military action against the Tamil Tigers. This dynamic remained largely unnoticed by well-meaning Western observers and activists. In this chapter, we will explore the Saṅgha opposition to federalism in detail, but instead of approaching the subject from the point of view of the Saṅgha, we will begin by reviewing the contents of the federal proposition and the trajectory of the federal debate in Lanka. As we noted in the introduction to this book, there were many good reasons why many voices within and outside Lanka would have considered federalism to be an appropriate and promising solution to the ethnic violence in the country. While the extreme position of the Saṅgha eventually proved decisive, it is instructive to trace the fate of federalism in Lanka because it enables us to shed further light on the Saṅgha and on federalism as a conflict resolution tool. As the federalism project failed in Lanka, what can we learn from this failure for the future implementation of federalism in other divided and war-torn countries?

Defining federalism

Academics, political activists, and leaders agree that federal arrangements are the best available democratic solution for societies that experience fragmentation, division and conflict (L. Anderson 2004, 2007a, 2007b; Erk and Anderson 2009; Burgess and Gagnon 2010;

Burgess and Pinder 2007; Kincaid and Stenburg 2011; Kincaid 2009, 2011; Barnes 2001; He, Galligan, and Inoguchi 2007; Hicks 2011; Horowitz 1993; Lijphart 2004, 1992; McGarry and O'Leary 1993; Roeder and Rothchild eds. 2005; Simeon 2009; Tillin 2007; Diamond 2008, 2002; Kymlicka 2009, 2007, 2005, 2000; Taylor *et al.* 2011). Federalism is evoked in the context of a wide range of conflicts including ethnic, religious, linguistic, and cultural conflicts. It is suggested as a solution during various stages of these conflicts, including pre-and post-conflict management, resolution and transformation.

There is a vast literature on federalism and the way it is defined.[1] Valerie Earle commented that federalism is marked by "infinite variety in theory and practice" (1968). William H. Stewart (1984) listed 326 varieties of federalism. Daniel J. Elazar, the chief editor of *Publius*, argued in the journal's first issue:

> Federalism, as we understand the concept in its political form, is related to the whole problem of the concentration, diffusion and, most particularly, the sharing of power in political and social systems. Federal principles grow out of the idea that free men can freely enter into lasting yet limited political arrangements to achieve common ends and protect certain rights while preserving their respective integrities. As the very ambiguity of the term "federal" reveals, federalism is concerned simultaneously with the diffusion of political power in the name of freedom and its concentration on behalf of energetic government. Institutionally, federalism is a form of political organization, which unites separate polities within an overarching political system so that all maintain their fundamental political integrity. It does so by distributing power among general and constituent governments in a manner designed to protect the existence and authority of all while enabling all to share in the system's decision-making and executing processes. In its most practical manifestations, the workings of federalism are reflected in the processes of intergovernmental relations and negotiated coordination among the general and constituent governments and the interests they represent.
>
> (Elazar 1971, 3)

In his much-quoted *Why Federations Fail* (1968), Thomas Franck noted:

> What this definitional problem suggests is not that a single, highly structured definition of federalism is needed. Rather it is that there be greater understanding of the nearly infinite number of variations that can be played on the federal theme and that the difficulties of engineering a union of nations only begins when the leaders agree to federate

1. For a list of recent literature, see http://www.pco-bcp.gc.ca/aia/index.asp?lang=eng&page=suggestions&doc=biblio/biblio-eng.htm and http://www.queensu.ca/iigr/pub/archive/bibliographies/pubBiblio/fedbio.pdf Accessed on Mar 10, 2010.

> and their subalterns sit down to work out what is too often called "the details." (Franck 1968, 169)

According to Burgess, "the study of federalism construed in its broadest sense is fraught with difficulties that are reflected in both theory and practice," and he goes on to elaborate:

> Part of the problem with studying federalism is that it is a microcosm of the problem with studying political science itself. Federalism deals simultaneously with fundamental moral questions as well as with amoral matter-of-fact issues. The former, like social diversity, individual, and collective identities, are highly charged emotional questions for many people while the latter involve the routine pursuit of economic profit and security and reflect for the most part calculated and dispassionate self-interest. The moral basis of federalism derives from certain inherent virtues such as respect, tolerance, dignity and mutual recognition, which lead to a particular form of human association, namely, the federal state or federation. The amoral foundation suggests that no such qualities inhere in federalism at all and that it is nothing more than a particular constitutional and/or political technique for achieving certain overarching goals such as territorial expansion or economic benefits and security. (Burgess 2006, 1)

One of the key questions, which surfaced already in our research and is highlighted by Burgess in the above quote, is the question of the normative core of federalism. Especially when it is introduced as a constitutional arrangement that is meant to manage diversity and to address possible conflicts, the indigenous political culture may consider the federal proposal as an alien imposition—the case of Lanka demonstrates this possibility. The fact is that whenever federalism is proposed, concrete people in concrete situations that are loaded with meaning propose it. Whether or not it constitutes in itself a "neutral" technique of power-sharing, as soon as it is "applied" to a concrete situation, it assumes a normative quality, which is reflected in the overall goals and ambitions of the political actors who become its advocates (or opponents). It is perhaps mostly in places where it is resisted, as in Lanka, that the normative dimension of federalism becomes obvious, raising the question of whether federalism itself originated from and reflects a particular set of ethical values contextualized in a political culture, which in turn may not be compatible with other political cultures. Elazar understands political culture as "the particular pattern of orientation to political action in which each political system is imbedded" (1966, 79). The expectation and delivery of politics, the nature and character of people who come forward to do politics and the policy outcomes are largely affected by this political culture, and federalism too is an expression of a particular political culture. Federalism, therefore, is not just a technical institutional arrangement; rather, it reflects the political aspirations—political virtues such as peace and justice-of a people.

It is well known, of course, that the historical origins of federalism are culturally specific. Wayne Baker emphasized the centrality of the notion of the "covenant" in federalism:

> The early federal idea and reality, as it developed from 1291 up to the sixteenth century, held the promise of the theological, political federalism that Heinrich Bullinger first formulated in Zürich in the 1520s and 1530s. [...] Combining his experience of living in a federal society with his perception of the biblical idea of the covenant, he developed a concept of the covenant that not only had theological meaning but also important social and political implications. In turn, this theological idea of federalism, as it developed more fully in the course of the sixteenth century, fed into and helped to create the modern political concept of federalism, especially in the thought of Althusius (Baker 1993, 20).

The covenantal basis of federalism extended to the Constitution of the United States:

> America's covenantal heritage inspired the public philosophy of federal liberty and the federal principle used to establish governments and political associations in colonial New England. The Puritans, as Tocqueville explained, created the bonds and the liberties of citizenship by their assent to eternal, transcendent principles, as well as by their consent to government. The principles of covenant ultimately provided the institutional and conceptual foundation of constitutional government, making America's federal democracy less vulnerable to possessive individualism and democratic despotism. (Allen 1998, 1)

The very history of the term, and the mutations it underwent because of its history, therefore suggest it is not a neutral technical label, but a political term with normative implications. Ronald Watt agrees:

> "Federalism" is basically not a descriptive but a normative term and refers to the advocacy of multi-tiered government combining elements of shared-rule and regional self-rule. It is based on the presumed value and validity of combining unity and diversity and accommodating, preserving and promoting distinct identities with a large political union. The essence of federalism as a normative principal is the perpetuation of both union and non-centralization at the same time. (2008, 6)

Karmis and Norman expressed the same idea from the point of view of citizenship:

> In its most general sense, federalism is an arrangement in which two or more self-governing communities share the same political space. Citizens of federal states (or super-states, as in the case of the European

Union) are members of both their subunit (sometimes called a province, canton, land or confusingly a state) and the larger federation as a whole.
(Karmis and Norman 2005, 1)

Our discussion of federalism in this chapter will take Watt's and Norman's definition as a guide, but we must stress that what exactly "federalism" meant—and to whom—in Lanka is an empirical question, not a theoretical stipulation.

Federalism without indigenous owners

As we have argued on several occasions throughout this book, federalism not only failed in Lanka; the federal proposal itself fuelled the conflict because it became a focal point for ethnic, religious and national agitation. Federalism came to symbolize, for the Saṅgha-led Sinhalas, everything that was wrong with ideas and practices that were not their own—practices, which they considered as threats, because the mere presence of difference reflected a departure from the unity and uniformity that their outlook and self-understanding demanded. In this section, we will briefly review some of the key reasons identified so far, as to why federalism came to play this role.

Political culture

The political culture reflected in the federal idea emphasizes bargaining and negotiation processes. There is nothing in the process itself; however, that guarantees a convergence of positions. For example, in the Norwegian-led negotiations, both parties for some time pretended to aim for a federal solution to the war. The LTTE demanded a Quebec-type federal devolution of powers as a minimum, while the Lankan government was not ready to agree even to a Pakistani-type federal arrangement as a maximum.[2] While both seemed to promote a federal solution, the range of options left enough room for a stalemate, and so they succeeded in deceiving the international community and the mediators. On paper, Chandrika's proposal for a union of five autonomous regions outlined a possible federal arrangement, but in practice no one believed that the proposal had any real chance of leading to a consensus among the conflicting parties especially the amongst the nationalist Sinhalas. Even the government's constitutional expert, Professor G. L. Peiris, who was the Minister of Constitutional Affairs and chief negotiator from 1994 to 2001, together with other architects of the proposals believed that it was "an excessive accommodation," which undermined the sovereignty of Lanka. In fact, while publicly displaying a liberal appreciation

2. For an introduction to the different types of federal governaces see Ronald L. Watts, Federalism, Federal political Systems, and Federations, *Annual Review of Political Science, 1998,* 1: 117–137.

for power-sharing, privately he expressed strong reservations. If there had been any chance that the proposals could have led somewhere, they would not have been made. As a discourse, therefore, federalism provided both parties with a playing field where they could hide their true positions and ambitions, while the well-meaning international community was eager to sustain the discourse in the mistaken hope that it had real substance. The situation seems to suggest that for the political culture of federalism to unfold, *it must already exist.* There are limits to the degree and nature of "political difference" that federalism can accommodate. Federalism only works where there is a willingness to share and thus to compromise. Where such willingness does not exist, or cannot be enforced, the discourse of federalism becomes a tool, which allows its users to hide their true intentions and manoeuvres. Even worse, where there is no will to compromise, external pressure may lead to a hardening of the underlying positions. The fact is that the federalist proposal in Lanka did not have any indigenous "owners."

Indigenous owners

The lack of indigenous ownership went hand in hand with the over-internationalization of the conflict. The Sinhalas perceived the international community and facilitators as pursuing their own interests, which were not necessarily in congruence with the interests of Sinhala Buddhism. During the period of 1994 to 2005, advocating federalism was very much the symbol of being "liberal" in Lanka—leading to various proposals such as the 1995 CBK proposal, the 2000 UPFA proposal, the 2003 ISGA proposal, and the 2004 PTOM proposals—but the Saṅgha and the majority of the Sinhalas came to consider the kind of liberal political culture that federalism seemed to manifest as a threat to their native culture. Moreover, the federal discourse was primarily concerned with question of peace and the ending of the war and thus partially ignored more substantial questions of justice. Whose peace should it be? The commitment of the international actors involved was looked at with suspicion. It is intriguing to observe that the many prominent supporters of the liberal peace projects and the many I/NGOs that not long ago wanted to be directly involved in the peace building process are no longer present in Lanka. Since the military conclusion of the conflict, neither Erick Solheim, Norway's Minister for International Development, the iconic figure representing the peace process, nor Yasushi Akashi, former UN Under-Secretary General and Japan's special peace envoy, have visited the island. The once-vibrant NGOs dedicated to promoting the peace process have disappeared as their foreign funding stopped. As a result, the Lankan government currently faces no external pressures to deal with the war victims, internally displaced persons, needs-based development, or to address wider issues such as the de-securitization of the North East or the downsizing of the swollen military, not to mention democratic and constitutional reforms that would include the respect for minority rights. Similarly, in spite of the 2012 March UN resolution, Lanka does not find it difficult to dismiss accusations of human rights violations and mass killings as part of an international conspiracy sustained by the Tamil diaspora. India's on-going involvement and its support for power-sharing arrangements reflect a tactical move aimed at satisfying Tamil Nadu sentiments. Similarly, the numerous visits of higher Indian officials to Lanka reflect India's concern with the growing Chinese influence in Lanka rather than with the situation of the Tamils. In the meantime, the Lankan government maintains a strong military presence in the Tamil areas. It seems that since the government's military victory, the agents of liberal peace have lost their sense of purpose in Lanka, which might suggest that with their well-meaning and flawed involvement in the "peace efforts" they responded to their own needs rather than the needs of the Lankan polity. These circumstances ensured that the religious, ethnic and nationalist forces could unite in their opposition to the federal proposal.

A pre-fab solution

The international debate on federalism in Lanka envisioned federalism as a normative extension of liberal governance. Initially, however, federalism was meant to end the war, to bring peace, which means it was a technical tool in the service of conflict mediation and resolution. Without indigenous ownership, the federal model implied in the peace process was a "mechanical" model, which if implemented would have amounted to an imposition of a template believed by its proponents to be of universal validity. In other words, the federal proposal in Lanka, embodying a distinct political culture, was always likely to be a purely "formal" proposal, which aimed at circumventing the intricacies of the Lankan situation precisely in order to achieve peace. Yet reduced to its "instrumentality" as a potential peacemaker, the federal idea failed to connect to the inner dynamics of the Lankan polity and to the self-understanding of any of its major actors. On the contrary, the emptiness of the proposed "formal," "mechanical" federalism made it an easy target for ethnoreligious nationalist agitation, thereby uniting the forces least interested in a resolution of the conflict based on the acceptance of "difference" in the name of peace. In other words, the federal discourse unleashed and elevated to the centre of political action precisely those forces it wanted and needed to contain.

Ignoring History

Throughout this book, we have emphasized the unique role that Lanka plays in the self-understanding of the Sinhalas and especially the Saṅgha as the home and "refuge" of pure Buddhism in the modern world as intended by Buddha himself. The political culture informed by this belief in Lanka as the manifestation of Buddhism in the world created both an informal and a formal structure whereby the kings and rulers on the one hand, and the Saṅgha on the other, mutually legitimized each other. It is this symbiotic relationship between power and Saṅgha—a defining feature of the Lankan polity—which the "mechanical" federalism of the peace process unintentionally (for the international community) or deliberately (for the liberals in the Lankan political spectrum) underestimated if not simply ignored. This, however, is not just a matter of ignoring or excluding important political actors from the political process, but is also a matter of failing to understand that the Lankan society, in the understanding of the Saṅgha, is a "cosmion," an analogue to the eternal cosmic order articulated in the teachings of Sinhala Buddhism.

The term "cosmion" was created by the Austrian philosopher Adolf Stöhr (1921) and then later developed by Eric Voegelin (Voegelin 1989). The purpose of a cosmion is to act as a shelter against the forces of disintegration, and it accomplishes its purpose by "simulating the wholeness of the cosmos by analogy" (Moulakis 1997, 18). A cosmion is always the product of the human imagination, but it manifests itself in history as a concrete political society with real political and social institutions.

> Out of the shapeless vastness of conflicting human desires rises a little world of order, a cosmic analogy, and a cosmion, leading a precarious life under the pressure of destructive forces from within and without. ... The function proper of order is the creation of a shelter in which man gives his life a semblance of meaning...thereby relieving his life from [the disordering aspects]of existence that always spring up when the possibility of the utter senselessness of a life ending in annihilation is envisaged.
> (Voegelin 1999, 226)

We need to stress the crucial importance of this fact. The Lankan polity is not just a historically grown community of people, who live together as a matter of fact, and convenience, and who over millennia have created their own culture, their own way of doing things. Rather, the political order in Lanka is an analogue to the cosmic order. Accordingly, the history of the country, too, has cosmic significance, in which adherence to cosmic principles is rewarded with well-being and prosperity and in which any departure from these principles is punished with chastisement and suffering. For the Saṅgha, the order of the land is not just "symbolic" of the order of the cosmos; rather, the relationship between the two "orders" is analogous and real. Within this context, clearly, the federal proposal too assumes cosmic significance and, to the extent that it is perceived as a threat, requires an existential and total response even at the expense of one's life. The stakes could not be higher: for the Saṅgha, federalism is not just a matter of war and peace. It is not only a form of neo-colonialism; far more seriously, it is an attempt by enemies of Sinhala Buddhists to hijack and hence divert the course of cosmic history.

Devaluing Buddha

As we noted, the *Mahāvaṃsa* is that record of the "cosmic history" of Lanka. We saw how the *Mahāvaṃsa* glorifies the Anurādhapura era, the longest of all in ancient Lanka (chapters 6 to 20), and two kings in particular: Duṭṭhagāmiṇi (chapters 12 to 18), and Parākramabāhu I (chapters 29 to 37). Their kingdoms were highly centralized and militarized; especially after the massive wars, they fought to "unite" the land under one strong Buddhist king (Cunningham 1996; Evers 1969, 1967). Chapters of the *Mahāvaṃsa* vividly narrate the wars fought by pious Buddhist kings against the Hindu Tamil rulers. These wars were fought in order to protect the dhamma, the śāsana, and the land—not merely to preserve political power. The *Mahāvaṃsa* thus indicates what kind of rule the Buddhist cosmion should adopt. Buddha's life, too, may be read as providing "models" of appropriate types of kingship. He lived at a time when there were several quasi-kingdoms that were often at war to restore and preserve territorial and ethnic/clan identities. Buddha himself came from the warring caste of Kṣatriyas. He met with, advised, and accepted invitations from kings. Richard Gombrich noted that Buddha, in many of his discourses, emphasized the importance of hierarchical order in political and administrative affairs. While his views were rather apolitical, Buddha did not radically dismiss the king's rule or his standing armies. In fact, Buddha agrees to the advice of King Bimbīsāra to avoid calling the soldiers into the order of Saṅgha (1988, 83–85). The significance of hierarchy is further underlined in the Dīpavaṃsa and the *Mahāvaṃsa*, because the hierarchy represents the fact that the dhamma is given the "foremost" place in a "united" land. The unity and uniformity of the land—the absence of difference—reflects the people's undiluted, pure, and undivided devotion to the faith. Moreover, in order to establish and sustain the purity of the dhamma, according to *Mahāvaṃsa* even Buddha used indirect force to either coercively expel or "integrate those outside the faith" (Clifford 1978, 40), suggesting to some that force and violence can be justified as long as they help sustain the hierarchy of the Buddhist dhamma. The realization of the federal proposal in Lanka would have undermined the Buddha's status and position within the Lankan cosmion.

Subverting the eternal order

The Saṅgha are the guardians of the Buddhist cosmion. They mediate between the political and cosmic order, and thus are the protectors of the analogy that must rule between the two orders. In some sense, these notions make the Saṅgha more powerful than the actual rulers of the polity, but we already noted that in practice their relationship tends to be one of mutual legitimization. The crucial link between worldly power and Saṅgha mediation is confirmed in many Theravāda texts, especially the *Mahāvaṃsa* (Collins 1998, 1992; Seneviratne 1978, 1977; Tambiah 1976, 1986; Wijeyeratne 2007). Modern Theravādins accept the rule of the Emperor Aśoka as the ideal model of governance. Asoka became a (Theravāda) Buddhist. He sponsored large amount of monasteries while building new temples and stupas. However, what makes Aśoka a great example in the minds of modern Buddhist is his commitment to expand the Buddhist ideology.

> The Ashokan period was then for Buddhism an axial moment, since not only was it changing from a regional Indian tradition to a pan-Indian one; but as a result of its encounter with Hellenism, which will be shown in this study, it thereby started to break away from its geographical-cultural Indian cocoon. In short, Buddhism started to reveal its cross-cultural and universalistic religious potential. (D. A. Scott 1985, 132)

Aśoka personified Buddhist political rule as no other ruler did. He tolerated non-Buddhist citizens, but only as long, they found and accepted their place in the highly centralized, hierarchical structure of the kingdom. He ensured that the dhamma reached all eight sections of his kingdom and gave his son and daughter to the śāsana, with missionary effort and sacrifice providing the ultimate legitimization of his rule. Aśoka understood himself, and was understood by those he ruled, not just as Buddha's agent but also as his placeholder, as his 'replacement', carrying the ultimate responsibility for ensuring the harmony between political and cosmic order. Wijeyeratne commented:

> The cosmic order of Sinhalese Buddhism is multi-layered and subdivided, but its fissiparous nature is "counteracted by the holistic framework within which it is understood, by the attributes of the Buddha, and by the principles and mechanisms which provide the pantheon with a unity of structure" (Roberts 1994, 62–63). Within this cosmological order, the Buddha is at the apex and the gods are in the middle, while the demonic forces of disintegration are at the base. This cosmic order is in a continuous state of flux as it moves between its hierarchical unifying aspects (associated with the Buddha), fragmentation, and reordering, with the ordering power of the Buddha ultimately encompassing the fragmenting logic of the demonic. (Wijeyeratne 2007, 162)

Nātha is the highest of the gods and in Sinhalese Buddhist tradition the next Buddha-to-be. He is "characterized as continually contemplating the teachings of the Buddha and as being so unattached to the matters of existence, that he is expected by the Sinhalese to be the next (Maitrī) Buddha. ... Vishnu is conceived of as the protector of Buddhism on the island; Kataragama is closely linked with the ancient Sinhalese Buddhist resurgence against Hindu Tamil domination; and Saman is the god of Adam's Peak, the site of Buddha's footprint and the Buddha's first visit to Sri Lanka" (Kapferer 1991, 159). Both Vishnu and Kataragama are concerned with affairs of the human world and combine both ordering and disordering powers "in their being" (Kapferer 1991, 160). The order of the land and the order of the cosmos are therefore not just "analogous," they are also closely linked via the actions of gods and humans, with the Saṅgha playing a crucial in-between role. The picture of the Sinhala order that emerges from these notions is thus one marked by unity, hierarchy and purity. The canonical narratives make it evident that the Buddha occupies the ultimate spiritual centre, with everything and everyone else, including *devas* and *arahaths,* being subjected to the centre in a hierarchical fashion which allows some to be closer to the centre than others (Gombrich 1998, 1971; Tambiah 1984, 1973). The journey towards the centre is an ascent, reflected in the Samsara journey towards nirvāna, which includes the six familiar steps: *Śrāvaka* (listener), *Dāyaka* (supporter), Saṅgha (renouncer), *Sōtapanna* (the one who had entered the stream of awakening), *Sakṛdāgāmin* (the one who will return only once more), *Anāgāmin* (the one who will not return), *Arahat* (the one who has attained). The same hierarchical order is also expressed in the notion of *simāmālā*, which recognizes the authority that radiates from the key temples. Even within the Saṅgha community we find a hierarchical order emphasizing age, experience, and gender. The equal power-sharing that is at the core of federalism seemed to directly negate this ideology of hierarchy as a principle of cosmic order.

Ignoring cosmology

Throughout this book, we have referred to the forces opposing federalism as representatives of "nationalism," or we have more appropriately referred to "ethnoreligious nationalism" as their underlying motivation. However, our previous discussion has also shown that in the case of Lanka, the forces of ethnicity, religion, and nationalism are the same. Applying the term "nationalism" to Lanka is, in some sense, an anachronism. The Lankan cosmion existed before nations and nationalism emerged, and accordingly it may be misleading to analyze it in terms of "nationalism." As Marshall Sahlins argued some time ago, the cosmion of Sinhala Buddhism is a "too dominant site of symbolic production, which supplies the major idiom of other relations and activities" (2013, 211). The language and ideology of a supreme ethnic race, Buddha's *dhammadīpa*, the warrior heroes, and their guardian Bhikkhus define the Sinhala polity. The centralization of all political power under Sinhala rule is not just a political "nationalist" notion but also the manifestation of a cosmology, which emphasizes unity, purity, and hierarchy—notions which to the Sinhalas seemed diametrically opposed to the notions of differentiation, plurality and equality highlighted by the federal proposals.

In light of these distinct features of the Lankan cosmion, we should not be surprised that federalism not only failed but that in fact its very proposal provoked the sensitivities of the Saṅgha and the Sinhalas, leading to a response that was both aggressive and defensive. This conclusion does not justify or sanction the Sinhala outlook, but it helps us raise the question of how one can politically engage with the Sinhalas.

Conclusions

In Sinhala society, the king, the Saṅgha and the people form a triangle, and it is primarily through their triangular relations that Sinhala society is to be modelled as an analogue to the cosmic order. The king is the ultimate centre of power, leader of the Saṅgha and the laity. He is to be a shadow of Buddha, while the laity who is to practice and embody the teachings becomes the symbol of dhamma. The Saṅgha, as we noted previously, occupy a crucial in-between position—between the king and the people, and also between the social order and the cosmic order. Any disturbance to the balance of these forces represents a challenge to an order that is not of man's making; it represents an affront to the divine order of the cosmos with consequences potentially much more serious than the human violence that the defenders of Buddhism may inflict on those they perceive as threats. The centralization of power corresponds to the central role played by Buddha. In *Dīgha Nikāya*, numerous verses are devoted to a justification of the "*Mahā-Saṃmata*", or the great chosen one and his centralized rule. The figure of the "*Mahā-Saṃmatha*" emerges from an election process and yet, once elected, it is his authority and power that moulds the realm into a cosmion. Tambiah (1977) and Roberts (1994) showed how most South/Southeast Asian states whose culture is dominated by Theravādian doctrine have come to adopt centralized political systems that reflect the above outlook.

Political centralization corresponds to the spiritual centrality of Buddhahood and nirvāna. Every individual in their entire cosmic journey through the cycle of births moves closer to that centre. The social and political order is subordinated to the overarching spiritual dynamics that underlies the overall direction of human lives. Ideally, the king is the caretaker or steward of the process of *Chakkavatti*—he is the turner of the wheel of dhamma. The king's palace becomes the capital not just for purposes of political administration but also as a place of spiritual significance, symbolized by the presence of the *Dhātu*-relics. Political society revolves around the centre, being drawn into its centripetal power field. This power field is a spiritual reality as much as it is a political reality.

It reflects the vision of an approved (*Saṃmatha*) and righteous king who holds everything under him in balance so as to assist the peripheries in completing their journeys towards Nirvāna. Politically, this vision may translate into rigid structures of control and even oppression. However, the spiritual legitimacy of the political order is conditional upon the king's righteousness, i.e. his ability to be Buddha's shadow. If he ignores his responsibility for maintaining the Theravāda cosmion, he cannot expect that his authority continue to be respected. It is especially with regard to this question—evaluating the righteousness of kingship—that the in-between position of the Saṅgha allows them to play a crucial role. Emperor Aśoka—the most idealized Buddhist king—was able to embody this idea of kingship. He came to power through ruthlessness and yet he was assured that his karma was nothing as he constituted and maintained the Buddhist cosmion.

As we noted throughout this book, these fundamental principles of the Buddhist cosmion are reflected in the *Mahāvaṃsa*. The central hero of the *Mahāvaṃsa*, king Duṭṭhagāmiṇi, acquires power by fighting wars against the Damilas—the Tamils—and by killing many who failed to support him in his crusade. As he doubted the purpose of his campaign in light of the suffering that it caused, the enlightened Buddhist Saṅgha (the Arahaths) reassures him:

> Only one and a half human beings have been slain here by thee, O lord of men. The one had come unto the (three) refuges, the other had taken unto himself the five precepts. Unbelievers and men of evil life were the rest, not more to be esteemed than beasts. But as for thee, thou wilt bring glory to the doctrine of the Buddha in manifold ways; therefore cast away care from the heart, O ruler of men. (Mhv. 25: 108–112)

Considering the stakes, no costs are too high to protect the cosmion. Charles Hallisay argued that Theravādin societies use Buddhist narratives in order to justify what he calls "ethical particularism" (1996).

The Buddhist cosmion in Lanka has survived into the present and continues to determine post-independence electoral politics. Leaders who position themselves outside this framework will ultimately fail to garner the support needed to implement their policies. They will provoke a response from the Saṅgha, who are the judges of Buddhist righteousness. This dynamics prevented CBK from implementing her proposal for Lanka, and it catapulted Rajapakse to power. In spite of the illiberal nature of their policies, he and his brothers were repeatedly elected because they were able to convey the image of the defenders of the cosmion. Rajapakse succeeded in defeating the LTTE, a fact that will cement his status within the Sinhala and Buddhist history of Lanka. It appears that his unwillingness to negotiate with the Tamil Tigers was corroborated in the latter's military defeat, turning Rajapakse into a modern *Duṭṭhagāmiṇi*-style leader. Opposition leaders such as Ranil Wickramasinghe, who campaigns for a market-based, western-style liberal order, ensure their political marginalization by ignoring the reality of the Lankan cosmion.

A federal peace

It was within the context of this deep-rooted and historically unfolding cosmion that an army of Western, liberal secularists injected federalist power-sharing as a one-size-fits-all solution to the violence of the war in Lanka. The power-sharing discourse came to a climax during the years from 1995 to 2005, which as a highlight saw the Ranil Wickramasinghe government agree to explore federalism as part of the solution proposed in the Oslo Communiqué. In light of the analysis provided in this book, it is not at all surprising that these proposals were unacceptable for the Sinhalas. From their point of view, they were held at gunpoint by the LTTE and put under pressure by the Western liberal peacemakers to change the very principles according to which they understood their society and polity. As they were looking to formulate a response, they turned again to their spiritual guides who mediate between cosmion and cosmos, the Mahā Saṅgha, restoring and rejuvenating the traditional position they held in Lankan society. In a historical process involving ceasefires, peace talks, the resumption of war, and the final military victory, we can see how the liberal peace agenda with federalism as its central proposal was ultimately self-defeating because it strengthened and revived the very forces it needed to contain.

The approach to conflict resolution and peace building that the international community brought to Lanka was exclusively defined in terms of Western scholarship and activism, emphasizing Western notions of minority rights, conflict resolution, democracy and federalist power-sharing. After the 1983 pogrom and the emergence of the LTTE, it seemed the peace building in Lanka required outside help. At first, India led the international efforts from 1984 to 1990.

During the Chandrika Kumaratunga presidency—primarily in response to demands from the Tamil diaspora and the LTTE—Western actors were invited to facilitate the peace talks. The fact that a large number of Tamils ended up in European states may have played a role in getting the Europeans involved in the negotiations. Moreover, when India's traditional ally, the USSR, collapsed, India's influence as a regional power was reduced. The globalization of market based economies and the concomitant desire for the creation of new markets and the expansion of existing markets led to what Roland Paris (2004) called "Wilsonian peacebuilding." This "liberal peacebuilding" (Duffield 2001; Richmond and Tellidis 2012) gained further momentum as a dimension of counter-terrorism measures as well as in the context of the "R2P" agenda—the "responsibility to protect"[3] (Bellamy 2015a, 2015b, 2014, 2010; Bellamy and Williams 2012; Cohen 2009). It is a distinctive feature of these efforts to involve non-state actors and indeed to involve them as partners who are as independent, autonomous and equal as sovereign states. In Lanka's cosmion, however, undermining state power is contrary to the order of things and thus is always likely to provoke resistance.

Furthermore, the peace process itself remained an élite-driven enterprise. Except for the president's office and the ministry of foreign affairs, hardly any other ministry or government agency was asked to take part in the process. The 2002 Ceasefire Agreement was largely an unknown document even to high-ranking officers in the Lankan army. Often senior public sector bureaucrats and administrators were asked to observe or take part in workshops conducted by a new breed of young, urbanized activists who preached the entire curriculum of peacekeeping, peacemaking, and peacebuilding from "early warning" to "post conflict-TRC mechanisms" and "distributive justice." An entirely new peace industry promoted Western concepts and methods of analysis, but to the extent that these notions were imposed from outside, they were also not just patronising but in fact dismissed the traditional order and its representatives.

The peacemakers approached their task with a rigid mind-set. They were determined to make permanent and far-reaching changes to the Lankan polity so as to accommodate their ideas. New actors were to be included, traditional actors were to be excluded, and federalism was to replace the traditional Sinhala hegemony. The peacemakers assumed that they had fully understood the internal conflict in Lanka. For them, the conflict was an example of the problems they had studied elsewhere, an "instance" of the theories they brought with them. Within their theories, they had ready-made "optimal" solutions, which they assumed would be appreciated by "rational" actors—implying that failure to accept their models would amount to irrationality. Accordingly, the peace process included individuals and organizations who sympathized with its overall framework and ambitions. These individuals and organizations were considered "supporters" and they were portrayed as international, enlightened, liberal and modern, while those who questioned, challenged, or even opposed the process were considered regressive, outdated "spoilers" (Newman and Richmond 2006). The process thereby managed to alienate precisely the very core of the Sinhala-Buddhist society—including the Saṅgha—and provoked a predictably hostile response.

3. R2P is a policy to intervene and protect the vulnerable section of a country when the state fails to do so. This was discussed by world leaders at the 2005 UN summit, See http://responsibilitytoprotect.org/world%20summit%20outcome%20doc%20 2005(1).pdf.

In the conditions of modernity, external observers have little choice but to approach the defenders of the Lankan cosmion as "nationalists" and yet this label reflects an anachronism. Nationalism is itself a modern category, while the mind-set that defines the cosmion in Lanka is, as we have shown, much older. The modern, liberal peacemakers were thus prevented from identifying the Lankan polity for what it is, adding another layer of misunderstandings to the situation. In response, Saṅgha led nationalist groups including the JVP, JHU, NMAT, and a plethora of other Saṅgha fronts united to condemn and agitate against the peace process, labelling the process a "sell out" to the LTTE and the foreign agents. The politicians and NGOs who promoted the peace process were demonized as traitors, who betrayed not just the politics of the country but the very fundamentals of Theravāda Sinhala Buddhism.

This binary opposition between inclusion and exclusion, supporters and spoilers, defenders of the faith and traitors, etc. structured the 2005 presidential election, ending with the defeat of Ranil Wickramasinghe of the UNF, who had supported a federal solution. Mahinda Rajapakse, who had presented himself as the protector of the land by distancing himself from the peace process, won the elections. It is ironic that the LTTE, which had eagerly worked with international actors in order to gain international recognition and publicity, entered into secret talks with Rajapakse as they too turned against Wickaramasinghe for his overtly pro-Western stance. In fact, although they fought against each other with extreme brutality and cruelty, the two warring parties in Lanka were still united in their opposition to foreign influence. Although they were driven by very different ambitions and objectives, they secretly agreed that federalism was against their desired goals.

The Saṅgha reinstalled and legitimized

One of the unintended and yet crucial results of the process was the restoration of the Saṅgha as a key formative influence on the Lankan polity. Not only did they survive in a concrete, "physical" sense in the post-LTTE social context while, in contrast, the Norwegians, the EU, the wide range of NGOs and INGOs engaged in peacemaking, as well as the Western scholars have disappeared from the country. Further, the Saṅgha have emerged from the process as the *legitimate* protectors of the Lankan cosmion. They emerge from this process with their traditional role and reputation intact, and they are probably the only actor in the process who can claim to have achieved this remarkable feat. Their in-between status allowed them to support Buddhist soldiers, as they had to reconcile their faith with the violence they endured and inflicted on others. On the one hand, they were able to commit to the *Panca Sīla*[4]—the

4. *Panca Sīla* are the five basic precepts of Buddhism: Do not kill (any living being),

five precepts of which the first is not to kill any form of life: *Pānātiāptā veramaṇī sikkhāpadam samāadiyāmi*—while on the other hand they could endorse the killing of thousands (Kent 2008). What is for outsiders a plain contradiction is a traditional paradox within the Lankan cosmion. Its particularized ethics applies within it; its ethics assumes the existence of the cosmion. If the cosmion itself is under threat, its normal ethical rules and precepts are suspended and it becomes not only possible but also indeed necessary to take whatever actions are required to restore and secure the cosmion.

We must stress at this point that it is not our intention to dismiss the achievements of the Western notions of peacebuilding and democratization altogether, but it is important to identify the limits of the Western approach. There is no question that in many other contexts, federalism has worked effectively and that liberal peacebuilding has achieved its intended purpose. However, this was not the case in Lanka, and this was because the very understanding of politics in the country differs from the modern understanding of national politics that prevails in many other countries. We also do not wish to romanticize or legitimize the Sinhala understanding of politics as the preservation of the cosmion. We do not doubt that under the disguise of spiritual politics, a considerable degree of "realpolitik" is taking place and self-interests are pursued even where the Saṅgha symbolize that the true protectors of the cosmion must first of all renounce themselves. Rather, what we wish to stress is that the "blind spot" of modern peacebuilding prevented the peacemakers from understanding and hence from effectively engaging with the Lankan polity. This, we argued, was because there were two different notions of "politics" involved. It is *this* insight that makes the Lankan case so significant for both political science scholarship and political practice.

We must also stress that not all Saṅgha were opposed to the peace process. Many Saṅgha, who lived in remote villages with a mixed ethnic demography such as Ampara, Degāmadulle, Galle, Trincomalee, and Vavuniya, were supportive of the idea of power-sharing and of a negotiated settlement with the Tamils. Some of them risked their reputation and lives as they attempted to engage in dialogues with the LTTE and with Sinhala society. Siyambalānduwē Mahinda, Mādapagama Assaji, Bäddegama Samita are three prominent Saṅgha amongst others less widely known who made their conviction public that peace must come from negotiation, compromise and power-sharing. However, these were the voices of individual Saṅgha without much state or nationalist élite support. And yet if only the international actors involved in Lanka had

---

do not take what is not given, avoid misconduct in sensuality, abstain from false speech and do not consume intoxicants.

taken the Saṅgha more seriously as political actors, they could have engaged with the Saṅgha hierarchy in Kandy and elsewhere by working with these pro-peace Saṅgha. As a result of this "blind spot," the exclusive, particularistic ethics of the Saṅgha seems more unitary than ever.

A way forward

Peacebuilding in conflict zones, particularly where new constitutional mechanisms such as federalism are introduced, is never a single-actor endeavour. A protracted conflict along ethnic and religious lines as in Lanka deepens the divisions between the communities, suggesting that solutions can only come from outside facilitation. There is no doubt that in many situations, external mediation and facilitation can be effective and beneficial. However, the case we explored in this book suggests that the effects of such interventions cannot only be ineffective but counterproductive; fuelling the very conflict, they were meant to resolve. The "blind spot" underlying the peace efforts in Lanka was not just, due to the fact that key actors were overlooked; rather, the issue is that the very nature of "politics" in the Lankan cosmion is different from the modern notions of politics on which those peace efforts were based. Arguably, there is no such separate realm of "politics" in Lanka as the modern discourse of "politics" implies. In Lanka, the political is a dimension of the spiritual. Accordingly, problems do not have technical, "political" solutions that can be separated from other dimensions of being. While it may be tempting for the modern mind to treat this mode of thinking as an outdated relic of the past, the case of Lanka shows that precisely this approach will confirm and reinforce this mode of thinking as a distinct and very real feature of the present.

It is important to understand the scope of our findings. Our main point is not that the techniques and methods of peace building need refinement—although this, too, is true. Rather, the entire project of Western style peace building and federalizing needs a thorough review in light of its unintended and yet very real effects on countries such as Lanka. The "blind spot" we have identified here appears to us as a general characteristic of the current Western approach to the world, with potentially tragic and unfortunate consequences—although there is not enough space here in this book to pursue this theme in greater detail.

The various forces in Lanka were able to use the war and the commotion surrounding it in order to assert them and (re)confirm their traditional roles. If it was the ambition of the peace builders to soften the positions of the traditional forces in the country, then it is fair to say that the very opposite was achieved. Instead of getting traditional actors to engage in a process of introspection, the situation in Lanka allowed them to fall back on their traditional roles. As we have seen, "reform" in Lanka will remain unlikely as long as the historical dynamic of the past continues. Crucially, the end of the war is not a new beginning, but precisely a continuation of the dynamic of the past. If the source of this dynamics is the Sinhala understanding of their polity as a cosmion, then it is there where "reform" needs to begin. For example, the present Sinhala understanding of the *Mahāvaṃsa* and related texts needs to be re-examined. This re-examination could be guided by the actual Pāli Theravādin teachings, in the light of which mythical-historical narratives acquire meaning. This process of re-reading, re-examining and re-interpreting is of a very different kind than the technical application of conflict resolution tools and universal peace building templates. The point of this re-reading is not to create a Western-style "consensus" but to use the reflective potential of Theravāda Buddhism itself in order to empower the Sinhalas to re-visit the by now taken-for-granted features of their self-understanding of them and other. Within the context of such a process, Western concepts and methods of analysis and interpretation may well be useful, but in their application, we will need to surrender to the process itself in order to let new meaning unfold.

— 6 —

Epilogue

By end of 2013, at the time of finalizing this book, Lanka and its Sinhala Saṅgha have gone through another wave of political unrest. The politically active Sangha who argued and worked so hard for a military victory became even more powerful. They received unrestricted aces in the new post-war political structure. Some of new but powerful political aspirants have decided to use the cultural power of the symbolic Sangha to advance their new power agendas.

New breeds of more militant Saṅgha groups have come forward with violent agitation against many issues. They have by the (in)direct support received from the state, positioned themselves as a cultural and social police force. Their campaigns have ranged against many social, political and cultural topics such as the Christian conversions, the economic and numeric growth of the Muslim minority, the existence of the provincial council system which aims to share administrative power with Tamils as well as some bizarre ethnocentric calls such as to prohibit Sinhala men and women from any form of birth control but to have more children.

Bodu Bala Sēnā, Rāvaṇa Balaya and Sinhala Rāvaya are few such Saṅgha led organizations openly operating with state protection. Their often-violent activities are not only unbuddhist they are blocking the path of peace/reconciliation and dismissing any stability in a state that is already so fragile by every socio-economic measurement.

Lanka also has faced mounting international pressure for the continued negative record on human rights. As of Sep 2013, there are two resolutions against Lanka at the United Nations Human Rights Council. Its High Commissioner, after her inspection tour of Lanka declared that Lanka is slipping into a dictatorial rule.[1]

It becomes therefore paramount now to further understand why and what (re)shapes the Sinhala Saṅgha ideology, its continued justification

1. http://www.ohchr.org/en/NewsEvents/Pages/Media.aspx accessed on 5 Sep 2013.

for violence where such ideology is stemming from. Such research is not easy but essential in order to detect the dynamics that controls the Saṅgha world that in returns influences the state of Lanka like no other factor.

Appendices

Appendix A

Constitutions of Sri Lanka

(All accessed on 10 January 2012)

Pre-Independence

1. The Colebrooke-Cameron Report of 1829–1831
2. The Donoughmore Report of 1927–1930
3. The Soulbury Report of 1944

Post-Independence

1. 1948 Independence Constitution
   http://tamilnation.co/srilankalaws/46constitution.htm
2. 1972 Republican Constitution
   http://tamilnation.co/srilankalaws/72constitution.htm
3. 1978 Executive Constitution
   http://www.priu.gov.lk/Cons/1978Constitution/CONTENTS.html

Proposed Constitutions

1. 1995 Chandrika Proposals
   http://tamilnation.co/conflictresolution/tamileelam/cbkproposals/95proposals.htm
2. 2000 Chandrika Proposals
   http://www.priu.gov.lk/Cons/1978Constitution/1978ConstitutionWithoutAmendments.pdf

Appendix B

Peace Agreements and Related documents (Post-Independence)

all accessed on 10 January 2012

1. 1956 Banda–Chelva Agreement
   http://www.tchr.net/rsdetr_banda_chela_pact.htm
2. 1965 Dudley- Chelva Agreement
   http://tamilnation.co/conflictresolution/tamileelam/65dudleychelvaagreement.htm
3. 1987 The Indo-Lanka Agreement
   http://www.satp.org/satporgtp/countries/shrilanka/document/papers/indo_srilanks_agreement.htm
4. 1987 Provincial Councils Act (as a result of the Indo-Lanka Agreement)
   http://www.priu.gov.lk/ProvCouncils/ProvicialCouncils.html
5. 2002 The Ceasefire Agreement
   http://news.bbc.co.uk/2/hi/south_asia/1836198.stm
6. 2003 The Oslo Communiqué on the possibility of a Federal solution
   http://tamilnation.co/conflictresolution/tamileelam/norway/021205oslodeclaration.htm
7. 2005 The LTTE Interim Self-Governing Authority (ISGA) proposal
   http://www.satp.org/satporgtp/countries/shrilanka/document/papers/LTTE_northeast.htm

References

Abeysekara, Ananda.

2011. "Buddhism, Power, Modernity: A Review Essay on Justin Thomas McDaniel's Gathering Leaves and Lifting Words: Histories of Buddhist Monastic Education in Laos and Thailand." *Culture and Religion* 12(4): 489–497.

2008. "Thinking the 'Question'of Religion: The Aporia of Buddhism and its Democratic Heritage in Sri Lanka." *Religion* 38(2): 174–180.

2004. "Identity for and Against Itself: Religion, Criticism, and Pluralization." *Journal of the American Academy of Religion* 72(4): 973–1001.

2002. *Colors of the Robe: Religion, Identity, and Difference.* Columbia: University of South Carolina Press.

2001. "The Saffron Army, Violence, Terror (ism): Buddhism, Identity, and Difference in Sri Lanka." *Numen* 48(1): 1–46.

2000. "Buddhist Fundamentalism and Minority Identities in Sri Lanka." *American Ethnologist* 27(2): 528–529.

Adamson, Fiona B.

2008. "Constructing the Diaspora: Diaspora Identity Politics and Transnational Social Movements." Paper Presented at the Annual Meeting of the ISA's 49 Annual Convention. March 26, 2008. San Francisco, CA.

Adamson, F. B. and M. Demetriou.

2007. "Remapping the Boundaries of 'State' and 'National Identity': Incorporating Diasporas into IR Theorizing." *European Journal of International Relations* 13(4): 489–526.

Adeney, Katharine.

2014. "Remapping India: New States and Their Political Origins." *Commonwealth & Comparative Politics* 52(4): 569–571.

Alagappa, Muthiah.

1995. *Political Legitimacy in Southeast Asia: The Quest for Moral Authority*. Stanford, CA: Stanford University Press.

Ali, Ameer.

1981. "The 1915 Racial Riots in Ceylon (Sri Lanka): A Reappraisal of Its Causes." *South Asia: Journal of South Asian Studies* 4(2): 1–20.

1984. "Islamic Revivalism in Harmony and Conflict: The Experience in Sri Lanka and Malaysia." *Asian Survey* 24(3): 296–313.

Allen, Barbara.
1998. "Alexis De Tocqueville on the Covenanted Tradition of American Federal Democracy." *Pulius* 28(2): 1–23.

Almond, Gabriel A., R. Scott Appleby and Emmanuel Sivan.
2003. *Strong Religion: The Rise of Fundamentalisms around the World.* Chicago, IL: University of Chicago Press.

Almond, Philip C.
2007. *The British Discovery of Buddhism.* Cambridge: Cambridge University Press.

Al Sayyad, Nezar and Manuel Castells.
2002. *Muslim Europe or Euro-Islam: Politics, Culture, and Citizenship in the Age of Globalization.* Lanham, MD: Lexington Books.

Amarasēkara, Guṇadāsa.
2003. *Out of the Darkness: Translation of Gunadasa Amarasēkara's Novel 'Asathya Kathāwak' and Its Sequel 'Premayē Sathya Kathāwa'.* Boralesgamuwa, Sri Lanka: Visidunu Publication.
1992. *Jāthika Chinthanaya Saha Jāthika Aarthikaya.* Nugegoda Sri Lanka: Chnthana Parshadaya.

Amunugama, Sarath.
1991a. "A Sinhala Buddhist "Babu": AngārikaDharmapāla (1864–1933) and the Bengal Connection." *Social Science Information* 30(3): 555–591.
1991b. "Buddhaputra and Bhumiputra?" *Religion* 21(2): 115–139.
1985. "Angārika Dharmapāla (1864–1933) and the Transformation of Sinhala Buddhist Organization in a Colonial Setting." *Social Science Information* 24(4): 697–730.
1979. "Ideology and Class Interest in One of Piyadasa Sirisena's Novels: The New Image of the 'Sinhala Buddhist' Nationalist." In *Sri Lanka: Collective Identities Revisited,* Volume 1, edited by Michael Roberts, 314–336. Colombo: Marga Institute.

Anagnost, Ann S.
1994. "The Politics of Ritual Displacement." In *Asian Visions of Authority: Religion and the Modern States of East and Southeast Asia.* edited by Charles Keyes, Laurel Kendall and Helen Hardacre, 221–254. Honolulu: University of Hawaii Press.

Anand, Dibyesh.
2000. "(Re)imagining Nationalism: Identity and Representation in the Tibetan Diaspora of South Asia." *Contemporary South Asia* 9(3): 271–287.

Anderson, Benedict R.
1983 *Imagined Communities: Reflections on the Origin and Spread of Nationalism.* London: Verso.

Anderson, Carol S.
1999. *Pain and Its Ending: The Four Noble Truths in the Theravāda Buddhist Canon.* Richmond, Surrey: Curzon.

Anderson, Lawrence.
2007a. "Theorizing Federalism in Iraq." *Regional and Federal Studies* 17(2): 159–171.
2007b. "Federalism and Secessionism: Institutional Influences on Nationalist Politics in Quebec." *Nationalism and Ethnic Politics* 13(2): 187–211.
2004. "Exploring the Paradox of Autonomy: Federalism and Secession in North America." *Regional & Federal Studies* 14(1): 89–112.

Appadurai, Arjun.
1996. *Modernity at Large*. Minneapolis: University of Minnesota Press.
1986. "Theory in Anthropology: Center and Periphery." *Comparative Studies in Society and History* 28(2): 356–374.

Appleby, R. Scott.
2000. *The Ambivalence of the Sacred: Religion, Violence, and Reconciliation*. Lanham, MD: Rowman and Littlefield.

Arasaratnam, Sinappah.
1972. "The Ceylon Insurrection of April 1971: Some Causes and Consequences." *Pacific Affairs* 45(3): 356–371.

Ardley, Jane.
2003. "Learning the Art of Democracy? Continuity and Change in the Tibetan Government-in-exile." *Contemporary South Asia* 12(3): 349–363.

Argenti-Pillen, Alex.
2002. *Masking Terror: How Women Contain Violence in Southern Sri Lanka*. Philadelphia: University of Pennsylvania Press.

Aung-Thwin, Maitrii.
2008. "Structuring Revolt: Communities of Interpretation in the Historiography of the Saya San Rebellion." *Journal of Southeast Asian Studies* 39(2): 297–317.

Bader, Veit-Michael.
2007. *Secularism or Democracy?* Amsterdam: University of Amsterdam Press.

Baharati, A.
1976. "Monastic and Lay Buddhism in the 1971 Sri Lankan Insurgency." *Journal of African and Asian Studies* 11: 102–112.

Bailey, Greg and Ian W. Mabbett.
2003. *The Sociology of Early Buddhism*. Cambridge: Cambridge University Press.

Bailey, Sydney Dawson.
1952. *Ceylon*. New York: Hutchinson's University Library.

Baker, Wayne J.
1993. "The Covenantal Basis for the Development of Swiss Political Federalism." *Publius* 23(2): 19–41.

Balasingham, Anton.

2004. *War and Peace: Armed Struggle and Peace Efforts of Liberation Tigers*. Mitcham, England: Fairmax Publishers.

Bandarage, Asoka.

2012. "Towards Peace with Justice in Sri Lanka: An Alternative Perspective." *India Quarterly* 68(2): 103–118.

2009. *The Separatist Conflict in Sri Lanka: Terrorism, Ethnicity, Political Economy*. London: Routledge.

1983. *Colonialism in Sri Lanka: The Political Economy of the KandyanHighlands, 1833–1886*. Berlin: Mouton.

Bandyopadhyay, Debashis.

2016. "In Defence of the Real: The 'Pathology'of Violence in Buddhist Folk Rituals and Statecraft of Sri Lanka: A Psychoanalytic Review." *Contemporary Buddhism*, 1–16. Online. doi: 10.1080/14639947.2015.1135534

Barker, Eileen.

2006a. "Bryan Wilson's Contribution to the Study of the New Religious Movements." *Social Compass* 53(2): 147–153.

2006b. "We've Got to Draw the Line Somewhere: An Exploration of Boundaries That Define Locations of Religious Identity." *Social Compass* 53(2): 201–213.

Barnes, Samuel H.

2001. "The Contribution of Democracy to Rebuilding Postconflict Societies." *The American Journal of International Law* 95(1): 86–101.

1997. "Electoral Behavior and Comparative Politics." In *Comparative Politics: Rationality, Culture, and Structure*, edited by Mark I. Lichbach and Alan S. Zuckerman, 115–141. Cambridge: Cambridge University Press.

Barron, T. J.

1988. "The Donoughmore Commission and Ceylon's National Identity." *Journal of Commonwealth and Comparative Politics* 26(2): 147–157.

Bartholomeusz, Tessa J.

2002. *In Defense of Dharma: Just-war Ideology in Buddhist Sri Lanka*. London: RoutledgeCurzon.

1999a. "First among the Equals: Buddhism and the Sri Lanka State." In *Buddhism and Politics in Twentieth Century Asia*, edited by Ian Harris, 173–193. London: Continuum.

1999b. "Mothers of Buddhas, Mothers of Nations: Kumaranatunga and Her Meteoric Rise to Power in Sri Lanka." *Feminist Studies* 25(1): 211–225.

1998. "Sinhala Anglicans and Buddhism in Sri Lanka: When the 'Other' Becomes You." In *Buddhist Fundamentalism and Minority Identities in Sri Lanka*, edited by Tessa J. Bartholomeusz, and Chandra R. De Silva, 133–146. Albany: State University of New York Press.

1994. *Women under the Bō Tree: Buddhist Nuns in Sri Lanka*. Cambridge: Cambridge University Press.

Bartholomeusz, Tessa J. and Chandra Richard De Silva, eds.
1998. *Buddhist Fundamentalism and Minority Identities in Sri Lanka*. Albany: State University of New York Press.

Barua, B. M.
1945. "Buddhadatta and Buddhaghosa: Their Contemporaneity and Age." *University of Ceylon Review* III(1): 77–88.

Basham, Arthur Llewellyn.
1951. *History and Doctrines of the Ajivikas: A Vanished Indian Religion*. New Delhi: Motilal Banarsidass.

Bastian, Sunil.
2011. "Politics of Market Reforms and UNF-led Negotiations." In *Conflict and Peacebuilding in Sri Lanka: Caught in the Peace Trap?*, edited by Jonathan Goodhand and Benedikt Korf, 132–149. London: Routledge.
2009. "Politics of Social Exclusion, State Reform and Security in Sri Lanka." *IDS Bulletin* 40(2): 88–95.

Bastian, Sunil, Sepali Kottegoda, Camilla Orjuela and Jayadeva Uyangoda.
2010. *Power and politics in the Shadow of Sri Lanka's Armed Conflict*. Edited by Camilla Orjuela. SIDA Studies 25. http://www.sida.se/contentassets/010b128fd4c544dca50548c2bbb04c56/power-and-politics---in-the-shadow-of-sri-lankas-armed-conflict_2891.pdf

Baumann, Martin.
1997. "Culture Contact and Valuation: Early German Buddhists and the Creation of a 'Buddhism in Protestant Shape'." *Numen* 44(3): 270–295.
1995. "Creating a European Path to Nirvana: Historical and Contemporary Developments of Buddhism in Europe." *Journal of Contemporary Religion* 10(1): 55–70.

Bayes, Jane H. and Nayyirah Tawḥīdī.
2001. *Globalization, Gender, and Religion: The Politics of Women's Rights in Catholic and Muslim Contexts*. Basingstoke: Palgrave.

Bayly, C. A.
1983. *Rulers, Townsmen and Bazaars: North Indian Society in the Age of British Expansion, 1770–1870*. Cambridge: Cambridge University Press.

Bechert, Heinz.
1992. "Buddha-field and Transfer of Merit in a Theravāda Source." *Indo-Iranian Journal* 35(2–3): 95–108.
1991. *The Dating of the Historical Buddha/Die Datierung des historischen Buddha*, part 1. Symposien zur Buddhismusforschung IV, 1–2. Göttingen: Vandenhoek und Ruprecht.
1978. "Beginnings of Buddhist Historiography: Mahavamsa and Political Thinking." In *Religion and Legitimation of Power in Sri Lanka*, edited by Bardwell L. Smith, 1–12. Chambersburg, PA : ANIMA Books.

1974. "Buddhism and Mass Politics in Burma and Ceylon." In *Religion and Political Modernization*, edited by D. Smith, 147–167. New Haven, CT: Yale University Press.

1973. "Saṅgha, State, Society, "Nation": Persistence of Traditions in "Post-Traditional" Buddhist Societies." *Daedalus* 102(1): 85–95

1970. "Theravāda Buddhist Saṅgha: Some General Observations on Historical and Political Factors in Its Development." *The Journal of Asian Studies* 29(4): 761–778.

Beckford, James A.

1999. "The Politics of Defining Religion in Secular Society." In *The Pragmatics of Defining Religion: Contexts, Concepts and Contests*, edited by Jan Platvoet and Arie L Molendijk, 23–40. Leiden: Brill.

1976. "Structural Dependence in Religious Organizations: From 'Skid Road' to Watch Tower. *Journal for the Scientific Study of Religion* 15(2): 169–175.

Bell, Bethia N. and Heather M. Bell.

1993. *H.C.P. Bell: Archaeologist of Ceylon and the Maldives*. Denbigh: Archetype Publications.

Bellamy, Allex J.

2015a. "A Chronic Protection Problem: The DPRK and the Responsibility to Protect." *International Affairs* 91(2): 225–244.

2015b. "A death foretold? Human Rights, Responsibility To Protect and the Persistent Politics of Power." *Cooperation and Conflict* 50(2): 286–293.

2014. "From Tripoli to Damascus & Quest; Lesson Learning and the Implementation of the Responsibility to Protect." *International Politics* 51(1): 23–44.

2010. *Global Politics and the Responsibility To Protect: From Words To Deeds*. London: Routledge

Bellamy, Alexander and Paul D. Williams.

2012. "On the Limits of Moral Hazard: The Responsibility to Protect, Armed Conflict and Mass Atrocities." *European Journal of International Relations* 18: 539–571.

Berkwitz, Steven C.

2008a. "Theravada Buddhism and the British Encounter: Religious, Missionary and Colonial Experience in Nineteenth-century Sri Lanka." *Religion* 38(1): 86–88.

2008b. "Resisting the Global in Buddhist Nationalism: Venerable Soma's Discourse of Decline and Reform." *The Journal of Asian Studies* 67(1): 73–106.

2006a. *The History of the Buddha's Relic Shrine: A Translation of the Sinhala Thupavamsa*. Oxford: Oxford University Press.

2006b. "Buddhism in Sri Lanka: Practice, Protest, and Preservation." *Buddhism in World Cultures: Comparative Perspectives*, edited by Steven C. Berkwitz, 45–72. Santa Barbara: ABC-CLIO

2004. *Buddhist History in the Vernacular: No. 23: The Power of the Past in Late Medieval Sri Lanka*. Leiden: Brill's Indological Library.

2003. "History and Gratitude in Theravāda Buddhism." *Journal of American Academy for Religions* 71(3): 579–604.

Bermeo, Nancy.

2002. "The Import of Institutions." *Journal of Democracy* 13(2): 96–110.

Bertelsen, Kristoffer Brix.

1997. "Protestant Buddhism and Social Identification in Ladakh." *Archives de sciences sociales des religions* 99(1): 129–151.

Beyer, Peter.

1999. "Secularization from the Perspective Of, Globalization: A Response to Dobbelaere." *Sociology of Religion* 60(3): 289–301.

Bhargava, Rajeev.

2009. "Why Not Secularism." Ethnicities 9(4): 553–560.

2007. "On the Persistent Political Under-Representation of Muslims in India." *Law & Ethics of Human Rights* 1(1): 76–133.

Bilimoria, Purushottama.

2008. "Nietzsche as 'Europe's Buddha' and 'Asia's Superman'." *Sophia* 47(3): 359–376.

Bischoff, Roger.

1995. *Buddhism in Myanmar: A Short History*. Kandy, Sri Lanka: Buddhist Publication Society.

Biswas, Bidisha.

2010. "Negotiating the Nation: Diaspora Contestations in the USA about Hindu Nationalism in India." Nations and Nationalism 16(4): 696–714.

2004. "Nationalism By Proxy: A Comparison of Social Movements Among Diaspora Sikhs And Hindus." *Nationalism and Ethnic Politics* 10(2): 269–295.

Blackburn, Anne M.

2010. *Locations of Buddhism: Colonialism and Modernity in Sri Lanka*. Chicago, IL: University of Chicago Press.

2001. *Buddhist Learning and Textual Practice in Eighteenth-Century Lankan Monastic Culture*. Princeton, NJ: Princeton University Press.

1999. "Looking for the Vinaya: Monastic Discipline in the Practical Canons of the Theravāda." *Journal of the International Association of Buddhist Studies* 22(2): 281–309.

Blackton, Charles S.

1970. "The Action Phase of the 1915 Riots." *The Journal of Asian Studies*, 2nd ser. 29: 235–254.

Blank, Jonah.

2001. *Mullahs on the Mainframe: Islam and Modernity among the DaudiBohras*. Chicago, IL: University of Chicago Press.

Bloss, Lowell S.

1973. "The Buddha and the Nāga: A Study in Buddhist Folk Religiosity." *History of Religions* 13(1): 36–53.

Bodhi, Bhikku.

2010. "The Revival of Bhikkhunī Ordination in the Theravāda Tradition." In *Dignity & Discipline: Reviving Full Ordination for Buddhist Nuns,* edited by Thea Mohr, Bhikṣuṇī Jampa Tsedroen and Dede Cummings, 99–142. Somerville, MA: Wisdom Publications.

Bond, George D.

2003. "The Contemporary Lay Meditation Movement and Lay Gurus in Sri Lanka." *Religion* 33(1): 23–55.

1998. "Conflicts of Identity and Interpretation in Buddhism: The Clash between the Sarvodaya Shramadana Movement and the Government of President Premadasa." In *Buddhist Fundamentalism and Minority Identities in Sri Lanka,* edited by Tessa J. Bartholomeusz and Chandra Richard De Silva, 36–52. Albany: State University of New York Press.

1992. *The Buddhist Revival in Sri Lanka: Religious Tradition, Reinterpretation and Response.* Delhi: Motilal Banarsidass Publishers.

Borchert, Thomas.

2007. "Buddhism, Politics, and Nationalism in the Twentieth and Twenty-first Centuries." *Religion Compass* 1(5): 529–546.

Borg, Marcus J.

1998. *Conflict, Holiness & Politics in the Teachings of Jesus.* London: Bloomsbury T&T Clark.

Bowden, Earnest W.

1893. "The Uposatha and Upasampadâ Ceremonies." *Royal Asiatic Society of Great Britain and Ireland* 1893: 159–162.

Braun, Erik.

2009. "Local and Translocal in the Study of Theravada Buddhism and Modernity." *Religion Compass* 3(6): 935–950.

Brekke, Torkel.

2009. "Beyond Theological Essentialism and Ethnic Reductionism." *International Journal of Buddhist Thought & Culture* 12: 125–155.

2007 "Bones of Contention: Buddhist Relics, Nationalism and the Politics of Archaeology." *Numen* 54(3): 270–303.

2002. *Religious Motivation and the Origins of Buddhism.* London: RoutledgeCurzon.

1999. "The Religious Motivation of the Early Buddhists." *Journal of the American Academy of Religion* 67(4): 849–866.

Brinkerhoff, J. M.

2008. "Diaspora Identity and the Potential for Violence: Toward an Identity-mobilization Framework Identity." *International Journal of Theory and Practice* 8(1): 67–88.

Broadhurst, Roderic.
2002. "Lethal Violence, Crime and State Formation in Cambodia." *Australian and New Zealand Journal of Criminology* 35(1): 1–26.

Bronkhorst, Johannes.
1998. *The Two Sources of Indian Asceticism*. Delhi: Motilal Banarsidass.

Brown, David.
2000. *Contemporary Nationalism: Civic, Ethnocultural, and Multicultural Politics*. London: Routledge.

Brown, Nathan J. and Amr Hamzawy.
2010. *Between Religion and Polity*. Washington, DC: Carnegie Endowment for International Peace.

Brun, Cathrine and Tariq Jazeel.
2009. *Spatialising Politics: Culture and Geography in Postcolonial Sri Lanka*. Los Angeles: Sage.

Buddhadatta, A. P.
1965. ලක්දිව බුරුම නිකායේ ඉතිහාසය [The History of Burmese Nikāya in Ceylon]. Colombo-Sri Lanka: Anula Press.
1952. "On a Burmese Mission to Ceylon 1896." *Ceylon Historical Journal* 1–2: 80–90.

Bühler, Georg.
1878. "The Digambara Jainas." *The Indian Antiquary* 7: 28–29.

Bullion, Alan.
2001. "Norway and the Peace Process in Sri Lanka." *Civil Wars* 4(3): 70–92.
1994. "The Indian Peace-keeping Force in Sri Lanka." *International Peacekeeping* 1(2): 148–159.

Bunnag, Jane.
1973. *Buddhist Monk, Buddhist Layman: A Study of Urban Monastic Organization in Central Thailand*. Cambridge: Cambridge University Press.

Bunt, Gary R.
2002. *Virtually Islamic: Computer-mediated Communication and Cyber Islamic Environments*. Cardiff: University of Wales Press.

Burgess, Michael.
2006. *Comparative Federalism: Theory and Practice*. London: Routledge.

Burgess, Michael and Alain Gagnon.
2010. *Federal Democracies*. London: Routledge.

Burgess, Michael and John Pinder.
2007. *Multinational Federations*. London: Routledge.

Burnouf, Eugène.
2010. *Introduction to the History of Indian Buddhism*. Chicago, IL: University of Chicago Press.

Carringer, Michael Blaine.

1979. *The Social Organisation of the Sinhalese* Saṅgha *in an Historical Perspective*. Volume 1. Oxford: Oxford University Press.

Cary, Nelson and Lawrence Grossberg, eds.

2005. *Marxism and the Interpretation of Culture*. Urbana, IL: University of Illinois.

Cesari, Jocelyne.

2009. *Muslims in the West after 9/11: Religion, Politics and Law*. London: Routledge.

Chabal, Patrick and Jean-Pascal Daloz.

2006. *Culture Troubles: Politics and the Interpretation of Meaning*. Chicago, IL: University of Chicago Press.

Chakrabarti, Dilip K.

1995. "Buddhist Sites across South Asia as Influenced by Political and Economic Forces." *World Archaeology* 27(2): 185–202.

Chakravarti, Uma.

1987. *The Social Dimensions of Early Buddhism*. Delhi: Oxford University Press.

Chandawimala, Rangama, Venerable.

2007. "The Impact of the Abhayagiri Practices on the Development of Theravada Buddhism in Sri Lanka. Unpublished PhD thesis, The University of Hong Kong.

Chandraperuma, C. A.

1991. *Sri Lanka, the Years of Terror: The J.V.P. Insurrection, 1987–1989*. Colombo: Lake House Bookshop.

Chatalian, George.

1983. "Early Indian Buddhism and the Nature of Philosophy: A Philosophical Investigation." *Journal of Indian Philosophy* 11(2): 167–222.

Chelvanayakam, S. J. V.

2005. "A Memorandum from the Tamils of Ceylon to all Delegates attending the 20th Commonwealth Conference in Sri Lanka." In *Dealing with Diversity: Sri Lankan Discourses on Peace and Conflict*, edited by G. Frerks and B. Klem, 275–290. The Hague: Netherlands Institute of International Relations Clingendael.

Christensen, Laurence W.

1999. "Suffering and the Dialectical Self in Buddhism and Relational Psychoanalysis." *The American Journal of Psychoanalysis* 59(1): 37–57.

Church, Clive and Paolo Dardanelli.

2005. "The Dynamics of Confederalism and Federalism: Comparing Switzerland and the EU." *Regional & Federal Studies* 15(2): 163–185.

Clarance, William.

2002. "Conflict and Community in Sri Lanka." *History Today* 52(7): 41.

Clark, Walter Eugene.

1930. "Some Problems in the Criticism of the Sources for Early Buddhist History." *The Harvard Theological Review* 23(2): 127–147.

Clements, Alan.

2006. *Instinct for Freedom: A Maverick's Guide to Spiritual Revolution.* London: New World Library.

1992. *Burma: The Next Killing Fields?* Berkeley, CA: Odonian Press.

Clifford, John Holt, Jacob N. Kinnard and Jonathan S. Walters.

2003. *Constituting Communities: Theravāda Buddhism and the Religious Cultures of South and Southeast Asia.* Albany: State University of New York Press.

Clifford, R. T.

1978. "The Dhammadīpa Tradition in Sri Lanka: Three Traditions within the Chronicles." In *Religion and Legitimation of Power in Sri Lanka*, edited by B. L. Smith, 36–47. Chambersburg, PA: Anima Books.

Cohen, Roberta.

2009. "The Burma Cyclone and the Responsibility to Protect." *Global Responsibility to Protect* 1(2): 253–257.

Collins, Steven.

2003. "What is Literature in Pali?." *Literary Cultures in History: Reconstructions from South Asia*, edited by Sheldon Pollock, 649–688. Berkeley: University of California Press.

1998. *Nirvana and Other Buddhist Felicities: Utopias of the PaliImaginaire.* Cambridge: Cambridge University Press.

1992. "Nirvana, Time and Narrative." *History of Religions* 31(3): 215–246.

1990. *Selfless Persons: Imagery and Thought in Theravada Buddhism.* Cambridge: Cambridge University Press.

Coleman, Simon.

2003. "Continuous Conversion? The Rhetoric, Practice, and Rhetorical Practice of Charismatic Protestant Conversion." In *The Anthropology of Religious Conversion*, edited by Andrew Buckser and Stephen D. Glazier, 15–27. Lanham, MD: Rowman & Littlefield.

2000. *The Globalization of Charismatic Christianity.* Cambridge Studies in Ideology and Religion 12 . Cambridge: Cambridge University Press.

Coningham, Robin A. E.

1995. "Monks, Caves and Kings: A Reassessment of the Nature of Early Buddhism in Sri Lanka." *World Archaeology* 27(2): 222–242.

Coningham, Robin, Prishanta Gunawardhana, Mark Manuel, Gamini Adikari, Mangala Katugampola, Ruth Young, Armin Schmidt *et al.*

2007. "The State of Theocracy: Defining An Early Medieval Hinterland in Sri Lanka." *Antiquity* 81(313): 699–719.

Coomaraswamy, Ananda Kentish.

1986. *Selected Papers: Traditional Art and Symbolism*. Edited by Roger Lipsey. Bollingen Series 89. Princeton, NJ: Princeton University Press.

1956. *Mediaeval Sinhalese Art*. New York: Pantheon Books.

1943. "Samvega: Aesthetic Shock." *Harvard Journal of Asiatic Studies* 7(3): 174–179.

1908. *The Village Community and Modern Progress*. Colombo: Apothecaries Company.

Coomaraswamy, Ananda Kentish and Sister Nivedita.

1967. *Myths of the Hindus and Buddhists*. New York: Dover Publications.

Cooper, Robert and Mats Berdal.

1993. "Outside Intervention in Ethnic Conflicts." *Survival* 35(1): 118–142.

Cooper, David Edward and Simon P. James.

2005. *Buddhism, Virtue and Environment*. Aldershot: Ashgate.

Coperahewa, Sandagomi and S. Arunachalam.

2002. සිංහල භාෂාවේ දමිල වචන. Colombo: S. Godage Brothers Publishers.

Cornwell, Benjamin.

2002. "The Protestant Sect Credit Machine Social Capital and the Rise of Capitalism." *Journal of Classical Sociology* 7(3): 267–290.

Crane, Robert I. and Norman Gerald Barrier.

1981. *British Imperial Policy in India and Sri Lanka: 1858-1912: A Reassessment*. Columbia: South Asia Books.

Crosby, Kate.

2008a. "Kamma, Social Collapse or Geophysics? Interpretations of Suffering among Sri Lankan Buddhists in the Immediate Aftermath of the 2004 Asian Tsunami." *Contemporary Buddhism* 9(1): 53–76.

2008b. "Changing the Landscape of Theravada Studies." *Contemporary Buddhism* 9(1): 1–6.

1999. "History versus Modern Myth: The Abhayagirivihāra, the Vimuttimagga and Yogāvacara Meditation." *Journal of Indian Philosophy* 26(6): 503–550.

Crotty, R.

1996. "Redefining the 'church and Sect' Typology." *Journal of Sociology* 32(2): 38–49.

Cuthbertson, Ian M.

2004. "Prisons and the Education of Terrorists." *World Policy Journal* 21(3): 15–22.

Darian, Jean C.

1977. "Social and Economic Factors in the Rise of Buddhism." *Sociological Analysis* 38(3): 226–238.

Dark, K. R.

2000. *Religion and International Relations*. New York: St. Martin's Press.

De Alwis, Malathi.

2002. "The Changing Role of Women in Sri Lankan Society." *Social Research* 69(3): 675–692.

Deegalle, Mahinda, The Venerable.

2011. "Politics of the Jathika Hela Urumaya: Buddhism and ethnicity." In *The Sri Lanka reader: history, culture, politics,* edited by J. Holt, 383–394. The World Readers. Durham, NC: Duke University Press.

2008. *Dharma to the UK : A Centennial Celebration of Buddhist Legacy.* London: World Buddhist Foundation.

2006a. *Popularizing Buddhism: Preaching As Performance in Sri Lanka.* Albany: State University of New York Press.

2006b. *Buddhism, Conflict and Violence in Modern Sri Lanka.* London: Routledge.

2004. "Politics of the Jathika Hela Urumaya Monks: Buddhism and Ethnicity in Contemporary Sri Lanka." *Contemporary Buddhism* 5(2): 83–103.

2003. "Buddhist heretics?" In *Pranamalekha: Essays in Honour of Ven. Dr. Medagama Vajiragnana,* edited by B. Wimalaratana, W. Wimalajothi, *et al.,* 141–144. London: London Buddhist Vihara.

2002. "'Asceticism: Buddhist Perspectives'; 'Death Rituals'; 'Marathon Monks'; 'Monasticism: Definitions of,'; 'Music: Buddhist Perspectives'; 'Sri Lanka: History'; 'Sri Lanka: Recent Changes'; 'Temple'; 'Virtues'.' In *Encyclopedia of monasticism.,* edited by W. Johnston. London: Fitzroy Dearborn.

2000. "From Buddhology to Buddhist Theology: An Orientation to Sinhala Buddhism." In *Buddhist Theology: Critical Reflections By Contemporary Buddhist Scholars.* editied by R. Jackson and J. Makransky, 331–345. Richmond: Curzon.

1999. "A search for Mahāyāna in Sri Lanka." *Journal of the International Association of Buddhist Studies* 22(2): 343–357.

1997. "Buddhist Preaching and Sinhala Religious Rhetoric: Medieval Buddhist Methods to Popularize Theravāda." *Numen* 44(2): 180–210.

1996. "The Moral Significance of Buddhist Nirvana." In *Pali Buddhism,* edited by F. Hoffman and M. Deegalle, 105–116. Curzon Studies in Asian Philosophy 3. Richmond: Curzon.

De Frantz, Monika.

2008. "New Regionalism Top Down: Mobilizing National Minority Culture." *Regional & Federal Studies* 18(4): 403–427.

De Jong, J. W.

1993. "The Beginnings of Buddhism." *The Eastern Buddhist* 26(2): 25–38.

1972. "Emptiness." *Journal of Indian Philosophy* 2(1): 7–15.

De Mel, Neloufer.

2003. "Agent or Victim? The Sri Lankan Woman Militant in the Interregnum." In *Feminists Under Fire: Exchanges Across War Zones,* edited by Wenona Mary Giles, 55–74. Toronto: Between the Lines.

2002. "Fractured Narratives: Notes on Women in Conflict in Sri Lanka and Pakistan." *Development* 45(1): 99–104.

2001. *Women & the Nations' Narrative: Gender and Nationalism in the Twentieth Century Sri Lanka*. Lanham, MD: Rowman & Littlefield.

De Silva, Chandra R.

2006. "Buddhist Monks and Peace in Sri Lanka." In *Buddhism, Conflict and Violence in Modern Sri Lanka*, edited by Mahinda Deegalle, 202–209. London: Routledge.

1997. *Sri Lanka, A History*. Delhi: Vikas Publishing House.

1995. "The Elections of 1994 in Sri Lanka: Background and Analysis." *The Round Table* 84(334): 207–217.

1979. "The Constitution of the Second Republic of Sri Lanka (1978) and Its Significance." *Journal of Commonwealth & Comparative Politics* 17(2): 192–209.

1974. "Weightage in University Admissions: Standardisation and District Quotas in Sri Lanka 1970–1975." *Modern Ceylon Studies* 5(2): 151–167.

De Silva, Chandra Richard and Tessa J. Bartholomeusz.

2001. *The Role of the Sangha in the Reconciliation Process*. Colombo: Marga Institute.

De Silva, K. M.

2005. *A History of Sri Lanka*. New Edition. New York: Penguin.

2001. "Grappling with the Past, Coping with the Present, Thinking of the Future: Culture, Tradition and Modernisation in Sri Lanka." *South Asian Survey* 8(2): 261–275.

1998. "Electoral Systems." In *Ethnic Diversity and Public Policy: A Comparative Inquiry*, edited by C. Young, 72–107. London: Macmillan.

1997. "Sri Lanka: Surviving Ethnic Strife." *Journal of Democracy* 8(1): 97–111.

1996. *Sri Lanka, Ethnic Conflict, Management and Resolution*. Vol. 1. Kandy, Sri Lanka: International Centre for Ethnic Studies.

1981. *A History of Sri Lanka*. Berkeley: University of California Press.

1979. "Political and Constitutional Change in Sri Lanka: The UNP Consolidates Its Position." *The Round Table* 69(273): 49–57.

De Silva, Nalin.

1990. "The Heritage of National Culture." "Alie's," *Economic Review* 16(2): 34–46.

De Silva, Padmasiri.

1979. *An Introduction to Buddhist Psychology*. New York: Barnes & Noble Books.

De Silva, Padmasiri and Kenichi Ishigaki.

2002. *Buddhism, Ethics and Society: The Conflicts and Dilemmas of Our Times*. Victoria: Monash Asia Institute, Monash University.

De Silva, Premakumara.
2006. "Anthropology of 'Sinhala Buddhism'." *Contemporary Buddhism* 7(2): 165–170.

De Winter, Lieven and Pierre Baudewyns.
2015. "Candidate Centred Campaigning in a Party Centred Context: The Case of Belgium." *Electoral Studies* 39: 295–305.

Demmers, J.
2002. "Diaspora and Conflict: Locality, Long-distance Nationalism and Delocalization of Conflict Dynamics." *The Public-Javnost* 9(1): 85–96.

Dep, Arthur C.
2001. *Ceylon Police and Sinhala-Muslim Riots of 1915*. Colombo: Sarvodaya Vishva Lekha.

Destradi, Sandra.
2012. "India and Sri Lanka's Civil War." *Asian Survey* 52(3): 595–616.

Devendra, D. T.
1959. "Seventy Years of Ceylon Archaeology." *ArtibusAsiae* 22(1–2): 23–40.

DeVido, Elise A.
2007. "Buddhist Nuns in Taiwan and Sri Lanka: A Critique of the Feminist Perspective - By Wei-Yi Cheng." *Journal of Chinese Philosophy* 34(4): 640–645.

DeVotta, Neil.
2010. "From Civil War to Soft Authoritarianism: Sri Lanka in Comparative Perspective." *Global Change, Peace & Security* 22(3): 331–343.
2009. "The Liberation Tigers of Tamil Eelam and the Lost Quest for Separatism in Sri Lanka." *Asian Survey* 49(6): 1021–1051.
2008. "Terrorism and Democratic Regression in Sri Lanka." *Economic and Political Weekly* 43(14): 15–17.
2007. *Sinhalese Buddhist Nationalist Ideology: Implications for Politics and Conflict Resolution in Sri Lanka*. Washington, DC: East-West Center Washington.
2005. "Civil Society and Non-Governmental Organizations in Sri Lanka: Peacemakers or Parasites?" *Civil Wars* 7(2): 171–182.
2004a. "Sri Lanka: Ethnic Domination, Violence, and Illiberal Democracy." In *Civil Society and Political Change in Asia: Expanding and Contracting Democratic Space*, by Muthiah Alagappa, 292–323. Stanford, CA: Stanford University Press.
2004b. *Blowback: Linguistic Nationalism, Institutional Decay, and Ethnic Conflict in Sri Lanka*. Stanford, CA: Stanford University Press.
2002. "Illiberalism and Ethnic Conflict in Sri Lanka." *Journal of Democracy* 13(1): 84–98.
2000. "Control Democracy, Institutional Decay, and the Quest for EELAM : Explaining Ethnic Conflict in Sri Lanka." *Pacific Affairs* 73(1): 55–76
1998. "Sri Lanka's Structural Adjustment Program and its Impact on Indo-Lanka Relations." *Asian Survey* 38(5): 457–473.

DeVotta, Neil and Jason Stone.

2008. "Jathika Hela Urumaya and Ethno-religious Politics in Sri Lanka." *Pacific Affairs* 81(1): 31–51.

Dharmadasa, K. N. O.

1998. "Formative Stages of Sinhala Journalism." In *Studies on the Press in Sri Lanka and South Asia,* edited by G. H. Peiris, 149–165. Kandy, Sri Lanka: International Centre for Ethnic Studies.

1992. *Language, Religion, and Ethnic Assertiveness: The Growth of Sinhalese Nationalism in Sri Lanka*. Ann Arbor: University of Michigan Press.

1989 "The People of the Lion Ethnic Identity, Ideology and Historical Revisionism in Contemporary Sri Lanka." The Sri Lanka Journal of Humanity 15 (1989): 1–35.

1977. "Nativism, Diglossia and the Sinhalese Identity in the Language Problem in Sri Lanka." *International Journal of the Sociology of Language* 1977(13): 21–32.

Diamond, Larry Jay.

2008. *The Spirit of Democracy: The Struggle to Build Free Societies Throughout the World.* New York: Times Books/Henry Holt and Co.

2002. "Thinking about Hybrid Regimes." *Journal of Democracy* 13(2): 21–35.

Dillon, Matthew.

2000. "Dialogues with Death: The Last Days of Socrates and the Buddha." *Philosophy East and West* 50(4): 525–558.

Dixit, Jyotindra Nath.

1998. *Assignment Colombo.* Delhi: Konark Publishers.

Dixit, Jyotindra Nath and Shailendra K. Singh.

2003. *External Affairs: Cross-border Relations*. Delhi: Roli Books.

Duara, Prasenjit.

2004. *Decolonization: Perspectives from Now and Then.* London: Routledge.

Duffield, Mark R.

2001. *Global Governance and the New Wars: The Merging Of Development and Security*. London: Zed books.

Duncan, James S.

2002. "Embodying Colonialism? Domination and Resistance in Nineteenth-century Ceylonese Coffee Plantations." *Journal of Historical Geography* 28(3): 317–338.

Dutt, Nalinaksha.

2003. *Mahayana Buddhism*. Revised edition. Delhi: Bhartiya Kala Prakashan.

1998. *Buddhist sects in India*. Delhi: Motilal Banarsidass Publishers.

1980. *Early History of the Spread of Buddhism and the Buddhist Schools.* New Delhi: Rajesh Publications.

1960. *Early Monastic Buddhism.* Calcutta: Calcutta Oriental Book Agency.

1945a. "The Buddhist Sects. A Survey." BC Law Volume, Part I, 282–292. Calcutta Indian Research Institute.

1945b. "Popular Buddhism." *Indian Historical Quarterly* 21: 251–256.

1941. *Early Monastic Buddhism*. Calcutta: Calcutta Oriental Book Agency.

Dutt, Sukumar.

1984. *Early Buddhist Monachism*. New Delhi: MunshiramManoharlal.

Earle, Valerie A. and George Wescott Carey.

1968. *Federalism: Infinite Variety in Theory and Practice*. Itasca, IL: F. E. Peacock.

Edrisinha, Rohan.

2005. "Multination Federalism and Minority Rights in Sri Lanka." In *Multiculturalism in Asia*, edited by W. Kymlicka and H. Baogang, 244–262. Oxford: Oxford University Press.

1999. "Constitutionalism, Pluralism, and Ethnic Conflict: The Need for a New Initiative." In *Creating Peace in Sri Lanka*, edited by Robert I. Rotberg, 169–187. Cambridge, MA: The World Peace Foundation.

1998. "Critical Overview: Constitutionalism, Conflict Resolution and the Limits of the Draft Constitution." *The Draft Constitution of Sri Lanka: Critical Aspects*, edited by Dinusha Panditaratne and Pradeep Ratnam , 13–37. Colombo: Law and Society Trust.

Edrisinha, Rohan and Naganathan Selvakkumaran.

2000. "The Constitutional Evolution of Ceylon/Sri Lanka 1948–98." In *Sri Lanka's Development since Independence: Socio-Economic Perspectives and Analyses*, edited by Weligamage D. Lakshman and Clement A. Tisdell, 95–112. New York: Nova Science Publishers.

Edrisinha, Rohan and Asanga Welikala, eds.

2008. *Essays on federalism in Sri Lanka*. Colombo: Centre for Policy Alternative.

Egge, James R.

2002. *Religious Giving and the Invention of Karma in Theravāda Buddhism*. Richmond: Curzon.

Eidelson, Roy J. and Judy I. Eidelson.

2003. "Dangerous Ideas: Five Beliefs That Propel Groups toward Conflict." *American Psychologist* 58(3): 182–192.

Elazar, D. J.

1987. *Exploring Federalism*. Tuscaloosa: University of Alabama Press.

1971. "The Themes of a Journal of Federalism." *Publius* 1(1): 3–9.

1966. *American Federalism: A View from the States*. New York: Thomas Cromwell Company.

Elbaum, Bernard and William Lazonick.

1984. "The Decline of the British Economy: An Institutional Perspective." *The Journal of Economic History* 44(2): 567–583.

Eliot, Charles.

1921. *Hinduism and Buddhism: An Historical Sketch*. London: E. Arnold.

Emmanuel, Benille Priyanka W. D. J.

2000. "Civilization on Its Own Words Archaeology of Ancient Sri Lanka." Unpublished PhD Thesis, University of California.

Esposito, John L., Darrell J. Fasching, Todd Lewis and Todd Vernon Lewis.

2007. *Religion and Globalization: World Religions in Historical Perspective*. Oxford: Oxford University Press.

Erk, Jan and Lawrence Anderson.

2009. "The Paradox of Federalism: Does Self-Rule Accommodate or Exacerbate Ethnic Divisions?" *Regional and Federal Studies* 19(2): 191–202.

Evans, Grant.

1998. *The Politics of Ritual and Remembrance: Laos since 1975*. Honolulu: University of Hawai'i Press.

Evers, Hans-Dieter.

1969. "Monastic Landlordism in Ceylon: A Traditional System in a Modern Setting." *Journal of Asian Studies* 28(4): 668–692.

1968. "Buddha and the Seven Gods: The Dual Organization of a Temple in Central Ceylon." *Journal of Asian Studies* 27(3): 541–550.

1967. "Kinship and Property Rights in a Buddhist Monastery in Central Ceylon." *American Anthropologist* 69(6): 703–710.

Evers, Hans-Dieter and Sharon Siddique.

1993. "Religious Revivalism in Southeast Asia: An Introduction." *Sojourn* 8(1): 1–10.

Fair, C. Christine.

2005. *Urban Battle Fields of South Asia: Lessons Learned from Sri Lanka, India and Pakistan*. Santa Monica, CA: RAND Corporation.

Fernando, P. T. M.

1970. "The Post Riots Campaign for Justice." *The Journal of Asian Studies* 29(2): 255–266.

1969. The British Raj and the 1915 Communal Riots in Ceylon Modern Asian Studies 3(3): 245–255.

Fernando. T.

1973a. Elite Politics in the New States: The Case of Post Independence Sri Lanka. *Pacific Affairs* 46: 361–383.

1973b. "The Western-Educated Elite and Buddhism in British Ceylon." *Contributions to Asian Studies* 4: 18–29.

Faist, Thomas.

2000. "Transnationalization in International Migration: Implications for the Study of Citizenship and Culture." *Ethnic and Racial Studies* 23(2): 189–222.

Findly, Ellison Banks. 1992. "Ānanda's Hindrance: Faith (*saddhā*) in Early Buddhism." *Journal of Indian Philosophy* 20(3): 253–273.

Fleming, A.

2006. "Post-processual Landscape Archaeology: A Critique." *Cambridge Archaeological Journal* 16(3): 267–280.

Flügel, Peter.

2006. "Demographic trends in Jaina monasticism." In *Studies in Jaina History and Culture: Disputes and Dialogues*, edited by Peter Flügel, 312–398. London: Routledge.

Foucault, Michel.

1978. "Nietzsche, Genealogy, History." *Semiotexte* 3(1): 78–94.

1985. *Discourse and Truth: The Problematization of Parrhesia*. Edited by J. Pearson. Evanston, IL: Northwestern University.

Fox, Jonathan.

2006. "World Separation oOf Religion and State into the 21st Century." *Comparative Political Studies* 39(5): 537–569.

2005. *Religion, Civilization, and Civil War: 1945 Through the New Millennium*. Lanham, MD: Lexington Books.

2004a. "The Rise of Religious Nationalism and Conflict: Ethnic Conflict and Revolutionary Wars, 1945–2001." *Journal of Peace Research* 41(6): 715–731.

2004b. "Religion and State Failure: An Examination of the Extent and Magnitude of Religious Conflict from 1950 to 1996." *International Political Science Review* 25(1): 55–76.

2004c. "Are Some Religions More Conflict-Prone Than Others?" *Jewish Political Studies Review* 16(1–2): 81–100.

2003. "Counting the Causes and Dynamics of Ethnoreligious Violence." *Totalitarian Movements & Political Religions* 4(3): 119–144.

2001. "Religion as an Overlooked Element of International Relations." *International Studies Review* 3(3): 53–73.

2000. "Religious Causes of Discrimination against Ethno–Religious Minorities." *International Studies Quarterly* 44(3): 423–450.

1999. "The Influence of Religious Legitimacy on Grievance Formation By Ethno-Religious Minorities." *Journal of Peace Research* 36(3): 289–307.

Fox, Jonathan and Shmuel Sandler.

2005. "Separation of Religion and State in the Twenty-first Century: Comparing the Middle East and Western Democracies." *Comparative Politics* 37(3): 317–335.

Franck, Thomas M., ed.

1968. *Why Federations Fail: An Inquiry into the Requisites for Successful Federalism*. Studies in Peaceful Change 1. Nedw York: New York University Press.

Freston, Paul.

1994. "Popular Protestants in Brazilian Politics: A Novel Turn in Sect-State Relations." *Social Compass* 41(4): 537–570.

Friedland, William H.

1994. "The New Globalization: The Case of Fresh Produce. In *From Columbus to ConAgra: The Globalization of Agriculture and Food*, edited by Alessandro Bonanno, Lawrence Busch, William H. Friedland, Lourdes Gouveia, Enzo Mingione, 210–231. Lawrence: University of Kansas Press.

Froese, Paul Christopher Bader and Buster Smith.

2008. "Political Tolerance and God's Wrath in the United States." *Sociology of Religion* 69(1): 29–44.

Frost, Mark.

2002. "'Wider Opportunities': Religious Revival, Nationalist Awakening and the Global Dimension in Colombo, 1870–1920." *Modern Asian Studies* 36(4): 937–967.

Frydenlund, Iselin.

2005. "The Sangha and Its Relation to the Peace Process in Sri Lanka." *PRIO Report 2*. Oslo: International Peace Research Institute (PRIO).

Gagnon, Alain.

2009. *The Case for Multinational Federalism: Beyond the All-encompassing Nation*. London: Routledge.

2007. "Democratic Multinational Federalism under Scrutiny: Healthy Tensions and Unresolved Issues in Canada." In *Multinational Federations*, edited by Michael Burgess and John Pinder, 17–30. London: Routledge.

Gagnon, Alain and James Tully, eds.

2001. *Multinational Democracies*. Cambridge: Cambridge University Press.

Gamage, Siri.

2009. "Economic Liberalisation, Changes in Governance Structure and Ethnic Conflict in Sri Lanka." *Journal of Contemporary Asia* 39(2): 247–261.

Gaus, G. F. and K. Vallier.

2009. "The Roles of Religious Conviction in a Publicly Justified Polity: The Implications of Convergence, Asymmetry and Political Institutions." *Philosophy & Social Criticism* 35(1–2): 51–76.

Geiger, Wilhelm.

1960. *The Mahāvaṃsa*. Colombo: Ceylon Governement Information Department.

1930. "The Trustworthiness of the Mahavamsa." *Indian Historical Quarterly* 6: 205–238.

Geiger, Wilhelm and Heinz Becchert, eds.

1960. *Culture of Ceylon in Mediaeval Times*. Wiesbaden: Otto Harrassowitz.

Geiger, Wilhelm and Mabel Haynes Bode.
1912. *Mahāvaṃsa: The Great Chronicle of Ceylon.* London: Published for the Pali Text Society by Oxford University Press.

Gellner, Ernest.
1997. *Nationalism.* New York: New York University Press.
1994. *Conditions of Liberty: Civil Society and Its Rivals.* New York: Allen Lane/ Penguin Press.
1987. *Culture, Identity, and Politics.* Cambridge: Cambridge University Press.

Giddens, Anthony.
1994. "Living in a Post-Traditional Society." In *Reflexive Modernization: Politics, Traditions and Aesthetics in the Modern Social Order,* edited by U. Beck, A. Giddens and S. Lash, 56–109. Cambridge: Polity Press.
1991. *The Consequences of Modernity.* Cambridge: Polity Press.

Goh, Geok Yian.
2007. "Cakkravatiy Anuruddha and the Buddhist Oikoumene: Historical Narratives of Kingship and Religious Networks in Burma, Northern Thailand, and Sri Lanka (11th-14th Centuries)." Unpublished PhD thesis, University of Hawaii.

Gokhale, B. Jayashree.
1986. "The Sociopolitical Effects of Ideological Change: The Buddhist Conversion of Maharashtrian Untouchables." *The Journal of Asian Studies* 45(2): 269–292.
1980. "Bhakti in Early Buddhism." *African and Asian Studies* 15(1): 16–28.
1969. "The Early Buddhist View of the State." *Journal of the American Oriental Society* 89(4): 731–738.
1966. "Early Buddhist Kingship." *The Journal of Asian Studies* 26(1): 15–22.
1965. "The Early Buddhist Elite." *Journal of Indian History* 42(2): 391–402.

Gombrich, Richard Francis.
2009. *What the Buddha Thought.* London: Equinox Publishing.
2006a. *How Buddhism Began: The Conditioned Genesis of the Early Teachings.* London: Routledge.
2006b. *Theravada Buddhism: A Social History from Ancient Benares to Modern Colombo.* London: Routledge.
2006c. "Is the Sri Lankan war a Buddhist fundamentalism?" In *Buddhism, conflict and violence in modern Sri Lanka,* edited by M. Deegalle. 22–37. New York: Routledge.
1998. *Kindness and Compassion as Means to Nirvana.* 1997 Gonda Lecture. Amsterdam: Royal Netherlands Academy of Arts and Sciences.
1996. *How Buddhism Began. The Conditioned Genesis of the Early Teachings.* London & Atlantic Highlands: Athlone
1995. *Buddhist Precept and Practice: Traditional Buddhism in the Highlands of Ceylon,* London: Kegan Paul International.

1992. "The Buddha's Book of Genesis?" *Indo-Iranian Journal* 35(2): 159–178.
1990a. "Recovering the Buddha's message." In *The Buddhist Forum* 1: 5–20.
1990b. "How the Mahayana Began." *The Buddhist Forum* 1: 21–30.
1988. *Theravāda Buddhism: A Social History From Ancient Benares To Modern Colombo*. London: Routledge & Kegan Paul.
1984a. "Notes on the Brahminical Background to Buddhist Ethics." In *Buddhist Studies In Honour of Hammalava Saddhatissa*, edited by G. Dhammapala, R. Gombrich and K. R. Norman, 91–102. Nugegoda, Sri Lanka: Hammalava Saddhātissa Felicitation Volume Committee.
1984b. "Temporary Ordination in Sri Lanka." *Journal of the International Association of Buddhist Studies* 7(2): 41–66.
1975a. "Buddhist Karma and Social Control." *Comparative Studies in Society and History* 17(2): 212–220.
1975a. "Ancient Indian Cosmology." *Ancient cosmologies* (1975): 112–113.
1988. *Theravāda Buddhism: A Social History from Ancient Benares to Modern Colombo*. London: Routledge & Kegan Paul.
1971. *Precept and Practice: Traditional Buddhism in the Rural Highlands of Ceylon*. Oxford: Clarendon Press.
1966. "The Consecration of a Buddhist Image." *The Journal of Asian Studies* 26(1): 23–36.

Gombrich, Richard F. and Gananath Obeyesekere.
1988. *Buddhism Transformed: Religious Change in Sri Lanka*. Princeton, NJ: Princeton University Press.

Gombrich, Richard and Sanjukta Gupta.
1986. "Kings, Power and the Goddess." *South Asia Research* 6(2): 123–138.

Goodhand, Jonathan.
2010. "Stabilising a Victor's Peace? Humanitarian Action and Reconstruction in Eastern Sri Lanka." *Disasters* 34: 342–367.
1999a. "From Wars to Complex Political Emergencies: Understanding Conflict and Peace-building in the New World Disorder." *Third World Quarterly* 20(1): 13–26.
1999b. "Sri Lanka: NGOs and Peace-building in Complex Political Emergencies." *Third World Quarterly* 20(1): 69–87.

Goodhand, Jonathan and Oliver Walton.
2009. "The Limits of Liberal Peacebuilding? International Engagement in the Sri Lankan Peace Process." *Journal of Intervention and Statebuilding* 3(3): 303–323.

Goodhand, Jonathan, David Hulme and Nick Lewer.
2000. "Social Capital and the Political Economy of Violence: A Case Study of Sri Lanka." *Disasters* 24(4): 390–406.

Goodhand, Jonathan, Bart Klem, Dilrukshi Fonseka, S. I. Keethaponcalan and Shonali Sardesai.
2005. *Aid, Conflict, and Peacebuilding in Sri Lanka, 2000–2005,* vol. 1. Colombo: Asia Foundation.

Goodhand, Jonathan, Benedikt Korf and Jonathan Spencer, eds.
2010. *Conflict and Peacebuilding in Sri Lanka: Caught in the Peace Trap?* London: Routledge.

Goonewardena, K. W.
2002. "Aborted Identity: The Commission and Omission of a Monument to the Nation, Sri Lanka, Circa 1989." *Radical History Review* 82(1): 141–156.

Goonewardena, K. W. and K. W. Goonewardene
1992. "Review of 'Robert Knox: The Interleaved Edition'." *Journal of the Royal Asiatic Society of Sri Lanka* (New Series) 37: 117–144.

Gooptu, Nandini.
1997. "The Urban Poor and Militant Hinduism in Early Twentieth-Century Uttar Pradesh." *Modern Asian Studies* 31(04): 879–918.

Gordon, Daniel V. and Wimal Rankaduwa.
1992. "Trade, Taxes and Debt Repayment in Sri Lanka." *Journal of Development Studies* 29(1): 148–165.

Grant, Patrick.
2009. *Buddhism and the Ethnic Conflicting Sri Lanka.* Albany: State University of New York Press.

Griffin, Roger.
2004. "Introduction: God's Counterfeiters? Investigating the Triad of Fascism, Totalitarianism and (Political) Religion." *Totalitarian Movements and Political Religions* 5(3): 291–325.

Grobar, Lisa Morris and Shiranthi Gnanaselvam.
1993. "The Economic Effects of the Sri Lankan Civil War." *Economic Development and Cultural Change* 41(2): 395–405.

Gromes, Thorsten.
2010. "Federalism as a Means of Peace-Building: The Case of Postwar Bosnia and Herzegovina." *Nationalism and Ethnic Politics* 16(3–4): 354–374.

Grossberg, Lawrence.
2006. "Does Cultural Studies Have Futures? Should It? (Or What's the Matter with New York?)." *Cultural Studies* 20(1): 1–32.

Gunasekara, Tisaranee.
1999. "Insurrectionary Violence in Sri Lanka: The Janatha Vimukthi Peramuna Insurgencies of 1971 and 1987–1989." *Ethnic Studies Report* 17(1): 65–88.

Gunasinghe , Newton.

2004. "The Open Economy and its Impact on Ethnic Relations in Sri Lanka." In *Economy , Culture and Civil War in Sri Lanka,* edited by Deborah Winslow and Michael D Woost, 99–114. Bloomington: Indiana University Press.

Gunawardana, R. A. L. H.

2003. "Roots of the Ethnic Conflict in Sri Lanka." *Journal of Buddhist Ethics* 10.

1995. *Historiography in a Time of Ethnic Conflict: Construction of the Past in Contemporary Sri Lanka.* Colombo: Social Scientists' Association.

1990. "The People of Lion: The Sinhala Identity and Ideology in History and Historiography." In *Sri Lanka: History and the Roots of Conflict*, edited by Jonathan Spencer, 45–78. London: Routledge.

1988. "Subtile Silk of Ferreous Firmness: Buddhist Nuns in Ancient and Early Medieval Sri Lanka and their Role in the Propagation of Buddhism." *The Sri Lanka Journal of the Humanities* 14: 1–59.

1985. "The People of the Lion: Sinhala Consciousness in History and Historiography." In *Ethnicity and Social Change in Sri Lanka*, edited by Social Scientists' Association. Colombo: Navamaga Printers.

1979. *Robe and Plough: Monasticism and Economic Interest in Early Medieval Sri Lanka.* Tucson: University of Arizona Press.

1978. "The Kinsmen of the Buddha: Myth as Political Charter in the Ancient and Early Medieval Kingdoms of Sri Lanka." In *Religion and Legitimation of Power in Sri Lanka*, edited by Bardwell L. Smith, 96–106. Chambersburg, PA: Anima Books.

1971. "Irrigation and Hydraulic Society in Early Medieval Ceylon." *Past and Present* 53(1): 3–27.

Guruge, Ananda W. P., ed.

1965. *Return to Righteousness: A Collection of Speeches, Essays, and Letters of the Anagarika Dharmapāla.* Anagarika Dharmapāla Birth Centenary Committee. Colombo: Ministry of Education and Cultural Affairs.

Habermas, Jürgen.

2006. "Religion in the Public Sphere." *European Journal of Philosophy* 14(1): 1–25.

1979. *Communication and the Evolution of Society.* Boston, MA: Beacon Press.

Hall, Rodney Bruce.

1999. *National Collective Identity: Social Constructs and International Systems.* New York: Columbia University Press.

Hallisey, Charles.

1996. "Ethical Particularism in Theravada Buddhism." *Journal of Buddhist Ethics* 3: 32–43.

1992. "Recent Works on Buddhist Ethics." *Religious Studies Review* 18(4): 276–285.

Hallisey, Charles and Anne Hansen.
1996. "Narrative, Sub-Ethics and the Moral Life: Some Evidence from Theravāda Buddhism." *Journal of Buddhist Ethics* 24(2): 305–327.

Hancock, Landon E.
1999. "The Indo-Sri Lankan Accord: An Analysis of Conflict Termination." *Civil Wars* 2(4): 83–105.

Haniffa, Farzana.
2011. "Three Attempts at Peace in Sri Lanka: A Critical Muslim Perspective." *Journal of Peacebuilding & Development* 6(1): 49–62.

Hansen, Thomas Blom.
2005. "Sovereigns Beyond the State: On Legality and Authority in Urban India." In *Sovereign Bodies: Citizens, Migrants, and States in the Postcolonial World*, edited by Thomas Blom Hansen and Finn Stepputat, 169–191. Princeton, NJ: Princeton University Press.
2001. *Wages of Violence: Naming and Identity in Postcolonial Bombay*. Princeton, NJ: Princeton University Press.

Harischandra, Walisinha.
1998. *The Sacred City of Anuradhapura*. New Delhi: Asian Educational Services.

Harpham, Geoffrey Galt.
1992. *Getting It Right: Language, Literature, and Ethics*. Chicago, IL: University of Chicago Press.

Harris, Elisabeth J.
2006. *Theravada Buddhism and the British Encounter: Religious, Missionary and Colonial Experience in Nineteenth Century Sri Lanka*. London: Routledge.
2001. "Buddhism In War: A Study of Cause and Effect from Sri Lanka." *Culture and Religion* 2(2): 197–222.

Harris, Ian Charles.
2007. *Buddhism, Power and Political Order*. London: Routledge.
2005. *Cambodian Buddhism: History and Practice*. Honolulu: University of Hawaii Press.
1999a. *Buddhism and Politics in Twentieth-century Asia*. London: Pinter.
1999b. "Buddhism in Extremis: The Case of Cambodia." In *Buddhism and Politics in Twentieth-century Asia*, edited by Ian Harris, 54–78. London: Bloomsbury.

Harvey, Peter.
2000. *An Introduction To Buddhist Ethics: Foundations, Values, and Issues*. Cambridge: Cambridge University Press.

Haynes, Jeffery.
2010. "Politics, Identity and Religious Nationalism in Turkey: From Atatürk to the AKP." *Australian Journal of International Affairs* 64(3): 312–327.

2008. *Routledge Handbook of Religion and Politics*. London: Routledge.
2007. "Religion, Ethnicity and Civil War in Africa: The Cases of Uganda and Sudan." *The Round Table* 96(390): 305–317.
2004. "Religion and Democratization in Africa." *Democratization* 11(4): 66–89.
2001. "Transnational Religious Actors and International Politics." *Third World Quarterly* 22(2): 143–158.

He, Baogang, Brian Galligan and Takashi Inoguchi.
2007. *Federalism in Asia*. Cheltenham: Edward Elgar.

Hellmann-Rajanayagam, Dagmar.
1990. *The Politics of the Tamil Past*. London: Routledge.

Hennayake, Nalini.
2006. *Culture, Politics, and Development in Postcolonial Sri Lanka*. Lanham, MD: Lexington Books.

Hennayake, S. K.
1989. "The Peace Accord and the Tamils in Sri Lanka." *Asian Survey* 29(4): 401–415.

Heyking, John Von.
2000. "The Harmonization of Heaven and Earth?: Religion, Politics and Law in Canada." *University of British Columbia Law Review* 33 (Special Issue): 663–697.

Hicks, Ursula K.
2011. [1961] *Federalism and Economic Growth in Underdeveloped Countries, a Symposium*. London: Routledge.

Hoffman, Yair.
1994. "Reflections on the Relationship Between Theopolitics, Prophecy and Historiography." In *Politics and Theopolitics in the Bible and Postbiblical Literature*, edited by Graf Henning Reventlow, Yair Hoffman and Benjamin Uffenheimer, 85–99. Sheffield: JSOT Press.

Höglund, Kristine.
2005. "Violence and the Peace Process in Sri Lanka." *Civil Wars* 7(2): 156–170.

Höglund, Kristine and Anton Piyarathne.
2009. "Paying the Price for Patronage: Electoral Violence in Sri Lanka." *Commonwealth & Comparative Politics* 47(3): 287–307.

Höglund, Kristine and Camilla Orjuela.
2011. "Winning the Peace: Conflict, Prevention after a Victor's Peace in Sri Lanka." *Contemporary Social Science* 6(1): 19–37.

Höglund, Kristine and Isak Svensson.
2009. "Mediating between Tigers and Lions: Norwegian Peace Diplomacy in Sri Lanka's Civil War." *Contemporary South Asia* 17(2): 175–191.

Holliday, Ian.
2007. "National Unity Struggles in Myanmar: A Degenerate Case of Governance for Harmony in Asia." *Asian Survey* 47(3): 374–392.

Holt, John Clifford.
1996. *The Religious World of Kirti Sri: Buddhism, Art, and Politics of Late Medieval Sri Lanka.* Oxford: Oxford University Press.

Hopgood, S.
2005. "Tamil Tigers, 1987–2002." In *Making Sense of Suicide Missions*, by Diego Gambetta, 43–76. Oxford: Oxford University Press.

Hopkins, Keith.
1998. "Christian Number and Its Implications." *Journal of Early Christian Studies* 6(2): 185–226.

Horowitz, Donald L.
1993. "Democracy in Divided Societies." *Journal of Democracy* 4(4): 18–33.
1985. *Ethnic Groups in Conflicts.* Berkeley: University of California Press.

Houtart, Francois.
1974. *Religion and ideology in Sri Lanka.* Bangalore: TPI Publisher.

Houtart, Francois and Genevieve Lemercinier.
1978. "Socio-Religious Movements in Kerala: A Reaction to the Capitalist Mode of Production: Part One." *Social Scientist* (1978): 3–34.
1977. "Theravada Buddhism and Political Power: Construction and Destructuration of Its Ideological Function." *Social Compass* 24(2–3): 207–246.
1976a. "Buddhism and Politics in South-East Asia: Part One." *Social Scientist* 5(3): 3–23.
1976b. "Weberian Theory and the Ideological Function of Religion." *Social Compass* 23(4): 345–354.

Hresko, Tracy.
2006. "Rights Rhetoric as an Instrument of Religious Oppression in Sri Lanka." *Boston College International Comparative Law Review* 29(1): 123–133

Hunt, Stephen.
2000. "'Winning Ways': Globalisation and the Impact of the Health and Wealth Gospel." *Journal of Contemporary Religion* 15(3): 331–347.

Iff, Andrea.
2013. "Peace-Promoting Federalism: Making Sense of India and Nigeria." *Publius* 43(2): 227–250 .

Ignatieff, Michael.
2001. *Human Rights As Politics and idolatry.* Edited and introduced by Amy Gutmann. Princeton, NJ: Princeton University Press.

Imtiyaz, A. R. M. and Ben Stavis
2008. "Ethno-Political Conflict in Sri Lanka." *Journal of Third World Studies* 25(2): 135–152.

Intirapālā, Kārttikēcu.

2005. *The Evolution of an Ethnic Identity: The Tamils in Sri Lanka C. 300 BCE to C. 1200 CE.* [Colombo]: M.V. Publications for the South Asian Studies Centre, Sydney.

James, Simon P.

2004. *Zen Buddhism and Environmental Ethics.* London: Ashgate.

Jayasuriya, Shihan De Silva.

1999. "Portuguese in Sri Lanka: Influence of Substratum Languages." *Journal of the Royal Asiatic Society* (Third Series) 9(2): 251–270.

Jayasuriya, J. E.

1977. *Educational policies and progress during British rule in Ceylon (Sri Lanka), 1796-1948.* Colombo: Associated Educational Publishers.

Jayawardena, Kumari.

2002. *Nobodies to Somebodies: The Rise of the Colonial Bourgeoisie in Sri Lanka.* London and New York: Zed Books.

1974. "Origins of the Left Movement in Sri Lanka." *Social Scientist* 2(6/7): 3–28

1972. *The Rise of the Labor Movement in Ceylon.* Durham, NC :Duke University Press

1970. "Economic and Political Factors in the 1915 Riots." *The Journal of Asian Studies* 29(2): 223–233.

Jeganathan, Pradeep.

1998. "In the Shadow of Violence, Tamilness and the Anthropology of Identity in Southern Sri Lanka." In *Buddhist Fundamentalism and Minority Identities in Sri Lanka*, by Tessa J. Bartholomeusz and Chandra Richard De Silva, 89–109. Albany: State University of New York Press.

1997. "After a Riot: Anthropological Locations of Violence in an Urban Community of Sri Lanka." Unpublished PhD thesis, University of Chicago.

Jeganathan, Pradeep and Qadri Ismail.

1995. *Unmaking the Nation.* Colombo: Social Scientists Association

Jenkins, Philip.

2002. *The next Christendom: The Coming of Global Christianity.* Oxford: Oxford University Press.

Jenkins, Richard.

2008. *Rethinking Ethnicity.* London: Sage.

Jennings, Ivor.

1954. "Politics in Ceylon Since 1952." *Pacific Affairs* 27(4): 338–352.

Jerryson, Michael.

2009. "Appropriating a Space for Violence: State Buddhism in Southern Thailand." *Journal of Southeast Asian Studies* 40(1): 33–57.

Jerryson, Michael K. and Mark Juergensmeyer.

2009. *Buddhist Warfare.* Oxford: Oxford University Press.

Jiggins, Janice.
2010. [1979] *Caste and Family Politics Sinhalese 1947-1976*. Cambridge: Cambridge University Press.

Joll, Christopher M.
2010. "Religion and Conflict in Southern Thailand: Beyond Rounding Up the Usual Suspects." *Contemporary Southeast Asia* 32(2): 258–279.

Jones, Richard H.
1979. "Theravāda Buddhism and Morality." *Journal of the American Academy of Religion* XLVII(3): 371–387.

Juergensmeyer, Mark.
2010a. *Terror in the Mind of God: The Global Rise of Religious Violence*. Berkeley: University of California Press.
2010b. "The Global Rise of Religious Nationalism." *Australian Journal of International Affairs* 64(3): 262–273.
2008. *Global Rebellion: Religious Challenges to the Secular State: from Christian Militias to Al Qaeda*. Berkeley: University of California Press.
2006. "Nationalism and Religion." In *The Sage Handbook of Nations and Nationalism,* edited by Gerard Delanty and Krishan Kumar, 182–191. London: Sage.
2005. *Religion in Global Civil Society*. Oxford: Oxford University Press.
2004a. "Is Religion the Problem?" *Hedgehog Review* 6(1). http://www.iasc-culture.org/THR/hedgehog_review_2004-Spring.php
2004b. From Bhindranwale to Bin Laden: The Rise of Religious Violence. Presentation at Arizona State University/National Bureau of Asian Research Conference, October 14–15, 2004, "Religion and Conflict in Asia: Disrupting Violence." http://escholarship.org/uc/item/7322q2p5
2002a. "Religious terror and global war." http://escholarship.org/uc/item/5k99k5mq
2002b. "A Gobal Antimodernism." In *Reflections on Multiple Modernities: European, Chinese and Other Interpretations*, edited by Dominic Sachsenmaier and Jens Riede, with S N Eisenstadt, 100–109. Leiden: Brill.
2001. "Terror in the Name of God." *Current History* 100(649): 357–360.
1995. "The New Religious State." *Comparative Politics* 27(4): 379–395.
1993. *The New Cold War?: Religious Nationalism Confronts the Secular State*. Comparative Studies in Religion and Society, vol. 5. Berkeley: University of California Press

Kannangara, A.P.
1984. "The Riots of 1915 in Sri Lanka: A Study in the Roots of Communal Violence." *Past & Present* 1(102): 130–164.

Kapferer, Bruce.
1988. *Legends of People, Myths of State: Violence, Intolerance, and Political Culture in Sri Lanka and Australia*. Washington: Smithsonian Institution Press.

1991. *A Celebration of Demons: Exorcism and the Aesthetics of Healing in Sri Lanka.* Providence, RI: Berg; Washington, DC: Smithsonian Institution Press.

Kapur, Devesh.

2010. *Diaspora, Development, and Democracy: The Domestic Impact of International Migration from India.* Princeton, NJ: Princeton University Press.

Karlhofer, Ferdinand.

2015. "Sub-national Constitutionalism in Austria: A Historical Institutionalist Perspective." *Perspectives on Federalism* 7(1): 57–84.

Karmis, Dimitrios and Jocelyn MacLure.

2001. "Two Escape Routes from the Paradigm of Monistic Authenticity: Post-imperialist and Federal Perspectives on Plural and Complex Identities." *Ethnic and Racial Studies* 24(3): 361–385.

Karmis, Dimitrios and W.J. Norman.

2005. *Theories of Federalism: A Reader.* New York: Palgrave Macmillan.

Kauffmann, Chaim.

1996. "Possible and Impossible Solutions to Ethnic Wars." *International Security* 20(4): 136–175.

Kearney, Robert N.

1978. "Democracy and the Stresses of Modernization in Sri Lanka. " *Journal of South Asian and Middle Eastern Studies* 3: 87–98.

1970. "The 1915 Riots in Ceylon: A Symposium." *The Journal of Asian Studies* 29(2): 219–222.

1964. "Sinhalese Nationalism and Social Conflict in Ceylon." *Pacific Affairs* 37(2): 125–137.

Kearney, Robert N. and Janice Jiggins.

1975. "The Ceylon insurrection of 1971." *The Journal of Commonwealth & Comparative Politics* 13(1): 40–64.

Keay, John.

2011. *India: A History: Revised and Updated.* London: Grove Press.

2001. *India Discovered: The Recovery of a Lost Civilization.* London: Collins.

Keddie, N. R.

1998. "The new religious politics: where, when and why do 'fundamentalisms' appear?" *Comparative Studies in Society and History* 40(4): 696–723.

Keerawella, Gamini and Rohan Samarajiva.

1995. "Sri Lanka in 1994: A Mandate for Peace." Special Issue: A Survey of Asia in 1994. *Asian Survey* 35(2): 153–159.

Keethaponkalan, S. I.

2011. "The Indian Factor in the Peace Process and Conflict Resolution in Sri Lanka." In *Conflict and Peacebuiling in Sri Lanka: Caught in the Peace Trap,* edited by Jonathan Goodhand, Benedikt Korf and Jonathan Spencer, 39–53. London: Routledge.

Kefale, Asnake.

2013. *Federalism and Ethnic Conflict in Ethiopia*: A Comparative Regional Study. Routledge Series in Regional and Federal Studies 20. London: Routledge.

Kemper, Steven.

1991. *The Presence of the Past: Chronicles, Politics, and Culture in Sinhala Life*. Ithaca, NY: Cornell University Press.

1984. "The Buddhist Monkhood, the Law, and the State in Colonial Sri Lanka." *Comparative Studies in Society and History* 26(3): 401–427.

1980. "Reform and Segmentation in Monastic Fraternities in Low Country Sri Lanka." *Journal of Asian Studies* 40(1): 27–41.

Kent, Alexandra and David P. Chandler.

2008. *People of Virtue: Reconfiguring Religion, Power and Morality in Cambodia Today*. Copenhagen: NIAS Press.

Kent, Daniel.

2010a. "Onward Buddhist Soldiers: Preaching to the Sri Lankan Army." In *Buddhist Warfare*, edited by Michael Jerryson and Mark Juergensmeyer, 157–177. Oxford: Oxford University Press.

2010b. "Proof of Buddhism: Interpreting the Bodies of Sri Lankan Buddhist War Dead." *The Sri Lankan Journal of Humanities* 36(1/2): 19–39.

2008. "Shelter for You—Nirvāna for My Son: Buddhist Practices in the Sri Lanka Army." Unpublished PhD Thesis, University of Virginia.

Keown, D.

2001. *The Nature of Buddhist Ethics*. New York: Palgrave.

Keyes, Charles F.

2013. "Buddhists Confront the State." In *Buddhism, Modernity, and the State in Asia*, edited by John Whalen-Bridge and Phatthanā Kiti'āsā, 17–39. New York: Palgrave Macmillan.

2011. "Buddhism, Human Rights and Non–Buddhist Minorities." In *Religion and the Global Politics of Human Rights*, edited by Thomas F. Banchoff and Robert Wuthnow, 157–192. New York: Oxford University Press.

1984. "Mother or Mistress but never a Monk: Buddhist Notions of Female Gender in Rural Thailand." *American Ethnologist* 11(2): 223–241.

1978 "Structure and History in the Study of the Relationship Between Theravāda Buddhism and Political Order." *Numen* 25(2): 156–170.

Keyes, Charles F. and E. Valentine Daniel.

1983. *Karma: An Anthropological Inquiry*. Berkeley: University of California Press.

Kiblinger, Kristin Beise.

2003. "Identifying Inclusivism in Buddhist Contexts." *Contemporary Buddhism* 4(1): 79–97.

Kincaid, John.
2011. *Federalism*. London: Sage Publishers.
2009. *Local Government and Metropolitan Regions in Federal Countries*. Kingston: McGill-Queen's University Press

Kincaid, John and Carl W. Stenberg.
2011. "'Big Questions' about Intergovernmental Relations and Management: Who Will Address Them?" *Public Administration Review* 71(2): 196–202.

King, Christine Elizabeth.
1982. *The Nazi State and the New Religions: Five Case Studies in Non-conformity*. New York: E. Mellen Press.

King, Preston T.
1982. *Federalism and Federation*. Baltimore, MD: Johns Hopkins University Press.

King, Sallie B.
2009. *Socially Engaged Buddhism*. Honolulu: University of Hawai'i Press.

Kinnvall, Catarina.
2006. *Globalization and Religious Nationalism in India: The Search For Ontological Security*. Routledge Advances in International Relations and Global Politics 46. London: Routledge.

Kitiarsa, Pattana.
2009. "Beyond the Weberian Trails: An Essay on the Anthropology of Southeast Asian Buddhism." *Religion Compass* 3(2): 200–224.
2005. "Magic Monks and Spirit Mediums in the Politics of Thai Popular Religion." *Inter-Asia Cultural Studies* 6(2): 209–226.

Kloppenborg, Rita.
2004. "A Buddhist=Christian Encounter in Sri Lanka: The Pānadurā Vāda." In *Religion: Empirical Studies*, edited by Steven J. Sutcliffe, 179–192. London: Ashgate Publishing Limited.

Kodikara, Shelton U.
1989. "The Continuing Crisis in Sri Lanka: The JVP, the Indian Troops and Tamil Politics." *Asian Survey* 29(7): 716–724.

Kongasthanne, Ananda. The Venerable.
1989. *Nikaya Sangrahaya*. London: Samayawardana Publishers.

Kosambi, D. D.
1969. "Indian Feudalism." In *Rural Sociology in India*, edited by A. R. Desai, 148–155. Bombay: Popular Prakashan.
1963. "The Beginning of the Iron Age in India." *Journal of the Economic and Social History of the Orient* 6(3): 309–318.
1955. "The Basis of Ancient Indian History, I." *Journal of the American Oriental Society* 74(4): 330–337.
1946. "The Bourgeoisie Comes of Age in India." *Science & Society* 10(4): 392–398.

Kosambi, D. D. and A. Kosala.
1952. "Magadha." *Journal of the Bombay Branch of the Royal Asiatic Society* 27: 180–213.

Kostal, R. W.
2005. *A Jurisprudence of Power: Victorian Empire and the Rule of Law.* Oxford: Oxford University Press.

Kriesi, Hanspeter and Alexander H. Trechsel.
2008. The politics of Switzerland: Continuity and Change in a Consensus Democracy. Cambridge: Cambridge University Press.

Krishan, Y.
1998. "Buddhism and Caste System." *East and West* 48(1–2): 41–55.

Krishna, Sankaran.
1999. *Postcolonial Insecurities: India, Sri Lanka, and the Question of Nationhood.* Minneapolis: University of Minnesota Press.

Krummel, J. W. M.
2005. "Praxis of the Middle: Self and No-self in Early Buddhism." *International Philosophical Quarterly* 45(4): 517–535.

Kukathas, Chandran.
2003. "Islam, Democracy and Civil Society." *Journal des Economistes et des Etudes Humaines* 13(2).

Kumarasingham, Harshan.
2006. "A Democratic Paradox: The Communalisation of Politics in Ceylon, 1911–1948." *Asian Affairs* 37(3): 342–352.

Kymlicka, Will.
2009. "Categorizing Groups, Categorizing States: Theorizing Minority Rights in a World of Deep Diversity." *Ethics & International Affairs* 23(4): 371–388.
2007. *Multicultural Odysseys: Navigating the New International Politics of Diversity*. Oxford: Oxford University Press.
2001. *Politics in the Vernacular: Nationalism, Multiculturalism, and Citizenship.* Oxford: Oxford University Press.
2000. "Nation-building and Minority Rights: Comparing West and East." *Journal of Ethnic and Migration Studies* 26(2): 183–212.
1996. "The Good, the Bad and the Intolerable: Minority Group Rights." *Dissent* (Summer): 22–30.

Kymlicka, W. and B. He, eds.
2005. *Multiculturalism in Asia.* Oxford: Oxford University Press.

Kymlicka, Will and W. J. Norman.
2000. *Citizenship in Diverse Societies.* Oxford: Oxford University Press.

Lambert, Yves.
1999. "Religion in Modernity as a New Axial Age: Secularization or New Religious Forms." *Sociology of Religion* 60(3): 303–333.

Leach, E. R.

1959. "Hydraulic Society In Ceylon." *Past and Present* 15(1): 2–26.

Levey, Geoffrey Brahm.

2008. "Multiculturalism and Australian national identity." In *Political Theory and Australian Multiculturalism*, edited by Geoffrey Brahm Levey, 254–276. New York: Berghahn Books.

2006. "Symbolic Recognition, Multicultural Citizens, and Acknowledgement: Negotiating the Christmas Wars." *Australian Journal of Political Science* 41(3): 355–370.

Levey, Geoffrey Brahm, Tariq Modood and Charles Taylor, eds.

2008. *Secularism, Religion, and Multicultural Citizenship*. Cambridge: Cambridge University Press.

Lewis, David.

2010. "The Failure of a Liberal Peace: Sri Lanka's Counter-insurgency in Global Perspective." *Conflict, Security & Development* 10(5): 641–671.

Lijphart, Arend.

2004. "Constitutional Design for Divided Societies." *Journal of Democracy* 15(2): 96–109.

1992. *Parliamentary Versus Presidential Government*. Oxford: Oxford University Press

Lilja, Mona and Joakim Öjendal.

2009. "The Never Ending Hunt For Political Legitimacy in a Post-Conflict Context: Cambodia A 'Hybrid Democracy'?" *Beyond Democracy in Cambodia: Political Reconstruction in a Postconflict Society*, edited by Joakim Öjendal and Mona Lilja, 297–312. Copenhagen : NIAS Press.

Lim, Youngil.

1968. "Trade and Growth: The Case of Ceylon." *Economic Development and Cultural Change* 16(2): 245–260.

Lincoln, Bruce.

2006. "An Early Moment in the Discourse of 'Terrorism': Reflections on a Tale from Marco Polo." *Comparative Studies in Society and History* 48(2): 242–259.

2003. *Holy Terrors: Thinking about Religion after September 11*. Chicago, IL: University of Chicago Press.

Ling, Trevor.

1983. "Kingship and Nationalism in Pali Buddhism." In *Buddhist Studies: Ancient and Modern*, editged by Philip Denwood and A. Piatigorsky, 60–73. Collected Papers on South Asia, Book 4. London: SOAS, Centre of South Asian Studies.

Linz, Juan J. and Alfred C. Stepan.

1996. *Problems of Democratic Transition and Consolidation: Southern Europe, South America, and Post-communist Europe*. Baltimore, MD: Johns Hopkins University Press.

Liston, Yarina.
2000. "The Transformation of Buddhism during British Colonialism." *Journal of Law and Religion* 14(1): 189–210.

Little, David.
2006. "Religion, Conflict and Peace." *Case Western Reserve Journal of International Law* 38(1): 95–103.

Liu, James H. and Denis J. Hilton.
2005. "How the past Weighs on the Present: Social Representations of History and Their Role in Identity Politics." *British Journal of Social Psychology* 44(4): 537–556.

Loganathan, Ketheshwaran.
1996. *Sri Lanka, Lost Opportunities: Past Attempts at Resolving Ethnic Conflict.* Colombo: University of Colombo.

Lopez, D. S.
1999. *Prisoners of Shangri-la: Tibetan Buddhism and the West.* Chicago, IL: University of Chicago Press.

Love, Thomas T.
1965. "Theravāda Buddhism: Ethical Theory and Practice." *Journal of the American Academy of Religion* 38(4): 303–313.

Lu, Catherine.
2008. "Shame, Guilt and Reconciliation After War." *European Journal of Social Theory* 11(3): 367–383.

Lustick, Ian S.
2005. "Negotiating Truth: The Holocaust, *Lehavdil*, and al-Nakba." *Exile and Return: Predicaments of Palestinians and Jews,* edited by Ann Mosely Lesch and Ian S. Lustick, 106–130. Philadelphia: University of Pennsylvania Press.
1996. "To Build and to Be Built By: Israel and the Hidden Logic of the Iron Wall." *Israel Studies* 1(1): 196–223.

Lyons, Terrence.
2007. "Conflict-generated Diasporas and Transnational Politics in Ethiopia." *Conflict, Security & Development* 7(4): 529–549.
2006. "Diasporas and Homeland Conflict." In *Territoriality and Conflict in an Era of Globalization,* edited by M. Kahler and B. F. Walter, 111–130. Cambridge: Cambridge University Press.

MacKinnon, Terri D.
2004. "Buddhists in Ethnopolitical Conflict: Examining Belief Systems of Non-Violence and Compassion." Unpublished PhD Thesis, Royal Roads University, Canada.

Macklem, Timothy.
2000. "Faith as a Secular Value." *McGill Law Journal* 45(1): 3–63.

Máiz, Ramón and Ferrán Requejo, eds.

2005. *Democracy, Nationalism and Multiculturalism*. Routledge Innovations in Political Theory 14. London: Routledge.

Malalgoda, Kitsiri.

1976. *Buddhism in Sinhalese Society, 1750–1900: A Study of Religious Revival and Change*. Berkeley: University of California Press.

1973. "The Buddhist-Christian Confrontation in Ceylon, 1800–1880." *Social Compass* 20(2): 171–200.

1970. "Millennialism in Relation to Buddhism." *Comparative Studies in Society and History* 12(4): 424–441.

Malalasekera, G. P.

1967. "'Transference of Merit' in Ceylonese Buddhism." *Philosophy East and West* 17(1/4): 85–90.

Manikkalingam , Ram and Prassanna Rathnake, eds.

1995. ලංකාවට අවශ්‍යය ෆෙඩරල් ක්‍රමය. Colombo: Social Scientists' Association.

Manoharan, Nagaioh.

2006. *Counterterrorism Legislation in Sri Lanka: Evaluating Efficacy*. Policy Studies 28. Washington, DC: East-West Center Washington.

Manor, James.

1989. *The Expedient Utopian: Bandaranaike and Ceylon*. Cambridge: Cambridge University Press.

1983. "Sri Lanka: Explaining the Disaster." *The World Today* 39(11): 450–459.

Manor, James and Gerald Segal.

1998. "Taking India Seriously." *Survival* 40(2): 53–70.

1985. "Causes of Conflict: Sri Lanka and Indian Ocean Strategy." *Asian Survey* 25(12): 1165–1185.

1979. "The Failure of Political Integration in Sri Lanka (Ceylon)." *Commonwealth & Comparative Politics* 17(1): 21–46.

Monshipouri, Mahmood and Claude Emerson Welch.

2001. "The Search for International Human Rights and Justice: Coming to Terms with the New Global Realities." *Human Rights Quarterly* 23(2): 370–401.

Marasinghe, Lakshman.

2002. "Constitutional Options for a Constitutional Settlement of the Sri Lankan Ethnic Problem Comparative Law." *Sri Lanka Journal of International Law* 14: 225–246.

Martiniello, Marco and Jean-Michel Lafleur.

2008. "Towards a Transatlantic Dialogue in the Study of Immigrant Political Transnationalism." *Ethnic and Racial Studies* 31(4): 645–663.

Marty, Martin E. and R. Scott Appleby, eds.
2004a. *Accounting for Fundamentalisms: The dynamic Character of Movements*, vol. 4. Chicago, IL: University of Chicago Press.
2004b. *Fundamentalisms Comprehended*, vol. 5. Chicago, IL: University of Chicago Press.
1997. *Religion, Ethnicity, And Self-Identity: Nations in Turmoil.* Hanover, NH: University Press of New England.

Mattes, Michaela and Burcu Savun.
2009. "Fostering Peace After Civil War: Commitment Problems and Agreement Design." *International Studies Quarterly* 53(3): 737–759.

Matthews, Bruce.
2007. "Christian Evangelical Conversions and the Politics of Sri Lanka." *Pacific Affairs* 80(3): 455–472.
1989. "Sinhala Cultural and Buddhist Patriotic Organizations in Contemporary Sri Lanka." *Pacific Affairs* 61(4): 620–632.

McCargo, Duncan.
2009a. "Thai Buddhism, Thai Buddhists and the Southern Conflict." *Journal of Southeast Asian Studies* 40(01): 1–10.
2009b. "The Politics of Buddhist Identity in Thailand's Deep South: The Demise of Civil Religion?" *Journal of Southeast Asian Studies* 40(1): 11–32.
2008a. "Buddhism, Democracy and Identity in Thailand." *Democratization* 11(4): 155–170.
2008b. *Tearing Apart the Land: Islam and Legitimacy in Southern Thailand.* Ithaca, NY: Cornell University Press.

McGarry, John and Brendan O'Leary.
2006. "Consociational Theory, Northern Ireland's Conflict, and its Agreement. Part 1: What Consociationalists Can Learn from Northern Ireland." *Government and Opposition* 41(1): 43–63.
1993. *The Politics of Ethnic Conflict Regulation: Case Studies of Protracted Ethnic Conflicts.* London: Routledge.

McGranahan, Carole.
2005. "Truth, Fear and Lies: Exile Politics and Arrested Histories of the Tibetan Resistance." *Cultural Anthropology* 20(4): 570–600.

McRoberts, Kenneth.
2001. *Catalonia: Nation Building without a State.* Oxford: Oxford University Press.

Mehretu, Assefa.
2012. "Ethnic Federalism and Its Potential to Dismember the Ethiopian State Progress." *Development Studies* 12(2–3): 113–133.

Mellor, Philip A.
1991. "Protestant Buddhism? The Cultural Translation of Buddhism in England." *Religion* 21(1): 73–92.

Mendelson, Edward Michael and John P. Ferguson.
1975. *Sangha and State in Burma.* Ithaca, NY: Cornell University Press.

Mendis, Garrett Champness.
1952. *Ceylon under the British.* Colombo: Colombo Apothecaries.
1932. *The Early History of Ceylon.* Calcutta: Y.M.C.A. Publishing House.
1931. "A Historical Criticism of Mahavamsa." Unpublished PhD thesis, University of London, School of Oriental and African Studies.

Mensing, John.
2010. "Understanding the Impulse to War in Terms of Community Consciousness and Culturally Specific Religious Values." In *Asian-Arab Philosophical Dialogues on War and Peace*, edited by Darryl R.J. Macer and Saad-Zoy, 40. Bangkok: UNESCO Bangkok.

Mills, Lennox A.
2012. *Ceylon under British Rule, 1795-1932.* London: Routledge.

Mitchell, Christopher R.
1991. "Classifying conflicts: Asymmetry and Resolution." *The Annals of the American Academy of Political and Social Science* 518(1): 23–38.

Monius, Anne Elizabeth.
2001. *Imagining a Place for Buddhism: Literary Culture and Religious Community in Tamil-speaking South India.* Oxford: Oxford University Press.

Moore, Mick.
1993. "Thoroughly Modern Revolutionaries: The JVP in Sri Lanka." *Modern Asian Studies* 27(3): 593–642.
1990. "Economic Liberalization Versus Political Pluralism in Sri Lanka?" *Modern Asian Studies* 24(2): 341–383.
1989. "The Ideological History of the Sri Lankan 'Peasantry'." *Modern Asian Studies* 23(1): 179–207.
1985. *The State and Peasant Politics in Sri Lanka.* Cambridge: Cambridge University Press.

Moreno, Luis and César Colino.
2010. *Diversity and Unity in Federal Countries.* Vol. 7. Kingston: McGill-Queen's Press.

Moulakis, Athanasios.
1997. "Introduction by the Editor." In *History of Political Ideas.Volume 1: Hellenism, Rome, and Early Christianity, Collected Works Volume 19*, by Eric Voegelin and Sivers Peter Von. Columbia: University of Missouri Press.

Murthy, Padmaja.
2000. "Sri Lanka's 'War Within' and India." *Strategic Analysis* 24(4): 773–795.

Muthiah, S.
2003. *The Indo-Lankans, Their 200 Year Saga : A Pictorial Record of the People of Indian Origin in Lanka from 1796.* Colombo: Indian Heritage Foundation.

Mayūrapāda, Thera.
2000. *Pūjāvaliya: a Sinhala Classic of the 13th Century*. Colombo: Department of Cultural Affairs.

Narayan Swamy, M. R.
2010. *The Tiger Vanquished: LTTE's Story*. London: SAGE Publications.
2005. *Inside an Elusive Mind Prabhakaran: The First Profile of the World's Most Ruthless Guerrilla Leader*. Colombo: Vijitha Yapa Publishers.
1999. *Tigers of Lanka: From Boys to Guerrillas*. Second edition. New Delhi: Asian Books.
1995. *Tigers of Lanka: From Boys to Guerrillas*. New Delhi: Asian Books.

Nelson, Cary and Lawrence Grossberg, eds.
2005. *Marxism and the Interpretation of Culture*. Urbana: University of Illinois.

Newman, Edward and Oliver P. Richmond.
2006. *Challenges to Peacebuilding: Managing Spoilers during Conflict Resolution*. Tokyo: United Nations University Press.

Nissan, Elizabeth.
1984. "Some Thoughts on Sinhalese Justifications for the Violence." In *Sri Lanka: In Change and in Crisis*, edited by James Manor, 175–195. New York: St. Martin's Press.

Nissan, Elizabeth and Roderick L. Stirrat.
1990. "The Generation of Communal Identities." In *Sri Lanka: History and the Roots of Conflict*, edited by Jonathan Spencer, 19–44. London: Routledge.

Nivette, Amy E.
2011. "Violence in Non-State Societies: A Review." *British Journal of Criminology* 51(3): 578–598.

Nolte, Insa.
2002. "Federalism and Communal Conflict in Nigeria." *Regional & Federal Studies* 12(1): 171–192.

Nussbaum, Martha Craven.
2007. *The Clash Within: Democracy, Religious Violence, and India's Future*. Cambridge, MA: Belknap Press of Harvard University Press.

Oberst Robert C.
1992. "A War Without Winners in Sri Lanka." *Current History* 91(563): 91–123.
1988. "Federalism and Ethnic Conflict in Sri Lanka." *Publius* 18(3): 175–194.
1985. "Democracy and the Persistence of Westernized Elite Dominance in Sri Lanka." *Asian Survey* 25(7): 760–772.

Obeyesekere, Gananath.
2003. "Buddhism, Ethnicity and Identity: A Problem of Buddhist Identity." *Journal of Buddhist Ethics* 10: 192–242.
2002. *Imagining Karma: Ethical Transformation in Amerindian, Buddhist, and Greek Rebirth*. Comparative Studies in Religion and Society 14. Berkeley: University of California Press.

1995. "Buddhism, Nationhood, and Cultural Identity: A Question of Fundamentals." In *Fundamentalisms Comprehended*, edited by Martin E. Marty and R. Scott Appleby, 231–256. Fundamentalism Project, volume 5. Chicago, IL: University of Chicago Press.

1979. "The Vicissitudes of the Sinhala Buddhist Dynasty, Through Time and Change." In *Collective Identities, Nationalism and Protest in Modern Sri Lanka*, edited by M. Roberts, 279–313. Colombo: Lake House Books.

1978. "The Fire-Walkers of Kataragama: The Rise of Bhakti Religiosity in Buddhist Sri Lanka." *The Journal of Asian Studies* 37(3): 457–476.

1977. "Social Change and the Deities: Rise of the Kataragama Cult in Modern Sri Lanka." *Man, New Series* 12(3–4): 377–396.

1974. "Some Comments on the Social Backgrounds of the April 1971 Insurgency in Sri Lanka (Ceylon)." *The Journal of Asian Studies* 33(3): 367–384.

1970. "Religious Symbolism and Political Change in Ceylon." *Modern Ceylon Studies* 1(1): 43–63.

O'Connor, Richard A.

1993. "Interpreting Thai Religious Change: Temples, Sangha Reform and Social Change." *Journal of Southeast Asian Studies* 24(2): 330–339.

O'Hanlon, Rosalind.

1985. *Caste, Conflict, and Ideology: Mahatma JotiraoPhule and Low Caste Protest in Nineteenth-century Western India*. Cambridge: Cambridge University Press.

Olupeliyawa, Asela, Kishara Goonaratne, Suchintha Tilakeratne, Kremlin Wickramasinghe, Indika Karunathilake and Dujeepa Samarasekera.

2007. "Graduates' Perceptions Regarding Their Final Year Training." *South-East Asian Journal of Medical Education* 1(1): 25–29.

O'Leary, Brendan.

1989. *The Asiatic Mode of Production: Oriental Despotism, Historical Materialism and Indian History*. Oxford: Blackwell.

Orjuela, Camilla.

2008. "Distant Warriors, Distant Peace Workers? Multiple Diaspora Roles in Sri Lanka's Violent Conflict." *Global Networks* 8(4): 436–452.

Ortner, Sherry B.

1995. "Resistance and the Problem of Ethnographic Refusal." *Comparative Studies in Society and History* 37(1): 173–193.

Osier, Jean-Pierr.

2007. "Blind Faith According to the Jainas: The Yama Case." *International Journal of Jaina Studies* 3(3): 1–12.

Palaniappan, Sudalaimuthu.

2008. "On the Unintended Influence of Jainism on the Development of Caste in Post-Classical Tamil Society." *International Journal of Jaina Studies* 4(2): 1–65. (Online)

Pandit, Moti Lal.

2005 *Encounter with Buddhism: A Study of the Evolution of Buddhist Thought.* New Delhi: MunshiramManoharlal Publishers.

Pandita, Venerable. (Burma).

2011. "The Buddha and the Māgadha-Vajjī War." *Journal of Buddhist Ethics* 18: 125–144.

Paris, Roland.

2004. *At War's End: Building Peace after Civil Conflict.* Cambridge: Cambridge University Press.

Peebles, Patrick.

2006. *The History of Sri Lanka.* Westport, CT: Greenwood Press.

Peiris, Roshan.

1997. "Ven Rahula: learned and forthright," Sunday Times, 21 September 1997, page 12, http://sundaytimes.lk/970921/news2.html.

Peleg, Ilan.

2004. "Jewish-Palestinian Relations in Israel: From Hegemony to Equality?" *International Journal of Politics, Culture, and Society* 17(3): 415–437.

Perera, Indu.

2001. සෝම හාමුදුරුවෝ *Soma Hamuduruvo: Pujya Gangodawila Soma Himi Caritapadanaya* [Reverend Soma: The Life Story of Venerable Gangodawila Soma]. Colombo: Dayawansa Jayakody.

Petito, Fabio and Pavlos Hatzopoulos.

2003. *Religion in International Relations: The Return from Exile.* New York: Palgrave Macmillan.

Pfaffenberger, Bryan.

1988. "Sri Lanka in 1987: Indian Intervention and Resurgence of the JVP." *Asian Survey* 28(2): 137–147.

1979. "The Kataragama Pilgrimage: Hindu-Buddhist Interaction and Its Significance in Sri Lanka's Poly-ethnic Social System." *The Journal of Asian Studies* 38(2): 253–270.

Phadnis, Urmila and RajatGanguly.

1976. *Religion and Politics in Sri Lanka.* Columbia, MO: South Asia Books.

1969. "Federal Party in Ceylon Politics: Towards Power or Wilderness." *Economic and Political Weekly* 4(20): 839–843.

Philipson, Liz.

2001. *Negotiating Processes in Sri Lanka.* Colombo: Marga Institute.

Pillai, M. S. Purnalingam.

2003. *Ravana the Great: King of Lanka.* New Delhi: Asian Educaional Services.

Ponnambalam, Satchi.

1983. *Sri Lanka: National Conflict and the Tamil Liberation Struggle.* London: Zed.

Prebish, Charles S.

1996a. "Ambiguity and Conflict in the Study of Buddhist Ethics: An Introduction." *The Journal of Religious Ethics* 24(2): 295–303.

1996b. *Buddhist Monastic Discipline: The Sanskrit Prātimokṣa Sūtras of the Mahāsāṃghikas and Mūlasarvāstivādins.* Delhi: Motilal Banarsidass Publishers.

1974a. "The Prātimokṣa Puzzle: Fact versus Fantasy." *Journal of the American Oriental Society* 94(2): 168–176.

1974b. "A Review of Scholarship on the Buddhist Councils." *The Journal of Asian Studies*33(2): 239–254.

Premasiri, P. D.

2006. "A 'Righteous War' in Buddhism." In *Buddhism, Conflict and Violence in Modern Sri Lanka*, edited by Venerable Mahinda Deegalle, 78–85. London: Routledge.

2003. "The Place for a Righteous War in Buddhism." *Journal of Buddhist Ethics* 10: 152–166.

Premdas, Ralph R. and S. W. R. De A. Samarasinghe.

1988. "Sri Lanka's Ethnic Conflict: The Indo-Lanka Peace Accord." *Asian Survey* 28(6): 676–690.

Proch, Jennifer Henry.

2009. *Steel Olcott: From Civil War Veteran to Sinhalese Buddhist Nationalist—A Case Study in International Religious Activism.* Richmond, VA: University of Richmond.

Prothero, Stephen.

1995. "Henry Steel Olcott and 'Protestant Buddhism'." *Journal of the American Academy of Religion* LXIII(2): 281–302.

1993. "From Spiritualism to Theosophy: 'Uplifting' a Democratic Tradition." *Religion and American Culture* 3(2): 197–216.

Queen, Christopher S., ed.

2000. *Engaged Buddhism in the West.* Boston, MA: Wisdom Books.

Rabasa, Angel, Cheryl Benard, Peter Chalk, C. Christine Fair, Theodore W. Karasik, Rollie Lal, Ian Lesser and David Thaler.

2004. *The Muslim World after 9/11.* Santa Monica, CA: RAND.

Radhakrishnan, Trinanjan.

2010. "A Cultural Analysis of the Ethno-Political Conflict in Sri Lanka." *Maritime Affairs* 6(2): 90–107.

Rāghavan, M. D.

1957. *Handsome Beggars: The Roḍiyās of Ceylon.* Colombo Book Centre.

Rāghavan, Suren.

2014. "Ethnoreligious Nationalism and the Rejected Federalism of Sri Lanka." In *Politics of Religion and Nationalism: Federalism, Consociationalism and Seccession*, edited by Requejo, Ferran and Klaus-Jürgen Nagel, 121–136. London Routledge.

2011. "Venerable Walpola Rāhula and the Politicization of the Sinhala Sangha." *Oxford Journal of Buddhist Studies* 1: 114–133.

2006. "Ethnonationalism in Sri Lanka: Can Federalism offer any Solutions?" Unpublished MA Thesis, University of Kent – Canterbury.

Rāghavan, V. R. and Volker Bauer.

2006. *Federalism and Conflict Resolution in Sri Lanka*. Chennai: Centre for Security Analysis.

Rāhula, Venerable Walpola.

1978. *Zen and the Taming of the Bull: Towards the Definition of Buddhist Thought*. London: Gordon Fraser.

1974. *The Heritage of the Bhikkhu: A Short History of the Bhikkhu in Educational, Cultural, Social, and Political Life*. New York: Grove Press.

1959. *What the Budhha Taught*. New York: Grove Press.

1956. *History of Buddhism in Ceylon: the Anurādhapura Period*. Colombo: M D. Gunasena Publishers.

1946. භික්ෂුවගේ උරුමය. 32nd Edition, 2009. Colombo: Godage Brothers.

Rajasingham-Senanayake, Darani.

2001. *Dysfunctional Democracy and the Dirty War in Sri Lanka*. Honolulu, HI: East-West Center.

Rambukwella, Sassanka Harshana.

2008. "The Search For Nation: Exploring Sinhala Nationalism and Its Others in Sri Lankan Anglophone and Sinhala-Language Writing." Hong Kong University Theses. Hong Kong University Theses Online.

Rao, P. Venkateshwar.

1988. "Ethnic Conflict in Sri Lanka: India's Role and Perception." *Asian Survey* 28(4): 419–436.

Rathana, Venerable Athuraliye.

2003. "A Buddhist Analysis of the Ethnic Conflict." *Journal of Buddhist Ethics* 10: 202–226.

Reat, Noble Ross.

1980. "Theravāda Buddhism and Morality: Objections and Corrections. *Journal of the American Academy of Religion* 48(3): 433–440.

Repplier, Agnes.

1932. *To Think of Tea!* Boston, MA: Houghton Mifflin.

Reynolds, Frank E.

1979. "Four Modes of Theravāda Action." *The Journal of Religious Ethics* 7(1): 12–26.

Richardson, John M.

2005. *Paradise Poisoned: Learning about Conflict, Terrorism and Development from Sri Lanka's Civil Wars*. Kandy, Sri Lanka: International Center for Ethnic Studies (ICES).

Richmond, Oliver P. and Ioannis Tellidis.

2012. "The Complex Relationship Between Peacebuilding and Terrorism Approaches: Towards Post-Terrorism and a Post-Liberal Peace?" *Terrorism and Political Violence* 24(1): 120–143.

Richter, Linda K.

1990. "Exploring Theories of Female Leadership in South and Southeast Asia." *Pacific Affairs* 63(4): 524–540.

Roberts, Michael.

2003. "Language and National Identity: The Sinhalese and Others Over the Centuries." *Nationalism and Ethnic Politics* 9(2): 75–102.

2001a. *Sinhala-ness and Sinhala Nationalism*. Colombo: Marga Institute.

2001b. "The Burden of History: Obstacles to Power Sharing in Sri Lanka." *Contributions to Indian Sociology* 35(1): 65–96.

1994. *Exploring Confrontations: Sri Lanka: Politics, History and Culture*. Amsterdam: Harwood Academic (Medical, Reference and Social Sciences).

1993. "Review Essay: Nationalism, the Past and the Present: The Case of Sri Lanka." *Ethnic and Racial Studies* 16(1): 133–166.

1982. *Caste Conflict and Elite Formation: The Rise of a Karāva Elite in Sri Lanka, 1500–1931*. Cambridge: Cambridge University Press.

1979. *Collective Identities, Nationalisms, and Protest in Modern Sri Lanka*. Colombo: Marga Institute.

Roberts, Michael, Ismeth Raheem and Percy Colin-Thomé.

1989. *People In Between: The Burghers and the Middle Class in the Transformations Within Sri Lanka, 1790s–1960, vol. 1*. Colombo: Sarvodaya Publication Services.

Rodriguez, Dylan.

2006. *Forced Passages: Imprisoned Radical Intellectuals and the U.S. Prison Regime*. Minneapolis: University of Minnesota Press.

Roeder, Philip G. and Donald S. Rothchild.

2005. *Sustainable Peace: Power and Democracy after Civil Wars*. Ithaca, NY: Cornell University Press.

Rogers, John D.

2004. Caste as a Social Category and Identity in Colonial Lanka." *Indian Economic & Social History Review* 41(1): 51–77.

1994. "Post-Orientalism and the Interpretation of Premodern and Modern Political Identities: The Case of Sri Lanka." *The Journal of Asian Studies* 53(1): 10–23.

1987a. "The 1866 Grain Riots in Sri Lanka." *Comparative Studies in Society and History* 29(3): 495–513.

1987b. "Religious Belief, Economic Interest and Social Policy: Temple Endowments in Sri Lanka during the Governorship of William Gregory, 1872–1877." *Modern Asian Studies* 21(2): 349–362.

1987c. "Social Mobility, Popular Ideology and Collective Violence in Modern Sri Lanka." *The Journal of Asian Studies* 46(3): 583–602.

Rostow, Walt Whitman.
1959. "The Stages of Economic Growth." *The Economic History Review* 12(1): 1–16.

Rouhana, Nadim N. and Daniel Bar-Tal.
1998. "Psychological Dynamics of Intractable Ethnonational Conflicts: The Israeli-Palestinian Case." *American Psychologist* 53(7): 761–770.

Rouhana, Nadim N. and Susan T. Fiske.
1995. "Perception of Power, Threat and Conflict Intensity in Asymmetric Intergroup Conflict." *Journal of Conflict Resolution* 39(1): 49–81.

Rowell, George.
2009. "Ceylon's Kristallnacht: A Reassessment of the Pogrom of 1915." *Modern Asian Studies* 43(03): 619–648.

Russell, Meg.
2005. "Women in the Party: The Quiet Revolution." In *Building New Labour: The Politics of Party Organisation,*" 96–128. Basingstoke: Palgrave Macmillan.

Ryan, Bryce.
1953. *Caste in Modern Ceylon: The Sinhalese System in Transition*. New Brunswick, NJ: Rutgers University Press.

Rhys Davids, T. W.
1972. *Lectures on the Origin and Growth of Religion, As Illustrated by Some Points in the History of Indian Buddhism*. Allahabad: Rachna Prakashan.

Sacks, Jonathan.
2002. *The Dignity of Difference: How to Avoid the Clash of Civilizations*. London: Continuum.

Sáez, Lawrence.
2001. "Sri Lanka in 2000: The Politics of Despair." *Asian Survey* 41(1): 116–121.

Sageman, Marc.
2004. *Understanding Terror Networks*. Philadeplphia: University of Pennsylvania Press.

Sahadevan, P.
2002. "Ethnic Conflicts and Militarism in South Asia." *International Studies* 39(2): 103–138.

Sahlins, Marshall.
2013. [1976] *Culture and Practical Reason*. Chicago, IL: University of Chicago Press.

Salgado, Nirmala S.

2004. "Religious Identities of Buddhist Nuns: Training Precepts, Renunciant Attire and Nomenclature in Theravāda Buddhism." *Journal of the American Academy of Religion* 72(4): 935–953.

Samaranayake, Gamini.

2008. *Political Violence in Sri Lanka, 1971-1987*. New Delhi: Gyan Publishing House

2007. "Political Terrorism of the Liberation Tigers of Tamil Eelam (LTTE) in Sri Lanka." *Journal of South Asian Studies* 30(1): 171–183.

1999. "Patterns of Political Violence and Responses of the Government in Sri Lanka, 1971–1996." *Terrorism and Political Violence* 11(1): 110–122.

1997. "Political Violence in Sri Lanka: A Diagnostic Approach." *Terrorism and Political Violence* 9(2): 99–119.

Samarasinghe, S. W. R. De A.

1994. "He 1994 Parliamentary Elections in Sri Lanka: A Vote for Good Governance." *Asian Survey* 34(12): 1019–1034.

Samaraweera, Vijaya.

1981. "Land, Labor, Capital and Sectional Interests in the National Politics of Sri Lanka." *Modern Asian Studies* 15(1): 127–162.

Sambanis, Nicholas and Jonah Schulhofer–Wohl.

2009. "What's in a Line? Is Partition a Solution to Civil War." *International Security* 34(2): 82–118.

Samuels, Jeffrey.

2008. "Is Merit in the Milk Powder? Pursuing Puñña in Contemporary Sri Lanka." *Contemporary Buddhism* 9(1): 123–147.

2007. "Buddhism and Caste in India and Sri Lanka." *Religion Compass* 1(1): 120–130.

2004. "Breaking the Ethnographer's Frames Reflections on the Use of Photo Elicitation in Understanding Sri Lankan Monastic Culture." *American Behavioral Scientist* 47(12): 1528–1550.

Sarkar, Goutam K.

1972. *The World Tea Economy*. Delhi: Oxford University Press.

Sarkar, Sumit.

1996. "Indian Nationalism and the Politics of Hinduttva." In *Contesting the Nation: Religion, Community, and the Politics of Democracy in India*, edited by David E. Ludden, 270–294. Philadelphia: University of Pennsylvania Press.

Sastri, Neelakanda K. A.

1977. *The Chōlas*. Madrass: Madrass Univeristy Press.

1976. *A History of South India: From Prehistoric Times to the Fall of Vijayanagar*. Oxford: Oxford University Press.

Savarkar, Vinayak Damodar.
2009. [1949] *Hindutva: Who Is a Hindu?* New Delhi: Hindi Sahitya Sadan.

Schaffer, Howard B.
1995. "The Sri Lankan Elections of 1994: The Chandrika Factor." *Asian Survey* 35(5): 409–425.

Schalk, Peter.
2014. "'The Vallipuram Buddha Image' Rediscovered." *Scripta Instituti Donneriani Aboensis* 16: 295–312.
1994. "Women Fighters of the Liberation Tigers in Tamil Ilam : The Martial Feminism of Atēl Pālacinkam." *South Asia Research* 14(2): 163–195.

Schaller, Mark and A. M. N. D Abeysinghe.
2006. "Geographical Frame of Reference and Dangerous Intergroup Attitudes: A Double–Minority Study in Sri Lank." *Political Psychology* 27(4): 615–631.

Scheible, Kristin.
2006. "Rethinking the Pali Mahavamsa." Unpublished PhD Thesis, Harvard University.

Schober, Juliane.
2011. "The Legacy of F.K. Lehman (F.K.L.U Chit Hlaing) for the Study of Religion and the Secular in Burma." *Journal of Burma Studies* 15(1): 43–58.
2008. "Communities of Interpretation in the Study of Religion in Burma." *Journal of Southeast Asian Studies* 39(2): 255–267.
1995. "The Theravada Buddhist Engagement with Modernity in Southeast Asia: Whither the Social Paradigm of the Galactic Polity?" *Journal of Southeast Asian Studies* 26(2): 307–325.

Schopen, G.
2002. "Counting the Buddha and the Local Spirits In: A Monastic Ritual of Inclusion for the Rain Retreat." *Journal of Indian Philosophy* 30(4): 359–388.

Schubring, Walther and Wolfgang Beurlen.
2000. *The Doctrine of the Jainas: Described After the Old Sources.* Delhi: Motilal Banarsidass.

Scott, David Alan.
1996. "Religion in Colonial Civil Society: Buddhism and Modernity in 19th–century Sri Lanka." *Cultural Dynamics* 8(1): 7–23.
1994. "Religion in colonial civil society: Buddhism and modernity in 19th century Lanka." *The Thatched Patio* 7: 1–7.
1992. "Conversion and Demonism: Colonial Christian Discourse and Religion in Sri Lanka." *Comparative Studies in Society and History* 34(2): 331–365.
1985. "Ashokan missionary expansion of Buddhism among the Greeks (in NW India, Bactria and the Levant)." *Religion* 15(2): 131–141.

Scott, David A. and C. Geertz.

1990. "The Demonology of Nationalism: On the Anthropology of Ethnicity and Violence in Sri Lanka." *Economy and Society* 19(4): 491–510.

Segamen, March.

2004. *Understanding Terror Network*. Philadelphia: University of Pennsylvania Press.

Sen, Amartya.

2005. "Why Exactly Is Commitment Important For Rationality?" *Economics and Philosophy* 21(1): 5–14.

1993. "The Threats to Secular India." *Social Scientist* 21(3/4): 5–23.

Senanayake, D. S.

1985. *Agriculture and Patriotism*. Colombo: Ministry of Lands and Land Development, Sri Lanka.

Senaratne, Jagath P.

1997. *Political Violence in Sri Lanka, 1977–1990: Riots, Insurrections, Counter-insurgencies, Foreign Intervention*. Amsterdam: VU University Press.

Seneviratne, H. L.

2001. "Buddhist Monks and Ethnic Politics: A War Zone in an Island Paradise." *Anthropology Today* 17(2): 15–21.

1999. *The Work of Kings: The New Buddhism in Sri Lanka*. Chicago, IL: University of Chicago Press.

1978. "Religion and Legitimacy of Power in the Kandyan Kingdom." In *Religion and Legitimation of Power in Sri Lanka*, edited by Bardwwell L. Smith, 177–187. Chambersburg, PA: ANIMA Books.

1977. "Politics and Pageantry: Universalization of Ritual in Sri Lanka." *Man* New Series 12(1): 65–75.

Seneviratne, H. L., ed.

1997. *Identity, Consciousness and the Past: Forging of Caste and Community in India and Sri Lanka*. Oxford: Oxford University Press.

Seymour, Michel and Alain Gagnon.

2012. *Multinational Federalism: Problems and Prospects*. Basingstoke: Palgrave Macmillan.

Shah, Samuel T. and Monica Doffy Toft.

2006. "Why God Is Winning." *Foreign Policy* 115: 39–43.

Shain, Yossi and Aharon Barth.

2003. "Diasporas and International Relations Theory." *International Organization* 57(3): 449–479.

Shastri, Amita.

2009. "Ending Ethnic Civil War: The Peace Process in Sri Lanka." *Commonwealth & Comparative Politics* 47(1): 76–99.

1999. "Estate Tamils, the Ceylon Citizenship Act of 1948 and Sri Lankan Politics." *Contemporary South Asia* 8(1): 65–86.

Shaw, Julia.
2004. "Nāga Sculptures in Sanchi's Archaeological Landscape: Buddhism, Vaiṣṇavism and Local Agricultural Cults in Central India, First Century BCE to Fifth Century CE." *ArtibusAsiae* 64(1): 5–59.

Silber, Ilana Friedrich.
1981. "Dissent through Holiness: The Case of the Radical Renouncer in Theravada Buddhist Countries." *Numen* 28(2): 164–193.

Silva, Kalinga Tudor.
1999. "Caste, Ethnicity and Problems of National Identity in Sri Lanka." *Sociological Bulletin* 48(1/2): 201–215.

Simeon, R.
2009. "Constitutional Design and Change in Federal Systems: Issues and Questions." *Publius: The Journal of Federalism* 39(2): 241–261.

Simpson, E.
2006. "The State of Gujarat and the Men without Souls." *Critique of Anthropology* 26(3): 331–348.

Singer, Marshall R.
1992. "Sri Lanka's Tamil-Sinhalese Ethnic Conflict: Alternative Solutions." *Asian Survey* 32(8): 712–722.
1991. "Sri Lanka in 1990: The Ethnic Strife Continues." *Asian Survey* 31(2): 140–145.

Sirimalwatta, Nisansala.
2009. "Sinhalese Nationalism and Its Interrelation with Identity, Peace and Conflict." Unpublished PhD thesis, Diplomarbeit, University of Vienna. Philologisch-Kulturwissenschaftliche Fakultät BetreuerIn: Graf, Wifried.

Sivasundaram, Sujit.
2010. "Ethnicity, Indigeneity, and Migration in the Advent of British Rule to Sri Lanka." *The American Historical Review* 115(2: 428–452.
2007a. "Buddhist Kingship, British Archaeology and Historical Narratives in Sri Lanka c.1750–1850." *Past & Present* 197(1): 111–142.
2007b. "Tales of the Land: British Geography and Kandyan Resistance in Sri Lanka, c.1803–1850." *Modern Asian Studies* 41(5): 925–965.

Slone, D. Jason and Joel Mort.
2005. "Sexism vs. Superhuman Agency in the Theravada Buddhist Ritual system." *Method & Theory in the Study of Religion* 17(2): 134–148.

Smith, Anthony D.
2001. *Nationalism: Theory, Ideology, History*. Malden, MA: Polity Press.
2000. *The Nation in History: Historiographical Debates about Ethnicity and Nationalism*. Hanover, NH: University Press of New England.
1986. *The Ethnic Origin of Nations*. Oxford: Blackwell.

Smith, Bardwell L.

1972. "Sinhalese Buddhism and the Dilemmas of Reinterpretation." In *The Two Wheels of Dhamma: Essays on the Theravada Tradition in India and Ceylon*, edited by Gananath Obeyesekere, Frank Reynolds and Bardwell L. Smith, 79–106. Chambersburg, PA: American Academy of Religion.

Smith, Bardwell L., ed.

1978. *Religion and Legitimation of Power in Sri Lanka*. Chambersburg, PA: ANIMA Books.

Smith, Donald. E.

1974. "The Dialectics of Religion and Politics of Sri Lanka." *Ceylon Journal of Historical and Social Studies* 4: 111–118.

Smith, Steven G.

2009. "Historical Meaningfulness In Shared Action." *History and Theory* 48(1): 1–19.

Smither, James George.

2007. [1894]. *Architectural Remains, Anuraďhapura, Ceylon; Comprising the Dágabas and Certain Other Ancient Ruined Structures*. [London]: Published by Order of the Ceylon Government. (Facsimile).

Snodgrass, Judith.

2007. "Defining Modern Buddhism: Mr. and Mrs. Rhys Davids and the Pāli Text Society." *Comparative Studies of South Asia, Africa and the Middle East* 27(1): 186–202.

Sōma, Venerable Gaṅgoḍawila.

2001. *Misaditu Bindina Handa: Bauddha Samajaye Mithya Visvasa Pilibanda Dharmanukula Vimasumak* [The Voice That Destroys False Views: An Examination in Accordance with the Dharma about False Beliefs in Buddhist Society]. Edited by Indu Perera. Colombo: Dayawansa Jayakody.

2002 දේශය සුරකින රන් අසිපත. *Desaya Surakina Ran Asipata* [The Golden Sword That Protects the Country]. Colombo: Dayawansa Jayakody.

Somasundaram, D. J. and S. Sivayokan.

1994. "War Trauma in a Civilian Population." *The British Journal of Psychiatry* 165(4): 524–527.

South, Ashley.

2008. *Ethnic Politics in Burma: States of Conflict*. London: Routledge.

Spencer, Jonathan.

2012. "Performing Democracy and Violence, Agonism and Community, Politics and Not Politics in Sri Lanka." *Geoforum* 43(4): 725–731.

2008. "A nationalism without politics? The Illiberal Consequences of Liberal Institutions in Sri Lanka." *Third World Quarterly* 29(3): 611–629.

1990a. *Sri Lanka: History and the Root of the Conflict*. London: Routledge.

1990b. "Writing Within: Anthropology, Nationalism and Culture in Sri Lanka." *Current Anthropology* 31(3): 283–303.

Spiro, Melford E.

1996. "Postmodernist Anthropology, Subjectivity and Science: A Modernist Critique." *Comparative Studies in Society and History* 38(4): 759–780.

1982. *Buddhism and Society; a Great Tradition and Its Burmese Vicissitudes.* New York: Harper & Row.

1978. "Reply to Professor Tambiah." *The Journal of Asian Studies* 37(4): 809–812.

1977. Review of "World Conqueror and World Renouncer: A Study of Buddhism and Polity in Thailand against a Historical Background. By SJ Tambiah. New York: Cambridge University Press, 1976. viii, 557 pp. Bibliography, Index. $37.50." *The Journal of Asian Studies* 36(4): 789–791.

Stark, Rodney and William Sims Bainbridge.

1980. "Networks of Faith: Interpersonal Bonds and Recruitment to Cults and Sects." *American Journal of Sociology* 85(6): 1376–1395.

Stein, Burton and David Arnold.

2010. *A History of India.* Oxford: Wiley-Blackwell.

Stewart, William H.

1984. *Concepts of Federalism.* London: Rowman & Littlefield.

Stirrat, R. L.

1999. "Constructing Identities in Nineteenth Century Colombo." In *Identity and Affect: Experiences of Identity in a Globalising World*, edited by John R. Campbell and Alan Rew, 39–63. London: Pluto Press.

1992. *Power and Religiosity in a Post-colonial Setting: Sinhala Catholics in Contemporary Sri Lanka.* Cambridge: Cambridge University Press.

Stöhr, Adolf.

1921. *Wege des Glaubens.* Vienna: W. Braumüller.

Stokke, Kristian.

2006. "Building the Tamil Eelam State: Emerging State Institutions and Forms Of Governance in LTTE-controlled Areas in Sri Lanka." *Third World Quarterly* 27(6): 1021–1040.

1998. "Sinhalese and Tamil Nationalism as Post-colonial Political Projects from 'Above', 1948–1983." *Political Geography* 17(1): 83–113.

1997. "Authoritarianism in the Age of Market Liberalism in Sri Lanka." *Antipode* 29(4): 437–455.

Strathern, Alan.

2009a. "The Vijaya Origin Myth of Sri Lanka and the Strangeness of Kingship." *Past & Present* 203(1): 3–28.

2009b. "Sri Lanka in the Long Early Modern Period: Its Place in a Comparative Theory of Second Millennium Eurasian History." *Modern Asian Studies* 43(4): 815–859.

2004. "Theoretical Approaches to Sri Lankan History and the Early Portuguese Period." *Modern Asian Studies* 38(1): 190–226.

2002. "Bhuvanekabahu VII and the Portuguese: Temporal and Spiritual Encounters in Sri Lanka, 1521–1551." Unpublished PhD thesis, University of Oxford.

Strenski, Ivan.
1983. "On Generalized Exchange and the Domestication of the Saṅgha." *Man* New Series 18(3): 463–477.

Stump, Roger W.
2000. *Boundaries of Faith: Geographical Perspectives on Religious Fundamentalism*. Lanham, MD: Rowman & Littlefield Publishers.

Sujato, Bhikkhu.
2008. "The Date and Cause of the First Schism." *Buddhist Studies Review* 25(2): 210–231.

Sullivan, Daniel P.
1999. "The Missing Pillars: A Look at the Failure of Peace in Burundi through the Lens of ArendLijphart's Theory of Consociational Democracy." *The Journal of Modern African Studies* 43(1): 75–95.

Sumathipala, K. H. M.
1969 "The Kotahena Riots and Their Repercussions." *Ceylon Historical Journal* 19: 65–81.

Swearer, Donald K.
1976. *Wat Haripunjaya: The Royal Temple-Monastery of the Buddha's Relic in Lamphun, Thailand*. Atlanta, GA: American Academy of Religion.
1970. "Lay Buddhism and the Buddhist Revival in Ceylon." *Journal of the American Academy of Religion* 38(3): 255–275.

Tamada, Y.
2009. "Democracy and Populism in Thailand." In *Populism in Asia*, edited by Kōsuke Mizuno and Phongpaichit Pasuk, 94–111. Singapore: NUS Press in Association with Kyoto University Press, Japan.

Tambiah, Stanley J.
1997. "On the subject of Buddhism Betrayed? A Rejoinder." *American Ethnologist* 24(2): 457–459.
1996. *Leveling Crowds: Ethnonationalist Conflicts and Collective Violence in South Asia*. Berkeley: University of California Press.
1993. "Buddhism, Politics and Violence in Sri Lanka." In *Fundamentalisms and the State: Remaking Polities, Economies, and Militance*, edited by Martin E. Marty and R. Scott Appleby, 589–619. Chicago, IL: University of Chicago Press.
1992. *Buddhism Betrayed?: Religion, Politics, and Violence in Sri Lanka*. Chicago, IL: University of Chicago Press.
1990. *Magic Science and Religion and the Scope of Rationality*. Cambridge: Cambridge University Press.

1989. "King Mahasammata: The First King in the Buddist Story of Creation, and His Persisting Relevance." *Journal, Anthropological Society of Oxford* 20: 227–234.

1987. *The Buddhist Conception of Universal King and its Manifestations in South and Southeast Asia.* Kuala Lumpur: University of Malaya.

1986. *Sri Lanka: Ethnic Fratricide and the Dismantling of Democracy*. Chicago, IL: University of Chicago Press.

1985. *Culture, Thought, and Social Action: An Anthropological Perspective.* Cambridge, MA: Harvard University Press.

1984. "The Buddhist Cosmos: Paradise Lost, Gained and Transcended." Review of "Three Worlds According to King Ruang, a Thai Buddhist Cosmology by Frank Reynolds and Mani B. Reynolds." *History of Religions* 24(1): 73–81.

1977. "The Cosmological and Performative Significance of a Thai Cult of Healing Through Meditation." *Culture, Medicine and Psychiatry* 1(1): 97–132.

1976. *World Conqueror and World Renouncer: A Study of Buddhism and Polity in Thailand against a Historical Background.* Cambridge: Cambridge University Press.

1973. "The Persistence and Transformation of Tradition in Southeast Asia, with Special Reference to Thailand." *Daedalus* 102(1): 55–84.

1970. *Buddhism and the Spirit Cults in North-east Thailand.* Cambridge: University Press.

1968. "The Ideology of Merit and the Social Correlates of Buddhism in a Thai Village." In *Dialectic in Practical Religion*, edited by Edmund Ronald Leach, 41–121. Cambridge papers in social anthropology, no. 5. Cambridge: Cambridge University Press.

Taylor, Charles and Amy Gutmann.

2011. *A Secular Age.* Cambridge, MA: Harvard University Press.

Tennekoon, Serena.

1990. "Newspaper Nationalism: Sinhala Identity As Historical Discouses." In *Sri Lanka: History and the Roots of Conflict*, edited by Jonathan Spencer, 205–226. London: Routledge.

Thapar, Romila.

2007. "Historical Memory, without History." *Economic and Political Weekly* September 29, 3903–3017.

2004. "The Future of the Indian Past." Seventh D. T. Lakdawala Memorial Lecture on February 21, 2004 at the FICCI Auditorium, New Delhi, India.

1989. "Imagined Religious Communities? Ancient History and the Modern Search for a Hindu Identity." *Modern Asian Studies* 23(2): 209–231.

1981. "State as Empire." In *The Study of the State*, edited by H. J. M. Claessen and Peter Skalník, 409–426. The Hague: Mouton.

1960. "Aśoka and Buddhism." *Past and Present* 18(1): 43–51.

Thapar R., J. M. Kenoyer, M. M. Deshpande, S. Ratnagar.
2007. *India: Historical Beginnings and the Concept of the Aryan*. New Delhi: National Book Trust.

Thomas, E. L.
1933. *History of Buddhist Thought*. London: Ulan Press.

Thomas, Martin.
2006. Crisis Management in Colonial States: Intelligence and Counter-Insurgency in Morocco and Syria after the First World War." *Intelligence and National Security* 21(5): 697–716.

Thompson, Mark R.
2002. "Female Leadership of Democratic Transitions in Asia." *Pacific Affairs* 75(4): 535–555.

Thompson, Spurgeon, Stavros St. Karayanni and MyriaVassiliadou.
2004. "Cyprus after History." *Interventions: International Journal of Postcolonial Studies* 6(2): 282–299.

Tibi, Bassam.
2002. *The Challenge of Fundamentalism: Political Islam and the New World Disorder*. Revised edition. Comparative Studies in Religion and Society 9. Berkeley: University of California Press.

Tilakaratne, Asanga.
2003. "The Role of the Sangha in the Conflict in Sri Lanka." *Journal of Buddhist Ethics* 10: 168–191.

Tillin, Louise.
2007. "United in Diversity? Asymmetry in Indian Federalism." *Publius* 37(1): 45–67.

Tiruchelvam, Neelan.
2000. "The Politics of Federalism and Diversity in Sri Lanka." In *Autonomy and Ethnicity: Negotiating Competing Claims in Multi-Ethnic States*, edited by Yash Ghai, 197–218. Cambridge: Cambridge University Press.

Tomalin, Emma.
2009. "Buddhist Feminist Transnational Networks, Female Ordination and Women's Empowerment." *Oxford Development Studies* 37(2): 81–100.

Trainor, Kevin.
1997. *Relics, Ritual, and Representation in Buddhism: Rematerialising the Sri Lankan Theravada Tradition*. Cambridge: Cambridge University Press.

Trawick, Margaret.
2007. *Enemy Lines Warfare, Childhood, and Play in Batticaloa*. Berkeley: University of California Press.
1997. "Reasons for Violence: A Preliminary Ethnographic Account of the LTTE." *South Asia: Journal of South Asian Studies* 20, Supplement 1: 153–180.

Trevithick, Alan.
2008. "The Theosophical Society and Its Subaltern Acolytes (1880–1986), Marburg." *Marburg Journal of Religion* 13(1), 32pp. http://www.uni-marburg.de/fb03/ivk/mjr/pdfs/2008/articles/trevithick2008.pdf

Turner, Bryan S.
2001. "Cosmopolitan Virtue: On Religion in a Global Age." *European Journal of Social Theory* 4(2): 131–152.

Turnour, George.
1837. *The Mahávaṇsa.* Colombo, Ceylon: Government Printer of Ceylon.

Ungureanu, C.
2008. "The Contested Relation between Democracy and Religion: Towards a Dialogical Perspective?" *European Journal of Political Theory* 7(4): 405–429.

Upadhyaya, Prakash Chandra.
1992. "The Politics of Indian Secularism." *Modern Asian Studies* 26(4): 815–853.

Uphoff, Norman.
1992. *Learning from Gal Oya: Possibilities for Participatory Development and Post-Newtonian Social Science.* Ithaca, NY: Cornell University Press.

Uyangoda, Jayadeva.
2011. "Sri Lanka in 2010." *Asian Survey* 51(1): 131–137.
2010. "Sri Lanka in 2009: From Civil War to Political Uncertainties." *Asian Survey* 50(1): 104–111.
2007. *Ethnic Conflict in Sri Lanka: Changing Dynamics.* (Policy Studies 32.) Washington: East-West Center.
2003. Pluralism, Democracy and Ethnic Conflict Resolution: Trajectories in Sri Lanka: Paper for the Conference "Democratizing and Developing Post-Conflict Sri Lanka," on May 06, 2003 at University of Oslo, Norway. http://www.constitutionnet.org/files/Uyangoda Sri Lanka.pdf
2000. "A State of Desire? Some Reflections on the Unreformability of Sri Lanka's Post-colonial Polity." In *Dilemmas and Prospects After 50 Years of Independence*, edited by Siripala T. Hettige and Marcus Mayer, 92–118. New Delhi: Macmillan.
1989. "The Politics of Sri Lanka in 1989." *Comparative Studies of South Asia, Africa and the Middle East* 9(2): 1–7.

Van De Voorde, Cécile.
2005. "Sri Lankan Terrorism: Assessing and Responding to the Threat of the Liberation Tigers of Tamil Eelam (LTTE)." *Police Practice and Research* 6(2): 181–199.

Varshney, Ashutosh.
2002. *Ethnic Conflict and Civic Life: Hindus and Muslims in India.* New Haven, CT: Yale University Press.

Veer, Peter Van Der.

2001. "Transnational Religion." Paper given to the conference on Transnational Migration: Comparative Perspectives. Princeton University, 30 June–1 July 2001. http://www.transcomm.ox.ac.uk/working%20papers/WPTC-01-18%20Van%20der%20Veer.pdf

1994. *Religious Nationalism: Hindus and Muslims in India*. Berkeley, CA: University of California Press.

Venugopal, Rajesh.

2011. "The Politics of Market Reforms at a time of Ethnic Conflict : Sri Lanka, in the Jayawardene Years." In *Liberal Peace In Question: Politics of State and Market Reform in Sri Lanka*, edited by Kristian Stokke and Jayadeva Uyangoda, 77–102. London: Anthem Press.

2010. "Sectarian Socialism The Politics of Sri Lanka's Janatha Vimukthi Peramuna." *Modern Asian Studies* 44(3): 567–602.

2008. "Cosmopolitan Capitalism and Sectarian Socialism: Conflict, Development and the Liberal Peace in Sri Lanka." Unpublished PhD thesis, University of Oxford.

Vittachi, Varindra Tarzie.

1962. *The Brown Sahib*. London: A Deutsch.

1958. *Emergency '58: The Story of the Ceylon Race Riots*. London: Andre Deutsch.

Voegelin, Eric.

2009. "Letter to Alfred Schuetz." In *Selected Correspondence 1924-1949, Collected Works Volume 29*. Edited by Juergen Gebhardt. Missouri: Columbia University Press.

1999. *History of Political Ideas, Volume 7 (Cw25): The New Order and Last Orientation (Collected Works Eric Voegelin)*. Edited by Juergen Gebhardt and Thomas Hollweck. Missouri: University of Missouri.

1989. *Collected works of Eric Voegelin*. Edited with an introduction by Ellis Sandoz. Baton Rouge: Louisiana State University Press.

1940. "The growth of the race idea." *The Review of Politics* 2(3): 283–317.

Wald, Kenneth D., Adam L. Silverman and Kevin S. Fridy.

2005. "Making Sense of Religion in Political Life." *Annual Review of Political Science* 8: 121–143.

Wallace, Vesna A.

2010. "Legalized Violence: Punitive Measures of Buddhist Khans in Mongolia." In *Buddhist Warfare*, edited by Michael K. Jerryson and Mark Juergensmeyer, 91–103. Oxford: Oxford University Press.

Wallis, Glenn.

2008. "The Buddha Counsels a Theist: A Reading of the Tevijjasutta (Dīghanikāya 13)." *Religion* 38(1): 54–67.

Walters, Jonathan S.

2000. "Buddhist History: The Sri Lankan Pali Vamsas and Their Community." In *Querying the Medieval: Texts and the History of Practices in South Asia,* edited by Ronald B. Inden, Daud Ali and Jonathan S. Walters, 99–164. Oxford: Oxford University Press.

1996. *The History of Kälaṇiya.* Colombo: Social Scientists' Association.

Warnapala, W. A. Wiswa.

1979. "Sri Lanka 1978: Reversal of Policies and Strategies."*Asian Survey* 19(2): 178–190.

1975. "The Marxist Parties of Sri Lanka and the 1971 Insurrection." *Asian Survey* 15(9): 745–757.

1973. "Sri Lanka in 1972: Tension and Change." *Asian Survey* 13(2): 217–230.

Warren, James H.

2004. "Contesting Colonial Masculinity/Constituting Imperial Authority: Ceylon in Mid-nineteenth-century British Public Debate." *New Zealand Journal of Asian Studies* 6(2): 39–62.

Watts, Jonathan S.

2004. "The 'Positive Disintegration' of Buddhism: Reformation and Deformation in the Sri Lankan Sangha." (Rethinking Karma: The Dharma of Social Justice, pt 2). *The World Fellowship of Buddhists Review* 41(4) and 42(1).

Watts, Ronald L.

2008. *Comparing Federal Systems.* Kingston: McGill-Queen's University Press.

1998. "Federalism, Federal Political Systems, and Federations." *Annual Review of Political Science* 1: 117–137.

Weber, Max.

2000. [1958] *The Religion of India: The Sociology of Hinduism and Buddhism.* Delhi: Munshiram Manoharlal Publishers.

1968. *The Religion of China: Confucianism and Taoism.* New York: Free Press.

1904. *The Protestant Ethic. "the Spirit of Capitalism."* New York: Scribners.

Weiss, Gordon.

2011. *The Cage: The Fight for Sri Lanka and the Last Days of the Tamil Tigers.* London: Bodley Head.

Whall, Helena J.

1999. "The Peace Process in Sri Lanka: The Failure of the People's Alliance Government-Liberation Tigers of Tamil Eelam (LTTE) Peace Negotiations, 1994-1995." Unpublished PhD thesis, University of London.

Whitehouse, Harvey.

2002. "Modes of Religiosity: Towards a Cognitive Explanation of the Sociopolitical Dynamics of Religion." *Method and Theory in the Study of Religion* 14(3/4): 293–315.

Whitehouse, Harvey and James Laidlaw.
2004. *Ritual and Memory: Toward a Comparative Anthropology of Religion*. Walnut Creek, CA: AltaMira Press.

Wickramasinghe, Nira.
2006a. *Sri Lanka in the Modern Age: A History of Contested Identity*. Honolulu: University of Hawaii Press.
2006b. "Sri Lanka's Conflict: Culture and lineages of the past." *Journal of International Affairs* 60(1): 107–124.

Wickremeratne, L. A.
1928. *Kandyan National Assembly, The Rights and Claim of the Kandyan People*. Kandy, Sri Lanka: Millers.

Wijeyeratne, Roshan De Silva.
2013. *Nation, Constitutionalism and Buddhism in Sri Lanka*. London: Routledge.
2007. "Buddhism, the Aśokan Persona and the Galactic Polity: Rethinking Sri Lanka's Constitutional Present." *Social Analysis* 51(1): 156–178.
2004. "On Being, Nation and Citizenship in Sri Lanka: Going Beyond the Ontological Hermeneutic of the Buddhist Cosmos." In *Critical Beings: Law, Nation, and the Global Subject*, edited by Peter Fitzpatrick and Patricia Tuitt, . London: Gower Publishing.
2000. "The Silent Echo of the Law: Phenomenology and the Cosomology of Buddism." *Law, Text, Culture* 5: 319–328
1998. "Citizenship Law, Nationalism and the Theft of Enjoyment-A Post-Colonial Narrative." *Law, Text, Culture* 4(2): 37–67.

Wijeyeratne, Roshan de Silva and John Strawson.
2003. "Tracks and Traces of the Law." *Griffith Law Review* 12(2): 157–165.

Williams, Andrew J.
2006. *Liberalism and War: The Victors and the Vanquished*. London: Routledge.

Williams, Rhys H. and Susan M. Alexander.
1994. "Religious Rhetoric in American Populism: Civil Religion As Movement Ideology." *Journal for the Scientific Study of Religion* 33(1): 1–15.

Wilson, A. Jeyaratnam.
2000. *Sri Lankan Tamil Nationalism: Its Origins and Development in the Nineteenth and Twentieth Centuries*. Vancouver: University of British Columbia Press.
1988. *The Break-up of Sri Lanka: The Sinhalese–Tamil Conflict*. London: Hurst.
1974. *Politics in Sri Lanka 1947–1973*. New York: St. Martin's Press.

Wilson, Bryan R.
1970. *Religious Sects*. London: Weidenfeld and Nicolson.
1961. *Sects and Society: A Sociological Study of the Elim Tabernacle, Christian science, and Christadelphians*. Berkeley: University of California Press

Wilson, Bryan R. and David A. Martin.

1981. *The Social Impact of New Religious Movements*. Barrytown, NY: Unification Theological Seminary.

Winter, J. Alan.

1996. "Symbolic Ethnicity or Religion Among Jews in the United States: A Test of Gansian hypotheses." *Review of Religious Research* 37(3): 233–247.

Wittfogel, Karl August.

1957. *Oriental Despotism; a Comparative Study of Total Power*. New Haven, CT: Yale University Press.

Woodhead, Holly Pearl.

2011. "Sri Lanka: Protracted Struggle To Decisive Defeat of the LTTE." Unpublished Thesis, Georgetown University.

Woodward, Calvin A.

1962. "The Trotskyite Movement in Ceylon." *World Politics* 14(2): 307–321.

Wriggins, Howard W.

1960. *Ceylon: Dilemmas of a New Nation*. Princeton, NJ: Princeton University Press.

Yalman, Nur.

1962. "The Ascetic Buddhist Monks of Ceylon." *Ethnology* 1(3): 315–328.

Yang, Fenggang and Helen Rose Ebaugh.

2001. Transformations in New Immigrant Religions and Their Global Implications. *American Sociological Review* 66(2): 269–288.

Young, R. F. and S. Jebanesan.

1995. *The Bible Trembled: The Hindu-christian Controversies of Nineteenth-century Ceylon*. Vienna: Sammlung De Nobilis.

Young, Richard Fox and G. P. V. Somaratna.

1996. *Vain Debates: The Buddhist-Christian Controversies of Nineteenth-century Ceylon*. Vienna: InstitutFürIndologie Der Universität Wien.

Zackariya, F. A. and N. Shanmugaratnam.

1999. "Sri Lanka Communalisation of Muslims in Sri Lanka: An Historical Perspective." *Dossier* 22: 66–98.

Zimmermann, Michael, Hui Ho Chiew and Philip Pierce.

2006. *Buddhism and Violence*. International Association of Buddhist Studies Conference. Lumbini International Research Institute Seminar Proceedings Series volume 2. Lumbini: Lumbini International Research Institute.

Zompetti, Joseph P.

1997. "Reading Postcolonial Identity: The Rhetoric of Devolution from Sri Lanka's President, Chandrika Kumaratunga." *Howard Journal of Communications* 8(2): 161–178.

Zvelebil, Kamil V.
1994. "Kanaka- Puranam–A Nineteenth Century Poetic Bibliograpghy of a Ceyylonese Devadasi." *Wiener Zeitschrift für die Kunde Südasiens/Vienna Journal of South Asian Studies* 38: 251–265.
1988. "Rāvaṇa the Great in Modern Tamil Fiction." *Journal of the Royal Asiatic Society* 120(1): 126–134.
1974. *Tamil literature.* Vol. 1. Wiesbaden: Otto Harrassowitz Verlag.

Index

References to illustrations, tables and notes are entered as, for example, *91*, 91t, 91n.

A

Abeysekara, Ananda 99–100
Abysinghe, A. M. N. D. 12
ahiṃsā xi, 39n, 44n, 101, 104
Ājīvakas 44n, 46
Akashi, Yasushi 188
Alagappa, Muthiah 177
Ali, Ameer 112
Allen, Barbara 186
Amarapura chapter 103–104
Amarasēkara, Gunadasa 14–15
Amnesty International 169
Amunugama, Sarath 121–122
Anagnost, Ann S. 176
Ānandá, Murithththettuwe 124
Anderson, Benedict 19, 110–111
Anderson, George 108
Aṅduren Eliyaṭa (TV show) 160–165
Anglicanism 74, 75, 111
Aṅguttara Nikāya 54–5
anti-Christian demonstrations 110–112, 174, 178
anti-colonialism 111–112
anti-Tamil riots 20–21, 22–23, 123–125
Anurādhapura 14, 17, 28, 69
Arya Ashtanga Mārga 48n
asceticism 17n, 43–44, 73, 147, 150
Aśoka, Emperor 2n, 28, 46, 52, 69, 71, 74, 192, 195
Assaji, Mādampāgama 136n
assassinations 1, 21, 61, 82, 120, 153, 171

B

Bahusrutas 43
Bailey, Greg 50
Baker, Wayne J. 186
Balasingham, Anton 13
Banda-Chelva Pact (1957) 27n, 30
Bandaranaike, Chandrika 34, 83–84, 87, 88, 149, 152–153, 160, 164–165, 170, 171–173, 175–178, 187, 195, 196–197
Bandaranaike, S. W. R. D. 1, 19–20, 26, 27n, 82, 115, 117–120, 152
Bandaranaike, Sirimāvo 21–22, 120, 121, 126
Bauer, Volker 26
Bechert, Heinz 36n
Berkwitz, Steven C. 92, 166
Bermeo, Nancy 4
Bhargava, Rajeev 5
Bhikṣuvagē Urumaya 141–152
Bhuddhacharitam epic 55
"Black July" (1983) 23
Blackburn, Anne 139
Borg, Marcus J. 46
Braun, Erik 39–40
Brekke, Torkel 53, 55
'British Buddhism' 57
British colonial rule 13, 16–18, 21, 26–27, 29, 42, 57, 66, 74–75, 76–79, 86, 104–115, 139–140

Buddha 12, 41–42, 43–44, 45, 47–48, 49–57, 59–60, 98, 191
Danta Dhātu 76, 106, 177
Buddharakkhita, Venerable Māpitigama 118–120
Buddhism 2n, 4–5, 36–42, 57–63, 70–89
anti-Christian demonstrations 110–112, 174, 178
asceticism 17n, 43–44, 73, 147, 150
and constitutional reform 21–22, 80
inculturalization 39–40, 81
"just war" thesis xi–xii, 129, 142–143
lay people 80–81, 84–85, 99, 129–130
and politics xi–xii, 17–18, 19–20, 21, 24–25, 36–42, 51–52, 58–63, 69–70, 83, 98–132, 174–179, 197–201, 203–204
"Protestant" Buddhism 64, 70, 75, 76–77, 79–85, 86, 93t, 96, 114, 128t, 140, 147, 163–164
theology 37, 38–42, 43–45, 47–48, 51, 53–56, 97–102, 109–110, 130, 135–6, 155, 177–178, 190–196
universalism 165–167
Western understanding of 57, 58
and women 156–157
Buddhist-Catholic riots (1883) 110–112
Buddhist-Muslim riots (1915) 112–115
Burgess, Michael 32, 185

C

caste system 37, 49n, 50, 54, 57, 60–61, 75–76, 80, 103–104, 109, 113, 115, 121, 129–30, 134–136, 167, 179, 191
Catholicism 75, 110–12, 121
Ceylon Parliamentary Elections (Amendment) Act no. 48 (1948) 19
Chakravarti, Uma 53
Chandanānda, Venerable Palipanē 124
charismatic Christianity 163–164
Chelvanayakam, S. J. V. 27n, 29–30, 119–120
Christensen, Laurence W. 53
Christianity 45–46, 74, 75, 80, 93t, 108–112, 128t, 141, 163–164, 174, 178
Citizenship Act No. 18 (1948) 19, 116
civilian casualties 1–2
Clark, Walter Eugene 49
Colebrook Commission (1832) 18, 106–107, 112, 127
colonial period 16–18, 26–27, 37–38, 41, 57, 66–67, 74–79, 86, 139–140
Communist Party 116, 167
constitutional reform 16–19, 21–22, 24, 30–32, 80, 125–127
cosmion, definition 190–191
cosmology 177, 190–196
Crosby, Kate 100

D

Danta Dhātu 76, 106, 177
Darian, Jean C. 50
Davids, Rhys 78
De Jong, J. W. 49
De Silva, K. M. 28, 106
De Silva, Nalin 14
democracy 6–8, 31–32, 37–38, 94–96, 169–170
Deshapremi Janathā Vyaparaya (DJV) 127
DeVotta, Neil 94
Dhammadīpa tradition 35, 67, 97, 131–132, 162, 175, 193–194
Dhammarakkhita, Attudāvē 104
Dhammasami, Venerable Khammai 43, 45
Dharmadasa, K. N. O. 160
Dharmapāla, Anagārika 17, 76–77, 78, 79, 80, 84, 86, 89t, 93t, 109, 113–14, 116, 140
Donoughmore Commission (1928) 16–17, 18, 26–27, 127
Dudley-Chelva Pact (1965) 27n, 30
duḥka 39, 44, 48, 53–56, 155, 156–157
Dutch colonial rule 75–76, 103, 111
Duṭṭhagāmiṇi, King 28, 65, 131–2, 195

E

Earle, Valerie A. 184
economics, and religion 45–47

economy 16, 24, 35, 53, 73, 81, 83, 106–107, 116, 118, 120, 122, 129, 152–154, 155, 156, 162, 164–165, 166–167, 171–172, 176, 178, 196–197
education 77, 81, 86, 114–115, 117, 148
Eksath Bhikṣhu Peramuna (United Saṅgha Front) 118–120
Elazer, D. J. 29n, 184, 185
elections 15, 19, 83, 115–116, 118, 123, 152–154, 171, 172–179
Elephant Pass attack (1999) 171
Equal Society Party (LSSP). *see* Lanka Sama Samāja Party (LSSP)
ethics 38–42, 97–99, 124–125, 135–136, 142–143, 145–147, 164–165, 175–179
ethnoreligious identity 5n, 11–12, 15, 16–25, 69–70, 91–132, 159–165, 197–201

F

Federal Party (FP). *see* Ilañgai Thamil Arasa Katchī (ITAK)
federalism 3–6, 9, 24–35, 61–62, 83–84, 94–96, 180, 183–201
  definition 3n, 29n, 183–187
Foucault, Michel 8
Franck, Thomas 184–185
fundamentalism 38, 87–89

G

Gagnon, Alain 32
Gal-Oya riots (1956) 20
Gampola 112
Gandhi, Mahatma 47
Gandhi, Ranjiv 27n, 31, 125
Gaṅgoḍawila, Venerable Sōma. *see* Sōma, Venerable Gaṅgoḍawila
Gautama Buddha. *see* Buddha
Geiger, Wilhelm 63n, 66, 67, 68–69
Gellner, Ernest 17
genocide 123
globalization 75, 128, 132, 136–137, 163–166, 196–197
Gokhale, B. Jayashree 50–51
Gombrich, Richard 45, 59, 75, 76–77, 87n, 191
Gromes, Thorsten 32
group identity 56–57
Guṇavardhana, R. A. L. H. 160
Gunawansa, Venerable Elle 91, *92*
Gunawardana, Phillip 141

H

Habermas, Jürgen 8
Hall, Rodney 177
Hallisay, Charles 195
Hinduism 13, 46, 49–50, 52, 80, 106
history 11–35, 36–38
  colonial period 16–18, 26–7, 41, 57, 66–67, 74–79, 86, 104–115, 139–140
  and politics 11–15, 35, 189–191
  post-independence 18–25, 35, 86–87, 115–132
  pre-colonial period 11–15, 28–29, 49–50, 52–53, 102–104
Hopkins, Keith 46
Human Rights Council (United Nations) 1–2, 189, 203

I

identity
  "double minorities" 12–13
  group identity 56–57
  and language 15, 19
  and nationalism 14–15, 17–18, 19–23, 69–70, 159–165
  "othering" 150–152
  and politics 2, 5–8, 11–12, 15, 16–25, 36–8, 41–2, 69–70, 91–132, 197–201
Ilañgai Thamil Arasa Katchī (ITAK) 27n, 29–30
"imagined communities" 110–11
independence 13
India, influence on Lankan politics 27n, 30–31, 33–4, 121–2, 125
Indian and Pakistani Residents (Citizenship) Act No. 3 (1949) 19
Indian religions 44, 45–47, 49–50, 52
Indo-Lanka Accord (1987) 27n, 30–31, 33, 82

Interim Self-Governing Authority (ISGA) 30
international peace process 28, 30, 34, 165–166, 172, 180–181, 187–189, 195–200
Islam 80, 112–115, 167, 171–172

J

Jaffna 14, 22, 23, 123
Jainism 44n, 46
Jana Vijaya 163
Janathā Miturō (JM) 168–170
Janathā Vimukti Peramuna (JVP) 33, 79, 82, 83, 120–127, 167, 168, 169n, 173, 176
Jāthika Chinthanaya movement 14–15, 169
Jāthika Helà Urumaya (JHU) 8, 79, 104, 151, 160n, 170, 172–179
Jayawardena, Kumari 148
Jayawardene, J. R. (JRJ) 20, 123, 125
Jinananda, Migeṭṭuvattē 173
"just war" xi–xii, 129, 142–143

K

Kandy 102–105
Kandyan National Assembly 26
Kapferer, Bruce 192–193
Kapilavastu 49–50
karma 48, 51
Karmis, Dimitrios 186–187
karunā 40, 70, 101
Kataragama (god) 193
Kemper, Steven 92
Keown, Damien 38n
Kīirti Śri Rājasiṃha 75–76, 102–103
kingship 37, 50–2, 59–60, 97, 102–105, 177, 191–196
Kumaratunge, Chandrika Bandaranaike. *see* Bandaranaike, Chandrika
Kymlicka, Will 34–35

L

Lambert, Iyes 162
land reform 119
land tenure 107
language policy 15, 19, 126
Lanka Eksath Bhikṣhu Mandalaya (LEBM) 144
Lanka Freedom Party (SLFP) 117–118
Lanka Muslim Congress 171–172
Lanka Sama Samāja Party (LSSP) 116, 173
Lanka Tamil State Party (Federal Party). *see* Ilañgai Thamil Arasa Katchī (ITAK)
liberalism 17, 80, 94–6, 159–60, 196–197
Liberation Tigers of Tamil Eelam (LTTE) 1–2, 7, 15, 23–25, 31, 33–34, 62, 82n, 88, 95, 96, 125–126, 130, 132, 149–150, 151, 165, 167, 168–169, 170–179
  and the peace process 30, 83, 125, 152–153, 187, 195–196, 198–200
Linz, Juan J. 31

M

Mabbett, Ian W. 50
Mahā Saṅgha. *see* Saṅgha
Mahājana Eksath Peramuna (MEP) 20–21
Mahāvaṃsa epic 10, 13, 17–18, 28–29, 35n, 38, 40, 41, 62, 63–73, 85–86, 87n, 91, 92, 96, 101, 106, 111–112, 114, 118, 129, 130, 131–132, 137, 142, 146, 148, 158, 175, 191, 192, 195
Mahendra Pact (1925) 26
Mahinda, Deegalle 136, 175, 176
maitrī 39n, 149–150, 151
Malalgoda, Kitsiri 74, 97, 108
Manor, James 117, 124
Marxism 45
mass communication 141–2, 160–165
Matālē Rebellion (1848) 107–108, 127
Mauvarungē Peramuna 169
Mawbima Surakeemy Viyapara (MSV) 126–127
methodology 8–11, 45, 94–96, 180–181
middle class 61, 80, 84–85, 163
minority rights 15, 19, 20–22, 29–30, 34–35, 81–82, 86, 169, 171–172, 189, 203
  "double minorities" 12–13

missionaries 75, 93t, 108–112, 128t, 141, 164
missionary schools 77, 81, 86, 114–115, 117
modernity 7–8, 75, 155, 157, 181, 198
Muslims. *see* Islam

N

Ñaṇavimala, Aṃgahapiṭiyē 104
Nātha (god) 192
national languages 15
nationalism 14–15, 17–18, 19–20, 21, 36–42, 86–89, 91–132, 159–165
Newman, Edward 197
Nietzsche, Friedrich 47–48
Nirvāna 37, 51, 98
NORAD (Norwegian Agency for Development Cooperation) 10–11
Norman, W. J. 186–187

O

Obeyesekere, Gananath 14, 75
Olcott, Henry 78, 84, 86, 93t, 110, 111, 113, 140
Oslo Communiqué (2002) 28, 196
"othering" 150–152

P

Pan-Sinhala Board of Ministers 18–19
Pānadura debates (1850-1870) 109–110
Paññadassi, Wëlletoṭa 173
Parākramabāhu I 74
Paris, Roland 196
passive protests 47–48
Peiris, G. L. 187–188
Peiris, James 26
Pentecostalism 163–4, 178
People's United Front (MEP). *see* Mahājana Eksath Peramuna (MEP)
Perera, N. M. 116, 141
pirivenas 78, 114, 116, 140n, 142, 144, 146
pluralism 80, 162
police 21, 22
politics
  anti-colonialism 111–112
  and Buddhism xi–xii, 17–18, 19–20, 21, 24–25, 36–42, 51–52, 58–63, 69–70, 83, 98–132, 174–179, 197–201, 203–204
  colonial period 16–18, 26–27, 37–38, 66–67, 74–79, 86, 104–115, 139–140
  communism 116, 167
  consequences of civil war 10–11, 196–201, 203–204
  constitutional reform 16–19, 21–32, 24, 30–32, 80, 125–127
  democracy 6–8, 31–32, 37–38, 94–96, 169–170
  and ethnoreligious identity 2, 5–8, 11–12, 15, 16–25, 36–38, 41–42, 69–70, 91–132, 159–165, 197–201
  federalism 3–6, 9, 24–35, 61–62, 83–84, 94–96, 180, 183–201
  and history 11–15, 35, 61–62, 189–191
  Indian influences on 27n, 30–31, 33–34
  international peace process 28, 30, 34, 165–166, 172, 180–181, 187–189, 195–200
  and language policy 15, 19, 126
  liberalism 17, 80, 94–96, 159–160, 196–197
  minority rights 15, 19, 20–22, 34–35, 81–82, 86, 169, 171–172, 189, 203
  passive protests 47–48
  pluralism 80, 162
  political culture 187–188, 189–191
  post-independence 13, 18–25, 86–87, 115–132
  Provincial Councils (PC) 30–31
  secularism 5–8, 78, 148, 161
  separatism 1, 6, 22–25, 62, 81–82, 125, 167
  Sinhalanization policies 19–23, 81, 129
  socialism 116, 120–122, 148, 168, 170, 173
  student activism 167–170

theocracy 97–102
and violence 1–3, 20–23, 33, 61, 82, 93–96, 100–102, 103–108, 110–115, 120–132, 142–143, 153, 198–199, 203–204
Polonnaruwa 14, 17
Ponnambalam, Satchi 13
Portuguese colonial rule 75, 111
post-Protestant Buddhism 79–85
post-secularism 100
power relations 12–13, 36–38, 41–42, 50–52, 58–63, 70–73, 127–132
Premadasa, Ranasinghe 33, 125
printing 141–142
"Protestant" Buddhism 64, 75, 76–77, 79–85, 86, 93t, 96, 114, 128t, 140, 147, 163–164
Protestantism 46, 74, 75, 111, 163–164, 178
Provincial Councils (PC) 27n, 30–31, 33, 125, 203
Pūjāvaliya 135–136

R

Rāghavan, V. R. 26
Rāhula, Venerable Walpola 9, 14, 42, 73, 114, 116–117, 121, 137–152
Rajapakse, Mahinda 25, 195–196
Rājasimha, Vickrama 104–105
Rajasundara, Suriyagoda 103
Ramanathan, Ponnambalam 26
Rathana, Venerable Athuraliyē 9, 151, 167–179
Rāvaṇa, King 13
rebellions 1, 33, 82, 103–104, 105–108, 120–107
religion. *see* entries for specific religions, e.g. Buddhism, Christianity; sociology of religion
religious pluralism 80, 162
research methodology 8–11, 94–96, 180–181
research questions xi–xii, 1–6
Revolt in the Temple (Wijewardene) 121–122
Richmond, Oliver P. 197
riots 20–21, 22–23, 110–115, 119–120, 123–125
Roberts, Michael 194
Rodiyas 16
Rutnam, James 26

S

Sahlins, Marshall 193
Saman (god) 193
Samarawickrama, E. J. 26
Samitha, Venerable Baddegama 136n, 173
Samuels, Jeffrey 135
saṃvega 54–55
Saṅgam literature 17n
Saṅgha 5–8, 43–89, 91–181
definition 3n
discipline 43–44, 48, 53–54, 60–61, 74, 145–147
and ethnoreligious nationalism 17–18, 19–20, 21, 36–42, 86–89, 91–132, 134–137, 159–165
and mass communication 141–142, 160–165
opposition to federalism 3–6, 9, 24–25, 61–62, 94–96, 180, 189–194, 197–201
and political violence xi–xii, 2–3, 8–9, 38–42, 61–63, 69–70, 93–96, 100–102, 103–108, 110–115, 120–132, 142–143, 175, 198–199, 203–204
relationship with the state/ruler 36–38, 41–42, 51–52, 58–61, 70–85, 98–132, 138–139, 177–178, 191–196
Venerable Athuraliyē Rathana 167–179
Venerable Gaṅgoḍawila Sōma 152–167
Venerable Walpola Rāhula 14, 42, 137–152
Saraṇaṃkara, Väliviṭa 102–103
Sarvodaya 84n
Sashtri, Amitha 116
Satyodaya Patrikā 141
Schaller, Mark 12

Scott, D. A. 192
secularism 5–8, 78, 148, 150, 161
Seeladharas 43
Senanayake, D. S. 112, 115–116, 117, 144
Senanayake, Dudley 27n, 117
Seneviratne, H. L. 50, 116, 139, 146–147
separatism 1, 6, 22–25, 62, 81–82, 125
shame culture 164–165
Sihala Urumaya 170–174
Sinhala language 14, 15, 19, 126
Sinhalas
  cultural influence of Tamils on 14
  diaspora 159–160
  ethnoreligious nationalism 14–15, 17–18, 19–22, 23, 36–42, 86–89, 91–132
  and federalism 4–8, 9, 24–35, 94–96, 180, 189–194
  history of 11–13, 17–25, 35, 66–67
  middle class 61, 80, 84–85, 163
  political violence 1, 20–21, 22–23, 33, 82, 110–115, 123–125
  population 12
Siyam Nikāya 76
Smith, Steven G. 11–15
Sōbitha, Venerable Maduluwawē 124
socialism 116, 120–122, 148, 168, 170, 173
society 47–61
  Buddha's society 49–61
  caste system 37, 49n, 50, 54, 57, 60–61, 75–76, 80, 103–104, 109, 113, 115, 121, 129–130, 134–136, 167, 179, 191
  counter-cultural resistance 57–63
  "othering" 150–152
  urbanization 53, 56–57
sociology of religion 45–47
Solheim, Erick 188
Sōma, Venerable Gaṅgoḍawila 9, 152–167, *153*, 178
Sōmārāma, Thudawē 82
Soulbury Commission (1946) 18, 22, 26–27, 115, 126
Sriwardhana, Holjoti Dines De Silva Jayatilaka 103
Stepan, Alfred C. 31
Stewart, William H. 184
Stöhr, Adolf 190
Strathern, Alan 66
Strenski, Ivan 73
student activism 167–170
suffering. *see duḥka*
Sumaṅgala, Hikkaḍuvē Śrī 17, 113
Sumaṅgala, Väligama Sri 113
Sutta Piṭaka 54n
Swearer, Donald 84–85

T

Tambiah, Stanley J. 59, 66, 87, 99, 194
Tamil Tigers (LTTE) 1–2, 7, 15, 23–25, 31, 33–34, 62, 82n, 88, 95, 96, 125–126, 130, 132, 149–150, 151, 165, 167, 168–169, 170–179
  and the peace process 30, 83, 125, 152–153, 187, 195–196, 198–200
Tamil United Liberation Front (TULF) 22–23, 30, 123
Tamils
  cultural influence on Sinhala 14
  discrimination against 20–23, 85–87
  and federalism 25–35, 62
  history of 13–15, 16, 17–19, 20–25, 85–86
  population 12
  Saṅgam literature 17n
  separatism 22–25, 62, 81–82, 125, 167
  violence against 20–21, 22–23, 123–125, 167
  voting rights 15, 19, 116
television 160–165
Thapar, Romila 53
theocracy 97–102
theology 37, 38–42, 43–45, 47–48, 51, 53–56, 97–102, 109–110, 130, 155, 177–178, 190–196
Thera, Venerable Kudapola 79
Theravada Buddhism. *see* Buddhism
Thero, Venerable Elle Gunawansa 91, *92*
Tilakarathne, Asanga 147
tooth relic 76, 106, 177
traditional societies, definition 5n

Turnour, George 66

U

United National Party (UNP) 19, 20, 27, 83, 115–116, 117, 122, 123–126, 152
United Nations Human Rights Council 1–2, 189, 203
universalism 165–167
urbanization 53, 56–7
Ūva Wellasa rebellion (1817–1818) 42, 105–107
Uyangoda, Jayadeva 94–95

V

Vaṃsa literature 36n, 64
vehicle registration 20–21
Vessantara Jātaka 59–60
Vibävé (monk) 106
Vickrama Rājasimha 104–105
Vidyālaṅkāra 78, 114, 116, 140, 142, 144, 146
Vidyodaya 78, 140n
vihāras 67–68
Vimalasāra, Hädigalle 171
Vinaya Piṭaka 39n, 43, 44, 45, 55n, 56–57, 73, 74, 98, 102–103, 145
Vinaya Vardhana 85
violence 93–96, 100–102, 103–108, 110–115, 120–132
  anti-Tamil riots 20–21, 22–23, 123–125
  assassinations 1, 21, 61, 82, 120, 153, 171
  and Buddhism xi–xii, 2–3, 8–9, 38–42, 61–63, 69–70, 129, 142–143, 175, 198–199, 203–204
  civilian casualties 1–2
  rebellions 1, 33, 82, 103–104, 105–108, 120–127
virtue ethics 39n, 40
Vishnu (god) 192–193
Voeglin, Eric 190
voting rights 15, 19, 116

W

Wallace, Vesna 142
Walter, Jonathan 121
war, ethical issues 38–42
Watts, Jonathan S. 78
Weber, Max 45, 46–47
Wickramasinghe, Ranil 196
Wickramasinghe, S. A. 167
Wijeratne, Roshan 177, 192
Wijewardene, D. C. 121
Wijewardene, Wimalā 119
women, in Buddhism 156–157

Y

Yaśodharā 156–157
youth rebellion (1971) 120–123
youth rebellion (1987–1989) 33, 82
yugapurusha 137–181

Lightning Source UK Ltd.
Milton Keynes UK
UKHW021812100319
338851UK00002B/36/P

9 781781 795743